ASIAN STUDIES ASSOCIATION OF AUSTRALIA
Southeast Asia Publications Series

THE EMERGENCE OF A NATIONAL ECONOMY

ASIAN STUDIES ASSOCIATION OF AUSTRALIA
Southeast Asia Publications Series

Titles in print
The Challenge of Sustainable Forests, F.M. Cooke
Fragments of the Present, Philip Taylor
The Riddle of Malaysian Capitalism, Peter Searle
The Seen and Unseen Worlds in Java, 1726–1749, M.C. Ricklefs
War, Nationalism and Peasants: The Situation in Java, 1942–1945,
   Shigeru Sato
Writing a New Society: Social Change through the Novel in Malay,
   Virginia Matheson Hooker

THE EMERGENCE OF A NATIONAL ECONOMY

An economic history of Indonesia, 1800–2000

Howard Dick
Vincent J.H. Houben
J. Thomas Lindblad
Thee Kian Wie

Asian Studies Association of Australia
in association with

ALLEN & UNWIN
and
UNIVERSITY OF HAWAI'I PRESS
HONOLULU

Published in Australia by
Allen & Unwin
83 Alexander Street
Crows Nest NSW 2065
Australia

Published in North America by
University of Hawai'i Press
2840 Kolowalu Street
Honolulu, Hawai'i 96822

National Library of Australia Cataloguing-in-Publication entry:

The emergence of a national economy: an economic history
of Indonesia, 1800–2000.

   Bibliography.
   Includes index.
   ISBN 1 86508 665 7.

   1. Globalization. 2. International economic integration.
   3. Indonesia—Economic conditions—19th century.
   4. Indonesia—Economic conditions—20th century.
   5. Indonesia—Economic policy. I. Dick, Howard.

330.9598022

Library of Congress Cataloging-in-Publication Data

The emergence of a national economy: an economic history of Indonesia, 1800–2000 /
Howard Dick . . . [et al.].
   p. cm. — (Southeast Asia publications series)
   Includes bibliographical references and index.
   ISBN 0-8248-2552-7 (alk. paper)
   1. Indonesia—Economic conditions. I. Dick, H.W. (Howard W.) II. Series.

HC447 .E495 2002
330.9598—dc21   2001052255

Set in 10/11 Times by Midland Typesetters, Maryborough, Victoria
Printed by SRM Production Services Sdn Bhd, Malaysia

10 9 8 7 6 5 4 3 2 1

Dedicated to the memory of
Professor Sumitro Djojohadikusumo (1917–2001)

Nationalist, pioneer of economic studies in Indonesia, founder of a strong
profession of Indonesian economists, several times minister, and ever a
forceful advocate of sound economic policies

Contents

Figures

Tables

Maps

Conventions

This book follows the current conventions of spelling Indonesian names of places and persons as applied since 1972. Exceptions are made only when the name of a city has actually been altered, notably in the case of Batavia/Jakarta, or when a person has preferred the traditional spelling, for instance Soeharto.

Abbreviations

ADB	Asian Development Bank
AFTA	ASEAN Free Trade Area
APEC	Asia-Pacific Economic Cooperation
ASEAN	Association of South-East Asian Nations
Bapindo	Bank Pembangunan Indonesia
Bappenas	Badan Perencanaan Pembangunan Nasional
BB	Binnenlands Bestuur
Bimas	Bimbingan Massal
BNI	Bank Negara Indonesia
BPM	Bataafsche Petroleum Maatschappij
BPPC	Badan Penyangga dan Pemasaran Cengkeh
BPS	Biro/Badan Pusat Statistik
BPU	Badan Pimpinan Umum
Bulog	Badan Urusan Logistik
CEPT	Common Effective Preferential Tariff
CGI	Consultative Group on Indonesia
CTC	Central Trading Company
EWNI	*Economisch Weekblad voor Nederlandsch-Indië*
FAO	Food and Agricultural Organisation
FDI	Foreign Direct Investment
FEUI	Faculty of Economics at the University of Indonesia
Finec	Financial-Economic Agreement
GATT	General Agreement on Tariffs and Trade
GDP	Gross Domestic Product
GNP	Gross National Product
GPP	Gross Provincial Product
HPAE	High-Performing Asian Economy
HYV	High-Yielding Variety
IDD	International Direct Dialling

IGGI	Inter-Governmental Group on Indonesia
Inmas	Intensifikasi Massal
Inpres	Instruksi Presiden
IRRI	International Rice Research Institute
ISD	International Subscriber Dialling
Jabotabek	Jakarta-Bogor-Tangerang-Bekasi
KKN	Korupsi, Kolusi, Nepotisme
KNAW	Koninklijke Nederlandse Akademie Van Wetenschappen
KNIL	Koninklijk Nederlandsch-Indisch Leger
KNILM	Koninklijke Nederlandsch-Indische Luchtvaart-Maatschappij
KPM	Koninklijke Paketvaart Maatschappij
LIPI	Lembaga Ilmu Pengetahuan Indonesia
MVA	Manufacturing Value Added
NEP	New Economic Policy
NHM	Nederlandsche Handel-Maatschappij
NIAS	Netherlands Institute of Advanced Study
NICA	Netherlands Indies Civilian Administration
NIE	Newly Industrialising Economy
NISN	Netherlands Indies Steam Navigation Company
NTB	Non-Tariff Barrier
ODA	Official Development Assistance
OPEC	Organisation of Petroleum-Exporting Countries
OPS	Organisasi Perusahaan Sejenis
PETA	Pembela Tanah Air
PIR	Perusahaan Inti Rakyat
PKI	Partai Komunis Indonesia
PNI	Partai Nasional Indonesia
PPN	Pusat Perkebunan Negara
PPP	Purchasing-Power Parity
PRRI	Pemerintah Revolusioner Republik Indonesia
PTP	Perseroan Terbatas Perkebunan
Repelita	Rencana Pembangunan Lima Tahun
RUSI	Republic of the United States of Indonesia
Seskoad	Sekolah Staf dan Komando Angkatan Darat
Seskoal	Sekolah Staf dan Komando Angkatan Laut
Seskoau	Sekolah Staf dan Komando Angkatan Udara
SME	Small- and Medium-Sized Enterprise
SOE	State-Owned Enterprise
SSN	Social Safety Net
STOVIA	School tot Opleiding Van Inlandsche Artsen
Supersemar	Surat Perintah Sebelas Maret
Susenas	Survai Sosial-Ekonomi Nasional
TNI	Tentara Nasional Indonesia
TPN	Timor Putra Nasional
VAT	Value-Added Tax
VOC	Vereenigde Oost-Indische Compagnie

About the authors

HOWARD DICK is an economist, economic historian and specialist on Indonesia and Southeast Asia. A graduate of the Australian National University, he is presently Associate Professor in the Australian Centre of International Business at the University of Melbourne, Australia. Since 1972 he has been researching Indonesia across a wide range of topics, including interisland shipping, public transport, deforestation, the new middle class, regional development, urbanisation and governance. Consultancies have included the World Bank, UNCTAD, Harvard Institute for International Development, and Australia's Department of Foreign Affairs and Trade. His other main books are *Surabaya, City of Work: A Twentieth Century Socioeconomic History* (2002) and *The Indonesian Interisland Shipping Industry* (1987, also 1990 in Indonesian translation) and, as joint editor, *Balanced Development: East Java under the New Order* (1993, also 1997 in Indonesian translation) and (with John Butcher) *The Rise and Fall of Revenue Farming: Business Elites and the Emergence of the Modern State in Southeast Asia* (1993).

VINCENT J.H. HOUBEN studied history and Indonesian languages at Leiden University, the Netherlands. In 1987 he finished his PhD on a study of the system of indirect rule in the Principalities of Central Java in the middle of the 19th century. This study was based on Dutch and Javanese primary sources and was published in English in 1994. From 1986 until 1997 the author worked as a lecturer of Indonesian history at Leiden University. Since then he moved to Germany to become a professor of Southeast Asian studies, first at Passau University, then at the Humboldt University in Berlin. He has published on a broad range of historical topics, mainly dealing with Indonesia. In the last few years he studied economic history topics, such as labour conditions of Javanese migrant workers in various parts of Southeast Asia. Recently, his research has encompassed the themes of political and economic culture after the Asian crisis.

J. THOMAS LINDBLAD is Swedish-born but lives in the Netherlands. He studied at Columbia University and the University of Amsterdam and obtained his PhD at the latter institution with a dissertation entitled *Dutch Trade with Sweden 1738–1795* (1982). Since 1975 he has been teaching at the University of Leiden, presently as a Reader in the Department of History and the Department of Southeast Asian Studies. His books include *Between Dayak and Dutch: The Economic History of Southeast Kalimantan 1880–1942* (1988) and *Foreign Investment in Southeast Asia in the Twentieth Century* (1998). He is the editor of several books including *New Challenges in the Modern Economic History of Indonesia* (1993, also 2000 in Indonesian translation), *Historical Foundations of a National Economy in Indonesia* (1996) and (with Vincent J.H. Houben) *Coolie Labour in Colonial Indonesia* (1999). Since 1995 he has been co-operating closely with the Department of History of Gadjah Mada University in Yogyakarta.

THEE KIAN WIE is an economic historian at the Economic Research Centre, Indonesian Institute of Sciences (PPE-LIPI), Jakarta. In 1969 he received his PhD in economics from the University of Wisconsin, Madison, Wisconsin, USA. His major research interests are industrialisation and foreign direct investment in the East Asian countries and Indonesia's modern economic history. His most recent publications include an edited book, *Indonesia's Technological Challenge* (co-editor with Hal Hill, 1998); and some papers, including 'Reflections on the New Order Miracle' in *Indonesia Today: Challenges of History* (editors Grayson Lloyd and Shannon Smith, 2001), 'The Impact of Foreign Direct Investment on Indonesia's Industrial Technological Development' in *The International Journal of Technology Management* (Special Issue, Summer 2001) and 'The Impact of the Asian Crisis on the Prospects for Foreign Direct Investment in Indonesia' in *Asian Growth and Foreign Capital* (editor Thomas Lindblad, 2001).

Preface and acknowledgments

Students of the history of Indonesia have for a long time been puzzled that this country, the world's fourth most populous, lacked an up-to-date standard work on its economic development. Until the appearance of Anne Booth, *The Indonesian Economy in the Nineteenth and Twentieth Centuries* (Booth 1998a), the most recent textbook had been D.H. Burger's two-volume study in Dutch, written in the 1950s and republished in 1975 following an earlier partial translation into Indonesian (Burger 1957/1975). Meanwhile, the study of Indonesian economic history had undergone a metamorphosis. Rapid economic development under Soeharto's New Order (1966–1998) revived interest in the historical context.

A new text (*handboek*) on Indonesian economic history was proposed by Cees Fasseur in June 1989, during informal talks on the shore of the North Sea among participants in a conference at the Netherlands Institute of Advanced Study (NIAS) on the late colonial state. The idea gained favour during the first international economic history conference in Indonesia, hosted by the Indonesian Institute of Sciences or LIPI (Lembaga Ilmu Pengetahuan Indonesia) in Jakarta in October 1991. Plans for a new textbook became more concrete during yet another two conferences on the economic history of Indonesia, held at Canberra in November 1992 and Amsterdam in September 1994. At the conclusion of the latter conference, sponsored by the Royal Netherlands Academy of Sciences or KNAW (Koninklijke Nederlandse Akademie Van Wetenschappen), the team of authors was formed with good advice from the other conference participants. Compilation of the text began in earnest in 1994/95, when the NIAS sponsored an extended retreat of three of the four authors in the pleasant surroundings of Wassenaar on the North Sea coast. Writing became part of a project of scientific cooperation between the Netherlands and Indonesia under the auspices of KNAW during the years 1995–2000.

We did not begin with a common view. This emerged gradually through several conferences, workshops, intensive editorial meetings in Jakarta, Canberra, Melbourne, Leiden, Amsterdam and Passau. Fortunately, our friendships survived intact. Many of the ideas were tried out in discussions with enthusiastic postgraduate students in three consecutive intensive courses run by the Department of History at Gadjah Mada University in Yogyakarta, in 1995, 1996 and 1997. The severe financial and economic crisis that hit Indonesia in mid-1997 occurred when the manuscript was well advanced. The author of the final New Order chapter, Thee Kian Wie, had the tough task of revising his chapter several times as events unfolded. The drama of economic crisis and regime change nevertheless served to bring the earlier period into sharper focus as well and to provide a robust test of our approach. Fittingly, the penultimate draft was presented to an international conference convened at Gadjah Mada University in July 1999 by Professor Djoko Suryo and Dr Bambang Purwanto. We gratefully acknowledge the strong support given from the outset by the late Professor Sumitro Djojohadikusumo, the late Professor Harsja Bachtiar and Professor Taufik Abdullah. We are particularly indebted to Professor Sumitro, who both funded the Indonesian participants in the international economic history conferences at Canberra and Amsterdam and provided financial assistance to the three intensive postgraduate courses on Indonesia's modern economic history given at Gadjah Mada University.

The universities of Melbourne, Passau, Leiden and LIPI in Jakarta supported the research for and writing of this book. Remko Blom and Bartel Stompedissel at the University of Leiden and Henriette Sachse, Anette Bloß and Dorothea Schöfter at the University of Passau assisted in the editing of the final versions of the manuscript. Generous encouragement and advice were given by colleagues in several countries. Heinz Arndt, Anne Booth, Pierre Van der Eng, Cees Fasseur, Hal Hill, Gerrit Knaap and Tony Reid deserve our special thanks.

Howard Dick
Vincent J.H. Houben
J. Thomas Lindblad
Thee Kian Wie
September 2001

Introduction
Howard Dick

Demise of Soeharto's New Order in May 1998 has revived Indonesian history as a field of critical study. The arrogant triumphalism of New Order development is no longer 'the end of history'. Authoritarian rule founded on military repression can no longer be excused as the price of development or a manifestation of 'Asian values'. Even before the June 1999 general elections restored party politics and gave voice back to the people, reassessment had begun of the 'Old Order', both Sukarno's Guided Democracy and the preceding period of parliamentary democracy. The necessity of revisiting the meaning and ideals of Independence draws attention even further back to the colonial period. Yet this is very much a revival of political history, for which there are rich veins of literature. By contrast, apart from the excellent pre-crisis study of Booth (1998a), there are no overviews of Indonesia's modern economic history. And even Booth's *The Indonesian Economy in the Nineteenth and Twentieth Centuries* is written for readers with some background in economics. The growing body of detailed academic literature has not been made accessible to the general reader. In light of the New Order's materialist preoccupation with economic development, this is quite puzzling and perpetuates a dangerous lack of understanding of the connections between political and economic development.

Economic history is a hybrid discipline, theorised by economists but also studied by historians. This book, which brings together both economists and historians, is a holistic study addressed to students with a background in history, economics and/or politics. The approach is broadly chronological, with the chapters integrated by three grand themes. First, by way of context, is globalisation — no new phenomenon but a centuries-long interaction between the region and the world economy; second, state formation, the gradual, trial-and-error construction of a colonial state that eventually became

1

the basis for the modern nation-state of Indonesia; third, the more belated and as yet incomplete emergence of a national Indonesian economy from the various local economies that once constituted the Malay archipelago. Each of these themes has its own logic and timing. By their interaction they give Indonesia's modern economic history its unique character.

Our guiding principle, vindicated by the recent crisis, is that economics and politics must be studied in conjunction. While economic development and political development are seldom synchronised, they always interact. Indeed, it is precisely the tensions generated by the imbalances — economic expansion and political repression in the late colonial period, mass mobilisation and economic breakdown during the Sukarnoist 'Old Order', development and repression under Soeharto's New Order — that has made Indonesia's 20th-century history so unstable.

The history of Indonesia's political development should begin by recognising that before the early 20th century Indonesia did not exist as a nation or even as a concept of nationhood. To project Indonesia further back into the past is to elevate ideology above scholarship. View of the critical 19th century is thereby distorted by false assumptions. 'Classical' writers such as Furnivall (1939/1944) recognised that the late colonial state had emerged by a gradual process. Subsequent writers who moved beyond the paradigm of colonial history rejected colonial scholarship as tainted: the colonial state was taken as given and the focus shifted to the origins and forms of resistance to it. Few authors argued for continuity, Willner (1981), Anderson (1983), Cribb (1994) and Booth (1998a) being rare exceptions.

Clarification of terms is a good starting point. Indonesia as a nation-state may be dated precisely to 1945. Before that time there was a territory defined by international treaty as the Netherlands (East) Indies (Nederlandsch-Indië), ruled by a colonial state but with sovereignty vested in the Dutch crown. Territory and state, however, also have origins. In 1800 the Malay archipelago, though claimed by the Dutch as a sphere of influence, was shared with the British, the Portuguese, and local rulers who had no intention of recognising Dutch sovereignty. During the 19th century the far-flung empires of trade were gradually, and with much conflict, consolidated into territorial imperia. International recognition of borders allowed the Dutch the freedom of action to bring all kingdoms within those borders firmly under the rule of the colonial state. Dutch control of Java was established following the Java War of 1825–1830. Control of Aceh, however, was bitterly contested for 30 years from 1873 to 1904. Other kingdoms such as in South Bali and Bone (South Sulawesi) were not conquered until 1906. A 20-year-old Balinese or Bugis in 1906 would have been around 55 when Dutch rule was abruptly terminated in March 1942. Across most of the archipelago, the notion of 350 years of Dutch rule is therefore quite misleading.

The vital institution that gave substance to Dutch rule was the colonial state. Around 1800 it scarcely existed (Chapter 3). Demise of the East India

Company or VOC (Vereenigde Oost-Indische Compagnie) had left a skeleton administration nominally supervising various local kingdoms. The Netherlands itself had been incorporated by Napoleon into the French empire, which caused Java in 1811 to be occupied by the British. The rudiments of a modern state, the first modern territorial state in Asia, were thus established on Java by a representative of the Napoleonic Empire, Governor-General Herman Daendels (1808–1811) and developed by British officials, most notably Thomas Raffles, during the interregnum (1811–1816). These reforms give the book its starting point as an economic history of modern Indonesia. Before 1800 there was an economic history of the Malay archipelago, which included both peaceful and violent interactions with Europeans, as also a more Eurocentric economic history of the VOC in the archipelago, but it is not our purpose to do more than sketch this background (Chapter 2).

To emphasise the European origins of the (colonial) state is unfashionable. After all, the claim that modern government began with Daendels in 1808 was made by Coolhaas (1956), an unreconstructed colonial historian, in his memorial history of the colonial civil servants in Nederlands-Indië (*sic*). Nonetheless, and despite the continuing influence of local models of kingship, it is a fundamental insight that the technology of the centralised Indonesian state and even the authoritarian New Order state are a product of modern European history. The modern colonial state with its Napoleonic pedigree was arguably the most fateful technology transfer between Europe and the archipelago in the 19th century. Java was precocious, not just within Southeast Asia but across East Asia. Except perhaps for the port town of Singapore, founded as a British settlement in 1819, the core regions of Southeast Asia did not acquire the basic institutions and organisation of modern government until after the 1870s, contemporary with the modernising reforms which flowed from Japan's Meiji Restoration of 1868. Thailand opened its ports to Western trade in 1855, but did not begin to modernise its administration until the 1870s, in the reign of Chulalongkorn. British involvement in peninsular Malaysia is dated from 1874, leading two decades later to formation of the Federated Malay States and the Malayan Civil Service. In the Philippines a modern bureaucratic state was established only after the American occupation in 1898.

Until the end of the 19th century, however, this adolescent state was virtually confined to Java. The Netherlands Indies guilder was not even common currency in the Outer Islands. Despite an ongoing process of reform, the patchwork of kingdoms and fiefdoms that constituted the 'Outer Islands' was only loosely integrated into the modern colonial state at the time of the Japanese occupation. The distinction between Java and Madura on the one hand and the Outer Possessions (literally *Buitenbezittingen*) on the other was not just a statistical convention but also a fairly accurate representation of the fault line between core and periphery (Chapter 1).

At Independence, the new Indonesian government set about the dual task of consolidating a centralised state and forging a nation, from which derived the preoccupation — even obsession — with national unity. Eventually, under the New Order, the older institution of the state prevailed over the newer community of nation (Anderson 1983). The Army, which had fought to establish the nation and then to defend it, now became integrated with the state from top to bottom under the principle of dual function (*dwifungsi*). When the effectiveness of the civilian state apparatus waned after the downfall of Soeharto, the Army showed itself willing to be utterly ruthless in defence of the state. Growing civilian ambivalence towards the centralised state suggests how much statism has become part of the *mentalité* of the Indonesian elite, literally a state of mind.

The lively interest of historians in the formation of the modern nation-state has been accompanied by a curious lack of interest on the part of economic historians and economists in the emergence of a modern national economy. The brilliant essay of Douglas Paauw, 'From Colonial to Guided Economy' (1963), which begins with this problem, is the one notable exception. Amid all the analysis of economic aggregates and the many sectoral studies of agriculture and manufacturing, the national economy has simply been taken for granted. This is intellectually unsound. If before 1945 there was no nation of Indonesia, neither could there be a national economy. At best there was within defined borders a colonial economy — or was it economies?

The convention of distinguishing even in the economic statistics between Java and Madura and the Outer Possessions suggests that officials of the colonial state did not recognise the phenomenon of a single or unified colonial economy. It therefore hardly makes sense retrospectively to invent a colonial economy on the grounds that postwar national income accounting gives plausibility to such a fiction. As a convention/fiction it may be valid for certain comparative or macroeconomic purposes to quantify the value or volume of all economic activity within a set of national borders. In terms of historical analysis, however, it is a subject of inquiry how there emerges the structure and dynamics of a national economy. This book contends that until almost the very end of the colonial period, globalisation in a virtually free trade regime integrated some — but not all — of its regions of the Netherlands Indies with the world economy, while generating little integration between the regions themselves. Only under the New Order was there at last manifest the structure and dynamics of a genuinely national economy.

The colonial state and later nation-state played a crucial role as the sometimes fickle handmaiden to the emerging colonial/national economy. Economic mobilisation under the Cultivation System in the 1830s, import substitution during the 1930s and rapid industrialisation under the New Order have been prime examples of the state striving to accelerate institutional change and economic growth. At other times, most notably during the period of Guided Economy (1959–1966) and the crisis of the late 1990s, the state has retarded economic growth. What gives the process its particular dynamic is that the colonial/national state has been the singular, defining pole to which all other local polities had ultimately to submit and conform. Except in brief periods of strife, such as the 1950s and post-1998, the centrifugal tendency has been weak. From the 1800s to the 1990s, the Netherlands Indies/Indonesian state has conformed to the centralist and centralising model. Whether post-Soeharto Indonesia will embrace a genuinely federal system of government remains to be seen.

The book's periodisation reflects the successive waves of globalisation or capitalist economic penetration that have washed through the archipelago. These waves have several important general features. First, each wave has been truly global. The penchant for national history leads into absurdity if that international context is not taken into account. Second, each wave has become shorter. The original wave lasted several centuries, the next around a century, and the latest about 50 years to date. Third, each wave ended in economic and political turmoil — the Asian crisis of the late 1990s now seems to have been a local adjustment rather than harbinger of a global crisis. Fourth, although each wave brought many benefits of prosperity, the rate of political innovation and economic restructuring also generated conflict, with profound consequences for local society, even if the consequences did not become apparent until the end of the cycle.

Before 1800, in what may vaguely be referred to as precolonial times, globalisation was essentially a matter of trade in high-value goods. The archipelago was well integrated into the world economy through networks across China, India and the Indian Ocean before the coming of the Europeans. From strategic bases the intruders sought to control empires of Asian trade but did not establish territorial control or, with a few notable exceptions, organise local production. This pattern will be reviewed briefly in Chapter 2.

During the 19th century, globalisation became a matter of large-scale commodity production. The quickening of trade and investment was a worldwide phenomenon associated with the industrial revolution in Europe and North America, and it sharpened the distinction between a European core and an Asian periphery. In Java, a better organised and more active colonial state combined with European capital to mobilise land and labour in a sophisticated plantation sector for the primary benefit of European interests (Chapter 3). Meanwhile, with the notable exception of the East Coast of Sumatra and a few mines, the 'Outer Islands' remained part of a trading world oriented towards the new free port of Singapore (Chapter 4). Not until the 1890s did the maturing Java-based colonial state begin to enforce political and economic hegemony over the 'Outer Islands', giving rise to a loosely integrated late colonial state (Chapter 5).

The influence of the last two waves of globalisation in the 20th century can be seen from an annual time series of national production or

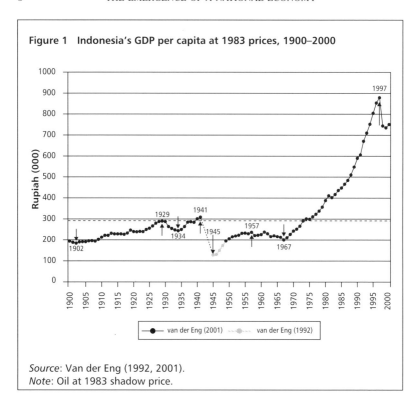

Figure 1   Indonesia's GDP per capita at 1983 prices, 1900–2000

Source: Van der Eng (1992, 2001).
Note: Oil at 1983 shadow price.

Gross Domestic Product (GDP) per capita (Figure 1). After late-19th-century stagnation caused by poor world commodity prices and crop failures (Chapter 3), economic growth was sustained to a peak in 1929 on the eve of the world Depression. Collapse of world commodity prices then pushed many primary exporting countries, including the Netherlands Indies, to switch to a more inward-looking trade regime of import substitution and industrialisation (Chapter 6). In the late 1930s Indonesia, like China, showed signs of being on the verge of an indus-trial revolution based on abundant cheap labour. Instead, in both cases, Japanese invasion followed by revolution brought about catastrophic economic decline.

After World War II there began a third wave of globalisation driven by economic boom in the United States and the rapid recovery of Western Europe. A newly independent Indonesia enjoyed a sudden boost from the Korean War boom of 1950/51 but during the 1950s and 60s was held back by political instability and a highly restrictive trade regime from reaping the benefits of expanding world trade (Chapter 6). The cost of this disengagement from the world economy was highlighted by the much greater prosperity of Malaysia (then Malaya). Only after 1967, under the authoritarian New Order, did a more liberal policy towards private investment and technology transfer, a fortuitous oil boom, and subsequently an outward-looking trade policy allow Indonesia to share in what was too breathlessly referred to as the 'Asian Miracle' (Chapter 7). Even so, it took until the early 1970s before GDP per capita recovered to the levels of 1929 and 1941. In economic terms, this meant 30 or 40 wasted years. In 1997/98 the Asian crisis and consequent political turmoil again weakened Indonesia's links with the global economy at a crucial time, when e-commerce and global logistics were rapidly changing the nature of international business.

A final issue is the extent to which Indonesia's economic history is like that of other countries. The answer depends on whether the criteria are partial or general. In area and population, Indonesia might be taken to resemble the USA, except that it is an archipelago like the Philippines and very poor. As a former colony and developing economy reliant on primary exports it bears comparison with other Southeast Asian and Third World countries (Brown 1997). During the rapid growth phase of the New Order, Indonesia was included by the World Bank in the category of High-Performing Asian Economies (HPAEs) (Chapter 7). Politically its experience since Independence has much in common with other authoritarian regimes, as more recently the transition to democracy. These and other criteria help to set up important comparative issues worthy of study. Overall, however, Indonesia is not like any other country. Its political history and economic history, and the interactions between them, are complex and unique and must be understood on their own terms. Because Indonesia is the fourth most populous of nations, a vast archipelago in a very strategic location, and at present a zone of great uncertainty, it is tremendously important that this background be more widely appreciated.

This book is not the only way that an economic history of modern Indonesia might be written. Addressing an audience literate in economic theory, Booth (1998a) examines key themes that highlight both continuities and discontinuities between the economic development of modern Indonesia and the colonial period. Nationalist historians are particularly mindful of the impact of colonial exploitation. Neo-Marxist historians would look more carefully at class formation. Anthropologists would remind us of the need to be more sensitive to local variation. Each approach has its own historiography, its own strengths and weaknesses. Our focus on (nation-)state and national economy is not intended as the meta-narrative for Indonesian economic history but as a consistent perspective on a remarkable two centuries. It is meant to be provocative, to stimulate research into new questions in Indonesia's economic history, and to provide a perspective on its future. Cribb's *Historical Atlas of Indonesia* (2000) may be found to be a useful supplementary reference work.

1

State, nation-state and national economy

Howard Dick

INTRODUCTION

The turn of a century should be just a numerical event, of no historical significance. In modern Indonesian history, however, the turns of recent centuries have been watersheds. Bankruptcy of the VOC at the end of the 18th century ushered in the age of modern colonial rule. The end of the 19th century was marked by a reassessment of colonial policy, giving rise in 1901 to announcement of a new Ethical Policy. Now the 20th century has ended with the sudden collapse of the authoritarian New Order and formation of a new government by popular election. Amid the drama of a change of regime, there is little time for historical reflection. Nevertheless, this book suggests that the unlamented demise of the New Order may bring to a close not only 32 years of 'stability and development' but also two centuries' aggrandisement of the centralised, Java-based state. The process began with Governor-General Daendels (1808–1811) and the British Governor Raffles (1811–1816), was accelerated after 1901 by the Ethical Policy, and taken to its ruthless, corrupt and personalised culmination by President Soeharto. The shape of a more democratic Indonesia is still hard to discern but it is likely to be less centralised, less authoritarian and more pluralistic — 'Diversity in Unity' rather than 'Unity in Diversity'.

Economic integration is more complex than political integration. The diffuse economic activities that take place within the boundaries of Indonesia's nation-state can be measured by a variety of indicators, which reveal interesting trends in growth and distribution. But does all this economic activity coalesce into some structure of a *national* economy? Are the islands of Indonesia parts of a cohesive national economy or are they still separate fragments? Are they more closely integrated with each other than with foreign countries, including Singapore and Malaysia? If such a national economy has by now emerged, by what process has it emerged and over what period of time? Such questions should be the starting-point for any economic history of modern Indonesia.

This introductory chapter argues that the emergence of an integrated national economy was a slow evolutionary process, not directly affected by the transfer of sovereignty, and that the structure of a national economy came into being only during the New Order. After briefly considering some methodological issues, it sketches the spatial structure of the Indonesian economy in the 1990s and then reviews how that national economy evolved from the early 19th century, focusing on the economic relationship between Java and the rest of the archipelago. It is argued that the foundations of the national economy were laid in Java during the 19th century in virtual isolation from the rest of the archipelago, that political and economic control over the foreign trade of the 'Outer Islands' was consolidated in the early decades of the 20th century, but that little substantive economic integration had been achieved by the end of the colonial era or indeed after two decades of independence. The spatial integration of production, consumption and interisland trade according to internal comparative advantage became apparent only from the 1970s in consequence of the rapid industrialisation of Java, a long-delayed second wave to the intensification of cultivation in the 19th century.

NATIONAL ECONOMY AND SPATIAL DISTRIBUTION

The concept of 'national economy' is a fairly recent one. Emergence of the modern nation-state gave rise to the need to define the economic space over which it claimed control. This economic space was delineated by frontiers. Goods and people were counted — and taxed — as they moved from one jurisdiction to the next. The idea of measuring the level of economic activity within those frontiers did not arise until after the world Depression of the 1930s, which was the catalyst for the formulation of interventionist macro-economic policies and the associated development of standard techniques of national income accounting. When the Indonesian nation gained international recognition in 1949, the national economy had statistically just been invented. In 1948 the Central Statistical Bureau of the Netherlands had prepared a set of modern national accounts and applied it to the Netherlands Indies for the year 1938 (Creutzberg 1979; Van der Eng 1997). Earlier pioneering estimates, though still sometimes referred to, were incomplete and not standardised (Van der Eng 1992). Statistical recognition of a national economy did not, however, mean that it yet had substantive form.

National income statistics are aspatial. They imply that economic activity is either concentrated at a single point or uniformly distributed. In a city-state such as Singapore, the former approximates reality. In as large a nation as Indonesia, however, neither implication is valid. Indonesia is the fourth most populous nation in the world, but about 80% of its claimed Exclusive Economic Zone is in fact sea (Map 1) (BPS 1992). The archipel-

Map 1   The Indonesian archipelago

ago is equivalent in extent to the USA but with a very different economic geography. Economic activity is spread unevenly across a large number of islands. Agricultural production is diffuse. Non-agricultural production, however, tends to cluster. This is most apparent in the case of large and medium-scale manufacturing, corresponding with the modern sector of manufacturing, which is heavily concentrated in and around the main cities.

To understand the spatial distribution of economic activity, it is necessary to disaggregate the *national* income (GDP) estimates. Figure 1.1 shows for 1996 the economic area of each main island or island group, scaled in proportion to its percentage share. Java (including Bali) stands out as by far the largest block of economic activity, being more than three-fifths of the national total. It is definitely the core of the national economy, with high population density, many cities, good infrastructure, and well-articulated transport networks. Greater Jakarta (Jabotabek) alone is almost as large an economy as the whole of Sumatra. Java/Bali and Sumatra together account for over four-fifths of the Indonesian economy, which therefore tilts heavily towards the west of the archipelago. Reflecting the underlying pattern of comparative advantage, Sumatra and Kalimantan do not trade much with each other but ship mainly raw materials to Java in exchange for manufactured consumer and capital goods.

The western economic bias of the archipelago has much to do with the regional context. Although neighbouring countries are left blank on most national maps, a proper economic map should take account of the city-state of Singapore, a world city, regional financial and business centre, and transshipment and logistics hub. Scaled at 'purchasing power parity' (Appendix 1.A), in 1996 Singapore was equivalent to 9% of the economic

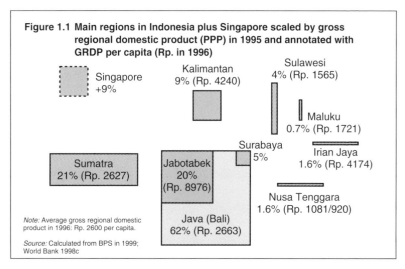

Figure 1.1 Main regions in Indonesia plus Singapore scaled by gross regional domestic product (PPP) in 1995 and annotated with GRDP per capita (Rp. in 1996)

Singapore +9%

Kalimantan 9% (Rp. 4240)

Sulawesi 4% (Rp. 1565)

Maluku 0.7% (Rp. 1721)

Surabaya 5%

Sumatra 21% (Rp. 2627)

Jabotabek 20% (Rp. 8976)

Irian Jaya 1.6% (Rp. 4174)

Nusa Tenggara 1.6% (Rp. 1081/920)

Note: Average gross regional domestic product in 1996: Rp. 2600 per capita.

Source: Calculated from BPS in 1999; World Bank 1998c

Java (Bali) 62% (Rp. 2663)

size of Indonesia, the same economic weight as Kalimantan or all the rest of Eastern Indonesia. Across Malacca Strait and including the northwestern part of Kalimantan, Malaysia would add another 25% to Indonesia's economic size. Western Indonesia (Sumatra, Kalimantan and Java/Bali) together with Singapore and Malaysia constitutes the economic core of Southeast Asia, along a main axis Kuala Lumpur–Singapore–Jakarta–Surabaya. This core is fairly well integrated. People and goods move with high intensity between Java and Singapore and from Sumatra and Kalimantan to both Java and Singapore. Sumatra and West Malaysia is also an important link.

Indonesia's vast eastern region, by contrast, has the misfortune to float in an economic vacuum. If Western Indonesia benefits from being part of the transnational core region of Southeast Asia, Eastern Indonesia suffers from being part of a transnational periphery. The Southern Philippines is held back by a 30-year separatist rebellion, Papua New Guinea is a weak economy, and Australia's northwestern and northern territories, though extremities of a prosperous economy, have no economic weight. Hence there is no growth stimulus and no regional coherence. The islands of Sulawesi, Maluku, Nusa Tenggara and Irian Jaya represent about half the nation's area of land and sea but a mere 8% of the economy. Its only substantial city is Makassar, formerly Ujung Pandang, the gateway to Eastern Indonesia but also the exit. Lying on the western edge of the region, it is too remote and too small to transform so poor and fragmented a region.

This core–periphery structure is reflected in regional income per capita. Figure 1.1 gives current rupiah income per capita for each main island in 1996, the year before the Asian crisis. Java/Bali and Sumatra are both around the national average of Rp. 2700, though Jakarta Capital City

Region is much higher, at Rp. 9000. Kalimantan is well above the average, mainly because of oil and gas revenues in East Kalimantan (Rp. 10 215); likewise Irian Jaya (Rp. 4174), because of oil and minerals. By contrast, Eastern Indonesia apart from Irian lies well below the national average, the poverty-stricken region of Nusa Tenggara being around only Rp. 1000. Though Indonesia may still be regarded as a poor country, it is therefore not uniformly poor (see also Hill 1996/2000a: Ch. 11). These wide differentials are part of the background to recent ethnic and religious strife and pressures for greater regional autonomy or, in Aceh and Irian Jaya (West Papua), for separation from Indonesia.

If economic geography enables us to identify patterns of development and underdevelopment, economic history requires us to explain how they came about. Why has Indonesia been so slow to develop into a modern national economy and why has the process been so uneven over time and across space? This chapter seeks to provide a framework for the following more detailed accounts that tell the story period by period. The essential argument is as follows. The core of both the modern state and the modern economy was moulded on Java during the course of the 19th century, with the development of the export economy under the Cultivation System being the formative experience. Regular communications between Java and the rest of the archipelago did not exist before the middle of that century and it took until almost the eve of World War I to impose colonial control over the entire country and to bring all parts into a transport and communications system focused on Java. The interwar years saw the culmination of efforts by the colonial government and private interests to divert the foreign trade of the rest of the archipelago away from Singapore and Penang to Dutch ports. By the end of the colonial era, however, interisland trade was still very modest and economic integration a dream for the future. The first three decades of independence saw a continued effort to direct Indonesia's foreign trade through Indonesian ports but, at least until the 1970s, little development of interisland trade. Progress towards economic integration awaited the second main phase in the modern economic development of Java, namely industrialisation, which built up self-sustaining momentum during the 1970s and in the 1980s turned outwards to international markets. This successful, albeit belated, exploitation of internal comparative advantage, accompanied by economic specialisation between Java and the rest of the archipelago, has for the first time provided the basis for the integration of a substantive national economy. Whether that basis can in fact be built on is something that will be determined very much by politics.

ORIGINS OF THE NATIONAL ECONOMY

The relationship between national economy and nation-state is more soluble than the age-old problem of the chicken and the egg. The state comes first and stakes its claim by delineating national boundaries. Without national boundaries there may be a great deal of economic activity but no national economy. The maritime world of Southeast Asia in the 16th and 17th centuries, described so well by Reid (1988, 1993a), was an example of a vigorous, seamless, well-articulated economy not partitioned by political boundaries. There were kingdoms and there were cities but trade was international by tradition and by default, as were the seas that unified the archipelago. Within Southeast Asia, the British free trade orthodoxy of the 19th century reinforced this much older local tradition and was actually subversive of the ambitious territorial claims of other European powers, not least the Netherlands. As the Dutch colonial government feared, Singapore became a centre of economic revolution.

National economies therefore emerged not as some natural evolution but as an unnatural distortion wrought by the force of arms of European powers. The often violent transition from an integrated maritime trading world to distinct colonial economies marked out by territorial boundaries, as also the tensions and conflicts which this created, are the stuff of the past 150 years of Southeast Asian economic history. Hitherto the Dutch, the British, the Spaniards and the Portuguese had maintained fortified trading posts but, except for Java and Luzon, had not sought to rule over extensive landed territories. Being naval powers, their main objective was to trade on privileged terms. As their powers to monopolise trade waned, they sought increasingly to profit from taxing the trade of others, most notably the Chinese. In the 19th century, there began a scramble among the European powers to mark out spheres of influence by precise boundaries acknowledged by international treaties. At first these claims were merely pre-emptive, but once the boundaries had been established they led inexorably to direct colonial rule. Thus the Anglo-Dutch Treaty of 1824 swapped the British settlement in Western Sumatra (Bengkulu) for the Dutch settlement on the Malay Peninsula (Malacca), thereby making the Straits of Malacca the boundary between Dutch and British spheres of influence, as formalised by the Sumatra Treaty of 1871.

Marking out a perimeter around a territorial sphere did not of itself, however, transform the pattern of economic activity inside it. In fact it is doubtful whether at first the intent was to establish anything more than prior international claim to foreign trade and resources within those boundaries. Until the 'pacification' of the 1900s, many indigenous rulers still regarded themselves as sovereign and were prepared to fight stubbornly to defend their autonomy from colonial encroachment. The Netherlands Indies, like British India, therefore resembled a patchwork rather than a unitary state. That heritage was reflected in the irregular pattern of direct and indirect rule right up to Independence. In terms of economy, the pattern of trade flows mocked colonial boundaries. Forceful intervention was needed to establish infrastructure, relocate production and refocus trade. A prerequisite was the consolidation of a political centre and economic core from which such control could be exercised.

THE CORE

The Dutch consolidated their rule on Java and developed its economic base almost in isolation from the rest of the archipelago. That the Vereenigde Oost-Indische Compagnie (VOC) in 1619 established its headquarters at Jakarta (Batavia) was due more to strategic convenience than to the importance of the Java trade. For ships rounding the Cape of Good Hope and picking up the northwesterly trade winds, Sunda Strait was the first Asian landfall. Jakarta was then just a small enclave in the jungle with almost no productive hinterland. Culturally and economically, it was not yet part of Java. Over the next two centuries, the VOC gradually became involved in local production, at first through 'forced deliveries' of trade goods but by the 18th century through the supervision of coffee cultivation in the Priangan highlands. Cattle-driven sugar mills were also set up by Chinese in the lowlands of West and Central Java. Nevertheless, until the demise of the VOC at the end of the 18th century, Dutch control over Java was tenuous except in the narrow strip along the North Coast. Indeed, during the Java War (1825–1830) the Dutch were almost overwhelmed in central Java, and hung on only at great human and financial cost. After 1830 under the Cultivation System the state mobilised the land and labour of Java to produce plantation crops, which were shipped to Europe by the monopoly Netherlands Trading Company, or NHM (*Nederlandsche Handel-Maatschappij*) (Chapter 3). Java became a much more ambitious version of the spice monopoly that the VOC had established in the Moluccas in the early 17th century.

   Apart from territory, an essential feature of a modern state is an effective administration. This was certainly not true of the VOC, which as a government relied heavily on the talents of a few officials and delegated most of the actual tasks of government to the indigenous aristocracy. The modernising republican Governor-General Daendels (1808–1811) laid the foundations for a modern bureaucracy by formalising the European civil service hierarchy and allocating 'prefects' (later known as 'residents') to defined territorial districts; he also restricted the powers and privileges of the Javanese aristocrats, who were unhappily demoted to the status of salaried civil servants (Sutherland 1979: 7–8). These reforms were carried through by Raffles during the British interregnum (1811–1816). After 1830 under the Cultivation System, the authority of European civil servants extended into every district outside the now much truncated Princely States (*Vorstenlanden*). Controleurs not only supervised the cultivation of export crops but also became involved in mobilising labour for the improvement of transport and communications. Nevertheless, as late as 1865 the territorial administration (*Binnenlands Bestuur*) still consisted of only 175 Europeans (Fasseur 1975/1992: 22).

   Rapid growth of the colonial bureaucracy began towards the end of the 19th century. One cause was the shift in local revenue collection from tax farming in mainly Chinese hands to direct taxation. This process was begun by Raffles, who replaced the customs revenue farm, and was completed in the 1900s with the closure of the last opium farms and the transfer of pawnshops to government control (Diehl 1993). Another cause was the increasing technical services of health, education, public works and other 'welfare' activities, which were promoted after 1901 as part of the 'Ethical Policy' (Sutherland 1979). The outcome was a sophisticated, modern bureaucratic state that by transfer of Dutch personnel and European institutional technology evolved almost simultaneously with the Netherlands. The outstanding and fateful difference was that in the Netherlands the aggrandising central bureaucracy encountered tenacious resistance from much older local authorities, whereas in the Netherlands Indies the colonial state simply swept aside local resistance. The New Order thus stands in direct line of descent from this colonial *Beamtenstaat* (Anderson 1983; Cribb 1994).

Along with the development of plantation crops and food output, the 19th century was a time of great improvement in Java's land-based communications. At the beginning of the century, communications along the coast of Java were almost entirely by ship, while the Solo and Brantas rivers were the main arteries of communication with the interior. As part of his program of strengthening the defences of Java, Daendels conscripted labour to build a wide post road along the north coast of Java via the Priangan highlands. Designed on the Napoleonic model, with regularly spaced relay stations, its purpose was to speed the conveyance of official mails and passengers. The movement of goods still relied on human porterage, pack animals, and prahu; wheeled carts were as yet uncommon. After 1830 under the Cultivation System, much labour was mobilised to improve roads and build bridges for transport of export crops by cart, usually to the nearest landing place on the river or coast. The first section of railway was opened in central Java in 1867. By 1880 lines had been completed into the interior from the main north coast ports of Jakarta, Semarang and Surabaya, and by the mid-1890s had become a linked network. Rail quickly supplanted river transport for freight to and from those ports. Meanwhile telegraphs had greatly hastened the speed of official communications beyond that of the post roads. The first telegraph line had been laid out in 1856 from Jakarta to the Governor-General's palace at Bogor. In 1871 Java was joined to the international network via Singapore, and a network of lines was gradually extended to all main towns throughout the island. In the 1880s telephone systems were installed in Jakarta, Semarang and Surabaya. And in 1899 Jakarta became one of the first cities in the world to enjoy the new technology of an electric tramway (*Encyclopaedie* 1921; Reitsma 1928).

The crucial aspect of these modern technologies is that they slashed the cost of transport and communications over land. Until the invention of railways in the mid-19th century, the ton-mile costs of transport over land were many times that for over water. The cost contours over land therefore lay close together, implying a very steep economic gradient. These high transport costs could be avoided only where there were valleys with navigable rivers or flood plains transected by canals, as in the Netherlands. Otherwise export production had to be located close to safe coastlines, an advantage to islands, which for any given land area enjoyed the maximum circumference of sea. This readily explains why island Southeast Asia had long been so favoured by international commerce. It also underlies the more than casual connection between the West Indies, where European capitalism first sank roots overseas, and the Netherlands Indies, where the Dutch sought by ingenious means to transplant plantation agriculture. Coffee was planted in the highlands, because it could bear the high cost of overland transport, and sugar in the plains along the coast or the great rivers. Java was probably the one feasible location for a plantation economy in the Netherlands Indies, not only because it was a fertile and accessible island but also because it had a large enough population to be exploited as corvee labour for cheap land transport to points of shipment. Technology closed the cost gap. By the end of the 19th century cane could be shipped by tramways from field to mill and raw sugar from mill to railhead, from where it was carried by main line to the great export sheds in the north coast ports. The spread of railway and narrow-gauge tramway networks allowed plantations to occupy any suitable terrain.

The first 300 years of the Dutch presence in the archipelago bore disproportionately on the Moluccas and Java. During the 19th century, politically, economically, socially and even culturally, Java was tugged farther away from island Southeast Asia, of which it had once been an integral part. In 1871 the first mail steamers to sail direct to Java through the Suez Canal closed the gap between the Netherlands and Java from around four months by sailing ship around the Cape of Good Hope to a timetable of 40 days by sea for passengers, mails and cargo (Brugmans 1950). The telegraph link opened in the same year reduced the transfer time for brief messages to an extraordinary 24 hours. That closure of economic distance led to a quickening inflow of Dutch capital into Java. The transfer of funds was facilitated by monetary reforms: the Netherlands guilder had been legal tender in Java since 1854 and after 1877 was tied to the international gold standard (Potting 1997). There was also a surge in European migration to Java. By the end of the 19th century urban Java was no longer a mestizo society. It had acquired a European veneer. The small European population had gained a tight hold on political and economic power. Holland in the Netherlands Indies, or more accurately Holland in Java, was now a palpable reality.

By 1900 Java was the most technologically modern and integrated economy between Bengal and Japan. The technology of the Industrial Revolution had been applied to a network of transport and communications, to an export-oriented sugar milling industry with giant factories commanding most of the best land on the island, to irrigation systems, to ancillary metal-working and heavy engineering industries, to the production of some urban middle-class consumer goods such as bread, soft drinks and ice, to construction materials such as bricks and timber and to public utilities such as gas and power. Excluding the tiny urban islands of Singapore and Penang, there was nowhere else like it in Southeast Asia. The west coast of Malaya would in time rank alongside Java, but in 1900, just four years after formation of the Federated Malay States and before the formative rubber boom had yet begun, the peninsula was still a string of rough tin mining towns whose only good transport link was by coastal steamer. In the Philippines the Americans had just established their occupation, but even the city of Manila was still fairly primitive by the standards of Java or the Straits Settlements, and except for one short rail line the island of Luzon was almost untouched by modern land-based transport and communications. Within the Netherlands Indies the only modern enclave outside Java was the rapidly growing plantation district around Medan on what was then known as the East Coast of Sumatra. Except perhaps for a few small coastal ports, the rest of the Indonesian archipelago was still on the periphery of the modern world.

THE PERIPHERY

The formation of the Indonesian nation involved not the reincorporation of Java into the archipelago but annexation of the other islands to Java. This historical process is obscured by the habit of juxtaposing Java and the 'Outer Islands'. It makes sense only if the standpoint is Java and there is some boundary that makes a set of Java and those 'Outer' islands. 'Outer' is necessarily 'Other', which is to say 'Other than Java', as the Indonesian term *Luar Jawa* (beyond Java) makes plain. Dutch colonialism turned the archipelago inside out, away from mainland Southeast Asia towards the small offshore island of Java. It helps to have some idea of scale. Java is much larger than Jamaica or Taiwan, about the same size as Cuba, its main rival as a sugar producer, or either island of New Zealand, but much smaller than Britain (England, Wales and Scotland) and Honshu (Japan). In terms of geographic area, the island is large enough to be a small country in its own right, much larger than the Netherlands and about the same size as Portugal.[1] By contrast, the Outer Islands cover a vast area of land and sea that merges physically and ethnographically with what are now neighbouring countries. The eastern coastline of Sumatra runs parallel with peninsular Malaysia, formerly British territory. But for the skyscrapers, Singapore is indistinguishable from any other island of the Riau archipelago. Kalimantan is divided into Indonesia and Malaysia by a border through the jungle. North Sulawesi is the back door to the Philippines; West Irian is culturally part of Melanesia; Bali and Nusa Tenggara, especially Timor, are the back door to Australia. These boundaries have always been porous. Trade and migration, official and clandestine, both acknowledge and mock these lines on the map.

While the Dutch were intensifying their exploitation of Java, the Outer

Islands remained part of a separate and much older economic system, the maritime economy of Southeast Asia that after 1819 was focused on Singapore. The Dutch presence outside Java was so marginal that as late as the mid-1830s it consisted of a string of only 15 small settlements throughout the entire archipelago: Padang, Bengkulu, Palembang, Muntok, Riau, Sambas, Pontianak, Banjarmasin, Makassar, Manado, Ternate, Ambon, Banda, Kupang and Bima, besides which the Portuguese occupied a small outpost at Dili in East Timor (Earl 1937/1971: 430n). Although the Dutch claimed sovereignty over more extensive territories (Vlekke 1945: 304 map), they had no means of administering them. Except for the spices of Banda and the tin of Bangka, these relics of the VOC's former trading empire had become outposts of little importance to Dutch trade. Nor did this situation change much during the period of the Cultivation System. The sparsely populated Outer Islands offered no supply of cheap labour. Compulsory coffee cultivation was introduced to West Sumatra in 1847 (Young 1990) and to Minahasa, but most of the rest of the archipelago was seen as 'an unprofitable burden' (Furnivall 1939/1944: 177). As late as 1870 the Dutch presence was depicted as 'officials planted out as animated coats of arms to warn off trespassers' (Furnivall 1939/1944: 178).

Thus by the late 19th century Java might be envisaged as occupying an economic location not in the middle of the Malay archipelago but closer to Ceylon, the first large island to the East of Suez. Lindblad (1996) has correctly pointed out that this is a relative perspective. By 1869 Java's exports had grown to equal the entire import trade of Singapore, and Java's economic importance was such that it also accounted for a third of Singapore's trade with the Malay archipelago. Nevertheless, most of Java's exports were shipped directly to the Netherlands, much less than 10% via Singapore. By contrast, virtually the entire trade of the Outer Islands, as far away as Makassar, was oriented towards Singapore and the smaller Straits Settlements of Penang and Malacca, where a large part was then absorbed in Asian markets. Table 1.1 shows how different were the trade patterns of Java and Singapore (Wong 1960: 219–30).

Table 1.1   Exports and imports of Singapore and Java by destination, 1869

Destination	Exports (%)		Imports (%)	
	Singapore	Java	Singapore	Java
Archipelago	33.5	12	31	36
Other Southeast Asia	15.5	1	11	1
China	13.0	1	12	2
India	12.0	–	12	2
Europe/North America	24.0	84	32	59
Other	2.0	2	2	–
Total	100	100	100	100

INTEGRATION AND FOREIGN TRADE

In the face of growing pressure by European powers, the Dutch had perforce to defend their sphere of influence. Except for Aceh, Sumatra had been regarded as secure since the treaty of 1824, but Brooke's intrusion into Sarawak in 1841 and the British claim to Labuan in 1846 jolted Dutch complacency. The poor communications between Java and the Outer Islands now became an urgent problem. Since 1830 a mail steamer had plied along the north coast of Java. When the European mails reached Singapore in 1845 by the British P&O line, the colonial government provided a steamer to carry the mails and cabin passengers on to Batavia and there to connect with the Java line. However, not until 1852 did government subsidies bring into being regular steamship links between Java and the Outer Islands (à Campo 1992). The official contract required two monthly lines, one from Batavia to West Sumatra (Padang), the other from Batavia to Makassar, Ambon, Ternate and Manado, with Banda being added in 1854 and Kupang in 1857; a third line from Batavia to West Kalimantan was opened in 1857. The benefits of this network, like Daendels' post road, were mainly administrative: official passengers and mail could now transfer to schedule between Java and the Outer Islands. The cargo of the Outer Islands, however, still flowed almost entirely to and from Singapore. This continued to be the case after 1865, when the more highly capitalised Netherlands Indies Steam Navigation Company (NISN) took over the mail contract. In the absence of cargo, the contract lines to and from Java would not have been viable without subsidy. Most non-contract lines were with Singapore.

The opening of the Suez Canal in December 1869, followed by commencement of a regular direct steamship service between the Netherlands and Netherlands Indies, reinforced this dual pattern. Passengers for Outer Island ports no longer had to transfer in Singapore to inferior local steamers but could travel in style to Java ports and then be carried on by the well-appointed NISN steamers. The impact on the flow of Outer Islands cargo, however, was negligible. The opening of the Canal allowed Chinese in Singapore and Penang to acquire second-hand steamers to replace European-rigged sailing ships in trades to Netherlands Indies ports, improving Singapore's cost advantage as a transshipment port (Bogaars 1955). In the 1880s, British and German European firms also put feeder ships on the berth to collect cargo for their larger steamers in the Singapore and Far East trade (Hyde 1957; Falkus 1990).

Improvements in the technology of transport and the consequent reduction in real transport costs therefore increased the density of shipping and trade networks based on Singapore and the volume of trade over those networks. Commanding the main artery of international commerce between Europe and East Asia, Singapore was the necessary port of call for the shipping of all flags. Moreover, in Singapore were the merchants who dealt in 'Straits produce', the products collected from the jungle and the sea throughout the archipelago and as far afield as Thailand and southern Indo-china. These products were sorted, processed, graded and repackaged for consignment to international markets. In Java, where merchants dealt in plantation products such as sugar, coffee, tobacco and indigo, those commercial facilities were lacking. Hence there was no natural process to redirect that trade back to Java ports, which were served almost solely by ships under the Dutch flag. Disengagement of the trade of the Outer Islands from Singapore would require very determined intervention, not only by commercial policy but also by force of arms.

Extension of Dutch political control over the archipelago was protracted and haphazard, almost absentminded (Chapter 4). In fact, Dutch writings of the 19th century attest to how much the Outer Islands were still being 'discovered'. Intervention was usually to forestall perceived foreign intrusion, mainly on the part of the British. For example, to hold the line against British penetration beyond Sarawak, the Dutch presence was strengthened in West Kalimantan, where Chinese were working the goldfields. However, there were also setbacks. In South Kalimantan Dutch coal mines were overrun and the Aceh War, which began in 1873, was not decided until 1904. The great Java War was settled in five furious and very costly years, whereas the Aceh War dragged on for three decades, which may be taken as some evidence of differing priorities. The 'high tide of Dutch expansion' was not until the very end of the century and was associated with J.B. van Heutsz, the conqueror of Aceh and later Governor-General (1904–1909) (Chapter 4). Mopping-up operations were carried out in the Southeast Moluccas and New Guinea until the eve of World War I. These conquests were significant in economic terms because they gave the colonial government leverage over commercial policy of the Outer Islands. Independent rulers had been able to hold the Dutch at bay by giving trade concessions or revenue farms to Singapore-based traders, mostly Chinese but also in a few cases Arab or European (Reid 1969; Van der Kraan 1980). These traders in turn used British-flag shipping based in Singapore. When these local rulers were defeated, the Dutch reallocated concessions to Dutch shipping lines, trading houses and banks based on Java.

Dutch commercial penetration was facilitated by the spread of Dutch currency into Sumatra, which hitherto had operated on a silver standard in a de facto common currency area with the Straits Settlements (Potting 1997). This silver-based currency also closely linked the trading sphere of Singapore and Penang with the China Coast. British efforts in 1903 to withdraw the old Trade dollar and Mexican dollar in favour of a new Straits dollar tied to the gold standard led to monetary turmoil in Sumatra and triggered the currency unification in North Sumatra in 1908. Dutch banks, in most cases incorporated in the Netherlands but with local headquarters in Jakarta, thereby strengthened their control over credit creation in the Outer Islands and, in conjunction with the trading houses, gained additional leverage over export production and foreign trade.

More direct mechanisms were needed to reorient the trade of the Outer Islands away from Singapore and Penang. The differential tariffs and export taxes or quantitative restrictions, as later applied during the 1970s, would have been flagrant breaches of commercial understandings with Great Britain. An alternative mechanism was applied through the private sector by means of differential freight rates. The mail contract for the archipelago, held since 1865 by the British-controlled NISN, lapsed at the end of 1890. In response to a strong campaign by Dutch shipowners, it was allocated to a new company, the Royal Packet Company, or KPM (*Koninklijke Paket-vaart Maatschappij*), controlled by the two Dutch lines that served the Java trade (à Campo 1992). Their intent, speedily put into practice, was to use transshipment contracts to redirect Outer Island cargo away from Singapore, where it was transshipped to steamers of rival British and German companies, to Java ports, where it could be loaded onto Dutch ships. The KPM therefore served not just as a contract carrier of passengers, mails and government cargoes like the NISN but also as a feeder network for export–import cargo. One of the first targets was the valuable tobacco trade of North Sumatra: by 1900 almost half of the export was being transshipped through Tanjung Priok (de Boer & Westermann 1941: 348). In this way trade was, in effect, induced to flow uphill.

This strategy of trade diversion had more success in the east than the west of the archipelago. The eastern archipelago (*Groote Oost*) became in time a Dutch lake. Suspension of sailings by German ships at the outbreak of World War I helped the KPM to eliminate all Singapore-based shipping east of Banjarmasin by 1915 and to secure for Dutch lines the trade of the whole eastern archipelago. Sumatran ports, however, were still contested. Over the shorter routes from eastern Sumatra across the Straits of Malacca, from the islands of Riau and from West and South Kalimantan, there was no cost advantage in redirecting trade to Java and Chinese commercial networks and shipping proved tenacious. The rubber boom tied these regions more closely to Singapore, a commercial reality which in time even the KPM was forced to concede by placing small, specially designed ships in the Singapore trades. In the interwar years Singapore was as busy a KPM hub as Tanjung Priok or Surabaya.

Table 1.2 Inward shipping by main port, 1903, 1929 and 1938			
	Thousand m³		
Port	1903	1929	1938
Jakarta	4.1	20.4	17.0
Surabaya	3.8	19.5	14.0
Belawan	0.7	10.1	10.0
Makassar	1.2	8.0	7.0

The commercial tactics of the Dutch lines were underpinned by public investment in strategic port development in the Outer Islands. The pioneer scheme, around the turn of the century, was the construction of a deepsea harbour at Sabang off the northern tip of Sumatra. Its rationale was to become the entrepôt for the foreign trade of Aceh, where the Dutch were still fighting a bitter war, and to restrict British-flag shipping operating out of Penang, which was seen as 'smuggling' supplies to 'the enemy' (Reid 1969: 268–70; à Campo 1992: 157–62). Sabang was declared a 'free port' in 1903, but without commercial networks never became more than a coaling station and transfer point for mails. The colonial government, nevertheless, held to the conviction that modern deepsea ports were the key to trade diversion. Coinciding with the end of military pacification, in 1909 the Dutch engineers Kraus and de Jongh were commissioned to design hub ports suitable to take the largest ships and to facilitate transshipment. Tanjung Priok, where construction of a deepwater port had begun in 1877, was extended with new harbour basins. Surabaya, hitherto a roadstead port, was developed as a complex of deepwater wharves, opened in 1917 and completed in 1925. In the western part of the archipelago, a new deepsea port was opened at Belawan (near Medan) in 1920 to capture the valuable plantation exports from North Sumatra, hitherto transshipped through Penang and Singapore. In the east, new deepsea wharves with huge godowns were opened in 1918 at Makassar, which since the 1900s had become the stapling point for the copra trade (de Boer & Westermann 1941: 233–7). Facilities including bulk handling for coal and oil were built at other ports around the archipelago, but these four ports remained the pivots of Dutch trade.

By the late 1920s a good deal of the trade of the Outer Islands had thereby been diverted into the hands of Dutch firms. An integrated network of interisland and deepsea shipping focused on the four main deepsea ports, whose infrastructure and customs procedures were designed to facilitate transshipment (Table 1.2; Knaap 1989: 73–9). This was supported by a sophisticated financial infrastructure of trading houses, banks and insurance companies. The stranglehold of Singapore over the foreign trade of the Outer Islands was thus broken for all main commodities except rubber. The trade of the eastern archipelago was shipped almost entirely through Makassar, that of the east coast of Sumatra mainly through Belawan. By 1929 the KPM fleet was almost 10 times larger than that of its predecessor

Table 1.3	Scale of interisland operations, NISN (1886) and KPM (1929)				
Company	Year	Ships	Tonnage	Miles (000)	Passengers (000)
NISN	1886	32	28 000	772	103
KPM	1929	137	268 000	4495	1203

(NISN) 40 years earlier, carried much more cargo and over 10 times as many passengers (Table 1.3; Knaap 1989: 69, 71).

INTEGRATION AND INTERISLAND TRADE

Dutch control over the foreign trade of the Outer Islands did not make the Netherlands Indies into an integrated economy. The trade of the separate islands was still oriented towards the outside world and very little with each other. That Sumatra, Kalimantan and Sulawesi had little to trade with each other is hardly surprising in view of their very similar resource endowment of abundant land and natural resources and sparse population. Because their local economies were still subsistence-oriented and had only small urban populations, the inwards trade was biased heavily towards essential items such as rice, sugar, salt and textiles. Between Java and the Outer Islands, however, there was a good deal of scope for specialisation according to comparative advantage. In Java the land frontier was closing, so that land was becoming more scarce and labour more abundant. This changing resource endowment offered scope for development of the manufacturing base, especially in the textile industry (Dick 1993d). The interest of Dutch textile manufacturers, however, was to keep open the Netherlands Indies market by low tariffs. There were no offsetting measures of industry policy to support the establishment of what would in the early years have been infant industries. Thus Java produced very little by way of manufactures that could have been exchanged for the raw materials of the Outer Islands.

An indication of the low degree of integration between Java and the Outer Islands is the value of interisland compared with foreign trade. The first usable interisland trade statistics date from 1914, by which time the whole of the archipelago except for Portuguese Timor had been brought under Dutch control. Even allowing for overstatement by inclusion of exports (including tin) and imports shipped on local bills of lading, in 1914 the value of interisland trade between Java and the Outer Islands was a mere 5.5% of the value of the foreign trade of the Netherlands Indies (Table 1.4; Korthals Altes 1991; BPS 1956; Rosendale 1978). It would have been more accurate to speak not of the Netherlands Indies economy but of the Netherlands Indies economies. Despite a common customs area (*tolgebied*) and a common currency and exchange rate, the former was still little more than an abstract concept.

The fragmentation of the archipelago shows up vividly from the dispersion of rail networks. Java had a particularly dense network of railways and tramways, whereas that of Sumatra was broken into three unconnected networks (Reitsma 1925). Elsewhere the only line was a short 47-km section from Makassar. Grand schemes to link the Sumatran networks and add spur lines to the ports of Sibolga, Tembilahan and Bengkulu came to nought because of the 1930s Depression, as also did plans to extend the

Sulawesi line from Makassar northwards and to construct new networks in South and West Kalimantan and in Minahasa. Instead the short Makassar line was closed as an economy measure. Even today the all-weather highway network has scarcely developed beyond the rail networks that had been planned in the 1920s. Intraisland trade continues to rely heavily on coastal shipping. The initial effects of administrative integration were underpinned by the period of autarky during World War I. Although the Netherlands stayed neutral in this conflict, the trade of the Netherlands Indies was greatly disrupted. By 1915 deepsea freight costs had begun to soar and from 1917 the Allied blockade interrupted most supplies, not only from Europe but also from the new sources of North America and Japan. Shipping to Europe did not resume until February 1919 and remained irregular for the rest of the year. All this conferred a suddenly high rate of natural protection on the Netherlands Indies and in Java gave rise to a certain amount of opportunistic industrialisation. Growth was most spectacular in the processing of vegetable oil (mainly coconut oil) and the manufacture of soap and margarine as new mills were built to fill the gap left by German factories, which on the eve of World War I had pressed most of the copra imported to Europe (Kamerling 1982). The engineering industry, which for several decades had concentrated mainly on repair work, now turned increasingly towards construction, and many new firms entered the industry. Other industries to become established under wartime conditions were chemicals, packaging materials, cement, cigarettes and rubber goods (NHM 1944). These goods were shipped from Java to the Outer Islands, with a reverse flow of fuel and raw materials. By 1921 the proportion of interisland to foreign trade had almost doubled, to 10% (Table 1.4).

That momentum was not sustained after return to normal international trading conditions. When international commodity prices and freight rates collapsed in 1920, wartime natural protection evaporated and hard-pressed manufacturers in Europe, North America and Japan competed with each other for the Netherlands Indies market. A few of the new manufacturing

Table 1.4   Ratio of interisland and foreign trade, 1914–1972

		Interisland trade	Foreign trade	Ratio interisland/ foreign trade (%)
1914	million	62	1114	5.5
1921	Dutch	247	2440	10.0
1929	guilders	310	2593	12.0
1939		211	1291	17.0
1955	million	10 400	17 973	58.0
1972	Rp.	372 000	1 422 000	26.0

plants survived, especially in the chemical industry, but entire infant industries succumbed, most notably the coconut oil industry. The local textile industry failed to progress much beyond the handicraft stage. As the separate local economies of the Netherlands Indies reverted to their usual pattern of export–import trade with the rest of the world, interisland trade grew no faster than foreign trade until the end of the 1920s.

Intensification of trade links between Java and the Outer Islands awaited an industry policy that would protect Java-based manufacturing industries against international competition. In terms that would become more familiar in the late 1970s, Java's labour was overpriced because rapid growth of Outer Islands exports sustained too high an exchange rate and price level. Manufactured imports were therefore too cheap, which made local manufacturing uneconomical. In that sense, by the 1920s Java was disadvantaged by incorporation into a wider Netherlands Indies economy at a single unified exchange rate. Had the Outer Islands been a separate colony or perhaps instead been incorporated with the similarly booming economy of British Malaya, the emerging weakness in Java's primary export capability, a consequence of growing land shortage, would have been accommodated either by a lower exchange rate or by deflation of wages and prices vis-à-vis the rest of the world.[2] Java's food crops and manufacturing industries would then have become more competitive and gained a larger share of the rapidly growing import demand of the Outer Islands. In the event, there was actually a perverse effect. The 'overvalued' exchange rate allowed the large population of Java, especially the prosperous European population, to maintain a higher rate of imports from the rest of the world. As late as 1939, Java ports accounted for two-thirds of the colony's imports but only one-third of its exports (Table 1.5; Indisch Verslag 1940). Even allowing for some redistribution of these imports to the Outer Islands, it would appear that the Outer Islands were already subsidising the imports of Java, a feature that would become more marked and more contentious after Independence.

Despite this exchange rate disadvantage, there is some evidence of a weak trend towards closer economic integration between Java and the Outer Islands during the 1920s. Although, as stated above, there was little gain in the size of total interisland trade relative to foreign trade, the balance of trade had begun to shift in Java's favour. In 1914 flows to and

Table 1.5   Share of exports and imports by main region, 1939

Region	% of exports	% of imports
Java	36	66
Western Outer Islands	50	25
Eastern Outer Islands	14	9

from Java were almost the same. In the early 1920s shipments into Java were much greater, but the direction switched in the mid-1920s and from 1927 onwards ran heavily in favour of Java (Korthals Altes 1991). The high level of aggregation makes it hard to determine the underlying causes, but three factors may be significant. The first is just a valuation effect arising from falling commodity prices in the late 1920s. This may have affected the value of foreign trade more than interisland trade. Second, a marked decline in the value of petroleum products shipped to Java from the Outer Islands at a time of rapidly rising consumption probably reflects rising production on Java, leading to virtual self-sufficiency (Lindblad 1989b: 59–60). Third, throughout the 1920s there was rapid growth in volume and value of cigarettes shipped from Java to the Outer Islands. By the end of the decade the value of 'cigarettes and cigars' was almost as great as 'textiles'; these two categories dominated the value (but not volume) of the outward trade from Java. Cigarettes were an early success of import substitution because the Java product, especially *kretek* (clove) cigarettes, was distinctive in taste and had no close substitutes among foreign brands.

The next stage in the integration of the archipelago was delayed until the early 1930s, and was a consequence of the world Depression. This 'crisis of capitalism' undermined the viability of the colonial import–export economy and called into question the *laissez-faire* assumptions on which it had rested since around 1870. The production of Java's staple export, sugar, collapsed from 3 million tons in 1928 and 1929 to just 0.5 million tons in 1935 (Creutzberg 1975). Exports from the Outer Islands, especially rubber and copra, were also badly affected. At the same time, Dutch consumer goods, particularly textiles, were almost driven from the Netherlands Indies market by cheap Japanese imports. In 1929 Japanese goods had held 10% of the market, but after the yen devaluation of January 1931 this share increased to almost one-third (Dick 1989). In these circumstances Dutch manufacturers had nothing to lose from protection of the Netherlands Indies market. The objections of the plantation and trading interests to any threat to 'cheap labour' were now muted.[3] Immediate survival required the sugar mills to renege on long-term land rental contracts and to forgo control over much of its labour force. Alternative employment opportunities were obviously essential.

Formulated by bureaucrats in the Department of Economic Affairs, the response was one of protection and import substitution in both industry and agriculture. To limit the penetration of Japanese imports, in 1933 the colonial government introduced import quotas by industrial product according to country of supply (see Chapter 6). The outcome was a boom in manufacturing output on Java, especially in textiles. Shipments of industrial goods from Java to the Outer Islands increased threefold between 1935 and 1941 (Sitsen 1943: 4). To ensure a livelihood for labour released by Java's sugar industry, the government also restricted the import of foreign rice, which caused rice shipments from Java to the Outer Islands to increase from around 30 000 tons in the 1920s to almost 200 000 tons in 1939

(Indisch Verslag 1940). Interisland sugar exports also increased. As evidence of closer economic integration, the proportion of interisland to foreign trade had by 1939 risen significantly, to 17% (Table 1.4).

More significant than the still modest degree of integration was the direction of the trend and the accompanying structural change. Java, the plantation economy which until the 1920s had been the powerhouse of the Netherlands Indies, was now disengaging from the international economy. Reversing the process that had begun in the 1830s, resources were being shifted out of plantation industries into food crops and also, from a very small base, into manufacturing. This marked belated recognition that population growth had shifted Java's underlying comparative advantage. In the 1830s labour had been the scarce resource and policy had been directed to harnessing that labour for export production through enforced corvée labour. By the 1930s the frontier had closed and land was the scarce factor. Population growth had made labour abundant, but it was not yet cheap. Rapid growth of Outer Island exports at a constant nominal exchange rate had inflated the domestic price level and thereby raised Java's wage rate relative to international levels (i.e. the real exchange rate). Although nominal rents and wages had been held down by the plantation interest backed up by administrative sanctions, sustained productivity growth through technological change had been necessary to maintain Java's share of world markets in the face of this disadvantage and falling commodity prices. The collapse of Java's sugar industry in the 1930s was therefore not a cyclical phenomenon but a fundamental structural adjustment (see Chapters 5 and 6).

The new interventionist economic policies of the 1930s marked belated recognition of an economic interest of the Netherlands Indies separate from that of the Netherlands (Chapter 6). Java had long been an engine to drive the Dutch economy. Now for the first time it was harnessed to drive an emerging Netherlands Indies economy. With sufficient protection to offset the exchange rate disadvantage, Java's abundant labour could be mobilised to develop manufacturing industries and obtain raw materials by trading with the Outer Islands, whose purchasing power could now be switched from foreign goods to cheaper domestic products. This was a virtuous cycle. Political trends, however, were reactionary. In most of the Outer Islands the once-disparaged expedient of indirect rule was reinforced during the 1930s (Benda 1966: 602–3). The modern functional bureaucracy of Java did not yet hold sway over a unitary state.

INDEPENDENCE

The trend towards economic integration probably accelerated after Independence. Autarky during the Japanese occupation was followed by foreign exchange restrictions and encouragement of import substitution. At face value, 1955 trade data show that the economy had become much more integrated since 1939 (Table 1.4), though comparison with more robust

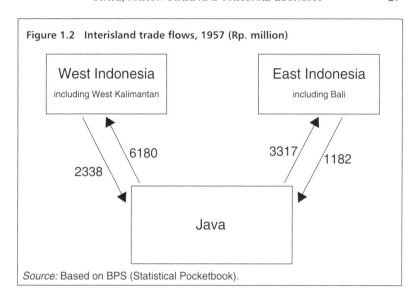

Figure 1.2   Interisland trade flows, 1957 (Rp. million)

West Indonesia
including West Kalimantan

East Indonesia
including Bali

6180

2338

3317

1182

Java

Source: Based on BPS (Statistical Pocketbook).

figures for 1972, when a realistic and unified exchange rate again applied, suggests that foreign trade was greatly understated. By 1955 the Indonesian rupiah was already quite heavily overvalued, thereby understating the official value of foreign trade. At the same time, smuggling was becoming a serious problem, especially from regions such as Central Sumatra and North Sulawesi, where the Army exercised de facto control. Foreign trade volumes were therefore also understated.

The 1957 interisland trade data, which for the first time are broken down by province, reveal the pattern of internal trade (Figure 1.2). Several features stand out. First, if the archipelago is broken into the three segments of West (Sumatra, Riau and West Kalimantan), Java, and East (South and East Kalimantan, Sulawesi, Maluku and Nusa Tenggara), it can be seen that most *inter*island trade was still between Java and the Outer Islands. Trade between West and East Indonesia was minimal. Second, Java now ran a huge export surplus with the Outer Islands, the outwards trade in foodstuffs and manufactures being almost three times the inwards trade in fuel and raw materials. Third, Java's trade was still heavily biased towards the West, which accounted for twice as much interisland trade as the East in both directions. Fourth, as a result of civil war, greater provincial autonomy, and smuggling, Makassar had greatly declined as an entrepôt for Eastern Indonesia. Fifth, western Indonesia still had no entrepôt of its own, that function being served by Singapore. The general impression is of an economy still 'under construction'.

From an economic perspective, the Permerintah Revolusioner Republik Indonesia (PRRI)-Permesta rebellions that convulsed Indonesia in 1958 may be seen in part as symptomatic of a country whose political integration had been pushed much faster than the economic integration needed to sustain it. Little had changed from the colonial situation whereby the islands of Indonesia, and indeed even separate parts of those islands, were fragments connected to each other by little more than geographic proximity and regular shipping lines. Some links had atrophied. For want of shipping, the Japanese had sought each island as far as possible to be self-sufficient. During the Revolution, political links with Java had also become tenuous. And when the Dutch re-established control over the Outer Islands, they encouraged a kind of puppet federalism that promised a degree of local autonomy with a demo-cratic façade (Yong 1982). Meanwhile, the British government in Singapore had surreptitiously encouraged local Chinese merchants to resume barter trade with Sumatra and Kalimantan by making available cheap ships that could slip through the Dutch blockade. Thus trade links with Singapore were re-established much sooner than links with Java. Regularised at Indepen-dence, they flourished during the Korean War boom, when many traders and shipowners made their fortune. During the 1950s, as the central government in Jakarta sought to tax exporters in the Outer Islands not only by direct export taxes but also by maintaining overvalued exchange rates, these Singapore merchants formed commercial alliances with local military leaders to turn a blind eye to smuggling in return for a share of the profits (Harvey 1977). Had the central government lacked the military forces or the will to overthrow the local military warlords, the actual political boundaries of the Republic might have contracted to Java and poorer parts of the Outer Islands such as Nusa Tenggara.

A clear insight into the commercial orientation of the Outer Islands was provided during Confrontation against Malaysia (1963–1966). Ships were forbidden to load cargo from Indonesian ports to Malaysia or to be admitted to Indonesian ports with cargo originating from or transshipped in Malaysia. These measures greatly disrupted the physical direction of trade and led to some increase in export cargo transshipped in Javanese ports. Nevertheless, with the connivance of local military commanders, other small ships continued to slip across the Straits to Singapore under cover of darkness with cargoes of rubber. However most foreign-flag ships previ-ously engaged in trade with Indonesian ports were simply transferred to Panamanian 'front' companies, repainted and renamed, and loaded for Hong Kong or Bangkok, where their cargoes were handled by the same Chinese networks as before. The foreign trade networks of the Outer Islands proved to be not only tenacious but also highly adaptable. The Indonesian government lacked the means to force trade into other channels. As the Dutch had found during the Revolution, it was impossible to impose a blockade across such a vast archipelago. Naval commanders, like their army counterparts, could be bought off by well-connected businessmen, often local-born Chinese. When the restrictions on trade with Malaysia were lifted in mid-1966 by the New Order government, the old principals shed their disguises and trade quickly slipped back into its familiar groove.

Over the next few years the Indonesian government, like the former colonial government, tried by various policy measures to redirect the country's foreign trade from Singapore to its own ports. Loading permits, introduced in 1964 to discriminate in favour of Indonesian deepsea shipping lines, were now applied to discourage transshipment through Singapore. In 1982 the Directorate-General gave this ad hoc protectionism the status of a 'gateway policy', whereby Indonesia's non-bulk exports were to be directed through Indonesia's deepsea ports of Tanjung Priok, Surabaya, Belawan and Makassar (Dick 1987a: 33–5; 1993b). The sanctions differed, but basic policy was little changed from colonial mercantilism.

By the 1980s, however, in the era of container shipping, a 'gateway policy' designed for the route patterns of conventional break-bulk cargo ships made little sense. After 1971 the Europe–Singapore–Far East trade was served not by 10 000-ton geared freighters but by giant 50 000-ton motherships. Closure of Indonesian ports to small feeder vessels denied Indonesian shippers the benefits of the much lower freight rates made possible by cargo consolidation in Singapore and consequent economies of scale. After the mid-1980s when the non-oil export drive became a national priority after the collapse of oil prices, these restrictions were swept away (Dick 1987a). Indonesia's trade with Europe and North America now moved almost entirely by transshipment via Singapore. This second attempt to eliminate Indonesia's trade dependence on Singapore, and thereby to cut adrift from the Southeast Asian trading system, thus became untenable under the pressures of technological change and globalisation. Trade could at some cost be pumped uphill but it could not in the long run be induced to flow uphill of its own accord.

Abandonment of the 'gateway' policy coincided with a new phase of national economic integration. As in the 19th century, when Java was consolidated as an economic core, the driving force has been the development on Java of massive new productive capacity. Since the late 1960s, Java has undergone a belated industrial revolution based on the resource of 'cheap labour' (Chapter 7). The first phase, from 1967 to the riots of January 1974, relied heavily on foreign investment. The second phase, lasting about 10 years over the second and third Five-Year Plans, involved import substitution behind a protectionist wall (Hill 1994). During both phases there was very rapid growth in interisland shipments of manufactures from Java to the Outer Islands and of raw materials and energy from the Outer Islands to Java (Dick 1995). Interisland commercial networks, which formerly redistributed imported goods, now handled similar local products. After the mid-1980s the Outer Islands could trade freely via Singapore, but continued to draw manufactured goods from Java. The differing resource endowments between Java and the Outer Islands were at last reflected in specialisation according to comparative advantage. Quite

Table 1.6   Destination of manufacturing sector output and origin of input by main island, 1987 (%)

	Intraisland	Interisland	Foreign	Total
Java				
output destination	80	15	6	100
input origin	64	13	23	100
Sumatra				
output destination	65	21	14	100
input origin	64	20	16	100
Kalimantan				
output destination	25	36	39	100
input origin	74	11	15	100

apart from residual tariff and non-tariff barriers, Java was now the least-cost producer of many of these items. At the same time, the explosive growth in the export of manufactures from Java flowed through into increasing demand for raw materials and energy from the Outer Islands, further boosting their demand for Javanese manufactures.

Quantifying the trend of integration beyond 1972 is difficult, because value data on interisland trade are no longer published (Table 1.4). However, some insight can be gained from input–output estimates by origin and destination for the manufacturing sector in 1987 (Table 1.6; Bappenas 1991).[4] The distribution of final manufacturing output from Java was heavily biased towards interisland trade, although inputs were still weighted towards imports. For Sumatra, both output and inputs were biased more towards interisland than foreign trade; Kalimantan's raw material shipments divided fairly evenly between interisland trade and exports. Other evidence of frequency of connections, tonnage of freight and number of passengers between Java and the Outer Islands confirms the dominance of Java in this booming interisland traffic.

Despite new pressures for greater regional autonomy, economic integration is unlikely to be reversed by the crisis of the late 1990s. Massive depreciation of the rupiah has boosted domestic integration through import substitution. Commodity exporters in the Outer Islands maximise their windfall gain in rupiah purchasing power through buying domestic consumer goods, which Java can now supply more cheaply than imports. Despite the obvious gaps in land transport in the Outer Islands, at the end of the 20th century the economic fragments of the colonial Netherlands Indies seemed at last to have welded into a substantive national economy. The irony is that at just this time the political unity of Indonesia was being challenged by separatists in Aceh and Irian.

CONCLUSION

The very long-term trends of the rise of a highly centralised nation-state and consolidation of an integrated national economy of Indonesia are the strong threads of the past two centuries of Indonesian history. Around 1800 at the beginning of our period, there was in the Malay Archipelago no modern state and no colonial/national economy. At the beginning of the 21st century there are four nation-states, among which Indonesia stands out by sheer size. Arguably it has become the world's most populous centralised state, for India and the United States are both federal systems, as de facto is China. Emergence of this nation-state and its associated national economy was no natural process but slow and often painful. It was moulded under tremendous pressure — political and military pressure from the European powers and later Japan and the USA, economic pressure from technological change and the forces of the global economy. As a locus of power, the modernising and centralising state used its formidable repressive apparatus to impose its will on society. Only when control of the state was contested during the Revolution and the early years of Independence did popular movements play a role.

The crisis of the late 1990s may turn out to have been a historical watershed. The downfall of Soeharto released popular frustration with overcentralisation of government and associated political repression. Like the former colonial state, the New Order state turned out to be remarkably fragile for want of broad-based institutions that embodied popular consent in that system of government. In May 1999 radical new laws were introduced to facilitate much greater regional autonomy. In June 1999 there were the first popular parliamentary elections since 1955. In the absence of a military coup, authoritarian centralisation is therefore unlikely to persist in the 21st century. The economy has become integrated to the point where it can sustain a more open and decentralised political system without the nation fragmenting. The great uncertainty is whether political instability will prevent the renewal of sustained economic growth.

Another new faultline is along a globalisation gap. Industrialisation in the form of large and medium-scale manufacturing, as well as associated financial and business services, have concentrated in a few urban agglomerations, most notably Greater Jakarta (Jabotabek) and Greater Surabaya. In 1930, at the end of a century of land-extensive agro-industrial expansion, the urban population of the entire Netherlands Indies was only 10% and Jakarta was a city of only 0.5 million. By 1995, Jabotabek's population of 20 million was itself 10% of the national population; its share of national product was 20% and of large and medium-scale manufacturing employment over 25% (BPS data). This capital city dominance reflects much more than centralisation of government. In an era of globalisation, Jakarta has become Indonesia's world city. Despite the achievement of national economic integration, Indonesia is therefore again subject to spatial stresses between the new globalised enclaves and the rest of the country. The tensions may become manifest between rich and poor, between the globalised, urban middle class and the mass of people still living around the poverty line, whether in the kampungs of Jakarta, the villages of Java, or in many parts of the Outer Islands. The character of this next transition, like that of many industrialising European countries or Japan in the first half of the 20th century, is still impossible to predict.

APPENDIX

1.A Purchasing-power parity

National income is calculated by summing the value added in each stage of production across a country for one year, giving a total in the currency of that country. For comparative purposes, these totals are then converted at official exchange rates into US dollars. In some countries, including Indonesia, this conversion gives rise to a distortion in comparative living standards because official exchange rates do not equate purchasing power in the two countries. Accordingly, the World Bank has developed an alternative conversion in terms of 'purchasing-power parity' (PPP), which equates one dollar of expenditure across countries (see also Appendix 7.B). For example, by the conventional GDP measure, in 1998 the economy of Singapore was 68% the size of Indonesia's; in PPP terms it was only 16% (World Bank 2000b).

2

The pre-modern economies of
the archipelago
Vincent J.H. Houben

INTRODUCTION

The economic history of Asia before the 19th century is increasingly being written from the perspective of world history. Product markets in Europe and Asia were interlinked. When European trading companies opened direct maritime trade routes to Asia, this connection intensified. Recent historiography on various Asian regions is displaying consensus that rapid economic growth was a regular feature of early periods. Colonial views that preindustrial economies were intrinsically static are no longer considered valid.

Asia's pre-modern economies shared many characteristics. In East Asia, close resemblances existed between the economies of Ming-Qing China (1368–1912) and Tokugawa Japan (1604–1867). Their high degree of integration in the world economy was connected to an important role of foreign trade, a highly commercialised agriculture, expanding handicraft production and a substantial growth in monetisation and urbanisation. Both relied on a rational management of human labour (Lee 1999: esp. 18). In Moghul India proto-capitalism developed from the 16th century, stimulated by a flourishing entrepôt trade through markets in the Indonesian archipelago and the Indian Ocean. This led to an increasing use of money, new forms of taxation, and hierarchic interdependencies between central and local markets (Perlin 1983). A similar picture has been given for Southeast Asia for the period between the 15th and 17th centuries.

Even the pre-1800 economic history of the Indonesian archipelago reflects the new vision of Asia as an integral and dynamic part of world history in the context of globalisation. This chapter outlines the main characteristics of the economies that occupied the area of modern Indonesia before Europeans established their hegemony in the 19th century. It identifies starting-points that would influence later developments. A thematic treatment is preferred to a chronological one, to avoid repeating similar features across many local regions. After a brief discussion of the economic geography of early Indonesia, demography, long-term economic trends, state formation and indicators of the level of precolonial economic development are discussed. This approach shows that Indonesia was a region full of economic opportunities and enterprise.

GEOGRAPHY

Any economic history must start with considerations of physical geography. The fundamental importance of the sea in Indonesian history is uncontested. Yet there were no clear boundaries that distinguished Indonesian seas from other ones (Wolters 1982: 39):

> The single ocean possessed a genuine unity of its own. The trading
> connections that linked the opposite ends of maritime Asia resemble links in a
> chain which would join together again even if one link were temporarily
> broken . . . In effect, the single ocean was a vast zone of neutral water, which
> rulers inside and outside Southeast Asia independently and for their own
> interests wanted to protect.

This perspective of the sea as a zone of neutrality bridged by a flexible chain of trading points suggests a basic problem in discussing the pre-modern early economy of Indonesia. Maritime sail transport and alternating monsoon winds determined the accessibility and defined zones, but the drawing of boundaries is problematic. The colonial boundaries of the future Indonesia were demarcated only at the end of the 19th century. How then to discuss Indonesia's pre-modern economic history without demarcation from the rest of insular Southeast Asia?

Historians have made various demarcations of their own. Some have studied both mainland and insular Southeast Asia together rather than using Indonesia as the unit of historical analysis. Some have argued the case for a single geographic and trading world extending from the mountains of the eastern Himalaya in the north to the volcanic arc of Sumatra/Java to Sumbawa in the south (Reid 1988: 1–3; 1993a). Others have accepted the Indonesian archipelago as a feasible historical category, being a distinct set of islands lying at the crossroads between the Indian Ocean and the South China Sea, with Java at its centre. This region can be subdivided into the Northeast Sumatran-Malay Peninsula region, the South Sumatran-West Java zone, the Java Sea (covering Central and East Java and South Kalimantan) and three separate regions east of Java, that is, Bali/Lombok/Sumba, then South Sulawesi, Sumbawa and Timor; and finally the Moluccan Sea linking North Sulawesi to Mindanao in the north and Banda in the south (Lombard 1990: I, 13–18).

Various types of ecological zones or 'landscapes' exist within Indonesia that, even today, allow for quite distinct patterns of human activity. Besides the interaction between water and land, most prominently at the mouths or lower reaches of navigable rivers, plains versus mountains, open terrain versus thick forest, swamps versus passable tracts of land resulted in spatial configurations of the economy that nowadays have been partly overlaid by modern technology and transport but in no way completely suppressed. The monsoon rainfall patterns of an equatorial climate, so vital for agriculture, add to the complexity of precolonial Indonesia.

The means of transport that allowed the exchange of goods determined much of economic activity in precolonial Indonesia. Movement from one island to another required navigation of sea lanes. The Indonesian islands, which form an arc from Sumatra in the northwest to New Guinea in the far east, give Indonesia a central axis around a number of smaller inner seas. Regional north–south maritime trade links were as important as the inter-regional east–west ones. The mountain ranges that cut through the main islands made coast-to-coast communication more difficult than traffic parallel to the coastlines. On the main islands of Sumatra, Java, Kalimantan and Sulawesi, rivers were the means of coast–hinterland links. Mountain ranges, swamps or other natural barriers delineated inner-island regions. Contact could be more easily made with adjacent islands than with neighbouring regions on the same island.

Another geographical complexity is the distinction between Java and the Outer Islands. Because of its relative abundance of resources and people, Java has dominated much of Indonesian history. Several geographical factors have to be taken into account here: the volcanic range in Java does not constitute a solid barrier of mountains as in Sumatra; its climate is more moderate than wet Sumatra or the dry Lesser Sunda islands and thus well suited to wet-rice cultivation; also its population has been much larger than that of Sumatra (Lombard 1990: I, 21–2). However, these geographical conditions alone do not explain Java's predominance. Also relevant is the nature of state formation on the island.

The geographical distinction between Java and the rest of the archipelago is reflected in indigenous culture. The ambiguous position of the Malay world vis-à-vis Java has often been portrayed in classical Malay literature. In the *Sejarah Melayu* there is an extensive description of the East Javanese court of Majapahit, when supposedly visited by Sultan Mansur Syah of Malacca, a central staple-port on the Malay Peninsula. Although full of irony, the Javanese arts are portrayed as being superior (Robson 1992: 38–40). Yet, from the perspective of economic history, it would make sense to consider Java, at least until the start of the 19th century, as a set of economic regions with similar characteristics to many of the 'Outer Islands'.

POPULATION GROWTH

Land and water were abundant in early Southeast Asia, but people were not. The availability of human labour was the critical economic constraint.

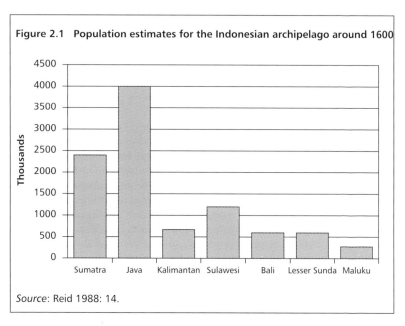

Figure 2.1 Population estimates for the Indonesian archipelago around 1600

Source: Reid 1988: 14.

The distribution of people over the Indonesian islands has always been uneven, Java being more densely inhabited than the Outer Islands. Nevertheless, the archipelago as a whole was relatively sparsely populated. The geographer Rigg states: 'Outside a few areas of high population density, such as Java and the Red River Delta of Vietnam, Southeast Asia was a low-pressure area when compared to its neighbours, India and China' (Rigg 1991: 16).

Pre-19th-century population figures for Indonesia are, with a few exceptions (Knaap 1995), either non-existent or highly unreliable. Royal tax lists exist but it is difficult to convert these into genuine population numbers. As a starting-point for his early period estimates, Reid takes data from the 18th and early 19th centuries — that is, just before the modern period of rapid population growth. These figures are extrapolated backwards, from 1800 to 1600, assuming an average rate of population growth of a mere 0.2% per year (Figure 2.1). A population estimate for the whole of Indonesia in 1600 would be about 10 million. Although the regions outside Java were together inhabited by more people than living in Java, Figure 2.1 confirms the demographic predominance of the latter. In terms of economic zones, the ratio of population numbers between the Malay, Java and Eastern Indonesia zones was something like 3:4:3. However, population density was much higher in Java than elsewhere, with most people living in the fertile valleys of the Solo and Brantas Rivers in Central and East Java, which were ideal for intensive wet-rice cultivation.

While some authors have raised objections, others have accepted Reid's projections as plausible. The low growth rate reflects a high death rate which offsets a high birth rate (Boomgaard 1989b: 335–7). Climatic variation and its influence on mortality have also attracted closer attention. Cycles in weather conditions of 50/51 or 88/89 years of length could be linked to droughts, harvest failures and famines, with wars (e.g. in the 17th century) following in their wake. Most epidemics followed also after years of anomalous weather conditions, although some such as smallpox normally preceded these and increased the virulence of the disease (Boomgaard 1996).

THE SECULAR TREND

The long-term economic trend or 'economic tide' is considered to be a reflection of slowly changing economic parameters, such as the size of production, the number of consumers or long-term price trends. In European history the hallmark of the secular trend is the price level of goods over time. However, for pre-modern Indonesia there are no such price lists. Data on economic growth are very unevenly scattered over time and place. The main parameter is that of population growth. It is assumed that the income elasticities of supply and demand for foodstuffs are low, whereas the elasticity of demand is high for manufactured goods.[1] Within these boundaries it is assumed that quick population growth caused real incomes to decline, and the reverse in the case of declining population.

A long-term economic or secular trend is assumed to have existed in the history of pre-modern Indonesia. From early history until the early decades of the 19th century the secular trend of economic development showed upward movement during the 7th–8th centuries, the periods 1450–1680 and 1750–1820s. Stagnation or decline can be assumed for the 1680–1750 period. In view of gradually expanding resources, it can be argued that by the early 19th century, the beginning of our period, the Indonesian economy had advanced beyond its starting-point in early history.

During the 7th and 8th centuries, trading activity grew in the regions of both the Malacca Straits and the Java Sea. This period is connected with the rise of the states of Srivijaya in Southeast Sumatra and Mataram in Central Java (Wisseman Christie 1995: 251, 264, 275). Not until the 'commercial revolution' of the 16th century did another growth spurt occur in both regions at the same time. Instead, a structure emerged in which the political and economic centre was situated either in the Malacca Straits or around the Java Sea. Srivijaya declined in the late 8th and 9th centuries, only to recover in the 10th. Its successor state and central marketplace of Malacca did not emerge until the 15th century.

Between 500 and 1500 Java may have experienced almost uninterrupted economic growth (Boomgaard 1993: 197–9). In the 11th century the economic centre of gravity moved from Mataram (South Central Java) towards the Brantas river basin (East Java), where in the 14th and

15th centuries the kingdom of Majapahit became pre-eminent. By the 14th century indigenous sources exist which reveal the existence of a developed pre-modern economy, with enough resources to maintain links with many areas outside Java (Hall 1985: 242–50).

According to Anthony Reid, during the period 1450–1680 a commercial revolution occurred across insular Southeast Asia. Reid argues that Southeast Asia played a critical role in the booming world economy of the 'long' 16th century. The most important long-distance trading products (pepper, cloves and nutmeg) came from this region, involving merchants, polities and cities and leading to rapid growth in all economic sectors (Reid 1993a: 1–2). Several features of the Indonesian economy in the 16th and 17th centuries are discussed in greater detail below. In the western part the archipelago trade was oriented towards Malacca, at least until 1511 when the Portuguese sacked the city. In 16th-century Java a string of harbours along the north coast (Pasisir) competed for commercial and political supremacy.

Before the mid-17th century a decline of Indonesian commerce set in, partly due to internal impediments, such as the struggle in Java of inland Mataram for coastal resources (Houben 1994b: 65), and partly because of the disruption caused by European trading companies. Other reasons for the decline of Indonesian high-seas commerce seem to be a shift in trade

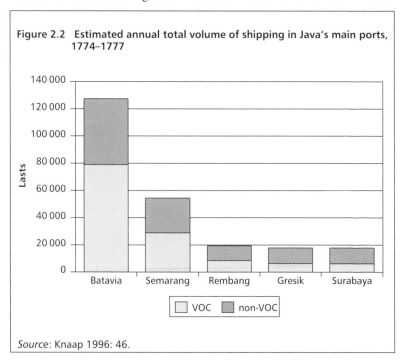

Figure 2.2   Estimated annual total volume of shipping in Java's main ports, 1774–1777

Source: Knaap 1996: 46.

networks away from Malacca towards Aceh and Banten, the upsurge of
Gujarat in the Indian Ocean trade, and Chinese junk trade in the South
China Sea (Manguin 1993: 201–4). Between the VOC and Chinese traders
a strategic alliance developed that was beneficial to both parties but
probably disadvantaged indigenous shipping. The Chinese junk trade to
Batavia prospered from 1690 to 1740 (Blussé 1986: 121–4).

There was no sharp distinction between European and Asian shipping.
European maritime technology was quickly applied to Indonesian shipbuilding. Javanese, Chinese, Malay and Bugis sailors were employed on
both Asian and VOC cargo ships. There existed many types of ship, of
which many displayed some sort of hybrid nature.

During the second half of the 18th century the Indonesian economy began
to recover while the VOC began to decline. By 1775 the total volume of
maritime traffic appears to have been substantially larger than in 1600
(Knaap 1996: 168). The decline of VOC trade volumes became apparent
only after 1780. A British naval blockade between 1795 and 1811 impeded
Dutch trade much more than indigenous maritime commerce. In a study
based on toll registers of harbour masters in the Java Sea area of around
1775, Knaap gives a detailed picture of the maritime trading network and the
dominance of the VOC. Nevertheless, indigenous shipping was much more
vigorous than was assumed on the basis of older studies. This is illustrated
by a comparison between the volume of goods transported by non-VOC and
VOC ships trading to and from Java (Figure 2.2). The VOC controlled about
half of the total trade volume out of Java ports and dominated the trade with
Batavia (Knaap 1996: 48). On the other hand, the trading connection
between central Java ports and the Malacca Straits was largely in the hands
of private non-VOC or 'Indonesian' shipping. The Malacca Straits were
clearly on the rise again due to the expansion of trading activities in Johore
and Palembang (Vos 1993; Watson Andaya 1993).

'POLITICAL ECONOMY': THE NATURE OF THE STATE

Economic development and state formation were closely connected.
Increasing fiscal resources empowered the political centre, which in turn
could more effectively control and protect market trade. The historiography
on the connection between early economic and political development
in insular Southeast Asia is fairly recent, since political and religious
explanations of state formation have long predominated.

By drawing together pieces of historical evidence, several basic
inferences regarding the nature of the very early economy can be put
forward (Wisseman Christie 1995: 272, 275):

1. There was a close link between maritime trade and state formation in
    the evolution of larger political entities from common local chiefdoms
    or port settlements.

2. The two key economic regions of insular Southeast Asia were the Malacca Straits and the southern end of the Java Sea. These economies slowly diverged, that of the Malacca Straits remaining totally dependent on trade, whereas in Java-Bali plural states developed where both external and internal resources were abundant. These different orientations were apparent until the end of the pre-modern era.

3. Both kinds of polity depended on control of the economic base, whether of adjacent ports or of the agricultural unit of production, the *wanua* or village community.

Later phases of pre-modern state formation fitted into the established pattern. While Srivijaya became the prototype for later Malay states, Mataram became the prototype for the Java-Bali region. Over time, states strengthened their control over natural and human resources in line with the growing number of people living on the shores of the Indonesian islands and with a growth in trade.

The two best documented precolonial states are Malacca in the western part of the archipelago and Majapahit in the Java-Bali region. How did their economic processes relate to political ones? Malacca owed its emergence in the 15th century as the dominant staple-port to several factors. The great maritime trade route between the Mediterranean, western Asia and India to China passed through the sheltered Malacca Straits, where a stopping-place was convenient to await the half-yearly change in the prevailing monsoon wind before sailing on into the South China Sea or the Bay of Bengal. Due to diplomatic relations and internal political control, one state in the Straits could dominate the others. Just as Srivijaya had owed its prominence to a special relationship with China, control over harbour chiefs and the *orang laut* (nomadic sea and riverine people), and its fame as a well-governed centre of high Buddhist standing, Malacca entered into fruitful diplomatic exchanges with the Ming dynasty, set up legal and political safeguards for peaceful trade and became part of the world of Islam.

The Malay polity was centred on the concept of *daulat*, the exclusive mandate to rule (Watson Andaya & Andaya 1982: 23–55, esp. 44–5). Milner has refuted Gullick's Western view of Malay politics as being a 'working system of political control' and has phrased it as the '*karajaan* system', in which the king is the source of honour, the bestower of titles and gifts and the constant recipient of homage (Milner 1982, 1995: 16). Trading activities, however, were largely regulated on royal behalf by the one or more *syahbandar* (literally 'harbour master'). These officials were often leading merchants of foreign origin, acting as intermediaries between ruler and traders and as surveyors of tradesmen. In Malacca there were four *syahbandar* of different origin, each of whom governed the activities of ethnically and spatially distinct trading communities, such as the Gujarati, Burmese, Javanese and Chinese (Watson Andaya & Andaya 1982: 42–3).

The key text for understanding Majapahit is the *Nagarakrtagama*. Written by the superintendent of Buddhist affairs and dealing mainly with King Rajasanagara's royal tour through East Java in 1359, this document is above all a praise of the king's excellent qualities as a ruler, thereby proving that he was an incarnation on earth of the highest divinity (Prapanca 1995: 5). Although there are several layers of meaning in this text, it connects with everyday reality as the poet saw it. Stanza 4 of canto 83 is of particular interest (Prapanca 1995: 85):

> And so constantly all kinds of people come from other countries in countless numbers -See: India, Cambodia, China, Annam, Champa, the Carnatic and so on, Gaur and Siam are their places of origin, sailing on ships with the merchants in numbers, monks and priests in particular, when they come they are given food and are happy to stay.

In local textual tradition, East Java's prominence was first and foremost connected to the advent of religious scholars from elsewhere. Commercial traffic itself was hardly mentioned, but only in the context of the economy prosperity of the Brantas valley could there emerge such a prominent royal state.

The Portuguese and subsequently the VOC interfered with the usual processes of state formation but did not suddenly introduce colonialism. The first author to break with the Eurocentric view that the Europeans simply replaced the indigenous fabric with a colonial one was J.C. van Leur. In his pioneering book on early Asian trade, the role of the Portuguese in Indonesian waters was described as follows (Van Leur 1934/1983: 117):

> After journeying through the inhospitable seas of southern Africa the Portuguese had come into regions where there was a complex of shipping, trade and authority as highly developed as the European: forms of political capitalism at least as large in dimensions as those of southern Europe, and probably larger; shipping in bottoms many of them carrying more than those used in European merchant shipping; a trade in every conceivable valuable high-quality product carried on by a great multitude of traders; merchant gentlemen and harbour princes wielding as great financial power as did the merchants and princes of Europe . . . The Portuguese colonial regime, built by and upon war, coercion, and violence, did not at any point signify a stage of 'higher development' economically for Asian trade. The traditional commercial structure continued to exist.

With regard to the situation much later in the 18th century, Van Leur argued that only a few European centres of power had yet been consolidated and that the 'Oriental lands' continued to play a very active role, economically and politically (Van Leur 1934/1983: 274). Van Leur's bold stance has since been modified but his thesis on the vitality of the indigenous Asian economy is undisputed.

Whether the period 1600–1800 constituted a watershed in the economic history of the archipelago depends on where we are looking. Only in part of Java and in the Moluccas did the VOC state effectively replace pre-existing polities and achieve territorial hegemony. There an infant colonial state could develop, with mechanisms of resource extraction, that in the 19th century would develop into a complete, integrated system of control. Outside Java and the Moluccas, the VOC destroyed rival kingdoms, such as Makassar in 1667 and Banten in 1683, or forced existing political entities to enter into alliances of an unequal nature, but without establishing territorial rule.

The VOC can be viewed as a precocious multinational corporation with features of an Asian state. Although its origins lay within Europe, it was a global organisation with vast resources. As an Asian state, the VOC reveals several features. First, the VOC organisation displayed a high degree of centralisation. Despite its many scattered possessions, orders and policies emanated from the Governor-General's office in Batavia and were expected loyally to be obeyed. Second, the VOC was an armed state. The large majority of its employees consisted of soldiers, and its powerful warships patrolled Asian waters. Violence was used wherever and to whatever degree was deemed necessary. All these characteristics were geared towards the single goal of maximum profit. This great degree of purpose and its global financial and economic resources made it a 'state of a different kind' from local polities in the tradition of Malacca or Majapahit. Because of its focus on trade and only limited territorial sway the VOC cannot be said actually to have controlled the entire archipelago, but its influence was undoubtedly substantial.

INDICATORS OF PRE-MODERN ECONOMIC DEVELOPMENT

Some picture of the level of economic development before the 19th century is necessary to put the modernisation of the past two centuries into perspective. The Indonesian economy evolved within an archipelago of shifting local, regional and global configurations which, at least until 1900, were rather open-ended. Many of the propositions made here are of a preliminary nature.

Despite the absence of reliable data, five key indicators can be identified as a basis for assessing the degree of economic development in the precolonial era:

1. The degree of *economic specialisation*. Market opportunities influenced the relative importance of agricultural production for export, the production of manufactures and the division of labour.
2. The range and differentiation of *commercial networks*. To what extent were trading links or market networks localised or integrated in the global economy? How sophisticated were transport facilities at the prevailing level of technology?

3. The level of *monetisation*.
4. The level of *urbanisation*.
5. The nature of *economic regulation*. What was the balance between protection and facilitation of economic activities versus extraction by political centres?

These indicators represent different aspects of the same historical reality.

The degree of economic specialisation

Before the 19th century there was already a marked orientation towards the world market. However, this orientation was neither universal nor uniform. Much of the archipelago remained, into modern times, a subsistence economy dominated by agricultural pursuits serving the basic demands of the local community and involving little trade with the outside world. A change from swidden to sedentary agriculture allowed for more mouths to be fed in a single locality and therefore larger communities to exist. Output growth did not involve technological advance but merely reflected population growth, which led to a further expansion of small-scale farming. In contrast, there were also pockets where favourable location and beneficial conditions for surplus production laid the foundations for an outward economic orientation.

Production for both the internal and the world market became an important feature of the economy at an early stage. Besides crops traded in bulk for domestic purposes — of which the staple food rice was the most important — there was a substantial supply of agricultural items to the global market, also recently imported ones such as tobacco (from America) and coffee (from Yemen). In part this was 'foreign trade' in precious products such as forest products from the Outer Islands (camphor, sandalwood), sea produce (pearls, shells) and gold (Sumatra), but above all in Moluccan spices. These goods attracted Chinese and Indian merchants long before Europeans came to the Indonesian archipelago. Pepper became a boom crop between the 15th and 17th centuries. There was extensive trading also of tobacco and *gambir* (leaves that produce an extract used for *betel* chewing). This kind of market orientation involved little capital, much share-cropping, use of migrant workers and local agricultural entrepreneurs (Reid 1984: 153–5). Because of lack of sources, it is difficult to quantify production, demand and price levels as a whole, let alone on a regional or local basis, but Bulbeck et al. (1998) is a first systematic attempt. The picture is of an already quite advanced, dynamic Asian economy, not fundamentally different from that of the contemporary Mediterranean.

Because regions specialised in particular marketable crops, it is possible to identify the trading networks by agricultural product. Rice and salt came from Java, while the plain near Makassar also produced rice. Spices (cloves, nutmeg and mace) originated from the Moluccas. Pepper was traded from Aceh, Jambi, Palembang and Lampung in Sumatra and from Banjar in South

Kalimantan. Minor items of indigenous trade were tobacco, *gambir* and coffee (Reid 1984: 153–5). An additional topography of trade includes the following products and destinations: Javanese cotton, fabrics and primary foodstuffs (rice, salt, dried fish, beans) were shipped to Sunda and to East and West Sumatran ports in return for pepper; products brought to Java by Chinese and Indian traders (silk, cotton cloth, porcelain) were transported with rice to the Moluccas and traded for cloves and nutmeg; spices were taken along with rice to Malacca or bought up by Chinese or Indonesians with porcelain, silk, precious metals or copper coins. Several side-branches were attached to the basic triangular format of trade between the Malacca Straits, Java and the eastern islands, for instance Sumatran pepper partly exported to Bali via Java in exchange for cotton fabrics, knives from Belitung and Karimata exchanged for sandalwood and wax on Timor. *Lacca* (fragrant wood) was imported from Lower Burma, *kesumba* (red dye) from Nusa Tenggara, and diamonds from Tanjungpura in East Sumatra and Martapura in South Kalimantan (Schrieke 1955–1957: I, 21–2).

The VOC traded not just in the archipelago but across the whole Asian economy. The archipelago was only part of a much larger network of factories and settlements from Japan to the Persian Gulf. Next to the Asian–European trade connection, intra-Asian trade was the central pillar on which this pre-modern multinational enterprise was built. The VOC had a profound impact on this elaborate trading network. Part of the indigenous trading network was brought under the control of the VOC. Elsewhere, the VOC bought goods either in exchange for goods in demand or by cash.

Backed by the coercive power of its warships and soldiers, the VOC also took steps to control production of some of the most valuable crops. In 1621 the VOC seized control of nutmeg production in the Banda Islands, which were managed like a plantation in the West Indies. In 1656 the VOC established a worldwide monopoly of clove production in the area around Ambon in the Central Moluccas, which was enforced by patrolling fleets of galleys (*hongi*). The case of pepper was somewhat different because the VOC did not control the whole of the Malacca Straits, so that the indigenous pepper trade was maintained. In Java, the north coast regents were compelled to deliver agrarian products — both foodstuffs and marketable cash crops — to the VOC (Nagtegaal 1996: 129–40, 168–74). Coffee cultivation was introduced to the Priangan highlands of West Java on such a scale that around 1725 it surpassed Yemen as the world's leading exporter of coffee. The coffee boom in the Priangan attracted migrants from north and central Java (Knaap 1986). This forced coffee cultivation became the model for the Cultivation System, which the Dutch introduced to Java on a huge scale after 1830 (see Chapter 3).

Local manufactures were also produced for the market. Except for cloth and pottery, most manufactures were produced by male artisans. Textiles functioned as a key indicator of wealth in pre-modern Southeast Asia.

Although much cotton and silk was imported from India and China respectively, a substantial indigenous textile industry had come into existence before 1800. In some regions — Java and Southwest Sulawesi — it had developed into a major export industry. The VOC and the British East India Company tried to procure cloth to trade for pepper and spices in their intra-Asian trading networks. Javanese batik was much in demand as a luxury item.

If local textiles were an item of mass consumption, the upper end of the market involved metal manufacture. Copper and lead were imported from outside Indonesia, whereas Kalimantan and Sulawesi provided iron. Located near royal courts, highly specialised villages or town quarters came into existence. Specific data are available on Makassar, where apparently a kind of guild operated, and Nagara in South Kalimantan at the royal capital of the sultan of Banjarmasin (Reid 1984: 155–61). In the 18th century, mining of tin commenced on the island of Bangka (Vos 1993).

After the VOC had acquired commercial predominance, the state of the economy can be generalised as follows. In areas under VOC control, a market orientation was often replaced by a more indirect relation through the use of intermediaries, either indigenous heads or Chinese, who were linked to the Dutch trading enterprise. Elsewhere, there was a range of outcomes: (a) the VOC had no impact because it did not interfere with the products of that particular locality or region; (b) market production was introduced by the VOC on top of an economy that was still predominantly subsistence-based; (c) the indigenous market-oriented production was exposed to VOC competition; (d) market orientation was wiped out (spices in the northern Moluccas). A reorientation of indigenous trade towards new economic niches could, at least in part, be a compensation for markets lost to the VOC.

Around 1750 the number of subjects under VOC jurisdiction in the archipelago numbered about 200 000 people: 60 000 in the Moluccas, 50 000 in South Sulawesi and some 100 000 in and around Batavia (Van Goor 1994: 135). Elsewhere, however, indigenous centres survived of political power and economic importance. In inland Java the Mataram empire retained a large rural economic base, even after its ports were brought under VOC control and despite much internal conflict between 1670 and 1755. Outside Java, Aceh was ascendant during much of the 17th century. So also was Makassar in South Sulawesi until its defeat by the VOC in 1667. At the river mouths of Sumatra, the Malay Peninsula and Kalimantan, smaller port polities continued to control much of the local coastal and river trade. During the 18th century Siak and Pontianak developed into substantial economic centres.

The range and differentiation of commercial networks

The rise of a dense market network in the archipelago from the 13th until the mid-17th century is well documented. Apparently starting from a few scattered harbours, a much more complex market system developed. This involved a web-like structure with a clear hierarchy of regional and central ports. Contacts with China and the Arab world increased significantly.

With the growing predominance of Majapahit during the 13th century and the ascendancy of the Pasisir coastal region 200 years later, Java itself developed into a maritime power. The 14th-century *Nagarakrtagama* manuscript mentions almost a hundred toponyms over which sovereignty was claimed, pointing to commercial contact in the form of state-supported embassies. In the 16th century along the north coast a string of mercantile cities developed, with a cosmopolitan population of merchants and their dependants (Lombard 1990: II, 31–50).

Overlapping this network of seaports there existed riverine and rice-plain exchange systems. The economic centre was based at a river mouth, while secondary and tertiary centres were located upstream, usually at junctions or watersheds. These were in turn fed by inland population centres or upriver villages. Economic centres like Srivijaya therefore possessed two hinterlands, the sea and the land.

The river-plain realms of Java displayed a different market configuration. Clustered villages or *wanua* possessed periodic markets (*pken*), which handled the flow of goods from coastal ports. Itinerant small merchants linked these communities of exchange into market networks. These peddlers were integrated in turn by intermediate market centres, inhabited by retail and wholesale traders as well as by artisans. Higher marketing centres, normally located at coastal ports, were run by large seafaring traders. This hierarchy facilitated trade (Hall 1985: 18):

> In the Javanese plains, free of physical constraints on the movement of goods
> from the hinterland, a number of periodic market centers connected to
> intermediate and higher order centers of exchange by a hierarchy of
> specialized and large-scale traders thus expedited the natural flow of goods
> destined to be sold to seafarers.

Transport systems underpinned these market networks. Sea transport was carried on mainly by small freight vessels of a distinct type called the 'Southeast Asian junk', which could carry 4–40 tons (Reid 1993a: 36–43). Inland river transport in Java was not so easy. Barges operated along the Brantas and Solo rivers, linking the plains of east and central Java with the sea, but deforestation of the river banks made them increasingly shallow and difficult to navigate. Land transport in Java was little developed until well into the 19th century. In the 17th century, inland Mataram was connected to the coast by only three adequate roads, from Mataram to Semarang, to Tegal in the northwest and to Gresik in the east. These roads permitted the passage of oxcarts, although passage was problematic during the wet season. Side roads were in general suitable only for transport by foot (Lombard 1990: I, 112, 114; see Appendix 2.B).

The rise of Islam in Indonesia, starting in northeast Sumatra in the 11th century and reaching the eastern archipelago in the 15th, indicates the growing commercial traffic over long distances, involving not only trading but also cultural transfer. The preponderance of Islamic trading communities in the port polities of the archipelago encouraged local rulers to convert to Islam. Not only could they then count on the support of religious brethren elsewhere — Islamic state philosophy also enabled local rulers to wield power more effectively. Islamic codified law offered many advantages for conducting business, as testified by the regulations of Malacca (*undang-undang Malaka*). Sophisticated commercial law, comprising rules on bankruptcy, collateral, borrowing and trusteeship, and maritime law were included in this codification, of which the core dates from the 15th century (Liaw 1976).

The expansion of Islam in the archipelago was like a slow wave, moving from West to East Indonesia and simultaneously moving from coastal areas to the interior of the various islands. Starting from North Sumatra, where Islamic polities may have existed as early as the 11th century, Islam reached Java in the 14th century and finally the eastern archipelago in the 15th. Trade contributed to the Islamisation of the archipelago and in turn benefited from the conversion of local powerholders to Islam. Muslim traders displayed a clear preference for doing business with fellow believers at trading sites controlled by Islamic law. Not only overseas relations but also contacts with hinterlands became easier through the religious connection. The egalitarian nature of the Islamic religion was an additional advantage for trade (Kathirithamby-Wells 1986).

Markets consisted of networks of people. Various groups specialised in maritime trade and their influence extended far beyond their home regions. Minangkabau traders were active on both shores of the Malacca Straits throughout the pre-modern period, establishing settlements on the west coast of the Malay Peninsula in early Malacca times. The Buginese, who became refugees from the Bone area in South Sulawesi during the civil wars in the latter part of the 17th century, were even more prominent. In the early 18th century Malacca's successor state of Johore came under their control. The number of Chinese in the archipelago also rose considerably, due to an upsurge in the junk trade with China.

After the Portuguese had conquered Malacca in 1511 and the VOC had taken control of Banda in 1621 and the Central Moluccas around 1650, both the eastern and western parts of the archipelago came under Western influence. The VOC's subjugation of Makassar in 1667 and the cession of Java's north coast by Mataram in 1743 altered the existing market networks in the centre of the archipelago. The consequences for trade differed according to product. In the case of the traditional export crops of the archipelago, the advent of the Europeans meant a reorientation of Asian trade. The European-led export of sugar and coffee produced dependency instead of strengthening indigenous trade. A statistical compilation of the values of four main export crops (cloves, pepper, sugar and coffee) shows that between 1540 and 1630 the output trend for both cloves and pepper was sharply upward; after the 1650s there was a prolonged slump, and these export values were not reached again until the 1720s (Bulbeck et al. 1998: 9–16, esp. 12–13). The salt trade, however, developed independently from Western interference. Java's salt exports rose from the end of the 17th to the end of the 18th century. In Java, distribution was increasingly taken over by Chinese, whereas in other islands Malay marketing networks remained viable (Knaap & Nagtegaal 1991: 156).

The level of monetisation

In the pre-modern archipelago there was a wide range of monetary systems, corresponding to the level of economic and market activity. Major trade items could be bartered directly, but many other transactions were realised only through the use of currency. In the Toraja area of Central Sulawesi there existed a system of exchange linked to funeral ceremonies; in Kalimantan Chinese ceramics were used as a currency. Precious metals played a role in higher-level markets. Until the 17th century Sumatra was a gold producer but little of it entered the monetary system, being used mainly for hoarding or status-enhancing display. The main local currency from the 13th century onwards was Chinese *picis*, which were copper — later a copper–lead alloy — coins with a punched-out centre that allowed them to be threaded into strings of cash (Blussé 1986). In a few localities locally minted coins also appeared. In Java *zimat* ('bringers of fortune') were struck on the model of the Chinese *pici*, and in Pasai (Sumatra) tin currency was produced. From the moment the Europeans arrived, their silver coins were much in demand and circulated widely. In the regulations of Malacca several sections were devoted to rules of currency exchange (Lombard 1990: II, 136–43).

During the 16th and early 17th centuries the expansion of production for the world market greatly enlarged the circulation of money throughout the archipelago. Silver, copper and lead were always in short supply and flowed into the region from the outside. As Reid writes: 'Chinese copper cash, and local coins modelled on them, were the basic lubricant for the increasing commercialisation of the region after 1400' (Reid 1993a: 95). From the late 16th century onwards there was a large influx of silver from Spanish America, transported by galleons heading for Manila and Japan. Although most of the silver was absorbed by the prosperous economies of India and China, some flowed into Southeast Asia and stayed there (Reid 1993a: 103). Because of the rising level of monetisation, this silver seems to have had no inflationary consequences.

The VOC tried to gain access to the economy of the Indonesian archipelago not only by controlling sea lanes but also by bringing in substantial amounts of copper and lead. Data on the tonnage of lead imported by the

VOC support the conclusion that about 350 tonnes of lead were required yearly to provide *picis* for its transactions in Indonesia. In the 17th century an estimated 800 million *picis* were in circulation for a total population of around 10 million (Reid 1993a: 99). Its monopoly of the production of lead coins helped the VOC to attract a good part of Indonesian shipping to Batavia. Monetary policies were thus a highly effective means of diverting trade to the benefit of the Europeans (Blussé 1986: 46–8).

The level of urbanisation

Cities were instrumental in the commercialisation of the precolonial economy. Estimates from both early European and indigenous sources of the size of 16th and early 17th-century Southeast Asian cities range from 100 000 to 800 000 (Reid 1993a: 71–2, table 7). These figures indicate that early modern Asian cities were at least as large as those in Europe, giving substance to the idea that commercialisation was accompanied by very rapid urbanisation (Reid 1993a: 68–70). Nevertheless, the high estimates by some European travellers cannot be accepted at face value. Pre-modern cities like Beijing and Istanbul were probably larger than the port polities of Indonesia. The morphology of Southeast Asian cities was different too, as stone houses and fortifications were absent. The concentration of scarce resources of manpower was of greater importance than putting much money into the establishment of solid buildings protected by brick walls.

If the high urbanisation thesis is accepted (see Appendix 2.D), it also seems likely that the decline of Asian trade after 1680 was accompanied by marked de-urbanisation. Dutch censuses at the end of the 17th century show that Malacca, Ambon and Makassar had only 5000 inhabitants each, and even Batavia's population was only 27 000 (Nagtegaal 1993: 49). Admittedly, most indigenous groups lived outside the area that the Dutch officially defined as urban, so that these figures are probably underestimates. Nevertheless, they are *prima facie* evidence for de-urbanisation.

The nature of economic regulation

Political structures depended on economic prosperity. State authorities had to seek a balance between promoting trade and extracting revenue from it. Growing expectations or the sheer greed of powerholders might disturb this balance, causing extraction to prevail over facilitation and eventually resulting in the decline of commerce. The period after 1450 seems to have been one of rapid commercialisation in the whole world, not only Southeast Asia. Local rulers profited from this and became stronger. Why did Europe manage to sustain economic development, whereas Southeast Asia or the Indonesian archipelago apparently did not?

One explanation for this fateful difference between Europe and Southeast Asia is in terms of 'property rights'. In much of Europe there was security of person and property; in Southeast Asia and especially Indonesia there was not. In northern Europe, cities developed autonomy from the ruler and could safeguard the interests of merchants and capitalists through legal codes, guilds, banks, stock exchanges, chartered companies and the like. Savings of both city-based merchants and the rural elite were mobilised for productive ends. By contrast, in Aceh, Banten and Makassar the trend was strongly towards personal rule. Through the opportunity to tap new sources of wealth, accompanied by a new arms technology imported from Europe, the merchants were increasingly squeezed by royal monopolies and driven away. Only rarely could a strong commercial class curtail the king's power. According to Reid, this was 'the most critical difference between Southeast Asia and Europe in this period' (Reid 1993a: 130, 245–66). Besides the impact of the European trading companies, this internal factor was a major cause for disengagement of the archipelago from the world economy and its subsequent decline.

Such analysis, although hypothetical, postulates a strong link between monopoly and absolutism and between absolutism and impoverishment. Economic growth increased the coercive powers of powerholders, who shortsightedly overtaxed the economy, thereby undermining growth. The damage wrought by the VOC on the early modern economy of the archipelago was therefore compounded by adverse political trends on the indigenous side. Royal monopolies strengthened the political role of kings and curbed the activities of merchants. At the same time, the disruption of trade by the Europeans may well have weakened the merchant class and hastened the rise of absolutism.

The link between VOC monopoly and impoverishment, on the other hand, seems less straightforward. The textile trade in the VOC era may point in another direction. Imports of Indian textiles to the archipelago started to decline as early as the 1650s. Challenging the thesis that Indonesians became so poor that they could no longer afford to buy imported cloth, Laarhoven argues the case for import substitution. Indonesians decided for economic and political reasons to produce their own textiles. The batik revival in Java, for example, was instigated by the Javanese rulers (Laarhoven 1994). At the beginning of the 18th century there were also economic interests that were pursued by both the VOC and the Mataram empire in Java alike, resulting in an alliance between the Dutch and the Javanese ruler Pakubuwana I. The two rulers joined forces in subduing the coastal regents in order to gain access to their resources (Nagtegaal 1996: 82–3). This alliance, however, broke down, and ultimately resulted in a situation in which the VOC received cash payments from the Javanese court and entrenched itself in the local economy of the island (Ricklefs 1993).

CONCLUSION

The precolonial archipelago consisted of a number of open economies, which experienced a high degree of commercialisation during periods of growth. The extent and nature of integration into the world market differed between regions within the Malacca Straits, the Java Sea and East Indonesia, but as a whole the core of insular Southeast Asia was heavily influenced by this early wave of globalisation. The period between 1450 and 1680 was one of great economic activity. A high degree of economic specialisation, a wide range of commercial networks, a high degree of monetisation and a rapid process of urbanisation were indicators of emerging capitalism. However, the combination of European encroachment on the Indonesian trading system and the rise of 'monarchical capitalism' caused the Indonesian economy to decline (Kathirithamby-Wells 1993: 136–43). Only after about 1750 did the economy of the archipelago seem to expand again. By then indigenous absolutist states had collapsed and the VOC was weakened by strong competition from the British, thus making room for new initiatives.

What then was the state of the economy in 1800, at the beginning of our modern period? It is hard to measure 'progressiveness' when we rely so much on modern economic concepts to depict a preindustrial, non-Western economy without time series on population, production and prices. Direct comparison with the European historical experience is difficult to sustain. Nevertheless, portrayal of a static, unmonetised economy no longer fits the qualitative evidence. In the case of mainland Southeast Asia, Lieberman (1995) has rejected Reid's trend of decline from the second half of the 17th century, arguing that there state formation and maritime trade continued in line with the experience in France and Russia. Historians of Outer Island Indonesia are similarly sceptical about the hypothesis on the region's long-term decline. Indonesia around 1800 may therefore be seen as a set of local economies that were, at least in part, quite vigorous and for the time quite modern.

APPENDICES

2.A   The debate on early demography

Boomgaard (1989b) argues that in 1600 Java had 5–6 million inhabitants. Lombard states that, before the advent of the Dutch (in 1596), Java 'could have numbered one or two million inhabitants' (Lombard 1990: I, 22), a much lower figure than Reid's estimate approximating Raffles' 4.6 million of 1815. Boomgaard (1989a: 166) assumes a number of 1.6 million for the north coast and Easthook of Java in 1795 and agrees, with others, that Raffles' 1815 figure for the whole of Java was far too low. If we inflate the figure for Java in 1800 and stick to an average population growth of 0.2% per annum, the backwards extrapolation delivers very different results. This would also alter the relative population density of Java versus the Outer Islands.

On the whole, Reid's estimates for 1600 are rather high, although Hugo's estimate gives a correspondingly high range of 3.4–5.0 million for 1600

(Hugo et al. 1987: 31). Of course, populations fluctuated sharply and could go down substantially if warfare was combined with crop failures and disease. For Java, the period 1675–1755 displayed such an adverse scenario, as the island suffered from a series of dynastic wars that ultimately split the Mataram kingdom. These 80 years could have offset the entire growth during the 120 years to 1675.

2.B   The 16th-century commercial revolution

Reid proposes the thesis of a pre-modern commercial revolution in Southeast Asia. The 1450–1680 period was labelled by him an 'Age of Commerce'. Rapid commercialisation did not occur in Southeast Asia alone but was a feature of world history: 'The entire period 1400–1630 was one of rapid monetisation and commercialisation of the economy' (Reid 1993a: 129). In contrast, the decline of Asian commerce was particularly evident from the second half of the 17th century onwards: '. . . the urban-centered world of Southeast Asia . . . had vanished by 1700. . . . The change of direction in the seventeenth century was not reversed until the twentieth' (Reid 1993a: 311).

Some authors challenge the view that everywhere in Indonesia the 'long' 16th century was associated with booming trade and rapid economic growth. Boomgaard sees the 16th century as a period of stagnation or low growth rates in Java, whereas outside Java Aceh and South Sulawesi were doing well. As far as the 1600–1800 period in Java is concerned, Boomgaard thinks it is almost impossible to decide whether it was one of economic growth, stagnation or decline. He concludes: 'Taken as a whole, the period 1500 to 1800 does not seem to have been one of expansion' (Boomgaard 1993: 203, 208).

2.C   The nature of Asian trade and the impact of Western trading companies

J.C. van Leur (1934/1983) was the first Western historian who tried to study the Asian trade system from within. Inspired by the example of the early modern Mediterranean, he argued that maritime trade in Southeast Asia was conducted by small-scale traders (pedlars) who went from harbour to harbour in order to sell high-quality luxury goods. This pattern of trade was continued under the Portuguese, who controlled part of the archipelago in the 16th century, and even under the VOC the Asiatic international trading system remained in place.

Meilink-Roelofsz modified the main propositions of Van Leur. She argued that Asian trade was not only a peddling trade in high-quality items but also included trade in bulk involving big traders and large capital. She also thought that Van Leur underestimated the impact of the European trading companies. The Portuguese possessed a huge preponderance in military technology. The VOC used its modern organisational structure to destroy part of the indigenous economy, so that Asian shipping was degrading long before 1800 (Meilink Roelofsz 1962: 5–11). Steensgaard postulates that Asian princes played a big role in Asian trade, offering trade protection against a fee. He argues that the Portuguese system and that of the princes did not much differ. By contrast, the VOC and British East India Company created a trade revolution, as they established a transparent staple market, price controls and internalised protection costs, which until then were higher than transport costs (Steensgaard 1973: 11, 40, 85–6, 96).

2.D   The Indonesian pre-modern city

There is considerable disagreement on the size and nature of the pre-modern Southeast Asian city. Some historians, particularly Reid, take at face value observations of contemporary European travel accounts, writing about wealthy Asian cities of staggering dimensions. From an economic point of view, the physical concentration of the most scarce factor of production, human labour, makes sense and corroborates evidence from the travel accounts.

Nagtegaal (1993), drawing in part on authors like Wisseman Christie, Boomgaard and others, argues that the pre-modern urbanisation of Southeast Asia was not at all impressive. Cities were in reality only small trading towns, with no more than 2000 inhabitants on average. There were three possible reasons for this. First, central markets were absent because of an efficient existing network of small markets dominated by small traders. Second, cities lacked a competitive edge over rural areas as economies of scale do not apply to wet-rice systems. Finally, Southeast Asian cities did not possess integrated urban functions. A role as military base was completely lacking, cities were not walled and were mostly abandoned on attack. Commercial and religious functions were not found together in one city.

3

Java in the 19th century: consolidation of a territorial state

Vincent J.H. Houben

INTRODUCTION

In 19th-century Java a threefold development took place that in retrospect can be seen as a precondition for the rise of the integrated, export-oriented economy that would eventually become Indonesia. The three interrelated developments were the establishment of a strong state, sustained population growth, and economic expansion associated with the input of capital and new technology. What happened in Java marked the beginning of massive expansion in primary production and export across most of Southeast Asia (Brown 1997: 1). Java took the lead in this process.

The starting-point was the establishment of a new type of state that proved much more effective than older indigenous states in mobilising local resources of land and labour to generate a sustained growth of output. The new colonial state can be defined as a modern, strongly bureaucratic, centralising polity that acted as an agent of the Netherlands. This modern state consolidated its power over Java's traditional rulers while drastically reorganising production and society to achieve its own ends. The outcome was a tremendous expansion of state-directed commodity exports produced by a steadily growing mass of rural manual labourers. In the last quarter of the 19th century, the colonial state gradually withdrew from direct involvement in production to facilitate and supervise private European capital, while restricting the role of Chinese capital.

The VOC had concentrated on maritime trade not just in the archipelago but throughout Asia. In the second half of the 18th century, by which time the Netherlands had ceased to be a centre for the world economy, the VOC empire went into decline. The British naval blockade and seizure of Ceylon (Sri Lanka) in 1795 triggered bankruptcy and in 1800 the VOC's remaining territorial possessions were taken over by the Dutch state. The Dutch role in Asia then contracted to exploiting the economic resources of just the one very fertile island of Java. Because Dutch trade was weaker than Dutch capital, resort was had to a system of belated mercantilism in an attempt to revive the Netherlands economy after the end of the Napoleonic wars. The complex trading system of the VOC was replaced by a dominant trading link with the Netherlands. These were the basic parameters of the Dutch colonial enterprise in the 19th century.

As the Dutch had lost much of their coercive power in the second half of the 18th century, the assertion of more direct colonial dominance over the people of Java provoked a vehement response. In 1825 the Yogyakarta prince, Diponegoro, started a large rebellion which led to a five-year war, costing up to 200 000 lives on the Javanese side and thousands on the European side. The Dutch were forced to mobilise all their national resources to defend their presence on the island. The causes for the outbreak of the Java War (1825–1830) are complex and lie in part in a feud over the succession to the throne of the Yogyakarta Sultanate. But the fact is that Diponegoro, who was seen as the *Ratu Adil* (messianic ruler), acquired the active support of the Javanese elite, Islamic teachers and the peasant population in large parts of Java. Never had a clash between Dutch colonialism and an indigenous population been more decisive. The fact that the Javanese lost the war meant that the Dutch could implement their policies in Java almost without restraint. Outbreaks of rural discontent were frequent but small scale and could easily be suppressed. The Javanese kingdoms of Central Java, descendants of the kingdom of Mataram, were preserved as semi-independent entities but were stripped of their four valuable outer districts of Bagelen, Kedu, Madiun and Kediri. The rump kingdoms were subsequently known as the Principalities (Houben 1994c). According to Booth (1988):

> At the beginning of the nineteenth century Java had an abundant land suitable for agriculture but not enough people to cultivate it. Much of the island was still jungle with plentiful wild animals like the much feared Javanese tiger. During subsequent decades the land–labour ratio steadily declined, so that at the end of the century there was a land shortage. Java's population grew from 6–10 million in 1815 to 20 million in 1880 and 28.3 million in 1900. The agricultural frontier closed in Central Java around 1880, though perhaps not until about 1920 in West and East Java.

Fertile lands and a large reservoir of rural labour were not enough to turn Java into a successful export-based economy. Investments by both the colonial government and private entrepreneurs helped to mobilise the rapidly expanding pool of labour (Appendix 3.A). At the same time, the foreign trade of the island was put under tight control by a system of trade barriers to assist Dutch shipping. Improvements of transport and communications facilitated the growth of a colonial economy that was geared towards export agriculture. The corporate plantation system was by

1900 the most technologically modern and integrated one in Asia (Dick 1996: 29–32; Knight 1996: 155–6). Besides realising rapid growth in output, the indigenous economy of Java became much more substantial in size and much more complex in nature in the course of the 19th century.

The consolidation as an integrated polity and economy is the dominant feature of 19th-century Java. Colonial state formation entailed a spread of control, both horizontally (the size of territory under effective rule) and vertically (the penetration of indigenous society and economy from the top downwards). Yet it remains extremely hard to generalise. Despite these unifying forces, huge differences continued to exist between the various regions. The mountainous area of the Priangan cannot be equated with the north coast plain (Pasisir), nor do the fertile *sawah* complexes of East and Central Java resemble the sparsely populated hills and highland areas of Banyuwangi in the eastern salient or Banten in western Java. Nevertheless, Java in 1900 was a far more integrated economy than a century earlier.

THE EXISTING INDIGENOUS ECONOMY

The economy of Java was already rather well developed before the 19th century, and was certainly no subsistence economy. In several areas substantial production for the domestic and even the world market had come into existence, despite the interference by the VOC. Rice from Java's north coast was exported to other parts of the archipelago. District chiefs in the same area stimulated the production of and trade in sugar, indigo and pepper (Nagtegaal 1996).

Research on the Principalities of Central Java has highlighted a few basic characteristics of the Javanese economy before 1830 that applied to much of inland Java. Forms of land tenure varied between regions and subregions but in the early 19th century landholding peasants paid crop tax (*pajeg*) in either produce or cash (later exclusively in cash). The peasant population was also liable for labour services to the village head and superior power-holders up to the ruler. Despite these burdens, peasants were able to generate surplus income through the cultivation of cash crops such as coffee, cotton and pepper. These products were bought up by travelling pedlars, who transported them to the coast. A barter and a cash economy existed alongside each other.

By 1810 Java's interior sustained a dense market network. At the district level there were permanent markets, while village markets opened one in every five days of the Javanese week and traders rotated between them. Goods imported from outside Java included iron, nails, Japanese copper, velvet, gold, diamonds and incense. Goods for interregional or foreign trade consisted of rice, tobacco, cotton, coconut and peanut oil. In Solo there was a thriving batik industry. Finally, there were goods for internal trade, which included rice, cattle, fish, fruit and peanut oil (Carey 1986: 88–96; Houben 1994c: 312–15).

The economy of the Pasisir was more developed because of proximity to the Java Sea. Priangan was dominated by forced coffee cultivation for the government and, near Batavia, by the estates of a Western/Eurasian/Chinese landed gentry. In Banten an indigenous economic system focused on the pepper-producing area of Lampung (South Sumatra). Pasuruan, in the Easthook, was still a frontier region during the first three decades of the 19th century, but its population grew quickly, boosted by immigration from Madura. Lands were reclaimed and the *pax Neerlandica* made the possession of land a solid investment for the peasantry. Production of saleable commodities was started on a large scale, although poor roads remained an obstacle (Elson 1984: 4–11).

Java's indigenous economy was dynamic but did not realise its full potential. Costs of production by non-industrial modes of organisation were too high to be competitive in the world market. Problems of transport, security and local taxation hindered further development. This gave an opportunity to the emerging colonial state to gain control and exploit the available land and labour.

ESTABLISHMENT OF THE MODERN COLONIAL STATE

The development of the colonial state in 19th-century Java was marked by several turning-points. Between 1800 and 1830 there was much internal discussion of the best colonial policy: a free trade system in combination with private entrepreneurs or a monopoly system run by the government. These systems imposed different institutional demands on the colonial state. H.W. Daendels (1808–1811), a supporter of Napoleonic political reform in Holland, and the British Lieutenant Governor-General Thomas Raffles (1811–1816) both tried to transform the corrupt, factionalised VOC-style administration into a modern, rational bureaucracy. The transition proved to be difficult. However, after establishment in Delft in 1842 of a training college for colonial civil servants, the recruitment of candidates for official appointment was no longer the prerogative of those with personal connections (Fasseur 1993).

Daendels and Raffles were the main architects of the new Dutch colonial state. Daendels reorganised both the central and regional colonial administration. At the top under the Governor-General he created a General Secretariat (*generale secretarie*), which devised the main policies and from which all directives emanated. The *Raad* Van *Indië* (Council of the Indies), which under the VOC had been a co-legislative organ of senior VOC officials, was turned into a consultative body. On the Napoleonic model, the territory of Java was divided into districts of more or less equal size, originally known as prefectures but later as *residencies*. Each district was headed by a European civil servant, who was directly responsible to the Governor-General. On paper the resident was responsible for a wide range of tasks, from agriculture to the administration of justice. Fixed salaries and

precise instructions were introduced to curb the formerly wide discretionary powers of colonial civil servants.

Raffles also sought to rule Java in a more modern way, and maintained
the principal features of Daendels' new administrative system. In 1812 he
issued an instruction by which residents were installed as head of a residency, under the direct authority of Batavia, on a fixed salary and without
entitlement to gifts. Residents were also given partial military authority
and instructed to submit a monthly report to the Governor-General on the
state of affairs in the area under their jurisdiction. Residents were given
support by the installation of assistant-residents. Finally, tax collectors
were appointed to collect a new land tax known as land rent (Van den Doel
1994: 38–45).

Daendels and Raffles also curtailed the powers of the Javanese district
chiefs (regents or *bupati*) as intermediaries between the European civil
service and the Javanese peasantry, while direct contact with village heads
was enhanced. These reforms broke with longstanding administrative
practice between Javanese rulers and their officials, and provoked much
opposition (Sutherland 1979: 7–9). These administrative reforms were
continued after Dutch rule was restored to Java in 1816. Residents,
supported by assistant-residents and *controleurs*, were the linchpin of
Dutch colonial administration. The system of rule was both direct and
dualistic, in that alongside the European hierarchy (*Binnenlands Bestuur*)
there coexisted an indigenous one (*Pangreh Praja*), ranging from the
Regent at the top, via the district head (*wedana*) in the middle, to the
village head (*lurah*) at the bottom. The regents, collectively known as
priyayi, originally constituted the group of aristocratic officials who ran
the Mataram administration. Based on the polite convention of older and
younger brother, colonial policies were implemented sideways by communication between European and indigenous officials of comparable rank.
Contrary to the objective of Daendels and Raffles, Javanese officials
retained much authority. Throughout the 19th century a gradual process of
bureaucratisation took place, so that both European and Javanese officials
became the executors of the will of centre, vested either in the person of
the Governor-General or in the Minister of Colonial Affairs in the Netherlands (Day 1904: 216–22; Burger 1939).

The increasing intervention by European colonial officials in the society
and economy of Java was reflected in their growing numbers. Although the
number of residents and subsidiary officials in Java stayed more or less the
same between 1825 and 1890, that of the middle ranks (assistant-residents
and *controleurs*) rose from 73 in 1825 to 190 in 1890. These mid-level
officials were the ones who stood in daily contact with the indigenous
bureaucracy, and their powers of coercion ensured the smooth running of
the colonial state, not least in generating revenue. Nevertheless, during the
19th century there were never more than several hundred European officials
in the colony, a tiny group to control many millions of Javanese.

Of course the strength of the colonial state cannot be judged solely from the number of European colonial civil servants. Throughout the 19th century a small professional standing army was kept at the disposal of the colonial authorities, especially as the Java War had shown the indigenous potential for massive revolt. The actual strength of the Netherlands East Indies army, or KNIL (*Koninklijk Nederlandsch-Indisch Leger*), was around 10 000 in 1820, whereas about 1875 its numerical strength passed the 30 000 mark (Bossenbroek 1992). This growth was necessitated by the increasing military activity in the Outer Islands after the Aceh War began in 1873, but at the same time a permanent military presence in Java gave the colonial administrators the muscle to impose their authority.

As in the Netherlands, the colonial bureaucracy functioned within a system of fixed rules laid down in regulations and legal codes. The Governmental Regulation (*Regeeringsreglement*) of 1854 became the crucial basic law on which rested all colonial institutions and their functions. Building on several earlier versions between 1818 and 1836, it fixed the instruments of state rule throughout the Dutch period and even after Independence. In the accompanying explanatory memorandum, Java was characterised as an 'area of exploitation' (*wingewest*), elevating conservative ideals of profit making above enlightened humanitarian interests, such as the need to develop the island for the sake of its inhabitants. The Governmental Regulation also confirmed the system of dual administration, whereby the Javanese population was primarily ruled by their own regents' class, giving these an important role in government. In 1854 the office of regent was officially declared hereditary.

A range of legally based racial distinctions was a cornerstone of Dutch colonial law. The basis for this was article 109 of the 1854 Governmental Regulation, in which a distinction was made between 'Europeans and those equated with them' on the one hand and 'Natives' on the other hand. The latter included Chinese, Arabs and others, who were later categorised as 'Foreign Orientals'. This led to a dual legal structure, in which administrative, civil and criminal law for both categories were kept separate. Ethnic descent and formal racial classification determined the group to which someone belonged.

POPULATION GROWTH

Java has been cited as a unique case of very rapid population growth in an allegedly pre-modern economy. Comparison of Raffles' population estimate of 1815 and the population census of 1900 suggests that the population grew extremely rapidly. However, it is likely that Raffles' rather crude count underestimated the true number of inhabitants, which would imply significantly lower growth rates. Historical demographers have come up with various explanations for Java's demographic performance. During

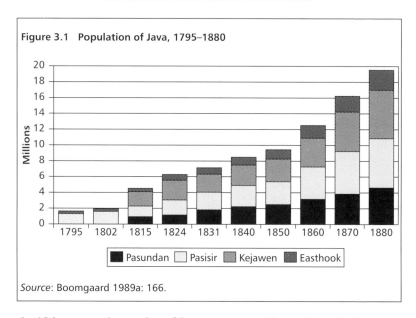

Figure 3.1   Population of Java, 1795–1880

Legend: Pasundan, Pasisir, Kejawen, Easthook

Source: Boomgaard 1989a: 166.

the 19th century the number of Javanese engaged in settled agriculture rose in comparison with the number of shifting cultivators. Part of the rising population numbers can be explained by a higher percentage of people being counted in tax lists. The death rate declined because of smallpox vaccination schemes (the first in Asia), improved communications, hence fewer crop failures and better nutrition from the greater area under wet-rice cultivation (Hugo et al. 1987: 32–6). A higher birth rate may be explained by improved living standards due to better health and nutrition. In times of prosperity, early marriages prolonged the female reproductive period, resulting in more children per woman.

Java's population growth was linked to economic development. Correlation coefficients reveal statistical relationships between demographic and economic variables. These involve patterns of landed tenure, population density, the percentage of families under the Cultivation System, the agricultural income per capita and demographic factors such as nuptiality, fertility and mortality (Boomgaard 1989a: 186). Accelerated growth can be explained through convergence of factors, whose relative importance changed over time. However, very detailed statistical data are needed to support such sophisticated analysis, and this is difficult for a period that is still prestatistical (Brown 1997: 92–3).

Population growth was uneven in time and across Java. Figure 3.1 (based on Boomgaard 1989a: 166) shows demographic development until 1880, distinguishing between Pasundan (West Java), Pasisir (Northcoast Java), Kejawen (the interior of central Java, including the Principalities) and the

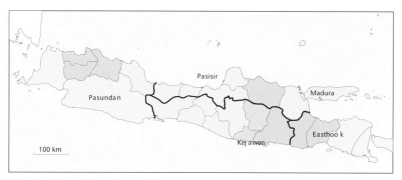

Map 2   The main regions of Java

Easthook (East Java) (Map 2). From this it appears that growth rates in Pasundan and the Easthook were higher than average, those in the Pasisir and Kejawen under the average. Sharp fluctuations in population growth were experienced during the Java War and during the localised famines and disease of the 1840s. Fluctuations in regional figures may also have been caused by population mobility, for instance from the densely inhabited Principalities to uncultivated lands in East Java, or from rural areas to coastal cities.

Whatever the exact rate and causes of Java's population growth, the supply of labour was greatly augmented during the 19th century. At the beginning of the 19th century the agricultural resources of the island had been underutilised, but by 1900 most of the agricultural frontier had closed and growing population pressure was being felt. Whereas in the first half of the century coercion was applied to tap the labour supply, towards the end of the century a free labour system offered all the labour needed for the smooth operation of Western agricultural enterprise (Elson 1986).

INSTITUTIONAL PATHS

In a context of rising budgetary expenditures and the aim of making Java a profitable colony, a stronger colonial state provided the means for an interventionist economic policy well beyond the modest fiscal systems in the contemporary Netherlands. Without regard to *laissez-faire* ideals, Java was subjected to an aggressive state which sought to mobilise the resources of the indigenous economy to its own advantage. The 19th century witnessed three phases in economic policy: the trial and error period 1810–1830; the years 1830–1870, dominated by the Cultivation System; and the years after 1870, conventionally referred to as the 'liberal' period.

Taxing possession of land (1810–1830)

The VOC profited from its territorial possessions in north Java by ordering the regents to compel the population to deliver goods (mostly rice and teak) and labour services. In the Priangan highlands coffee had been planted as a compulsory cash crop. After liquidation of the VOC, Dutch political circles debated what should follow next. Some wanted to continue the VOC monopoly system in a modified form, others, in particular liberals headed by Dirk Van Hogendorp, wanted to leave the economic relationship between the Netherlands and colonial Indonesia in the hands of private merchants. After a short interventionist period under Governor-General Daendels, the liberal solution carried the day.

The British conquered Java in 1811, and Lieutenant Governor-General Raffles introduced a land rent (i.e. tax) system based on free trade principles. He obliged peasants to pay a rent for the possession of their land equivalent to the value of two-fifths of the annual harvest, either in kind or, preferably, in cash. This system was inspired by the tax system of British Bengal but proved difficult to transplant to Java. There was little accurate knowledge of the size and fertility of arable lands, regents tried to siphon off a portion of the tax revenues, and peasants often became indebted to Chinese moneylenders, especially in times of crop failure when they could not pay their land rent on time. Despite the obvious shortcomings in the land rent system, it was continued well into the 20th century.

Taxing labour: the Cultivation System (1830–1870)

Loss of much of its foreign trade to the British, the impact of the Napoleonic wars and the Belgian secession of 1831 brought the finances of the Dutch kingdom to the verge of ruin. After several decades of vehement discussions between proponents and opponents of free trade, King Willem I decided that the colony of Java should contribute substantial revenues to the state. In 1830 Governor-General Johannes van den Bosch installed a state monopoly on the cultivation of export crops in Java, known as the Cultivation System. Van den Bosch's concept was very simple. He argued that the land rent system could be converted into something more beneficial to both the colonial government and the Javanese peasant. Instead of demanding two-fifths of the value of the harvest, only one-fifth would be required. But this reduced tax rate would have to be delivered not in kind (rice) nor in money but in export crops, of which the kind and quantity would be specified by colonial officials. In practice, this simple scheme had vast and quite varying consequences. Moreover, contrary to Van den Bosch's original plan, the land rent tax was maintained in Java, on top of the compulsory cultivation of cash crops and traditional corvée labour services (*heerendiensten*).

Under the Cultivation System the Javanese peasant population was required to produce cash crops, such as coffee, sugar cane and indigo, on their fields and to deliver them to government warehouses scattered throughout Java. In return the peasants received crop payment, an arbitrarily fixed compensation in cash that bore no direct relation to the value of the produce on the world market. To stimulate production, both European and Javanese officials were paid cultivation percentages (*cultuurprocenten*), payments related to the quantity of cash crops delivered to the government in their respective districts. Under the so-called consignment system, the products were sent for auction in the Netherlands by ships of the NHM, a semi-public trading company established in 1824 on the initiative of King Willem I, who was himself a major shareholder. The financial results of the system were impressive. Between 1832 and 1852 the benefits from the colony constituted around 19% of the total state income. At its height, between 1860 and 1866, one-third of Dutch state revenue was derived directly from the Cultivation System (Fasseur 1975/1992).

The essence of the system can be summarised from the viewpoint of labour as follows. Building on contractual arrangements within Javanese society and based on VOC experience, Van den Bosch levied tax and tribute by mobilising labour and receiving the fruits of this labour in kind. For Java the Cultivation System was essentially a labour-tax system, for the Netherlands it was late mercantilism.

As the Cultivation System encompassed cash crops requiring quite distinctive ways of cultivation, and because it built on local arrangements between Javanese powerholders and the Javanese peasantry, the precise form of the forced cultivations cannot be generalised. Nevertheless, there were various phases. It started as a peculiar set of arrangements combining the colonial state apparatus with three other 'stakeholders': Javanese powerholders, private European and Chinese entrepreneurs, and the centre of the colonial state in Batavia (Elson 1996: 126–32). These arrangements worked smoothly during the first decade, but from 1840 onwards problems emerged in the form of rising rice prices, crop failures and even famines. Greed and bureaucratic overexploitation resulted in a failure to balance the labour and material resources needed by peasants for their subsistence on the one hand and for the benefit of the Cultivation System on the other. The centre could not control the blurring of private and public interests, especially on the part of the indigenous elite. In the early 1850s the Cultivation System was reformed but the old coalition of stakeholders collapsed, leaving the colonial state as the dominant player. At the same time state contractors processing state sugar cane in private factories were allowed to keep part of the sugar to trade on their own account. This began a process of privatisation, in which the colonial state gradually transferred export production to Western entrepreneurs hiring free wage labour.

Exploiting land with labour (1870–1890)

After 1850 the proportion of agricultural exports on private account rose steadily versus that from compulsory cultivation. Several minor compulsory crops were phased out. In the Dutch parliament the liberal critics of the Cultivation System gradually gained ground. Published in 1860, Multatuli's novel *Max Havelaar* shocked the Dutch public by its portrayal of abuse of power by Javanese regents and the high level of colonial taxation, but without much influencing political discussion in the Netherlands. Not until 1870 was there a decisive shift towards an era in which European private capital could freely enter the colony. The Agrarian Law of that year at last made it possible for European entrepreneurs to lease *sawah* land from the indigenous population on an annual basis. 'Waste' land or allegedly uncultivated lands could be leased from the colonial government under hereditary lease (*erfpacht*) for a period up to 75 years, but such leases did not confer access to unpaid labour services. The colonial administration kept a register of all lease contracts and prescribed that the entrepreneur would not demand more labour from the local village population than was justified by existing customary rights.

Even after 1870 the switch from state-run cultivation to private enterprise was hardly abrupt. The Sugar Law of that year began the gradual abolition of the forced production of sugar cane, but the process took two decades. After 1890 only coffee remained a compulsory crop. Thus the crop on which the Cultivation System had been modelled also long outlasted it, the last remnants of the old Priangan system not being dismantled until the 1910s. Thereafter the colonial state merely supervised relations between Western enterprise and the rural population.

Institutional arrangements did not radically change after 1870. In Europe and especially Amsterdam, business networks among the well-established merchant elite remained intact. The NHM continued to be preferred by the colonial government in state contracts, combining a wide range of activities. It acted as a large trading company with branches throughout the Outer Islands, as well as in almost every port city in the Asia-Pacific region. It also developed itself into a commercial bank with extensive interests in Javanese plantations.

Older paths: West and South-Central Java (1810–1890)

After 1830 two parallel Western systems of production for the world market were in operation. One was the above-mentioned Cultivation System, involving Javanese peasants, village heads and regents and the emerging colonial state. The other and rather older one involved private Western entrepreneurs associated with trading agencies in the north coast port towns. Whereas the weight of the Cultivation System was on Central Java and the Easthook residencies, private plantations were prevalent in West Java and the Principalities of South Central Java.

Around Batavia (the *Ommelanden*), manorial estates (*landerijen*) had been sold off by Daendels and Raffles with quasi-feudal rights over the resident population and virtual autonomy from colonial administration. There mainly Eurasian and Chinese owners collected land rent in the form of rice and other products and in labour services. These tax burdens were often heavy and in 1886, on the Ciomas estate in West Java, a major revolt occurred. After 1900 private estates were gradually bought back by the state and restored to direct colonial administration.

In the Principalities of South Central Java (Solo and Yogyakarta), around 1816 private European entrepreneurs began leasing appanage land from the nobility. As on the manorial estates, lessees gained rights to the obligatory labour services of the resident population, but in this case to produce export crops of coffee and sugar cane. Tensions arose when the colonial government in 1823 banned such leases, depriving the court elite of a valuable source of monetary income. This contributed to the outbreak of the Java War two years later. In 1827 leasing was again permitted and plantation agriculture continued to expand. When the compulsory planting of indigo was abolished in 1851 on lands under the Cultivation System, the private entrepreneurs of Yogyakarta were quick to take over. Before 1870 the major export products of the Principalities were coffee and indigo, thereafter sugar cane, tobacco and rubber (Houben 1994c: 257–68).

By 1850, exports from Java classified as 'private' amounted to one-third of total exports. Whereas sugar production by forced culti-vation produced high yields, private production (mostly by government contractors themselves) reached almost the same level in 1860. When state-controlled production in the framework of the Cultivation System went into decline, the experience with private enterprise in Central Java served as a springboard for a similar development elsewhere. It can only be speculated how different the history of Java might have been had the young colonial state continued to alienate or allow the lease of private estates throughout the island instead of switching to the state-directed Cultivation System. The experience of the Philippines suggests that much more highly concentrated landholdings and a powerful landed gentry would have been likely outcomes.

ECONOMIC EXPANSION: THE WESTERN SECTOR

The intrusion of the Western sector

Export-oriented agricultural production expanded in a framework of increasing colonial domination. The colonial state either acted as an entre-preneur or facilitated the commercial interests of Western private entrepre-neurs. The common view is that this commercialisation opened Java's economy to the world market. Colonialism was thereby interpreted as a necessary first step on the road to economic development (Burger 1939). This picture is too simplistic, because the indigenous economy of Java was already partially commercialised. Under colonial domination, however, the Western sector developed lopsidedly as the main avenue to the world market. This interpretation is crucial to understanding the structure of Java's colonial economy.

Agrarian export volumes show that the Western sector in Java expanded dramatically throughout the 19th century. As extensive lands were still available, its success has to be attributed to the forced mobilisation of labour. Production figures for the three main export crops of coffee, sugar cane and tobacco over the period 1840–1890 are given in Figure 3.2. The Cultivation System clearly boosted production for the world market. The most dramatic increase in export production took place between 1830 and 1840, when staples (including rice) grew more than 13% per annum and in 1840 directly involved around 12% of Java's total population. As world prices declined, indigenous officials were pressed to demand more corvée labour, but output growth remained slower until the liberal era began in 1870. In the part of the economy that was monetised, real per capita output growth rose an estimated 2% per year between 1850 and 1873 (Booth 1998a: 17–23). The gradual shift from state monopoly to private production stimulated a new boom in output. Between 1870 and 1885 the production of sugar cane in Java more than doubled, while coffee production remained of secondary importance only.

The three main ports of the north coast (Batavia, Semarang and Surabaya) functioned as main transit points for an increasingly complex system of arteries into the hinterland. In these towns one could find the main offices of the colonial government but also banks and private merchant houses, providing credit to Western entrepreneurs and facilitating shipments to foreign markets. Grand office buildings of the former colonial banks, trading houses and plantation management agencies can still be seen in the old central business districts.

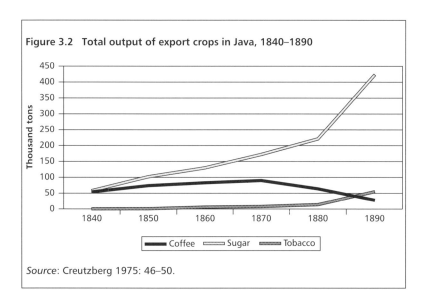

Figure 3.2   Total output of export crops in Java, 1840–1890

Source: Creutzberg 1975: 46–50.

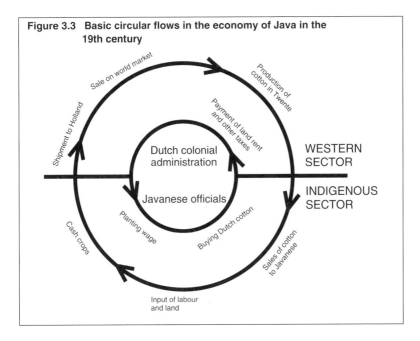

Figure 3.3 Basic circular flows in the economy of Java in the 19th century

The economic circular flow

The Western sector introduced an economic circular flow that was largely self-sustained and closed in character. Supply and demand were controlled by the Dutch, marginalising third parties. This structure was erected after the colony was returned by the British in 1816 and was strengthened during the era of the Cultivation System. After 1870, when private enterprise prevailed in the Western sector, the closed circular flow was entrenched in the economic system as a whole. The state facilitated and supervised the unequal bargaining position of indigenous supply versus Western demand, thereby creating a dual economy in which the indigenous and Western sector became largely separate entities.

The main features of the economic circular flow are represented in Figure 3.3. With regard to the flow of labour and goods, Javanese produced crops for the world market which were transported to the Netherlands on NHM-chartered ships and sold there. However, besides exporting goods the Dutch began to import cotton goods from a nascent cotton industry in Twente, a region in the east of the Netherlands. In the 1830s the value of cotton imports to Java rose rapidly. While high-quality English imports faced no competition, Dutch manufacturers gained control of the large mass market (Figure 3.4). These cheap cotton goods were sold in large consignments either to Dutch trading houses or direct to Chinese intermediaries. Javanese cloth was still produced with handlooms but at higher cost. With

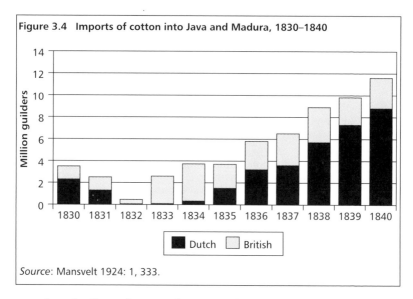

Figure 3.4 Imports of cotton into Java and Madura, 1830–1840

Source: Mansvelt 1924: 1, 333.

regard to the flow of money, it appears that much of the wages paid to peasants for planting and harvesting must have been used to pay the land rent. The remainder must have been spent on clothing and other goods provided for by the Western sector.

This closed economic system consolidated a dominant nexus of trade between Java and the Netherlands. From 1818 onwards, non-Dutch competitors were discouraged by placing trade to and from Java under tight control. Batavia was designated as the exclusive port of entry for imports, while exports could be shipped only through Batavia, Semarang or Surabaya. A system of differential duties was levied whereby Dutch imports on Dutch ships were exempt, foreign imports on Dutch ships were subjected to 6% duty, Dutch products on foreign ships to 9% and foreign goods on foreign ships to 12% import duty. Port dues for foreign ships were also higher than for Dutch ships (Knaap 1989: 19).

Until the 1860s, most of the export of leading commodities was actually in government hands. Exports on private account, especially sugar exports via Singapore, became more important during the 1840s, but as late as 1850 the government's share of exports was still 72%. By 1859 it had fallen to below 58% and this trend continued during the 1860s. In 1874 the system of differential duties was abolished, so that henceforth all manufactures, Dutch or foreign, paid the same 6% duty. By then Dutch private trade had been consolidated and this shift towards trade liberalisation had no dramatic impact (Korthals Altes 1991: 13–15).

Java's product mix changed over time. The early years of the Cultivation System were dominated by coffee and indigo. Indigo production declined

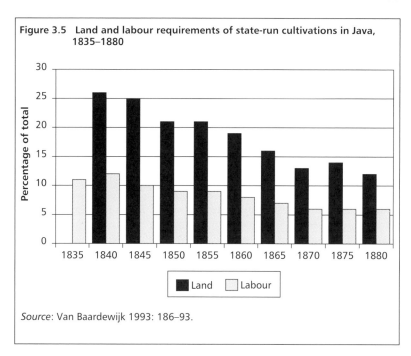

Figure 3.5   Land and labour requirements of state-run cultivations in Java, 1835–1880

Source: Van Baardewijk 1993: 186–93.

after the early 1840s, whereas that of coffee remained fairly stable. Formerly a minor crop, tobacco surpassed indigo production in the mid-1840s. The most remarkable performance, however, was that of sugar. Production exceeded that of coffee in the 1840s and grew continuously until the end of the 19th century. From only 20 000 in 1835, Java's sugar output reached 100 000 tonnes in 1857 and 744 000 tonnes in 1900 (Van Baardewijk 1993: 225–36, 249–60, 278–305). Revenues for individual products fluctuated over time, depending on world market prices.

The major inputs into the system were Java's land and labour. In absolute terms the input levels of land and labour were remarkably stable between 1840 and 1880. However, Figure 3.5 shows that the percentage of total arable land taken up in forced cultivation peaked at around one-quarter of the total in 1840, as did the number of hands required to run the system. After 1840 the relative impact of forced deliveries of cash crops therefore gradually declined as the colonial economy expanded through growth of private agricultural enterprise.

In the early 1880s Java's plantation economy was hit by multiple crises. Depressed by subsidised production of European beet sugar, the world market price for sugar collapsed suddenly in 1884, falling below the cost of production. To make matters worse, harvests were destroyed by *sereh* disease in the sugar leaf. *Arabica* coffee plantations had also been wiped out by the 1890s and had to be replaced by the less flavoursome but resistant *Robusta* variety. Only after 1895 did the export trade revive.

The crises of the mid-1880s necessitated a thorough restructuring of Java's plantation enterprises. Individual planters gave way to limited liability companies, which in turn associated with colonial banks, trading houses and management agencies. More attention was paid to scientific principles, to product quality, and to costs of production. However, as can be inferred from the names of directors and commissioners, now mainly living in the Netherlands, the involvement of established merchant families or 'gentlemanly capitalism' persisted (Bossenbroek 1996).

Technological innovation through the Western sector

During the 19th century, colonial state formation and private capital investment were underpinned by heavy investment in new technologies of transport and communications (see also Chapter 1). The first big initiative was the Great Post Road, built on the orders of Daendels to extend over a distance of 1000 km along the north coast of Java, from Anyer in the west to Panarukan in the east. According to the Napoleonic model, its purpose was to convey official messages and personnel quickly across the island or to enable the prompt movement of army units. This road was reserved for official traffic, while private access was restricted by law. For the movement of goods, transport by sea and river was much cheaper. After 1830 along the north coast of Java, after 1845 to and from Europe via Singapore, and from 1852 between Java and the Outer Islands, the mail was carried by regular steamers. The speed of transmitting official messages increased again in the mid-1850s, when the first telegraph line was opened between Batavia and Bogor. A network was soon extended across the island and in 1871 joined to the international system. These innovations combined to allow colonial officials in Batavia to exercise much closer control of their island realm.

Java's increasingly capital-intensive Western sector was able to benefit from modern European technologies, ahead of Chinese and indigenous sectors. Telegraphs put Western business in daily contact with world markets, and regular steam packets allowed an orderly conduct of business. The inadequacies of Java's rivers and roads in shipping goods to and from the north coast ports led merchants and planters to lobby for the construction of railways. A private railway between Semarang and the Principalities of Central Java was opened between 1867 and 1873, followed by lines in West and East Java; despite different gauges, these were soon linked to a Java-wide network (Knaap 1989: 28–9).

The development of Java's sugar industry in the 19th century illustrates how technological innovation was biased towards the Western sector. In the early phases of the Cultivation System the colonial government, not Chinese or European manufacturers, played the key role in the introduction and diffusion of technological innovations. From the 1840s onwards, the Netherlands Indies government and the Ministry of Colonial Affairs set up an information exchange network to promote the introduction of vacuum pans to increase both the quantity and the quality of the production. Technical progress in Europe's beet sugar industry provided an impetus for the colonial government to introduce better sugar-processing machinery. Later private manufacturers and the managers of the sugar factories joined forces in sharing knowledge from European scientists and engineers to improve the production process. Between 1870 and 1900 experimental stations were established through private initiative, in particular to breed higher-yielding cane varieties that were also more resistant to disease (Leidelmeijer 1997).

The role of intermediaries

The Western economic sector relied heavily on intermediaries. Regents and subordinate Javanese heads acted as brokers between European colonial officials and the Javanese population. As Javanese heads were drawn more and more into the orbit of the colonial administration, the Javanese elite (*priyayi*) became its instrument and lost part of their prestige as indigenous leaders (Sutherland 1979).

In the economic sphere, foreign minority groups (Chinese, Arabs and Indians) acted as brokers between the Javanese peasant, the colonial sector and the world market. The Chinese, who numbered 175 000 in 1870, were in absolute terms a tiny minority amid Java's 16 million indigenous inhabitants, but in the coastal towns their proportion was much higher. In 1890 the Chinese of Batavia constituted one-quarter and in Semarang almost one-fifth of the total urban population (Boomgaard & Gooszen 1991: 110, 127, 220). Dutch attitudes were ambivalent. On the one hand, the Chinese were seen as indispensable to the smooth running of the colonial economy; on the other, they were viewed with suspicion as usurers, who disrupted the supposed harmony of Javanese rural society. Dutch fears of Chinese economic domination were cloaked in reproaches for cheating the ignorant Javanese in the countryside.

Java's Chinese community had a long and complex history, which predated the colonial era. During the VOC period, immigration from the coastal province of Fukien had grown rapidly, so that in the towns of the Pasisir Chinese traders were more numerous than Javanese ones. Chinese networks controlled the trade of inland Java, particularly that of rice. Rivalry ensued between acculturated *peranakan* (Chinese with a Javanese mother who had become partly Javanised) and new immigrants (*totok*) (Nagtegaal 1996: 94–101). In the 19th century there was again an increasing migration of Chinese to the port towns of Java. In 1854 Chinese were separately classified as 'Foreign Orientals' under Netherlands Indies law, but until the early 20th century they were still obliged to live in special quarters. Since VOC times, these Chinese communities had been administered by their own headmen, rich tycoons who were granted official status and rank as Chinese lieutenants, captains and majors.

Chinese headmen were often leading members of farm syndicates (*kongsi*), which collected many of the taxes levied by the colonial state. Between 1816 and 1885 such revenue farms contributed 15–25% of revenue collection. The most important revenue farm was opium. After 1834 the rights to retail opium and collect the tax in each residency were auctioned as fixed-term franchises to the highest bidder (Rush 1990). Associated with the main opium farm and often held by the same principals were minor revenue farms, ranging from a market tax (abolished in 1851) to pawn shops and cattle slaughter. In 1870 around 7000 Chinese were involved in tax farms (Diehl 1993).

Tax farms and restrictions on the Chinese communities together helped the rich headmen to control their countrymen and the local economy (Butcher & Dick 1993). For example, Chinese needed a pass to travel in the interior, but privileged access was enjoyed by tax farmers and members of their syndicates. Farmers were also allowed to maintain private police forces of thugs and spies (*mata mata*) to supervise the farms and suppress smuggling, especially of opium (Rush 1990). Major and minor tax farms were therefore the basis of networks of patronage and protection which allowed farmers to control the wholesale and retail trade and moneylending of entire residencies (Diehl 1993). Chinese headmen and tax farmers sponsored new immigrants and found them employment in their farms or as local pedlars. While most Chinese were poor, patronage networks provided channels of upward mobility whereby a few quickly attained wealth and elite status.

With the strengthening of the colonial state and colonial capital, the 'marriage of convenience' between the state and leaders of the Chinese community began to come apart (Dick 1993a: 11). Towards the end of the 19th century, as Dutch capital began to challenge Chinese capital for control of the commanding heights of the colonial economy and for access to the local Javanese economy, anti-Chinese sentiments became virulent. The opium farm in particular was identified as the key to Chinese economic dominance and in the mid-1890s two detailed reports by the colonial official Fokkens (see Butcher & Dick 1993) provided the basis for their phasing out in favour of a state opium monopoly (*regie*) and more modern taxes, such as personal income tax and business tax (Diehl 1993). The last opium farm was terminated in 1904. Deprived of state patronage, Chinese networks fragmented.

By the turn of the century the Chinese on Java were thus constrained to an essential middlemen role between colonial capital, which controlled the gateways to the world market, and the petty producers and consumers of Java's rural economy. Relying now on credit from European banks and trading houses, Chinese family firms in Batavia, Semarang and Surabaya still controlled the wholesale supply of goods, with distribution networks extending throughout their hinterlands. These towns also had many artisans of Chinese descent engaged in small-scale industry, such as furniture making.

Arab traders and entrepreneurs were less numerous than the Chinese but were involved in similar business activities. Immigration mainly from the Hadramaut coast of the Arabian peninsula grew after the mid-19th century. Concentrating in the north coast towns of Java, they acquired wealth and status as traders, tax farmers, moneylenders, shipowners and landholders. Like the Chinese community, they enjoyed a good deal of local autonomy under their own headmen, but as Muslims they were well respected by the local population, with whom they intermarried (Clarence Smith 1997).

ECONOMIC EXPANSION: THE INDIGENOUS SECTOR

The rise of the Western export agriculture in 19th-century Java had a profound impact on the indigenous sector. Not just production for the market but the whole fabric of society was affected. There are two basic problems in assessing the extent of change in the indigenous economy: the lack of reliable information, and the degree of regional and even local variation. Integration of Java's four economic zones was a gradual process, driven by the infrastructure investments and extractive activities of the colonial state, which sought to establish an integrated economy suited to even more lucrative exploitation. Yet despite the growing predominance of the Western export sector, the indigenous economy continued to display its own dynamics.

Improved transport infrastructure

Java's transport infrastructure was greatly improved in the course of the 19th century, to the benefit of both Western and indigenous sectors. The two main navigable rivers, the Solo and Brantas, which flow from the centre of the island to the Java Sea, had silted up because of deforestation of their watersheds, much of it clearance for upland plantations. Nevertheless, in the wet season they continued to serve as the main arteries for shipping bulk products, including export sugar. Around 1860 the lowest 80-km reach of the Solo River was navigable by Javanese wooden sailing boats (*prahu*), with a cargo capacity up to 90 tons; on the whole route from Surabaya to the town of Solo the largest *perahu* could carry only half this amount (Houben 1994c: 73).

Transport of bulk goods by road was even more seasonal. During the wet monsoon, major and minor dirt roads were impassable to heavy carts. Nineteenth-century population growth and extension of cash crop agriculture therefore required the road system to be extended and upgraded. During the Cultivation System, traditional corvée labour services were applied to public works, especially to extend, upgrade and maintain roads.

Regional and local roads were the responsibility of the indigenous admin-istration. As roads were improved, animal-drawn carts could be used instead of inefficient human porters or packhorses. Despite the construction of railways during the last decades of the century (Chapters 1 and 6), the road system was further extended. Colonial statistics show that between 1872 and 1892 the total length of public roads in Java and Madura grew from 7600 to almost 20 500 km (Knaap 1989: 81).

Better transport infrastructure stimulated the indigenous economy, allowing Javanese to respond to market opportunities, either by provid-ing goods that were in demand or by offering labour where it was scarce, in the transport sector itself or in other sectors outside of agriculture.

Monetisation and purchasing power

The history of monetisation in 19th-century Java is still a neglected topic. Before 1800 currencies such as lead *picis* and silver coins were widely used in indigenous trade. During the 19th century monetisation increased to the point where even village-level transactions involved cash. The use of money was probably more widespread along the north coast, with its many port towns, and in Central Java, because of landleasing in the Principalities, than

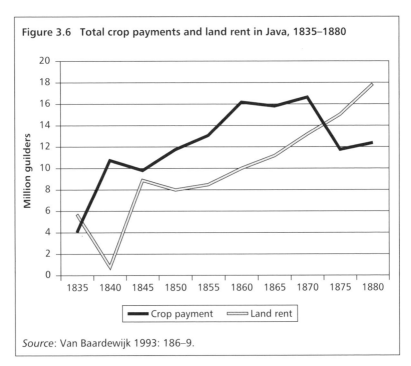

Figure 3.6   Total crop payments and land rent in Java, 1835–1880

Source: Van Baardewijk 1993: 186–9.

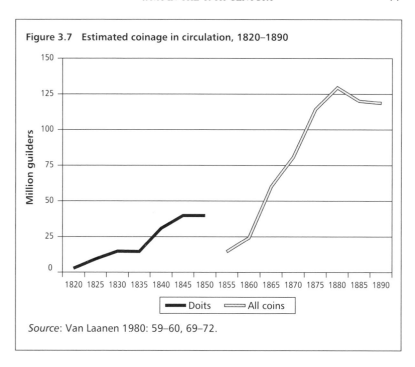

Figure 3.7   Estimated coinage in circulation, 1820–1890

Source: Van Laanen 1980: 59–60, 69–72.

elsewhere in Java. The Cultivation System stimulated monetisation of the rural economy. Between 1840 and 1870 for all Java, crop payments exceeded land rent, which must have left a small cash surplus in the hands of the peasant population, even though crop failures between 1846 and 1850 resulted in a worsening balance (Figure 3.6). The circulation of currency, predominantly copper doits (*duiten*), rose steadily, except for a fall around 1850 caused by a purge of inferior copper–lead coins (Figure 3.7). Expansion of indigenous commerce, especially items like rice and textiles, reflected the growth of purchasing power (Elson 1994: 199–200).

The impact of monetisation on buying power can be measured against price levels and quantities supplied of major trade items. Rice consumption is a good indicator, the sale of opium another, although exact figures cannot be given due to large-scale smuggling. Rice prices tended to rise in Java from 1850 onwards (Figure 3.8). Although prices could differ and therefore represented a variable share of spending, the dependence on bought rice was growing and therefore must have partly offset any extra money earned through the Cultivation System. On the other hand, when ricefields were claimed for compulsory cash crop cultivation, farmers could still switch to planting secondary food crops (*palawija*) on drylands.

Development of the non-agricultural sector of the rural economy

Recent historiography has highlighted the increase in off-farm employment in 19th-century Java. Whereas in the 1820s nearly all peasant
households met their own basic material needs and only a small fraction
of the population were non-agricultural workers, by the 1880s nearly a
quarter of all economically active Javanese were non-agricultural workers
(Fernando 1996: 78). Change began in the 1830s and 1840s because of
the need for skilled labourers in the plantation sector. However, from the
early 1850s onwards, manufacturers, traders and labourers found a wider
market. As the rural economy broadened, an increasing number of manufacturers and craftsmen could earn a living, both in the towns and in rural
areas. Javanese petty traders found opportunities in the burgeoning local
markets (*pasar*). Transport work proved to be in increasing demand. An
index has been constructed of the sectoral distribution of the indigenous
economy for 1880, just prior to the Depression of the mid-1880s. Besides
agriculture, which still accounted for three-quarters of Java's total
workforce, manufacturing accounted for 4%, services 7% and trade 11%
(Fernando 1996: 106–7).

Surplus from the non-agricultural sector was an alternative source of
income in the indigenous economy. No clear boundary can be drawn with
the agricultural sector, as many agricultural labourers could engage in non-
agricultural pursuits on a seasonal basis, but components of the

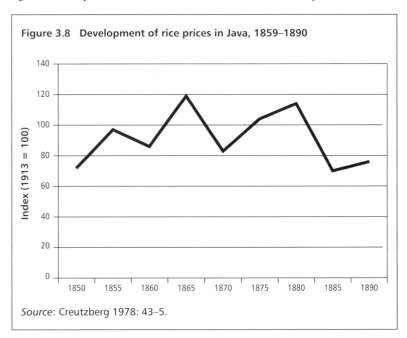

Figure 3.8   Development of rice prices in Java, 1859–1890

Source: Creutzberg 1978: 43–5.

non-agricultural sector can be identified. The main primary activities outside agriculture were fishing and salt making. Industrial establishments associated with the Cultivation System (sugar and indigo factories) were located in rural areas and required substantial input of labour, partly permanent and partly seasonal. The secondary sector was, however, far from undeveloped: already in 1820 there were mills for sugar, rice and oil, there were shipyards, sawmills, arrack distilleries, candle workshops, batik and textile workshops and potteries. From the mid-19th century the production of *kretek* cigarettes was started in Central and East Java. Larger industries were mainly in the hands of Europeans and Chinese, whereas small-scale industries were operated by Javanese. In these industries wage labourers carried out tasks assigned to them side by side with their corvée labour. The number of people involved in the tertiary sector must also have been substantial, for the need for trade and transportation grew as the colonial economy expanded (Boomgaard 1989a: 111–13, 119–34).

Non-agricultural output and export are useful criteria of economic development. The growth of off-farm employment was possibly the most important single development in Java's peasant society in the 19th century. It was born out of opportunity but also reflected the growth of landlessness and declining farm size in consequence of population growth. This process started earlier in Java than almost anywhere else in Southeast Asia. Around 1900, more than one-third of the labour force earned most of its livelihood outside agriculture (Elson 1997: 173).

LATE 19TH-CENTURY JAVA: A MISSED OPPORTUNITY?

Java's economy at the end of the 19th century was more productive and better integrated than in 1810, and had fulfilled the necessary preconditions for industrialisation. An integrated, modern Western sector had emerged that was well connected to both the world market and the local economy. The sugar industry was particularly advanced and became the leading sector. By 1900 only Cuba exported more. Huge amounts of capital had been invested to upgrade factories and supply them with very modern machinery, suggesting that a combination of high-level processing with control of rural resources was the key to success (Knight 1996).

At the same time, the indigenous economy, especially the non-agricultural sectors, had displayed great dynamism. The diversification of occupational structure was only partly explained by the increasing demand of the Western agricultural sector for skilled workers and carriers. Rising demand from the Javanese themselves also played a role. Because of the 1880s crisis, however, much of the momentum was lost. There was concern over food production on the island and the first complaints of the 'declining welfare' (*mindere welvaart*) of the indigenous population were brought forward by Dutch colonial specialists. Java had not yet recovered by the turn of the century.

The progress of both Western and indigenous economies disproves the Geertzian thesis that the rural economy of Java was characterised by a process of involution (see also Chapter 5). An alternative perspective would emphasise three features:

1. The colonial economy experienced rapid growth between 1810 and 1885 because of the stimulus of the colonial state and its success in mobilising indigenous labour resources. In the first few decades of the Cultivation System this was realised by creating a precarious balance between several stakeholders within Java; after 1850 the colonial state promoted private enterprise. At the same time, population growth ensured that the supply of labour would henceforth exceed demand, so that the dependence on intermediary activities of the indigenous elite became largely obsolete.

2. The indigenous economy developed partly alongside and partly subsidiary to the colonial economic system. Growth of non-farm employment was a dynamic trend but the welfare of the rural population depended increasingly on the dynamics of the Western sector, which provided much of the monetary earnings and purchasing power. Java's indigenous economy was therefore hardly static, but the terms on which it participated in the world market were set within a colonial relationship.

3. Instead of treating the whole of Java as identical and starting from a duality between Western and indigenous sectors (Appendix 5.D), we should look at specific avenues of modernisation or specific leading sectors involving both Western and indigenous components. The sugar industry is one good case of substantial structural and technological change.

Although by 1890 Java had fulfilled a number of the conditions for sustained growth, contrary to what might have been expected, 'take-off' was not realised for another 75 years. Dick (1993d) argues that colonialism as such cannot be blamed for Java's failure to take advantage of its lead in industrialisation. A spatial-sectoral matrix identifies the rural-based sugar industry as the leading sector, but because it was spread out in three geographical clusters (north coast, Principalities, East Java), externalities and stimuli for other infant industries were diffused instead of being concentrated in urban centres. The 'surplus' purchasing power of the Indonesian population was insufficient to generate the rise of a large domestic mass market, such as for textiles, while the open trade regime and support for the textile industry in the Netherlands discouraged local production. Thus, at the end of a century of economic expansion, officials warned of the depth of rural distress among the Javanese population and were pessimistic as to the prospects for continued growth.

Nevertheless, Java's 19th-century transformation laid much of the foundations for the future Indonesian nation and national economy. First, a modern bureaucratic and centralised state after contemporary European models took root, and firmly subordinated and co-opted traditional Javanese centres of power. Second, after much experimentation, it was determined that the resources of Java would be made accessible to exploitation by private foreign capital but on terms laid down by the state. Thus land could be leased but not sold to private plantation companies, thereby preserving a peasantry while restricting the market opportunities for smallholder enterprise. Third, a racially defined intermediary class of mainly Chinese entrepreneurs was perpetuated and given new opportunities in this new capitalist system. Finally, administrative modernisation and integration was matched by economic integration underpinned by massive investments in the infrastructure of transport and communications. All this gave Java the features of an economic core on a colonial periphery. In the Outer Islands, by contrast, the colonial state and capitalist economy had still acquired only rudimentary features (Chapter 4). The big issue for the new century was how Java's quasi-modern state and economy would be grafted onto the rest of the archipelago.

4

The Outer Islands in the 19th century: contest for the periphery

J. Thomas Lindblad

INTRODUCTION

In the 19th century the Outer Islands were still an integral part of a wider Southeast Asian trading system, and for the most part were only very loosely subject to Dutch colonial rule. National borders were porous and there was still no clear political distinction between, for instance, Sumatra and the Malay peninsula. Trade links ran between major port cities rather than between national capitals. There was a strong commercial tradition in local economies to produce for the market rather than focusing primarily on subsistence agriculture.

Two dynamics determined the long-run development of what became the Outer Islands or Outer Possessions of the Netherlands Indies. The first was the establishment in 1819 of Singapore, which strengthened the economies of the many kingdoms throughout the Outer Islands and enhanced their political leverage against the Dutch colonial power based on Java. The second dynamic was the gradual extension of Dutch influence beyond Java, culminating in territorial conquest and the application of an unrestrained capitalist mode of production for exports as private investors followed in the wake of the colonial administrators. These two forces interacted because the growing assertiveness of indigenous leverage outside Java provoked the Dutch to expand and consolidate their colonial territory and economic influence.

The British occupation of Java in 1811 had already brought sleepy Batavia back into the mainstream of an Asian trading world extending from British-controlled India to the southern Chinese entrepôt of Canton (Guangzhou). Restitution of Dutch authority in 1816 led the British to look for an alternative Southeast Asian port to develop the link between British and Asian commerce. In 1819 the former Lieutenant Governor-General of Java, Thomas Raffles, found what he believed to be the ideal location on the little island of Singapore, which commanded the entry to the Straits of Malacca and the South China Sea. From that time onwards, most of the Malay archipelago was caught up in fierce Anglo-Dutch commercial and political rivalry. The Treaty of London (1824) swapped British and Dutch settlements in Sumatra and the Malay Peninsula, separating British and Dutch spheres of influence along the Straits of Malacca, but not until the Sumatra Treaty (1871) was the present Indonesian archipelago reserved unambiguously for Dutch colonial expansion. British declaration of the Federated and Unfederated Malay States in 1896 unequivocally separated the Malay Peninsula from the Dutch archipelago. Dutch authority was challenged during the Padri War in West Sumatra (1821–1837), the Banjarmasin War in South Kalimantan (1859–1863) and the Aceh War (1873–1904). Nevertheless, by 1900 effective Dutch colonial rule was being extended throughout virtually the entire Indonesian archipelago.

Precolonial trade links between the Outer Islands and the wider region of Southeast Asia (Chapter 2) were disrupted and gradually modified in the course of the 19th century. The Outer Islands were, in effect, pulled away from the the wider region and integrated with the Dutch colonial state that was being welded on Java. This was an important first step in the long process towards the formation of a national economy in the Indonesian archipelago (Chapter 1). It coincided with innovations in export production initiated by private Western enterprises operating in the exceptionally liberal economic climate that prevailed in the colonial state from about 1870 (Chapter 3), and that laid the basis for rapid economic expansion and closer integration with the world economy in the early decades of the 20th century (Chapter 5). This process gives rise to the three key themes for this chapter: slowly declining integration in the trading network of the wider region of Southeast Asia; increasing integration with the emerging Dutch colonial state and Java-based economy; and reorientation towards economic expansion and globalisation. Some conclusions are presented in the final section. Because the Outer Islands are a relatively new object of study in Indonesian economic historiography, this chapter presents new evidence and tries out new methodological approaches (Appendix 4.A).

THE MALAY SPHERE

The Outer Islands occupy an immense territory. The distance from west to east is the same as from western Ireland to eastern Turkey and more than that from coast to coast in the USA. Their Indonesian population had probably grown from some 7.5 million around 1850 to around 13 million in 1900. However, these are crude estimates, based on a backward extra-polation from early 20th-century census figures and assuming a constant annual rate of growth (Lindblad 1993: 245–6). This population was unevenly distributed across the various islands and within individual regions. Densities were higher in coastal areas at the mouths of the rivers (*ilir*) than in the uplands along rivers in the interior (*ulu*). Minority immigrant groups, who lived almost exclusively in coastal ports and towns, together comprised only 150 000 individuals in 1880 but doubled to reach 300 000 by the turn of the century. About 90% of the immigrant population were of Chinese descent, but Europeans, Arabs and Indians were also counted in this group (Boomgaard & Gooszen 1991: 226–30). Altogether they still represented only 2.3% of the total Outer Islands population.

During most of the 19th century, the colonial state scarcely existed in the Outer Islands except in the Moluccas. The authority of the Dutch residents and assistant-residents was generally restricted to the port towns. Their knowledge of matters such as the size of the interior population was scant. According to colonial administrators, the Indonesian population in about half of the regions among the Outer Islands amounted to 1.5 million in 1880 but grew to 3 million in 1900. Such figures grossly understate more reliable census data from the early 20th century.

Kingdoms and statelets headed by indigenous sultans formed a patchwork throughout the archipelago. Their rulers sought to maintain the appearance, if not the substance, of sovereignty. (The Sultan of Riau in Central Sumatra, for one, flew his own flag until challenged on it by the Dutch administrator in 1911.) Nevertheless, they were reluctant to join forces against external enemies. This gave rise to a very fluid political situation in which commerce took place in virtual disregard of formal political boundaries.

Singapore became the foremost entrepôt in the Malay world almost immediately on its foundation in 1819. Its geographic location at the tip of the Malay Peninsula was more advantageous than that of the older British settlement of Penang, which was too distant from most ports in the archipelago. Singapore's lively interregional trade sustained busy ports in the Outer Islands, including Kampar (East Sumatra), Jambi and Palembang (South Sumatra), Muntok (Bangka), Pontianak (West Kalimantan), Banjarmasin (South Kalimantan), Samarinda (East Kalimantan), Makassar (Sulawesi), Kuta (Bali) and Ampenan (Lombok). The trade of all these ports was oriented towards Singapore, just as formerly they had been closely linked with Johore, Malacca and Penang. The three main ports along the north coast of Java, namely Jakarta (Batavia), Semarang and Surabaya, were also tied into this regional network of shipping and trade.

The traditional staples of the Outer Islands were forest and sea products. Such exports included *gambir*, *damar*, rattan, resin, rhinoceros horns and elephant tusks from the forests in the interior of the larger islands, as well as fish, *trasi* (fish paste) and tortoise shells from coastal regions. Other traditional staples were pepper from Aceh and South Kalimantan, tin from Bangka, nutmeg and cloves from the Moluccas, coffee from West Sumatra and Bali and rice from Lombok. Tin and spices were still engrossed by the Dutch trading monopoly, a remnant of the privileged position once enjoyed by the VOC (Chapter 2). A wide assortment of unprocessed exports found

Figure 4.1 Origin of imports into Singapore, 1829–1869

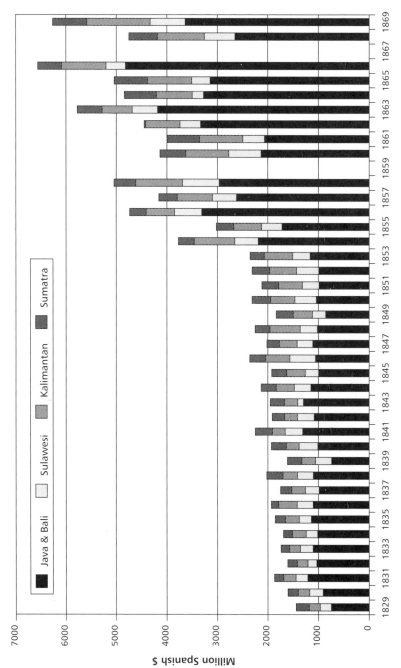

Source: Wong 1960: 219–30.

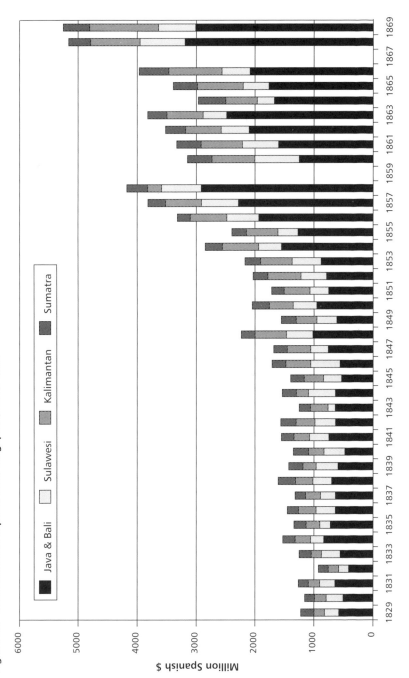

Figure 4.2 Destination of exports from Singapore, 1829–1869

Java & Bali Sulawesi Kalimantan Sumatra

Million Spanish $

Source: Wong 1960: 219–30.

their way to customers in Asia, in particular through the entrepôt of Singapore. The reverse flow of trade, from mainland Southeast Asia to the Outer Islands, included European and Indian textiles, raw silk, wool, salt, tobacco, iron, steel, copper, alum, porcelain, firearms and opium. Singapore's exports to Indonesian ports consisted almost exclusively of goods imported from third countries.

The various economies in the Outer Islands differed by strength of demand for foreign imports and the extent of export specialisation. This is reflected in their volume of trade with Singapore (Figures 4.1 and 4.2; based on Wong 1960: 219–25, 229–30). In most years Sulawesi ranked first, as Makassar served as the gateway for trade with the entire eastern part of the archipelago. Sumatra occupied a less impressive position in the Singapore trade, as trade of the northern part of this island was directed to Penang (Reid 1996: 284–5). Singapore's trade with Kalimantan was about the same size as that with Sumatra (see Appendix 4.B; Wong 1960: 90).

Bali and Lombok were located much further away from Singapore, yet also benefited from the boom in interregional commerce during the 1820s. Direct trade links sprang up between Singapore and the ports at Badung and Kuta in Bali and Ampenan and Labuan Haji in Lombok. The rice trade was particularly lucrative, as Singapore prices were two or three times local prices. Bali and Lombok also prospered as the backdoor to Java: smuggling of opium and coffee added to the profits (Rush 1990: 65–82). Total exports from Bali and Lombok to Singapore grew fivefold between the early 1830s and mid-1840s and together accounted for about 10% of the total trade between Singapore and the Indonesian archipelago (Wong 1960: 62–4; Van der Kraan 1993: 95–8).

Singapore's share of the total trade of the Outer Islands was much larger than its share of the trade of Java. The Outer Islands absorbed a substantial proportion of all imports entering the Indonesian archipelago from Singapore: about two-thirds in the second quarter of the 19th century and possibly slightly more than 50% during the 1850s and 60s. In the reverse flow of exports destined for Singapore from the Indonesian archipelago, the Outer Islands supplied about one-half, possibly slightly less, throughout the period between the 1820s and the 1860s (Figures 4.1 and 4.2; see also Appendix 4.B). The volume of trade between the Outer Islands and Singapore was therefore of approximately the same magnitude as that between Java and Singapore. Although Java's exports were much larger than those of the Outer Islands — in the 1890s, more than three times — most were shipped direct to the Netherlands (Korthals Altes 1991: 72; also Chapter 1).

The trade of the Outer Islands was maritime trade. Lively shipping connections were maintained with Singapore and to a lesser extent Penang. In the early 1830s several vessels called at Singapore every day to or from the Indonesian archipelago. At least half probably came from the Outer Islands. Most of the ships were small *prahu* of about 20 tons, often from Sumatra or Kalimantan. However, in the 1830s, the fleet already included some European-styled square-riggers with a capacity of 200 tons or more, often from Makassar. The total capacity of the fleet was about 50 000 metric tons.

The decades from the 1830s to the late 1860s witnessed a rapid expansion in shipping between Indonesian ports and Singapore. The total number of ships rose to about 2000 per year, or six per day on average. Half probably still came from the Outer Islands, considering an increasing proportion now consisted of square-rigged vessels. Growth in cargo-carrying capacity was especially rapid in the 1850s and 60s, rising to some 200 000 metric tons by the late 1860s (Wong 1960: 280–4). The opening of the Suez Canal in December 1869 redirected shipping through the Straits of Malacca. Steamships from Europe now crossed the Indian Ocean via the coaling stations of the Red Sea, Ceylon and Penang instead of the much longer sailing ship route via the Cape of Good Hope.

Traders and trading networks   Shipping and trade in the Outer Islands consisted of multilayered maritime networks. Parallel trading systems were organised along ethnic lines. For example, Ampenan (Lombok) in the 1840s had three distinct trading systems: long-distance European trading reaching as far as China and New South Wales; Chinese and Bugis trading within the wider Southeast Asian region; and, finally, local shipping plying between Lombok and adjacent islands (Schulte Nordholt 1981). Large square-rigged ships were employed in European or Chinese long-distance trading, whereas the Bugis from Sulawesi and local traders relied on small *prahu*.

The foundation of Singapore gave a powerful impetus to Chinese trade across the South China Sea as well as between mainland Southeast and the Indonesian archipelago. The Chinese in the Outer Islands were part of a vast regional network extending from the Philippines to Vietnam and Burma. By 1880 there were an estimated 135 000 Chinese in the Outer Islands (Boomgaard & Gooszen 1991: 228), corresponding to slightly less than one-tenth of the Chinese population of Southeast Asia at that time (based on Hicks 1993: 4). Chinese traders in the archipelago drew on a centuries-long tradition that leveraged from old settlements in the western part of the archipelago, such as Palembang (since the eclipse of the Sriwijaya empire), Bangka (for tin mining) and Pontianak (close to the gold mines in Sambas). The Chinese fleet grew quickly in the first half of the 19th century as traditional junks were replaced by square-rigged vessels (Reid 1993b: 24–8; Poelinggomang 1991: 61–5, 113–15). Chinese shipping reached further than Indonesian shipping, and Chinese merchants were as quick as their European rivals in adopting modern technology.

The Outer Islands were firmly rooted in the Malay sphere. This held true not only of commercial relations but also of cultural impulses. Traders from Siak or Riau in Sumatra, Pontianak or Banjarmasin in Kalimantan, Makassar or Lombok were active in the interregional trade of the Outer Islands. Malays throughout the archipelago were exposed to the modern world through the city of Singapore, where they came either as traders or as pilgrims on their way to Mecca. Their *prahu* sailed with the monsoon winds and had a smaller cargo-carrying capacity than European-style square-rigged vessels, let alone the steamships that increasingly appeared in the archipelago in the last quarter of the 19th century. The diffusion of modern technology favoured Chinese and European shipping, but Indonesian *prahu* shipping also benefited from the boom in trade and found niches in the maritime network of the archipelago in peripheral routes and feeder lines (à Campo 1993). *Prahu* shipping continued to play an important role in Indonesian waters until far into the 20th century (Dick 1975, 1987b).

Most *prahu* owners and operators were themselves traders. In their regions of origin they dealt direct with suppliers of export produce and local retailers interested in the return goods from the international market. These captains-cum-traders constituted a separate trading system that was tied into the Chinese trading system operating out of Singapore. As Raffles had envisaged, they interlinked local trade with trade in the wider region of Southeast Asia. They were more inclined to apply traditional technology and business practices subject to *adat* law as opposed to European law. For protection and privileges they tended to rely on Malay rulers, with the local *syahbandar* (harbour-master) often acting as an intermediary.

Among indigenous traders, the Bugis had the most extensive archipelago-wide trading networks. Their contacts with mainland Southeast Asia and Java dated back several centuries. During the 17th and 18th centuries, the parent kingdom of Bone in South Sulawesi had served as the main ally of the VOC in extending and defending its territorial claims in the archipelago. In the 18th century infiltration of local politics also secured them a strong-hold in Riau and Johore. By 1745, the Bugis *raja muda* (crown prince), acting behind the scenes, was known to be the real power in the Johore sultanate and to look after the commercial interests of his countrymen (Watson Andaya & Andaya 1982: 82–5). Arguably their technology of ships and firearms was advanced by the standards of the time, and they were renowned as good navigators and fearsome soldiers (see also Reid 1993a: 48–51; Leirissa 1993).

The foundation of Singapore offered the Bugis new opportunities. Raffles initially thought they, and not the Chinese, were the key to the trade of the Indonesian archipelago and granted them special privileges. In the 1820s a substantial Bugis *kampung* arose on the Kallang River, commemo-rated in today's Bugis Street shopping centre. Local merchants hailed the annual 'Bugis season' when these traders arrived as a 'golden harvest' with profits to 'compensate for all their losses throughout the other parts of the year' (Wong 1960: 65). Bugis ships conducted the bulk of trading between Bali and Singapore, and Bugis traders controlled much of the trade along the eastern coast of Kalimantan. In 1827, an early overseas visitor to Kutai (East Kalimantan) counted more than 300 Bugis *prahu* in the harbour of Samarinda alone (Lindblad 1988a: 11).

After the mid-19th century, however, the Bugis lost ground. First, the alliance with the Dutch broke down. The Bugis came to be seen as commercial allies of the British and the kingdom of Bone as a threat to Dutch suzerainty in the area. Despite Dutch military campaigns in South Sulawesi, both during the Java War and in the late 1850s, Bone remained autonomous until 1906, but Bugis power was weakened (Locher-Scholten 1991). Towards the end of the 19th century, Bugis traders were challenged by Chinese merchants on the coast of Kalimantan. In long-distance trade they suffered from lack of the commercial contacts and sources of credit needed to keep abreast of other Asian competitors. Nevertheless, as a heritage of this glorious past and more recent emigration, Bugis settlements are today scattered throughout Indonesia.

The example of the Bugis was emulated, albeit on a modest scale, by the Selayarese from the island of Selayar just off the southwestern peninsula of Sulawesi. Like the Bugis, the Selayarese established an elaborate network of small satellite communities scattered over a vast area. In fact, Selayarese and Bugis settlements were often located next to one another. Satellites sprung up in such varied locations as Manggarai (West Flores), Ampenan (Lombok), Banjarmasin and Pagatan (South Kalimantan) and Sumbawa. The numbers of registered *prahu* operated by Selayarese captains-cum-traders exceeded 400 in the late 1870s (Heersink 1995: 98–100).

The Banjarese of South Kalimantan are known as enterprising merchants, willing to migrate and always alert to trading opportunities. They draw on a tradition of long-distance commerce extending back to the 17th and 18th centuries, when they exported pepper from Banjarmasin to mainland Southeast Asia. In the 19th century they switched to light manufactured goods, such as weapons, textiles, pottery and mats produced in their heartland Hulu Sungai in the interior of South Kalimantan. These goods were marketed throughout the Outer Islands. Their success is in part explained by the political autonomy which they enjoyed until the eclipse of the Banjar sultanate in 1860. As in the case of the Bugis, the link between politics and economics is crucial to understanding commercial rivalries in the archipelago. Indigenous communities could thrive commercially as long as their regions were not incorporated into the Dutch colonial state. However, ultimately they succumbed to the superior military technology, international networks and economic resources of the colonial power and expanding Chinese intermediary networks.

The surrender to the Dutch colonial authorities after the Banjarmasin War induced many Banjarese to move northwards, where they founded the *kampung* Muara Muntai (named after Amuntai in Hulu Sungai) on the Mahakam River. Fierce competition ensued over the control of the coastal and riverine trade, with Bugis traders already operating in East Kalimantan. Migration towards the end of the 19th century brought Banjarese traders to Riau in eastern Sumatra and even to Perak in Malaya

(Potter 1993: 264–74). The Banjarese trading system was less extensive than the Bugis system, but links with production sites in the interior of their heartland were probably stronger.

The Minangkabau were to West Sumatra what the Bugis were to South Sulawesi and the Banjarese to South Kalimantan. The Minangkabau traditionally engaged in riverine trade from the highlands of West Sumatra to ports in eastern Sumatra. Dutch military interference during the Padri War (1821–1837) and subsequent commercial restrictions forced the Minangkabau to look west. Conducting trade from what was generally perceived as the wrong side of Sumatra, they established a commercial hierarchy extending from producers and consumers in the interior through retail traders in inland markets to large wholesale traders in Padang. Copra, cinnamon and coffee were exchanged against textiles and an assortment of foreign consumer goods. The Minangkabau were said to be capable of competing with Chinese traders on equal terms. They secured control over much of the regional trade in West Sumatra (Dobbin 1983: 218–19; Colombijn 1994: 79–82). The range of Minangkabau trading was more limited than in the case of Bugis or Banjarese, but through a high degree of vertical integration they probably exerted a stronger influence on economic life in their region of origin than did any of their counterparts in Sulawesi or Kalimantan.

Incessant rivalries between Chinese, Bugis, even Selayarese, Banjarese and Minangkabau in the ports of the Outer Islands and the Malay peninsula added drama to commerce in the wider Malay sphere. This also testifies to the dynamism of Indonesian entrepreneurship that flourished in the political vacuum before the Dutch conquered the Outer Islands. Ports and markets in the Outer Islands were melting pots, often displaying a great variety of traders of different ethnic origin, which as such was nothing new (Chapter 2). Two examples illustrate this dynamism.

In Palembang retailers from Muara Dua in the interior competed with Minangkabau, Chinese, Arabs and Indians. Eventually each group of traders would find a niche of its own. However, such a balance of vested commercial interests could easily be disturbed by external interference. Menggala, a port on the Tulang Bawang River in the southern tip of Sumatra, emerged in the 1850s as the major trading centre of the Lampung region. Local Indonesian merchants controlled most of the pepper trade. Yet by the early 20th century Menggala had become a ghost town, superseded by Telukbetung, terminus of the new South Sumatra railway and a focal point for Chinese trading (Purwanto 1993: 120–2).

European traders played only a marginal role in the Outer Islands during most of the 19th century. The leading Dutch commercial enterprise in the archipelago, the NHM, incorporated under royal charter in 1824, estab-lished branches outside Java, including Padang (1826), Palembang (1839) and Banjarmasin (1840), but met with little success. The Palembang and Banjarmasin factories even closed for lack of business. The few European vessels calling at ports in the Outer Islands, as sighted for instance in the harbour of Ampenan in the 1840s, were almost irrelevant to the busy commerce of the Outer Islands.

Nevertheless, the political vacuum provided opportunities for individual Western adventurers to set up on remote locations in close cooperation with local rulers. One of the first was George Peacock King, who had started out in Lombok in the 1830s and became the first European to engage in riverine trade in East Kalimantan — so fearing for his safety that he usually stayed on board his sailing vessel in the Mahakam River (Lindblad 1988a: 11). He was followed by William Lingard, the English *raja laut* (sea king) in the sultanate of Gunung Tabur (northeastern Kalimantan), who became the prototype for the hero in Joseph Conrad's novel *An Outcast of the Islands*. Some of these pioneers had political aspirations, such as Adam Wilson, who settled at Siak in eastern Sumatra in the 1850s and tried to emulate James Brooke's success in Sarawak. These early adventurers, often of British descent, added to the romantic lure of pioneering in the Outer Islands but themselves had a very limited impact on local life.

Singapore was the fulcrum of the general expansion of trade and shipping in Southeast Asia during the 19th century. The total turnover of foreign trade passing through Singapore increased fivefold between the early 1820s and the late 1860s, a very substantial increase in real terms considering the low rate of inflation at the time (Wong 1960: 254). Despite the acceleration of trade expansion in the 1850s and 60s, the share of the Indonesian archipelago stayed high, at about 20% (Wong 1960: 219–25, 229–30). In the late 1860s, probably around 10% of all Singapore trade was with ports in the Outer Islands (Lindblad 1996).

In the 1820s the turnover of foreign trade at Penang was of approximately the same magnitude as at Singapore, even though its trade with the archipelago was confined to northern Sumatra and in particular Aceh. Pepper from Aceh was one of Penang's main export staples, being exchanged against European and Indian consumer goods and tin from southwestern Thailand. In the late 1820s Sumatra supplied as much as 20% of all foreign imports entering Penang. By the late 1860s its share had dropped to about 10%, about the same as the proportion of the Outer Islands in the total trade of Singapore (Wong 1960: 55; Booth 1998a: 26).

Singapore and Penang were important trading partners to the Indonesian archipelago in general and to the Outer Islands in particular. In the early 1870s, Singapore (together with Penang) received 12% of all exports from the Indonesian archipelago while delivering 23% of all imports entering the archipelago (Korthals Altes 1991: 87–8, 100–2; see also Appendix 4.B). These figures reinforce the impression of rapid commercial expansion, accompanied by a high degree of economic integration between the Outer Islands and mainland Southeast Asia that continued well into the second half of the 19th century.

THE JAVA SPHERE

In the early 19th century, effective Dutch colonial authority outside Java was restricted to the Moluccas and a few ports and their immediate hinterlands, such as Padang and Palembang in Sumatra, Pontianak and Banjarmasin in Kalimantan, Makassar and Manado in Sulawesi. Dutch rule was restored after the British interregnum (1811–1816), but its restoration was slow and often incomplete. In Banjarmasin the former British administrator, Alexander Hare, stayed on for several years, emulating local Malay rulers. He maintained a court with a harem of his own until finally expelled by the Dutch. The Treaty of London, negotiated on the other side of the world and signed between Great Britain and the Netherlands in 1824, applied the rather ambiguous formulation that the Dutch would hold sway in 'islands south of the Straits of Singapore'. Sources of conflict thus remained in northern Sumatra and Borneo, both technically located to the *north* of Singapore. This ambiguity profoundly affected the political development of the archipelago during the 19th century.

The Dutch policy of abstaining from interference with local affairs (*onthoudingspolitiek*) remained the official guideline for Dutch colonial administrators in the Outer Islands until well into the second half of the 19th century. It was widely felt that the scarce resources of the small Dutch nation ought to be reserved for Java, even if Governor-General Van den Bosch in 1830 contemplated extending the Cultivation System and the Dutch sphere of influence to Sumatra. In 1841 abstention was elevated to official policy, applying to all parts of the Outer Islands. The Minister of Colonial Affairs, J.C. Baud, expressly forbade any further colonial expansion outside Java. In the early 1870s a proposal to sell some remote territories in the Outer Islands to Italy was not immediately rejected.

Abstention was the official ideology behind Dutch colonial policy outside Java even after the Aceh War had broken out in 1873. In 1878, when the European colonial powers were getting ready for the 'scramble of Africa', the Dutch Parliament still advised against any aspirations in terms of colonial expansion outside Java. Otto Van Rees, shortly afterwards Minister of Colonial Affairs, stated: 'If colonial administrators are found in the Outer Islands who wish to take this path of action [extension of colonial authority], whether out of ambition or bellicosity, then such tendencies should be repressed' (Kuitenbrouwer 1985: 77). In this tradition the Dutch colonial state should be confined to Java; Dutch settlements in the Outer Islands were considered to be *lastposten*, literally nuisances, for which costs ran higher than gains.

Nevertheless, change was afoot. The emerging Dutch colonial state, its authority unchallenged in Java after the conclusion of the Java War (1825–1830), was gradually extending its control over the rest of the Indonesian archipelago. It was a long process, facilitated by the political fragmentation of the Outer Islands. To all intents, the only modern state in the Indonesian archipelago during the 19th century was the Dutch colonial state, with its centre in Java.

During the initial phase of Dutch expansion, commercial policy was of greater concern than the extension of formal political authority. Commercial aims sometimes combined with Dutch military intervention in drawn-out local conflicts, such as the Padri War in West Sumatra between 1821 and 1837 (Dobbin 1983). Here the colonial authorities sought to discourage traditional riverine trade connecting the Minangkabau Highlands to the eastern shore of Sumatra and from there across the Straits to the Malay Peninsula and Singapore. The aim, ultimately achieved, was to divert Minangkabau trade to Batavia (Colombijn 1994: 44–5).

Bali and Lombok were similarly drawn into the sphere of Java. Military intervention in Bali in 1848 gave the Dutch control of the north coast ports, after which commercial policy reserved trade between Bali and Java and other parts of the Indonesian archipelago for Dutch vessels. These measures impinged on shipping with Singapore and disrupted the further integration of Bali and Lombok with the world economy. Bali and Lombok thus became economically dependent on Java even before establishment of colonial rule, which subsequently further retarded their long-run economic development (Wong 1960: 65–7; Van der Kraan 1993).

Sulawesi attracted the special attention of the Dutch colonial authorities in the 1830s and 1840s. Makassar benefited substantially from the general expansion of trade and shipping centred on Singapore. These two ports worked like eastern and western nodes of a vast maritime network around the Java Sea. They both gained by virtue of a liberal commercial climate. Singapore was acclaimed as 'the freeest of the free ports in the world' (Wong 1960: 196). Makassar, on the other hand, profited from the weak Dutch grip on local commerce. Around 1840 as much as two-thirds of all commodities traded in the Makassar market escaped registration by Dutch customs. Dutch control of surrounding waters was so scant that pirates were sighted from the city shore as soon as the one Dutch man-of-war stationed there had sailed out (Poelinggomang 1991: 163–4; Heersink 1995: 73). The rise of Singapore and the lack of control over affairs at Makassar were both sources of irritation to the Dutch colonial government.

Makassar became a free port in 1847, although not as free as Singapore, for preferential treatment was given to goods carried on Dutch vessels. This measure had a dual aim: to increase Makassar's trade in general, and to divert it away from Singapore. The former aim was achieved but not the latter. Total trade grew but Sulawesi's share in the total trade on Singapore remained high. The colonial authorities soon concluded that the expansion in Makassar's trade benefited Singapore more than Batavia. Makassar's status as a free port was unnecessary, though not until 1906 was it suspended (Poelinggomang 1993).

From the Dutch point of view, colonial commercial policy succeeded in West Sumatra and Bali and Lombok but not in Makassar. After the middle of the 19th century, the colonial state made more effort to control production, not only in Java but also in the Outer Islands. In West Sumatra the continued Dutch military presence also after the Padri War paved the way for the establishment of forced coffee cultivations in 1847. The estates were modelled after the Cultivation System in Java (Chapter 3) and remained in operation until 1908. State-run cultivations were also located in the Minahasa (North Sulawesi). The local population probably gained little from these cultivations, whether in West Sumatra or in North Sulawesi (Young 1990; Schouten 1995).

Elsewhere the focus of commercial policy was mining. The state alluvial tin mines in Bangka, inherited from the VOC, were enlarged and the output shipped direct to Europe. There was no opportunity for Singapore or Penang Chinese to play an intermediary role as the colonial state wished to reap all the profits, also from the processing of the ore (Somers Heidhues 1992: 36–7). Introduction of steamships led the state to open coalmines in South Kalimantan; in 1849 Governor-General J.J. Rochussen travelled several days upriver by *prahu* to the mines in the interior. These had to be abandoned during the Banjarmasin War (1859–1863). Strife over the succession to the Banjar throne prompted the colonial government to intervene militarily and abolish the sultanate altogether.

Dutch private capital became involved in the economic development of the Outer Islands after the mid-19th century. Colonial authorities endorsed the first concessions for mining and estate agriculture granted by local rulers during the 1850s and 1860s. The Billiton Company's tin mining concession on Belitung Island off the eastern Sumatra coast was authorised in 1852 and held by a combination of Dutch entrepreneurs, including the younger brother of King Willem III. Mining began in 1860. In 1863 Jacob Nienhuys obtained a concession from the sultan of Deli (East Sumatra) for the 'Deli' tobacco estate. This launched a spectacular economic expansion in that region (see the next section).

The first phase of Dutch expansion into the Outer Islands ended in the early 1870s. It had then lasted for more than half a century. During this phase, interference by the Dutch colonial government with economic matters outside Java slowly increased but military intervention was still occasional. The aspirations of other European powers were not yet a source of alarm. Foundation of the Brooke sultanate in Sarawak in 1841 caused much annoyance in Batavia and The Hague, but no military action was taken. In 1858, however, suspicions about British ambitions in northern Sumatra, across the waters from the Malay Peninsula, prompted the formal incorporation of the Siak sultanate into the Netherlands Indies.

The second phase began with the outbreak of the Aceh War in 1873 and lasted for almost a quarter of a century until 1896. The problem with the demarcation between British and Dutch spheres of influence in the archipelago had at long last been settled through the Sumatra Treaty, concluded in November 1871. Henceforth, all of Sumatra fell within the Dutch sphere of influence. This ruled out international complications in the event of a

Dutch military offensive against Aceh. Dutch historians still dispute whether the attack on Aceh in 1873 was prompted by real or perceived threats of foreign intervention, as also the seriousness of the alleged internal political strife in Aceh (Kuitenbrouwer 1985: 59–67). At any rate, a devastating war began that was to last for more than three decades, absorb an ever-increasing proportion of the colonial budget and, most importantly, inaugurate a more aggressive type of Dutch imperialism in the archipelago.

Dutch colonial expansion became more determined during the second phase of penetration, but overt military aggression did not extend much beyond Aceh. This phase was a rather peculiar one and there has been much discussion, primarily among Dutch historians, as to how to classify it. Was the Aceh War a 'false start' on the road to aggressive imperialist expansion or a stage in which Dutch imperialist ideology was underpinned by vested economic interests (Appendix 4.C)? Colonial expansion generally took the form of enforcing authority over territories in the Outer Islands that were claimed but not yet effectively controlled. This was a defining characteristic of the specific Dutch version of modern imperialism (Ricklefs 1981: 125). Local economic and political interests often interacted to spark colonial expansion. Military aggression had begun but was not yet full-scale. Politics were important, but not with respect to aspirations of other imperialist powers or in response to external threats. Economic factors were important too but were now more strongly linked to territorial expansion than before (Lindblad 1989a; Locher-Scholten 1994a).

The period between the early 1870s and the mid-1890s saw several initiatives taken by the colonial government or private businessmen to further economic expansion through trade and foreign investment. Such initiatives were accompanied by extension of colonial control in the regions concerned. The Siak sultanate in eastern Sumatra was pushed as a potential 'second Deli' and in 1873 made into a separate residency, but results were disappointing. In 1887 the Dutch administrator moved to Medan. Arrival of the British North Borneo Company in present-day Sabah in 1878 set in motion a chain reaction. Mining prospectors and Dutch colonial officers were dispatched to the three remote sultanates of Bulungan, Gunung Tabur and Sambaliung in northeastern Kalimantan. In Gorontalo in North Sulawesi Australian gold diggers went ashore in the late 1880s, which in turn prompted the Dutch colonial administrators to start exercising control over the area. Military expeditions to Flores followed in 1889 and 1890 in the wake of prospectors searching for tin in the inaccessible interior of the island. No tin was ever found but colonial rule remained.

Government economic policy fluctuated between restraint and intervention. Authorisation of mining and agricultural concessions was held up for some years because the government felt unable to guarantee the safety of men and property on remote sites. In West Sumatra, it took 20 full years of deliberation before the government finally, in 1892, assumed responsibility for exploitation of the newly discovered Ombilin coalmines and construction of the necessary railway to the coast (Colombijn 1996: 389–90). In West Kalimantan in the late 1880s, the sultans of Pontianak and Sambas received assistance in advertising for private capital in the Netherlands. About a hundred concessions for mining and agriculture were authorised with unusual speed, and the local administrative apparatus was enlarged. Few, if any, of the private firms made profits or stayed long in the region (Lindblad 1989a).

Continued military action in Aceh and more active involvement in the economic development of the Outer Islands both pointed in the same direction — the political and economic integration of the Outer Islands into the emerging colonial state. This process of incorporation combined Dutch colonial rule with exploitation of the Outer Islands' rich natural resources by private foreign capital. Yet as late as the 1890s vast territories in the Outer Islands fell under Dutch jurisdiction only in name: actual Dutch authority was scarcely exercised. Private foreign investment had been encouraged since 1870 but was remarkably slow in forthcoming. At the end of the 19th century, foreign-held assets in the archipelago amounted to about 750 million guilders ($300 million), of which the overwhelming majority was invested in Java (Lindblad 1998: 48). A strong nexus between political expansion and vested private economic interests was not yet established.

The colonial government also had fiscal motivations for encouraging economic development and private investment in the Outer Islands. After 1870 the gradual abolition of the Cultivation System in Java meant less revenue from sales of export produce and greater dependence on taxes. The share of taxes in total government revenue grew from 33% in 1867 to 58% in 1897 (Furnivall 1939/1944: 341). The best way to ensure a wider tax base in the future was to improve the investment climate. This presupposed effective colonial rule.

The Lombok incident in 1894 foreshadowed a crucial change in the character of Dutch imperialism. A military expedition had been mounted on the pretext of internal conflict. Dutch soldiers met with unexpected resistance and were defeated in their first attempt at invasion. Public outcry in the Netherlands generated support for the subsequent conquest of the island. The Cakranegara Palace in Mataram was burnt and Lombok brought under effective colonial rule.

The shift of public opinion at home towards aggressive imperialism led in 1896 to escalation of the war on Aceh after 23 years of indecisive warfare. The colonial lobby in the Netherlands, representing vested economic interests in the Indonesian archipelago, urged military action. A foremost proponent was the Royal Dutch (*Koninklijke*), whose oilfields in East Sumatra were drying up; concessions in East Aceh remained inaccessible as long as the war was going on (Ismail 1991: 151–5; Bakker 1989). Massive military resources were deployed and by 1904 the entire province of Aceh was declared to be fully under Dutch military control.

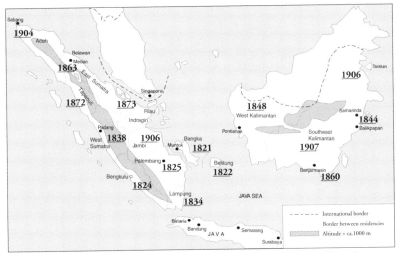

Map 3   The extension of Dutch colonial authority in western Indonesia

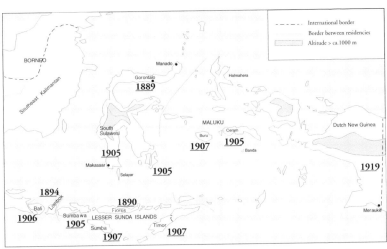

Map 4   The extension of Dutch colonial authority in eastern Indonesia

Escalation of the war on Aceh inaugurated the third and final phase of Dutch expansion into the Outer Islands. Full-scale, aggressive imperialism, known euphemistically as 'pacification', lasted throughout the first decade of the 20th century, by which time colonial rule had been imposed on the entire Indonesian archipelago (Maps 3 and 4). The expansion culminated during the years 1904–1909 when the former commander-in-chief in Aceh, General J.B. van Heutsz, held the office of Governor-General. The annexations of formerly autonomous kingdoms into the Netherlands Indies made liberal use of a standardised contract for acknowledging Dutch suzerainty, the so-called Short Declaration (*Korte Verklaring*).

The conquests extended to all parts of the archipelago. Occupation of the Batak lands in the interior of northern Sumatra followed in the wake of the escalation of the war on Aceh. In Jambi in southern Sumatra the deposed Sultan Taha had been exercising authority for decades in disregard of asserted colonial claims. His rule was broken by invading units from the colonial army in 1904, the aged sultan was killed in ambush, and Jambi was brought under effective colonial rule. Here also an economic motive played a part, as rich oilfields had just been discovered in the interior of Jambi and were awaiting exploitation. However, the economic motive for Dutch colonial expansion in Jambi had first to be 'politicised' before military action could be justified (Locher-Scholten 1994b: 243–63, 1996). In 1907 Dutch soldiers reached the Kerinci valley close to the border with West Sumatra. Remaining 'white spots' in interior Sumatra were incorporated into the colonial state.

In upriver South Kalimantan, the resistance of supporters of the former sultanate of Banjarmasin was crushed by 1907. The Bugis and Makassarese states in southwestern Sulawesi fell in 1905 and 1906. The fiscal motive for imperialist expansion was conspicuously present in the Dutch military expedition to Bone in South Sulawesi in 1905. Here the local *raja* allegedly declined to cede the right to collect export and import duties (Locher-Scholten 1991). Meanwhile Dutch soldiers ventured into the Toraja lands in interior Sulawesi. Sumbawa was brought under Dutch rule in 1905. Sumba and Timor followed in 1907. The latter year also saw Dutch flags flown in Buru and Ceram in the Moluccas. Only West New Guinea (later Irian Jaya) remained largely outside the realm of effective colonial rule until far into the 1920s.

Private European investors trickled into the Outer Islands along with colonial administrators. A vast new network took shape, extending through the entire Indonesian archipelago. It was above all a maritime network. Here also important changes took place towards the end of the 19th century. Between 1865 and 1890 the interisland mail contract had been held by the British-owned NISN. However, Chinese and Arab steamers dominated the carrying trades with Singapore, despite intensifying competition from British- and German-owned vessels. Indigenous *prahu* owners did not make the switch to steamships. In 1888 a fully Dutch-owned shipping concern, the KPM, was founded to take control of interisland shipping from British and Chinese lines based on Singapore (see also Chapter 1).

Commencing operations in 1891 by taking over the network and contracts of the HNISN, the KPM enjoyed special privileges, including a monopoly on the transport of mail and official goods and personnel. In return the KPM promised to maintain less profitable shipping lines to remote locations where a Dutch presence was deemed necessary. Expansion was quick, and within two decades the number of ports of call had increased from 100 to 225. A high degree of interdependence developed between three overlapping networks: maritime, political, and economic.

This can even be statistically corroborated between seats of colonial administration on the one hand and ports of call and centres of economic activity
on the other (à Campo 1992: 579–612, 636–41). The tripartite network
emerged as the convergence of administrative ambition, shipping interests
and private pioneering.

Dutch expansion into the Outer Islands was a long process that gained
momentum only towards the end of the 19th century. The Dutch colonial
state extended fitfully beyond Java, even if trade and shipping were still
largely dominated by non-Europeans, which also held true for the mining
settlements in West Kalimantan and Bangka. Sumatra occupied a separate
position within this whole process. Here we find the chief exception to the
long-honoured policy of abstention from military intervention outside Java
(the Padri War), also the turning-point in the evolution towards a more
aggressive imperialism (Aceh in 1873) as well as, finally, the cradle of a
new type of economic expansion in the Outer Islands (Deli).

A NEW ERA IN PRODUCTION

Expansion in world trade slowed down between the 1870s and mid-1890s,
the period conventionally labelled the 'Great Depression'. Despite the

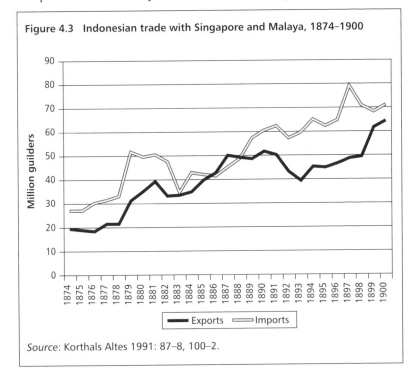

Figure 4.3   Indonesian trade with Singapore and Malaya, 1874–1900

Source: Korthals Altes 1991: 87–8, 100–2.

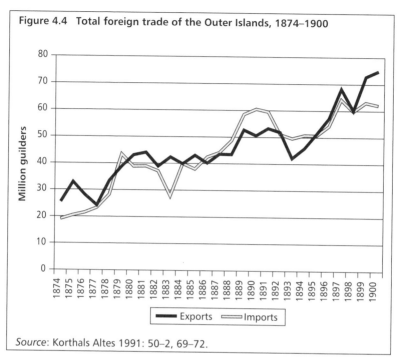

Figure 4.4 Total foreign trade of the Outer Islands, 1874–1900

Source: Korthals Altes 1991: 50–2, 69–72.

lower freight rates that flowed from the opening of the Suez Canal and
the switch to steamships, international trade remained sluggish. Markets for
primary products were especially affected. Not until the mid-1890s was the
downward trend in international trade reversed. Southeast Asia was now
more fully drawn into the world economy. A new international division of
labour evolved in which Asian economies supplied raw materials for industrial production in Europe and the USA (Sugihara 1986). These changes, in
both economic climate and patterns of international trading, were of utmost
importance to the economic development of the Outer Islands.

The slowdown applied also to trade between the Indonesian archipelago
and mainland Southeast Asia. Over the final three decades of the 19th century,
trade volumes continued to rise but much more slowly than in the 1850s
and 1860s (Figure 4.3; Korthals Altes 1991: 87–8, 100–2). The foreign
trade of the Outer Islands was still mainly a host of minor trades in forest
and sea products. The Outer Islands continued to run a trade deficit with
Singapore and Malaya (largely Penang). Singapore's function as a distribution centre for foreign imports into the Outer Islands was therefore still
more important than its role as a transshipment port for their export of
primary products.

At the end of the 19th century, the Outer Islands were still highly
integrated with mainland Southeast Asia. This may be inferred from a

comparison of the total trade of the Outer Islands with that of the whole Indonesian archipelago with Singapore and Malaya (Figure 4.4; Korthals Altes 1991: 50–2, 69–72). These trade volumes were by and large of the same magnitude. Singapore (and Malaya) probably accounted for about one-half of the total trade of the Outer Islands alone. This implies a strong systematic relationship between the trade of the entire archipelago with Singapore and Malaya on the one hand and the total foreign trade of the Outer Islands on the other (Lindblad 1996: 539–45).

In the second half of the 1890s, exports from the Outer Islands began to grow much faster than exports from Java. This acceleration coincided with two simultaneous processes of integration, one external and one internal. The former refers to the closer integration of parts of the Outer Islands into the world economy. The latter refers to the formation of the Dutch colonial state, a process of integration with Java which, as elaborated above, culminated in the 'pacifications' of the late 1890s and first decade of the 20th century. The two processes were linked in the sense that the integration of the Outer Islands into the world market formed the macroeconomic framework of Dutch imperialism. By 1909, the Outer Islands already accounted for one-third of all exports leaving the Indonesian archipelago, compared with just over one-fifth in 1894 (Korthals Altes 1991: 72–3).

The rise of the Outer Islands as an important producer for the world market was furthered by changes in both the range of products and the system of production. At the turn of the century forest products still predominated among exports from the Outer Islands, but even within the traditional mode of collection innovations did take place. The foremost new forest product in the late 19th century was gutta percha, a resin exceptionally well suited to insulating undersea telegraph cables. It had been discovered in 1843 and was allegedly first used for the telegraph connection between Singapore and Johore. Demand increased in the 1870s, and more dramatically in the 1890s. Gutta percha was a new product but the organisation of production was very traditional.[1] The product was collected by Dayaks in the interior, specifically gangs of young men who roamed through the jungle for months on end, reputedly sometimes combining forest collection with head-hunting. The activity was financed by Chinese traders, who advanced foreign consumer goods to Malay suppliers in the coastal towns of Kalimantan and then made almost exclusive use of Singapore as the gateway to the world market.

Copra was another new product in the range of exports from the Outer Islands. It was obtained from the coconut palm that grew abundantly in the eastern part of the archipelago. The coconuts were broken open and the white flesh extracted and dried. European mills extracted the coconut oil for a variety of industrial uses, including food preparation (copra oil and margarine) and personal care (soap). Exporting regions included West Sumatra and parts of Sulawesi. In the late 1870s Selayar, off the south-western peninsula of Sulawesi, served as the regional centre for this still minor trade (Heersink 1995: 107–8). In the 1880s and 1890s, however, the Minahasa in the Manado region became the leading suppliers from the Indonesian archipelago. Here a system of production developed in which local Indonesian entrepreneurs contracted with both smallholder culti-vators and foreign purchasers (Leirissa 1996). Around 1900, copra accounted for about one-quarter of total foreign exports from the Outer Islands (see also Chapter 5).

Tobacco was not a new product, but the organisation of the Deli estate in East Sumatra after 1863 differed from that of plantations in Java. In Deli the emphasis was on large-scale production, which allowed rationalisation of processing and distribution and lower overhead costs. The heavy capital investment needed to clear land for cultivation and erect the necessary infrastructure required financing from sources in the Netherlands and effectively reserved this line of production for Western entrepreneurship. The Deli Company (*Deli Maatschappij*) was founded in 1869 on the basis of the original concession granted to Nienhuys. Between the 1870s and the 1890s, it was followed by many other tobacco companies. Deli tobacco leaf, especially suited for wrapping cigars, gained a worldwide reputation for high quality.

The success of the Deli Company and its followers had important repercussions for the region of East Sumatra and beyond. A pioneer society evolved in the region, complete with heavy-handed European planters, well-connected Chinese traders, Dutch administrators and formal financial institutions (Thee 1977). The seat of the Resident of East Sumatra was moved to Medan in 1887 and a branch office of the NHM opened its doors in 1888. Several attempts were made to emulate the success of Deli, both nearby in the sultanate of Siak and further afield in South and West Kalimantan. Most of these initiatives failed for the simple reason that the soil was not as good. Nevertheless, Deli set an example and paved the way for the later massive influx of foreign investment into the Outer Islands.

Labour mobilisation was one of the most critical issues in implementing large-scale export production in the Outer Islands (Breman 1989). In this respect, Deli acquired a notorious reputation. For countless poor Chinese and Javanese labourers, the word 'Deli' became synonymous with brutal repres-sion, deceit and maltreatment. The tobacco companies in Deli urged special measures to safeguard the supply of labour in the thinly populated area where they were starting operations. The legal basis was the Coolie Ordinance of 1880, which granted employers extreme legal powers to deal with immigrant employees. These included the so-called penal clause (*poenale sanctie*) that allowed for criminal prosecution if employees were judged, by the employers, to have failed to fulfil their contractual obligations. This much-hated and ill-reputed legal weapon remained in force until 1931.

The Coolie Ordinance and the penal clause were defended as indispen-sable to recovering the investment in overseas recruitment and transport of coolies to East Sumatra. Significantly, the Coolie Ordinance was issued for the Outer Islands only one year after a similar regulation had been abolished in Java. However, shortage of local labourers was not the only reason for Western enterprises to rely on coolies imported from China or Java. In Aceh after the war, for instance, local residents were not prepared to work for Western firms even if it meant remaining at a lower income level in the ailing pepper cultivation (Ismail 1991: 245–6). Few attempts were in fact made by Western employers to recruit locally. The choice of immigrant coolies was deliberate, as employers expected them to be more easily controlled away from their original surroundings. Such a strategy was also reflected in the increasing preference for Javanese coolies over Chinese ones: the former were said to be less industrious but also less inclined to offer resistance.

By the first decade of the 20th century, the number of coolies working in the Outer Islands exceeded 100 000, about 80% in East Sumatra alone (Houben, Lindblad et al. 1999). The colonial authorities assisted the recruitment of coolies by sending emissaries to poverty-stricken regions in South China and setting up depots in the main ports of Central Java. Government support became controversial in the early years of the 20th century. In 1902 the employers in East Sumatra were charged with gross abuse of coolies. An investigation was ordered, but the contents of the resulting report were not disclosed even to members of the Dutch Parliament. Later publication of the report showed that the accusations were well founded (Breman 1989: 179–205). Although since the 1880s the government had maintained facilities in Medan to give the appearance of official protection to newly arrived coolies, not until 1908 did the government in fact take action by establishing a Labour Inspectorate for the Outer Islands. Its specific task was to alleviate abuses and check whether contractual obligations were being met by employers.

Tin counted among the most traditional of export products delivered by the Outer Islands, but also here innovations occurred in the organisation of production. In the late 19th century the two foremost producers, the islands of Bangka and Belitung, both switched to large-scale production and intensive use of Chinese coolie labour. In both cases there were substantial capital outlays on machinery and infrastructure. The colonial government remained in charge of the Bangka mines, whereas the private Billiton syndicate ran the mines on the neighbouring island. The entire output was exported to overseas refineries, first at Singapore, later in the Netherlands. Billiton's profits were so extraordinary that in 1882 political controversy arose about the renewal of the company's concession, due to expire in 1892. More than one high-ranking official had to resign and the government gained a larger share of dividends.

Oil epitomised the progress of export production in the Outer Islands. The commodity itself was included in the export range of the Outer Islands only in the early 1890s. There was a separation between exploration and drilling sites in the interior and refineries at the coastal ports of

Pangkalan Brandan (North Sumatra) and Balikpapan (East Kalimantan). Refineries applied sophisticated technology and were highly capital-intensive. Exploitation required massive capital injections from Europe and called for complex business organisations. Coolie labour was generally used, though wages formed a much smaller proportion of total costs than on the tobacco estates. Locally recruited coolies were on occasion employed for exploration and pipeline construction.

The original market leader was the Royal Dutch (*Koninklijke*), founded in 1890 to exploit a number of concessions in East Sumatra and East Aceh. From 1898 Royal Dutch also exploited rich oilfields in the sultanate of Kutai in East Kalimantan. The years around the turn of the century saw cut-throat competition and a proliferation of newcomers. The largest refinery in the archipelago was built at Balikpapan by the British-owned Shell Transport and Trading. Heavy demands in terms of capital endowment and managerial skills eventually forced a concentration of resources. In 1907, Royal Dutch and Shell joined forces by establishing a number of joint subsidiaries, in which the Dutch partner held 60% and the British one 40%. Their common production company, the Batavian Petro-leum Company, or BPM (*Bataafsche Petroleum Maatschappij*), soon gained a virtual monopoly in the Indonesian oil industry and became the single largest private corporation in the archipelago.

Gutta percha, copra, tobacco, tin and oil all contributed to a renewal and extension of the basis for production for foreign markets in the Outer Islands towards the end of the 19th century. Four of them (excluding gutta percha) were to remain important throughout the late colonial period. Oil and copra and later rubber together brought the Outer Islands into the position of dominating the foreign exchange of the archipelago.

CONCLUSION

The 19th century was a tumultuous epoch in the development of the Outer Islands. It was a time of continuous competitive strife between Chinese and indigenous traders, among indigenous traders, between Chinese and Euro-peans, among British and Dutch. It was also a time of warfare and violence, on many occasions and in several locations. When the century began, politi-cal fragmentation prevailed and it was by no means certain what type of nation-state, if any, would evolve. Commercial rivalry and imperialist expansion, whether overt or disguised, both thrived. As the century drew to a close the Outer Islands were a frontier of unrestrained capitalism in the course of being forcefully incorporated into the hitherto Java-based Dutch colonial state.

Local traditions of trading, Western capitalism and Dutch imperialism combined to give the processes of state formation and economic integration a unique flavour in the Outer Islands. Unlike in Java, the frontier economy in the Outer Islands was at first an arena for incessant competition but

eventually consolidated into parallel modes of export production, indigenous next to Western, each viable in its own right (Chapter 5). The late
incorporation into the colonial state implied much less alignment with the
centre of power than was the case in Java. Here are the historical roots
of tendencies towards separatism that came to the fore after Independence
(Chapter 6). The striking example is Aceh, where forces of resistance
remained strong and popular support for secession was manifest again as the
20th century drew to a close.

At the epicentre of rapid export expansion, Deli, the three main trends
in the development of the Outer Islands were juxtaposed: interregional
integration, interinsular integration within the Indonesian archipelago, and
increasing integration with world markets. The economy and society of
East Sumatra's plantation belt were both strongly oriented towards the
Malay Peninsula. English was widely used by the planters and the Straits
dollar remained the main local currency until 1907, when the region was
also in monetary terms incorporated into the Dutch colonial state (Potting
1997). Nevertheless, Deli was from the outset more firmly rooted in the
realm of Java's Dutch colonial state than anywhere else in the Outer
Islands. Planters received strong support from colonial administrators and
benefited from the close links between overseas capital owners and the
Colonial Office in The Hague (Bossenbroek 1996).

This chapter puts forward three propositions. The first is the continuity
in terms of integration between the Outer Islands and the wider region of
Southeast Asia. This was a heritage from the past, and continued to apply
throughout most of the 19th century. A second proposition refers to a
movement in opposite direction, namely the extension of colonial control
over the Outer Islands. This raised the degree of interinsular integration,
but the process was slow for most of the century. The third and final proposition refers to the establishment of a new basis for export expansion
in the Outer Islands. Extensions in the range of export commodities and
innovations in the organisation of export production were stimulated by a
new kind of globalisation, one that reached further than Southeast Asia.
New directions for the future were charted: away from the Malay sphere,
towards the Java sphere, and also towards the sphere of the world economy.

APPENDICES

4.A   The Outer Islands in historiography

In the literature on 19th-century Indonesian history, the Outer Islands
have remained in the shadow of Java. There have been no heated debates like
that over the Cultivation System in Java. Dutch scholars have shown interest
in the Outer Islands primarily as the venue for Dutch imperialism (see
Appendix 4.B). This preoccupation may have perpetuated a Eurocentric
approach to Indonesian history among foreign scholars. Indigenous economic

development in the Outer islands left few primary sources for the historian. It is too readily assumed that little happened because little was recorded.

Reliance by default on information gathered by colonial officials introduces another bias — that is, to consider the Outer Islands solely in relation to Java. The islands beyond Java are seen as regions yet to be incorporated and as examples of development differing from that of the core of the embryonic colonial state. Dick distinguishes three approaches in the literature on the Outer Islands in the late colonial period (Dick 1993c):

1. colonial history, describing how Western private capital penetrated the Outer Islands;
2. local history, focusing on individual regions and how they responded to exogenous impulses;
3. case studies, in which concepts from economic theory or political economy are applied to regional development.

The three categories are not mutually exclusive. They overlap when, for instance, economic analysis is applied to Western pioneering in a local region. All approaches have in common that Java is prominent, whether as the base for Western expansion, as a model for future development, or as the core of a larger national economic system still under construction. Dick concludes by advocating a fourth approach, which disregards national boundaries but considers the Outer Islands as part of Southeast Asia (see also Chapter 1). Such an approach fits into the historiographic tradition established by Reid's Braudelian work on precolonial Southeast Asia, and can incorporate studies of areas bordering on Indonesia, for example Warren's study of maritime trade in the Sulu Sea of the southern Philippines during the 19th century (Warren 1981).

There is now growing appreciation of the economic vitality of the Outer Islands in the 19th century. These islands possessed a multifaceted economic life that often escaped the attention of colonial administrators. Research in this vein has unearthed much interesting information that is still awaiting a broader synthesis. Asian trading networks in the Outer Islands in the 19th century were outward-looking but geared more towards Singapore and Penang than to Java. Coconuts from Selayar, rice from Lombok, gutta percha from West Kalimantan, coffee from southern Sumatra, pepper from Aceh — these are all cases in point (Heersink 1995: 69–120; Van der Kraan 1993; Purwanto 1993; Ismail 1991: 66–82).

The juxtaposition of Asian entrepreneurship and the wider East Asian region remains important also when moving beyond the strict confines of the 19th century. Such an approach is indispensable for a full understanding of the export-driven expansion of the Outer Islands up to the Depression of the 1930s. This Asian perspective leads into study of the development of Japanese business interests throughout the Indonesian archipelago. This process started in the very early 20th century and continued up to the Pacific War. Post in particular has stressed the early presence of Japanese businessmen in the Indonesian archipelago and the unique Japanese capability of making use of local trading networks in penetrating Indonesian markets for imported consumer goods (Post 1996).

4.B Statistics on 19th-century trade

The description of foreign trade developments between the Indonesian archipelago and mainland Southeast Asia during the 19th century draws on two main statistical sources. The first is the published foreign trade statistics of Singapore, running from the 1820s up to 1869. The second source is the official foreign trade statistics of the Netherlands Indies, which start in 1823 but contain information on the trade of the Outer Islands only from 1874. Both series have peculiarities that must be taken into account when combining them.

The trade statistics for Singapore are especially useful for the period up to the 1870s because the colonial foreign trade statistics were then confined to Java and Madura. However, those using the Singapore statistics meet some problems with geographical classifications. The island of Borneo is consistently treated as a single unit, whereas from the mid-1840s Bali, Lombok and Sumbawa are combined with Java. Any estimate of the total trade between the Outer Islands and Singapore must therefore make an assumption about how to split the Borneo total between Sarawak and Brunei on the one hand and Dutch Kalimantan on the other. Wong (1960: 90) suggests that the Borneo total could be split equally. The most reasonable assumption with respect to Bali, Lombok and Sumbawa after the mid-1840s is that their combined share remained constant over time.

In the early colonial foreign trade statistics compiled by customs officers at Batavia between 1823 and 1873, the Outer Islands are treated as if they were a foreign country and show up only as a trading partner of Java. This procedure demonstrates, albeit unintentionally, the lack of economic integration in the Indonesian archipelago during most of the 19th century.

The consolidated colonial statistics from 1874 onwards contain a wealth of information. Unfortunately, breakdowns by trading partners are given only for the entire Indonesian archipelago, not for the Outer Islands alone. This makes it impossible to isolate the trade between the Outer Islands and mainland Southeast Asia. A plausible assumption is that the share of the Outer Islands in the Indonesian archipelago's total trade with Singapore stayed the same, approximately one-half, as may be inferred from the trade statistics of Singapore for the earlier period. An additional drawback of colonial trade statistics is that Singapore cannot be distinguished from Malaya (including Penang). This makes it very difficult to link the Singapore and Batavia statistics into a consistent time series that would clearly identify the long-term trade development of the Outer Islands (Lindblad 1996).

4.C Debates about Dutch imperialism

The debates about the character of Dutch imperialism in the Indonesian archipelago have been pursued almost exclusively within Dutch historiography. Most contributions have been in the Dutch language, with English-language surveys appearing only recently. The discussion consists of two separate debates that occasionally interlink. One debate concerns whether modern Dutch imperialism was unique or not. The other addresses the conventional key question in the international literature about modern imperialism: was overseas expansion caused by economic or political factors?

The claim that Dutch imperialism differed fundamentally from other imperialisms can be traced back to the time of expansion itself. Around 1900 people defended the Dutch military offensive against Aceh in northern Sumatra while condemning British aggression in South Africa. The claim of Dutch uniqueness remained in force throughout the late colonial period. It was put forward again as the national debate in the Netherlands about the colonial past was reopened in the early 1970s, when the trauma of decolonisation had faded. The claim to uniqueness rested on several grounds, including the following:

1. the rather formalistic observation that Dutch expansion outside Java at the end of the 19th and early 20th century entailed no new acquisition of territory because the entire archipelago had been bequeathed to the Dutch state when the VOC went bankrupt in 1799;
2. the ethical aspirations of the colonial government, as laid down in the Ethical Policy from 1901. This appeared to contrast with the more crude ambitions of other imperialist powers;
3. the reluctance of the colonial government to extend the area under its effective control outside Java. This abstention coincided with the intensification of imperialist expansion by other European powers in the second half of the 19th century.

The third argument has become the most important one. It was elevated by Wesseling and others to a 'continuity hypothesis'. Throughout the era of modern imperialism the Dutch colonial government in the Indonesian archipelago stayed reluctant to intervene militarily unless provoked (Wesseling 1988). The 'continuity hypothesis' was contrasted with the 'contiguity hypothesis' — that is, an extension of authority from a territory already under control.

The traditional view of Dutch imperialism was challenged by Kuitenbrouwer, who compared the Dutch record of expansion with that of Britain and Portugal and found a greater resemblance with the British case than with the Portuguese. Dutch expansion in the Indonesian archipelago around 1900 fitted a broad definition of imperialism as an 'acceleration of colonial expansion'. The only uniquely Dutch aspect was that it started so late

(Kuitenbrouwer 1985: 215–25). Outbreak of the Aceh War in 1873 has been labelled a 'false start' before the 'real' turning-point of the invasion of Lombok in 1894, though some would argue that this is too late (Locher-Scholten 1994a).

The second debate touches on the rationale for imperialist expansion and stirs up controversy because of the emotional content of charges that the mother country enriched itself at the expense of the colony. Traditionally the divide between advocates of economic and political causes of imperialism coincided with the distinction between those inspired by Marxist theory and liberalism in Dutch historiography. A less stereotyped proposition was formulated by Van Tijn in the early 1970s, being that only the economic factor could explain the gap between the outbreak of the Aceh War in 1873 and the launching of the Ethical Policy in 1901 (Van Tijn 1971).

The matter can be resolved only by good case studies. Such research has highlighted both the coexistence of economic and political moti-vations, and the interplay between the two in the same location. The first line of argument has been explored, distinguishing between conditions under which ambitious local administrators took the first step and situations where the initiative came from private business (Lindblad 1989a). The transformation of economic motivations into political and territorial aspirations was described in detail by Locher-Scholten with respect to Jambi in southern Sumatra around 1900 (Locher-Scholten 1994b: 203–93; 1996).

A third debate is at present taking shape. This debate leaves aside the contrast between Dutch imperialism and other imperialism or quibbles about the primacy of politics above economics. Instead it focuses on the macro-level process of colonial state formation. Integration of a cohesive entity with its own identity is stressed above isolated instances of Western expansion. À Campo depicts this process as one with the three distinct dimensions of maritime, economic and political or administrative networks. These networks evolved in the Indonesian archipelago during the 1890s and 1900s. According to à Campo, the final outcome of early expansion was a 'technological system' containing three networks that overlapped and reinforced one another (à Campo 1992). This original approach may revitalise the imperialism debate.

5

The late colonial state and economic expansion, 1900–1930s

J. Thomas Lindblad

INTRODUCTION

The period from the late 1890s until the onset of the world economic Depression in the 1930s was one of converging and conflicting trends. The political integration of Java and the Outer Islands into a single colonial polity was largely achieved. At the same time, rising Indonesian nationalism foreshadowed the eventual demise of this polity. The process of globalisation, based on further integration with world markets, gathered momentum and generated an impressive export-led economic expansion. Yet dependence on external markets increased the vulnerability of the emerging colonial economy, foreshadowing the need for a fundamental reorientation after independence (Chapter 6). Such was the rhythm of this period: on the surface a steady consolidation of the colonial state and economy, but under the surface the emergence of powerful new currents that would eventually lead to dramatic change.

By the late 1920s, the colonial state was firmly rooted and gave the outward appearance of having integrated the vast archipelago into one coherent whole. This colonial society was highly stratified, but the coexistence of the various population groups suggested peace and order (*rust en orde*). These were the 'good old days' (*tempoe doeloe* in traditional Indies parlance) that have since been much romanticised. Indonesians also looked back to a state of normality (*zaman normal*). These images of the past contrasted starkly with the confusion of decolonisation and the poverty of newly independent Indonesia. Thus arises probably the single most important question in modern Indonesian economic history: why at Independence was Indonesia so poor, despite an impressive economic performance over several decades of the late colonial period? This chapter addresses that question within the context of internal and external integration, both inside the colonial state and with respect to the world economy.

The survey begins around the turn of the century, when the Dutch were consolidating their rule throughout the archipelago and initiating a new phase of export-led economic expansion, and runs through to around 1930, when the world economic Depression started to bite. Two important trends gave this period its unique character. One concerned policies pursued by the Dutch colonial authorities: the emphasis shifted from the ambitious Ethical Policy, launched in 1901 and implemented during the subsequent two decades, to a far more repressive regime in the 1920s. The other was the emergence of the Indonesian nationalist movement. Its birth is conventionally located as the foundation of the study club *Budi Utomo* in 1908, but establishment of the Indonesian National Party, PNI (*Partai Nasional Indonesia*), by Sukarno in 1927 was a more dramatic step. Three main themes are discussed: the colonial regime, export-led economic expansion, and the integration of the colonial economy and segmentation of economic life. Several appendices detail the historiography and discuss key themes in the literature. To maintain continuity to the end of the colonial period and to link up with Chapter 6, the statistics of Figures 5.1–5.7 run, where applicable, to the end of the 1930s.

THE LATE COLONIAL REGIME

Traditional policies of only selective intervention outside Java were abandoned in the 1890s in favour of outright territorial conquest (see Chapter 4).

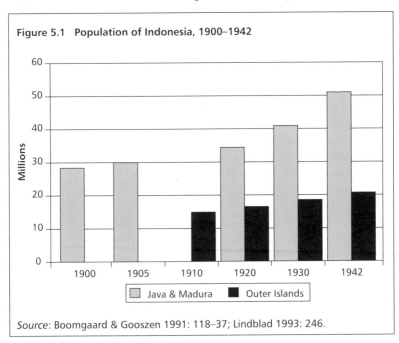

Figure 5.1   Population of Indonesia, 1900–1942

Java & Madura   Outer Islands

Source: Boomgaard & Gooszen 1991: 118–37; Lindblad 1993: 246.

Effective colonial rule was extended quickly throughout the entire Indonesian archipelago, reaching a climax during his term as Governor-General (1904–1909) of former Aceh commander General J.B. van Heutsz. The process of political, economic and maritime integration eventually produced a cohesive polity which can be defined in technological, economic, political and even ethnic terms. It is referred to here as the colonial state (see also Appendix 5.A). It was more than a colonial possession, more than an overseas appendage to the mother country, yet obviously less than a sovereign nation. Almost simultaneously, the colonial state stirred into being a new type of modern nationalism, which eventually would give birth to the independent nation-state of Indonesia.

Though smaller in population than British India, the Netherlands Indies was a vast and populous colony. The total population rose from 42 million in 1900 to 60 million by 1930 (by comparison, the total population of the Netherlands in 1930 was less than 10 million, in an area corresponding to only one-third of Java). The population of the archipelago grew at an average rate of 1.4% *per annum*. As population growth was almost as fast in Java as in the Outer Islands, the geographical distribution of the population remained fairly stable, at two-thirds in Java and one-third in the Outer Islands (Figure 5.1; Boomgaard & Gooszen 1991: 118–37, 222–30). Population growth was in fact more rapid among Europeans and Chinese than among indigenous Indonesians. This is explained by both immigration and natural increase in the rising numbers of Chinese and European family households. The non-indigenous population doubled in size, from 0.7 million in 1900 to 1.5 million in 1930, or 2.6% of the total. Though tiny compared with the indigenous Indonesian population, it dominated the economic and political life of the colonial state.

Racial classification had been the cornerstone of the colonial administration since 1854 (see also Chapter 3). The law differentiated three population groups: Europeans; 'foreign orientals' (*vreemde oosterlingen*), who were primarily ethnic Chinese but also Arab; and Indonesians or indigenous peoples. Ethnic stratification applied to all parts of colonial society, including jurisdiction, education, taxation and civil service employment. Legal segregation was accompanied by informal modes of ethnic discrimination that pervaded daily social life, most notably in the strict dress codes prescribed for the different groups in colonial society.

The gap between Europeans and Indonesians widened in the first half of the 20th century as the former society was transformed from one of single men, often living with local partners, to nuclear family households. In cities and towns, where most Europeans resided in suburban comfort, transport, entertainment and clubs were effectively segregated. For example, in Padang (West Sumatra) there was a clear distinction between two types of seats in the downtown cinema, the uncomfortable cheap front rows, labelled *kelas kambing* (goat class), where the Indonesians sat, and the better, more expensive seats that were in practice occupied only by

Europeans. In this provincial capital there were also two separate swimming pools, the *Julianabad* for Indonesians and the baths at Belantung Street for Europeans (Colombijn 1994: 72–4).

Yet ethnic segregation was not uncontested. In the early 20th century, it became the subject of heated discussion in the colony, especially among young Javanese intellectuals, who had been educated in Dutch schools but then confronted the harsh realities of underlying discrimination in a racially segregated society. The best-known example from Indonesian literature is Pramoedya Ananta Toer's hero Minke (Pramoedya 1982). Educated Indonesians began dressing in a European way, which could signify many things: emancipation from traditional Javanese or Islamic values, accommodation to Dutch colonial rule, or defiance of Dutch rule and refusal to accept cultural inferiority (Van Dijk 1997: 53–71). The Chinese minority was also enraged by the granting of 'European' status to Japanese immigrants in 1899. In the event, some compromises were made. In 1913 non-Europeans became eligible, at least in principle, for appointment to all functions in the colonial administration, with the sole exception of the office of Governor-General. In 1920 differential taxation was abolished. Henceforth, a uniform income tax was levied on all population groups. But then the reforms came to a halt. The final decades of Dutch colonial rule were marked by futile protests from Chinese and Indonesian intellectuals against the rigidity of institutionalised segregation along ethnic lines (Fasseur 1994).

Consolidation of the Dutch colonial state in the 1900s necessitated rapid enlargement of the colonial bureaucracy. Mechanisms for exercising colonial authority were further extended and ever more ambitious targets of colonial policy were formulated. This reflected a deeply felt Dutch commitment to the colony. It was tacitly assumed that Dutch rule would last for a very long time. However, the strengthening of the colonial regime fostered widespread resentment among Indonesians. This found expression in the rising nationalist movement. But intensified colonial rule and resistance to it were mutually incompatible. One presupposed continued Dutch rule for decades, perhaps even centuries to come; the other called for independence as soon as possible.

The early decades of the 20th century saw two competing tendencies in the evolution of the colonial bureaucracy. In the first place there was a tendency towards liberalisation. This included experiments with quasi-democratic institutions such as the advisory People's Council (*Volksraad*), founded in 1918. The conflicting tendency was a strengthening of the administrative apparatus and procedures. It reinforced the so-called *Beamtenstaat*, a German term to describe a type of government giving highest priority to effective bureaucratic administration in a tradition dating back to Napoleonic times. This style suited very well the interests of the colonial bureaucracy (Benda 1966; Booth 1998a: 154). Reformism and decentralisation at first had the upper hand, but in the 1920s the *Beamtenstaat* was restored to full glory. The numbers of administrators had grown fast since 1900 but no liberalisation was permitted to infringe the strict racial segregation within the civil service (Houben 1996b: 62–4). The decisive turn away from reformism came with the Communist rebellions in 1926/27.

The colonial bureaucracy nevertheless had two unique elements. The first was the figure of the *controleur*, the lowest level of European colonial administration. The *controleur* was entrusted with a great variety of tasks in the minutiae of local affairs (Furnivall 1939/1944: 193–4). He could in the morning hours preside over a local court or appear at a formal reception for village heads, then in the afternoon go on horseback to a remote *sawah* to supervise the construction of an irrigation dam. The *controleur* reported to the assistant-resident and thereby to the resident, but enjoyed considerable discretionary powers due to his specialist local knowledge. Preparation included language training and instruction about Indonesian law and society, usually at the School of Indology at the University of Leiden in the Netherlands.[1]

The second unique feature was the parallel arrangement between Dutch and Indonesian civil servants, each with his own pyramidal structure of authority, together constituting the so-called *Binnenlands Bestuur* (BB), literally the domestic civil service (Van den Haspel 1985: 87–9). In this model the Javanese regent (outside Java the Malay sultan) was expected to play the role of a 'younger brother' to the Dutch civil servant, even if the former was much the senior in age and experience as well as a nobleman. Lower-ranking Javanese civil servants usually belonged to the educated *priyayi*, the administrative upper class in Javanese society. The idealistic myth about their role as buffer between the Dutch authorities and their Indonesian subject does not always stand up to critical examination. Abuse of power often lay beneath the surface (Sutherland 1976).

The Dutch colonial regime differed from those elsewhere in Southeast Asia. Involvement with local society and economy was probably more far-reaching than in British Malaya, but there was no intention of granting limited autonomy in preparation for eventual independence or fostering an indigenous business class as in the Philippines under American rule. However, the bias in favour of exclusive ties with the European mother country was less strong than in the case of French Indochina. Such differences in the style of colonial rule had important consequences for the economic climate at the time (Lindblad 1998: 60–93). In a longer time perspective it also shaped the path of economic development after independence (Booth 1991).

Liberalism was the credo of the colonial state. The general policy was one of *laissez-faire*, or non-intervention in economic life. It held sway over colonial economic policy for a very long time, from about 1870 to 1933, reflecting the prevailing ideology but flexible in application. In economic policy liberalism provided a favourable climate for foreign investment and a free trade regime conducive to economic expansion.

However, it was not designed to protect Indonesian producers against competitors at home or abroad.

The expanding colonial state offered an increasingly favourable investment climate for foreign private capital, especially of Dutch origin. The safety of personnel and property could now be guaranteed even in the most remote locations. The tax system encouraged private investors by allowing a substantial proportion of gross earnings to be retained in the business or to be repatriated to overseas owners. Standardisation of legal and administrative arrangements across regions facilitated the extension of corporate business networks throughout the archipelago. Against non-Dutch foreign capital there was little overt discrimination, but Dutch enterprises were advantaged by their familiarity with Dutch procedures, institutions and jurisdiction. The position and operations of domestic investors differed too, depending on whether they were European or Chinese immigrants or ethnic Indonesians. The conventional dichotomy between foreign and domestic capital is therefore not easily applied to capital investment in the colonial state. It is better to apply a sliding scale by degree of foreignness. At one extreme of the scale are investors from third countries, in the middle are investors operating out of the mother country, and at the other extreme are investors of European, Chinese or Arab origin who have become permanent residents of the colony (Lindblad 1998: 72–3).

Accumulated foreign investment in the Indonesian archipelago rose from 750 million guilders ($300 million) in 1900 to about 1.7 billion guilders ($675 million) in 1914 and further to a peak at some four billion guilders ($1.6 billion) in 1930 (Lindblad 1991: 189). The corporate network was highly segmented. Dutch-owned firms ranged from a small number of large corporations run from the Netherlands to a very large number of small firms that were enmeshed in the colonial economy. By the late 1920s the former made up 23% of all firms but held 71% of registered equity, whereas the latter were twice as numerous but controlled less than 15% of all equity (Lindblad 1998: 74, 78). Chinese firms formed a separate category. These numerous enterprises, mainly specialising in trade, made up 25% of the total number but only 4% of total equity. The balance of equity, about 10% of the total, was held by Western firms with non-Dutch owners, primarily British and American corporations. The corporate network included hardly any Indonesian enterprises, as these businessmen did usually not choose the legal form of incorporation.

The trade regime was exceedingly liberal. There were scarcely any tariffs or other trade barriers to imports of any origin. This situation lasted for six full decades, from the repeal of the differential tariffs in 1874 to the Crisis Import Ordinance of 1933. Free trade implied that no protection was given to imports from the Netherlands. Suppliers of Dutch textiles, for instance, had to compete with foreign rivals, first from Britain, later also from Japan. Eventually the textile market in the colony was split up into three segments of about equal size. The factories in the eastern Dutch province of Twente supplied more expensive bleached goods and sarongs, whereas other more expensive qualities were delivered from Lancashire in Britain. Lower qualities at a lower price came from Japan. Because local producers received no more than the natural protection of ocean freight rates, there was little scope for import-substituting industrialisation until the 1930s (Segers 1987: 27–31). The extreme openness of the domestic market forestalled any restructuring of the economy away from agriculture and primary production towards manufacturing (see also Chapters 1 and 6).

The liberal economic policy allowed for selective government intervention of two main types. One was short-run and ad hoc, the other long-term and institutionalised. An example of the former was the regulation of the rice market in 1911 and again towards the end of World War I, when the Allied blockade stopped imports of foreign rice and acute shortages appeared in several regions. In 1918 a special agency was entrusted with the task of handling rice imports and redistributing rice across the archipelago (Prince 1993: 167–8; see also Uemura 2000). Such direct market interventions remained exceptional. Government intervention of the second type, geared towards the achievement of long-run developmental objectives, mainly grew out of the Ethical Policy. This was the facet of government policy that attracted most attention from contemporary observers, both at home and abroad. It determined Dutch colonial ideology for several decades. The Dutch had a mission to fulfill by 'uplifting', in the terminology of the time, the Indonesian peoples (Locher-Scholten 1981).

The Ethical Policy

Queen Wilhelmina announced the Ethical Policy in her speech from the throne in 1901. The original conception had two essential elements — Christian ethics, and the obligation of the Netherlands towards the Indonesian people. Its origins can be traced back to a public discussion in the late 1890s in the Netherlands about the responsibility of the Dutch state to protect the 'common man' in Java against oppression by feudal Javanese overlords. In 1899 the parliamentarian C.Th. Van Deventer argued that the Netherlands, having reaped such large financial benefits from the Cultivation System in Java, should now pay something back, especially at a time when the colony had to borrow from the mother country to cover recurrent deficits in the colonial budget (Appendix 5.B). He described this as a 'debt of honour' (*ereschuld*).

The goal of the Ethical Policy was to raise the prosperity of the Indonesian population. The means were direct state intervention in economic life, which was promoted under the slogan 'irrigation, education, emigration'. Better irrigation facilities would raise agricultural productivity; emigration to the Outer Islands would reduce population pressure in crowded Java; education meant more opportunities for Indonesians, both to transmit the fruits of Western civilisation and to train a skilled labour force to work for colonial enterprises. The Ethical Policy was even claimed to provide the Indonesian population with legal and administrative protection against the adverse effects of colonialism itself (Cribb 1993: 226–30). Such were the best aspirations of Dutch colonial rule. The driving force was the enlightened A.W.F. Idenburg, Colonial Minister (1902–05, 1908–09 as well as 1918–19) and Governor-General (1909–1916), with support from his successor as Governor-General, Count J.P. van Limburg Stirum (1916–1921).

The Ethical Policy had its immediate impact on colonial administration. Numerous government bodies were created or reconstituted. This included the Department of Agriculture, Industry and Trade (1904), the Department of Public Works (1908) and the Department of Education (1908). New specialist agencies included the Agricultural Extension Service (*Land-bouwvoorlichtingsdienst* 1910), the Civil Medical Service (*Burgerlijke Geneeskundige Dienst* 1911) and the People's Credit Banks (*Volkskred-ietwezen* 1912). These organisations were entrusted with the responsibility for implementing the Ethical Policy. The Decentralisation Law (1903) provided a legal basis for decentralisation of authority to the local level. After 1905 municipal governments (*gemeenten*) were created in most of the main cities and towns, later also regency councils in rural areas.

Over the first decade, implementation of the Ethical Policy was constrained by lack of finance. The colonial budget remained at around 200 million guilders ($80 million) until the early 1910s and grew rapidly only from 1914 (Figure 5.1; Creutzberg 1976: 64–7). However, by 1920 the record level of revenues (700 million guilders or $280 million) and expenditures (1000 million guilders or $400 million) contained a large inflationary component arising from the postwar boom. Expenditures rose faster than revenues, which caused an accumulating deficit that had to be covered by loans from the Netherlands. The indebtedness to the mother country was mirrored by the debt of honour of the mother country to the colony. Responsibility for the debt to the Netherlands became a source of much contention at the time of decolonisation in the late 1940s (see further Chapter 6).

Sources of colonial revenue changed rapidly. In the 1890s about 20% of revenue consisted of proceeds from revenue farming. This system involved subcontracting to Chinese middlemen the collection of taxes and income from the state monopolies of opium and salt. By the 1920s, however, such arrangements had been replaced by direct state administration of opium and salt monopolies. The fiscal base of the colonial state was strengthened by expanding state enterprises such as railways, telegraphs and mines. Income, property and consumption taxes increased somewhat faster than total revenue, so that their combined share rose from 45% in the 1890s to 50% in the 1920s (Diehl 1993: 208; see also Rush 1990).

The composition of government expenditure also changed. In 1905, at the height of the 'pacification' campaign, 40% of the colonial budget was spent on warfare and administration, which by 1921 had fallen to only 20%.

Outlays on public works and state enterprises displayed the opposite trend, rising from 20% of total expenditures in 1905 to 40% in 1921. The share of funds allocated to education in particular, however, remained low (Booth 1990b: 224). The priorities of the Ethical Policy were reflected in budgetary restructuring only to the extent that public investment was directed towards irrigation dams rather than productive capacity in state enterprises. On the level of the local economy, improvements often appeared hardly connected at all with the Ethical Policy (Kuntowijoyo 2000).

Institutional reform and budgetary expansion both came to a halt in the early 1920s, when the postwar recession of 1920–1923 transformed the fiscal outlook. The newly appointed Governor-General, D. Fock (in office 1921–1926), insisted on balancing the budget. Total expenditures were cut back drastically to about 700 million guilders ($280 million), though revenues rose towards 800 million guilders ($320 million). In the years 1924–1926 the colonial finances were in surplus. Amid renewed economic expansion, public expenditure as a proportion of national income declined from 14% at the peak in 1921 to 10% in the mid-1920s (Booth 1998a: 145). As in the early days of the Ethical Policy, the scope for government action was again severely constrained.

The political will to carry on ethical programs waned as the colonial government became increasingly repressive in response to nationalist opposition, especially after the Communist rebellions in 1926/27. Disillusionment and disappointment proliferated among colonial administrators and observers, who came to the view that the Ethical Policy had been overly ambitious (Booth 1989b: 114–15; Cribb 1993: 240–4). Things did not change for the better in the second half of the 1920s, when the conservative Governor-General A.C.D. de Graeff (in office 1926–1930) did no more than allow expenditures to rise in line with revenues. By the time it was officially abandoned in the 1930s, it was already a remnant of the past.

Of the main initiatives of the Ethical Policy, investment in irrigation consumed the most funds and probably had the most tangible and lasting impact. Irrigation was favoured in the allocation of funds through the powerful vested interest of the engineering corps of the Public Works department (*Burgerlijke Openbare Werken*). About 125 million guilders ($50 million) were spent between 1913 and 1924 alone. By 1920 the total harvested area from irrigated land was 50% larger than in 1900 and expansion continued, though more slowly, in the 1920s. From the late 19th century to the eve of the Pacific War, irrigated *sawah* area in Java increased by 1 million hectares, corresponding to 30% of the island's total arable *sawah* land (Boomgaard 1986: 70–2; Booth 1988: 38; Van der Eng 1993a: 71, 112). Some of the benefits from the irrigation facilities accrued to the sugar industry, but the evidence suggests that rice cultivators gained the most (Van der Eng 1993a: 57–60, 72).

Nevertheless, growth in agricultural productivity was slow and fostered disillusionment with the efficacy of the Ethical Policy (Van der Eng 1993a:

72, 149; Booth 1989b: 115). The colonial government made efforts, but on too small a scale. The Agricultural Extension Service sought to upgrade techniques and organisation in food crop agriculture. The emphasis was on what was 'practicable' and 'socially desirable' rather than on technology as such (Prince 1993: 172–6; Van der Eng 1991). It was a far-sighted and commendable approach, but the agency itself remained seriously understaffed. In the 1920s, after almost two decades of operations, the Agricultural Extension Service employed less than 70 consultants. The most tangible results were probably the promotion of secondary food crops (*palawija*) (Van der Eng 1993a: 92–7).

Another policy was to set up credit institutions to stimulate Indonesian entrepreneurship at the village level, thereby also often displacing Chinese intermediaries (Sumitro: 1943: 14–18). In 1930 there were almost 6000 village 'banks' in Java and 600 in the Outer Islands. However, most were so small as scarcely to deserve the epithet 'bank' at all, while bureaucratic procedures restricted farmers' access (Van der Eng 1993a: 123, 129–30; Cribb 1993: 236–7; Booth 1998a: 303–6). Traditional sources of credit therefore remained popular. In addition, pawnshops still catered to large numbers of Indonesian customers (Margono 1970). Especially in the Outer Islands, Indian and Chinese moneylenders met the credit needs of Indonesian smallholders (Potting 1997: 255–70). Interest rates were higher for such transactions but there were no bureaucratic obstacles.

Education was one of the most publicised targets of the Ethical Policy. However, strict ethnic segregation ensured that educational opportunities were highly unequal, and the Ethical Policy did little to correct this. Numerous primary schools were set up, but still less than 7% of the indigenous population (excluding infants) had attained literacy by the time of Independence. Dutch education was enjoyed by only very small numbers of non-Europeans. Scarcely more than a thousand Indonesians each year graduated from Dutch-language secondary schools and few progressed to some form of tertiary education (Booth 1989b: 117–18). In 1938 the share of Indonesians in higher education enrolments was only 7% (Baudet & Fasseur 1977: 330). This has been attributed to the colonial authorities seeking to avoid an Indonesian intellectual proletariat with European aspirations but without a European income (Van der Veur 1969; Wertheim 1956: 147–8). The demand that more Indonesians be allowed to learn Dutch was brought forward by Indonesian nationalists with the same fervour that nationalists in British India used to urge the right of instruction in a vernacular language (Sartono 1986).

Emigration under the aegis of the Ethical Policy anticipated the New Order's transmigration schemes to establish Javanese settlements in the Outer Islands. Recipient regions included Lampung and Bengkulu in southern Sumatra, West and South Kalimantan and Sulawesi. Contemporary observations and piecemeal demographic evidence suggest that the policy fell far short of achieving its targets. By 1941 the total Javanese population of colonisation settlements outside Java amounted to only about 250 000 persons, of whom more than one-half were in Lampung (Cribb 1993: 237; Hardjono 1977: 18). This was just a small fraction of Java's population growth between 1901 and 1941.

The broad Ethical Policy objective of protecting Indonesian subjects against hardships imposed by either colonialism or feudalism was the least convincing facet of the entire program. Its main effect was to cause frictions with both Indonesian spokespeople and Western private entrepreneurs. The former found the reforms hopelessly inadequate, while the latter felt betrayed by colonial officials, who failed to side unequivocally with European business interests.

From its inception in 1901 to its abandonment in the 1920s, the Ethical Policy gave rise to expectations of improved living standards and more political freedom. Reformist zeal, decentralisation and a limited political representation for the colonised people all pointed in the direction of a less repressive type of colonial rule. The Ethical Policy gave impetus to the development of political consciousness in the tiny Indonesian intellectual elite. The Indonesian nationalist movement was, as Legge nicely puts it, 'the product of the virtues rather than the vices of Dutch rule' (Legge 1980: 123).

Indonesian nationalism

The birth of Indonesian nationalism is conventionally located in 1908, when the association Budi Utomo was founded by students at the training school for indigenous physicians, STOVIA (*School tot Opleiding* Van *Inlandsche Artsen*), in Jakarta. The founders were aware of developments abroad, such as the Philippine Revolution of the late 1890s and Japan's victory in the Russo-Japanese War (1904–1905), as well as the more progressive intellectual climate at home. Javanese aristocrats (*priyayi*) dominated the daily affairs of Budi Utomo (Van Miert 1995: 19–39). From 1918 it operated as a moderate political organisation within the Volksraad (Nagazumi 1972). A political tradition was established in which cooperation with the Netherlands was envisaged as a pathway towards Indonesia acquiring some measure of independence.

In the wake of Budi Utomo there emerged the first mass political party, Sarekat Islam (Islamic Union). Founded in Surakarta in 1911 as Sarekat Dagang Islam (Islamic Trading Union), it began by articulating resentment against Chinese domination of the local batik industry and seeking economic emancipation of indigenous entrepreneurs (Shiraishi 1990). Under the leadership of Tirtoadisoerjo, a former STOVIA student, publisher-writer and founder of local trading organisations, Sarekat Islam quickly developed popular political consciousness of a radical tendency, a process in which the vernacular Malay press played a key role (Adam 1995). The Muhammadiyah, founded in 1912, was also strongly

Islamic, whereas the Indische Partij (1912) and the Indonesian Association of Social Democrats (*Indische Sociaal-Democratische Vereniging*; 1914) drew heavily on Western political ideology. Internal strife within the last-mentioned organisation led in 1920 to formation of the Indonesian Communist Party, PKI (*Perserikatan*, later *Partai Komunis Indonesia*), which quickly became prominent in the young trade union movement.

Although at first the colonial government took a permissive approach to Indonesian political organisation, tensions mounted during the 1910s and exploded in the following decade. Ideological radicalisation combined with disappointment at the slowing pace of political reform to culminate in the Communist uprisings in West Java and West Sumatra in 1926/27. These were violently suppressed, leading to surveillance and repression of virtually all opposition to Dutch rule by the Political Intelligence Service (*Politieke Inlichtingen Dienst*) (Frederick 1989; Poeze 1994). The shift to conservatism and outright repression antagonised more moderate nationalist leaders and radicalised the entire nationalist movement. In 1927 the nationalists reacted by establishing the Indonesian Nationalist Party, PNI (*Partai Nasional Indonesia*), with full Indonesian independence as its prime goal (Moedjanto 1988: 25–53; Ingleson 1979).

An important date in the history of the Indonesian nationalist movement was 28 October 1928, *Hari Sumpah Pemuda* (Youth Oath Day), when at a congress of youth organisations the oath was sworn that Indonesia was to be one nation and one country with one language (*Bahasa Indonesia*). The anthem *Indonesia Raya* was played and the red-and-white flag (*merah putih*) was flown for the first time. The following years, however, saw increasing repression of the nationalist movement. The young leader of the PNI, Sukarno, was imprisoned for years at a time. His later associate Mohamad Hatta, originally from West Sumatra, was deported to the prison camp *Boven Digoel* in New Guinea shortly after returning from studies in the Netherlands.

Nationalists tried to evade political repression by taking economic and social initiatives to raise popular awareness and develop organisational capabilities. The foremost economic initiative during the 1920s and 30s was support of the cooperative movement. Hatta, for instance, was an outspoken advocate of cooperatives (Ingleson 1979: 167). The colonial authorities were ambivalent. Cooperatives were favoured in line with official policy of stimulating Indonesian economic activity. Rural credit certainly enabled Indonesians to compete more successfully with Chinese traders. Restrictive legislation was relaxed in 1927 but cooperatives continued to be viewed with suspicion because of their close links to the nationalist movement (Boomgaard 1986: 75–7). Numbers rose from less than 150 in 1921 to almost 600 by 1939, by which time more than 50 000 Indonesians were participating. but the overall impact on the local economy was marginal (Sumitro 1943: 180–94; Van der Eng 1993a: 126–7). The significance of the cooperatives was more political than economic.

Cooperatives often linked up with nationalist social initiatives in education, notably the 'free' (*wilde*) schools and adult education.

Like so many governments, the colonial state tried to reconcile motivations and approaches that were mutually incompatible. Administrative reform embraced both decentralisation and bureaucratic rigidity. Economic liberalism did not prevent the colonial authorities from interfering with the minutest details of local society and economy. An ethically inspired reform policy was accompanied by fiscal restraint and increasing political repression. In the end no-one was satisfied, and tightening repression was the only way to maintain colonial authority.

EXPORT-LED EXPANSION

Accelerating construction of the colonial state after the mid-1890s coincided with a new boom in the world economy. This phase of economic expansion was sustained for more than a quarter of a century, from shortly after 1900 to the eve of the worldwide Depression in 1930. GDP per capita rose by two-thirds in real terms, or by 1.8% on average each year between 1900 and 1930 (Van der Eng 1994a: 102). This rate of growth was about twice as fast as that applying to the entire period 1880–1940 and compared favourably with rates in other Asian countries, such as Thailand and India (Booth 1998a: 14).

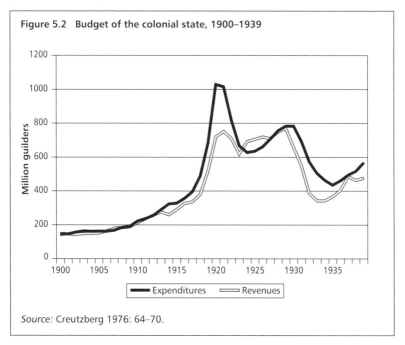

Figure 5.2   Budget of the colonial state, 1900–1939

Source: Creutzberg 1976: 64–70.

Economic expansion was export-driven and began with a smooth and gradual increase in foreign trade volumes up to 1917. During these years the Indonesian archipelago benefited from an improvement in its commodity terms of trade, meaning that the index of export prices rose faster than the index of import prices. This was a powerful impetus for export producers to supply more to the world market. As total exports grew faster than total imports, an increasing surplus was generated in the balance of trade with the outside world. Total exports climbed from 300 million guilders ($120 million) in 1905 to almost 800 million guilders ($320 million) in 1917, while total imports increased from 200 million guilders ($80 million) to nearly 500 million guilders ($200 million) in the same period (Korthals Altes 1991: 72–5).

The last two years of World War I saw an extraordinary development. In 1917/18 Germany's unlimited submarine warfare combined with an Allied blockade to bring trade between Europe and the Netherlands Indies to a virtual standstill. Even telegraph communications were broken off for weeks or months. Dutch imports were replaced by imports from third countries or by an increased production in the colony's embryonic manufacturing sector (Dick 1993c: 135–7). Cessation of hostilities in 1918 was followed by extreme price inflation. The total value of exports from the

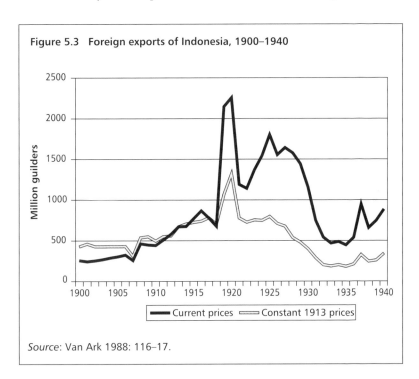

Figure 5.3   Foreign exports of Indonesia, 1900–1940

Source: Van Ark 1988: 116–17.

Netherlands Indies soared to two billion guilders ($800 million) in 1919 and 1920, much of which was due to the huge short-run price effect (Figure 5.3; Korthals Altes 1991: 72–5) (see further Appendix 5.C).

The immediate postwar boom was followed by a world recession in 1921–1922. Export values collapsed, whereas the value of imports stayed more or less at boom levels, turning the usual surplus in the balance of trade into a rare deficit. Exports recovered to an average of about 1.5 billion guilders ($600 million) during the years 1923–1929, and a large surplus in the balance of trade was restored. However, after 1921 the commodity terms of trade, which had been so favourable for a quarter of a century, continued to move against the Indonesian archipelago. Apart from a sharp spike in rubber prices in 1925, export prices lagged behind import prices and even started to decline during the second half of the decade. The deterioration in terms of trade meant that export producers in the archipelago had to supply ever larger quantities in order to pocket the same revenue. Java was particularly affected because of falling prices for its main export commodity, sugar.

Before the terms of trade started to turn against the Netherlands Indies, the export expansion was propelled by a rapidly increasing demand for goods that the Indonesian archipelago could supply. A larger demand abroad induced export suppliers in the archipelago to invest in productive capacity so that more could be supplied in the future. In the words of the economist C.P. Kindleberger, 'demand was right abroad and supply was right at home' (Kindleberger 1962: 211). This applied to both the traditional Java-based agricultural goods and additions to the range of exports procured from the Outer Islands.

Foreign demand for Java sugar grew especially fast after 1902, when the artificial protection of continental European beet sugar was terminated, allowing international sugar prices to rise. Rapid population growth, income growth and rising living standards also boosted demand in Asia, where soon Java's most promising markets were found. The volume of sugar exports from Java doubled between 1902 and 1914, stabilised, and then doubled again during the second half of the 1920s. By 1929, Java's annual sugar exports exceeded three million tonnes. Sugar remained the single most important export product in most years, its average share in total exports declining marginally from 32% in the 1910s to 28% in the 1920s (Figure 5.4; Lindblad 1988b: 286–9).

Total export volumes of the other two Java-based agricultural export crops, coffee and tobacco, were far smaller but values per ton were higher than in sugar. Volumes were more erratic compared with sugar exports (Figure 5.4; Clemens, Lindblad & Touwen 1992: 60–5). Exports of tobacco and coffee both suffered severely from the virtual standstill in trade with Europe in 1917/18 and quantities also declined in the early 1920s. From 1925, however, coffee joined sugar in a very rapid enlargement of output, whereas tobacco continued to be supplied in far smaller volumes than had been the case in 1920. Prices for agricultural products had then started to

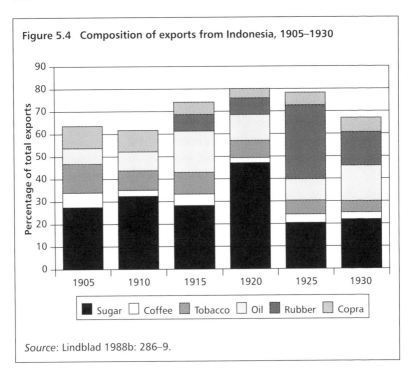

Figure 5.4   Composition of exports from Indonesia, 1905–1930

Source: Lindblad 1988b: 286–9.

fall and compensation was sought in raising volumes. The fall in unit prices was steeper for sugar and coffee than for tobacco.

Despite the importance of sugar in total exports, the Indonesian archipelago was much less dependent on a few leading export commodities than most tropical economies. The key to success was supplementing rather than replacing old export goods with new ones. The share of the five first-ranking commodities in total exports dropped below 70% in 1900 and stayed at that level, or slightly above, until the end of the colonial period (Booth 1998a: 207–8). Diversification had begun already in the late 19th century, when oil and copra from the Outer Islands were added to the largely Java-based assortment of sugar, coffee and tobacco (see also Chapter 4). Early in the 20th century came the rubber boom — another commodity primarily, but not exclusively, supplied by the Outer Islands. Yet another new commodity was palm oil from Sumatra, which however gained importance only towards the very end of the colonial period.

The most powerful impetus to export expansion came from the rise of the automobile industry in the industrialised countries, and especially the USA. Demand for oil, both crude and refined, and rubber increased dramatically during the first two decades of the 20th century. The consequence was higher prices, at least up to the mid-1920s, and great scope for producers in the Outer Islands to raise output (Clemens, Lindblad & Touwen 1992: 66–70). The bottleneck was the productive capacity of the export industry. In the oil industry, huge investments were needed to extend fields and enlarge refineries. In rubber a gestation period of five to seven years had to lapse before latex could be tapped from newly planted trees.

The rubber tree originally grew in the jungle of Brazil, but seeds were secretly transmitted via Kew Gardens to British Malaya where the newly established estates caught the attention of Indonesian traders on their way home from a pilgrimage to Mecca. Rubber was introduced to southern Sumatra and West and South Kalimantan in the first decade of the 20th century. Eventually it was grown in several other regions, including East and West Java. As in British Malaya, Western estate firms at first dominated the industry and much British and American capital was invested, especially in East Sumatra (Lindblad 1998: 46). This international flavour distinguished the large rubber estates from the Dutch-dominated tobacco plantations in East Sumatra and the sugar factories in Java. Rubber exports were from the very beginning oriented towards the American market, which led to the opening of new shipping lines to the USA.

A parallel Indonesian smallholder mode of rubber production for export emerged, especially in Palembang and Jambi in southern Sumatra and in West and Southeast Kalimantan. Local cultivators sought employment as day labourers in nearby rubber estates only long enough to learn the techniques of planting and tapping, and could then set up their own plantations or transmit the acquired skills to other locals against payment, usually about 2.50 guilders ($1) (Lindblad 1988a: 61). Connections with the international market at Singapore were established and maintained through *haji* passing through and Chinese middlemen. The latter played a leading role by supplying credit, seeds and import goods (Cator 1936).

Expansion was accelerated in the rubber industry during the 1920s. The booming American economy continued to bolster demand. In 1922 competitors in the world rubber market, especially in the British colonies, combined in the Stevenson Rubber Restriction Scheme in an attempt artificially to raise unit prices by slowing down the increase in quantities supplied. Producers in the Indonesian archipelago did not participate but seized the opportunity to increase output. This held especially true for smallholder producers in Sumatra and Kalimantan (see the next section). In 1925, when rubber prices were exceptionally high, rubber alone accounted for one-third of all export revenues accruing to the Indonesian archipelago. Rubber was then firmly established, together with sugar and oil, as a foremost earner of foreign exchange in the colonial economy. The Stevenson Scheme was discontinued in 1928, when it became clear that rubber prices were falling rather than rising and that Dutch and Thai producers outside the scheme had enhanced their share in world exports (Barlow & Drabble 1990).

Export expansion boosted demand for imports. Imports increased as incomes rose. In the 1910s and 20s, textiles and an assortment of other consumer goods accounted for about 40% of all imports. Rice imports, on the other hand, declined as a proportion of total purchases from abroad, from 10% in the 1910s to 5% in the 1920s (Lindblad 1994: 105). Demand was highly elastic for textiles and other consumer goods but relatively inelastic for foodstuffs.

The propensity to import was far higher in consumption than in investment. The share of capital goods in total imports was below 20% in the 1910s and rose only marginally in the 1920s (Booth 1998a: 35). This testifies to the labour-intensive technologies employed in most export production. Apart from sugar milling and oil refining, little processing of raw materials took place before export. The expansion of exports as such therefore did not encourage much investment in manufacturing production.

Trade expansion in the early 20th century was accompanied by reorientation in the direction of trade, both outside and inside the archipelago. In 1903, A.W.F. Idenburg, then Minister of Colonial Affairs, spoke at length in the Dutch Parliament about the great importance of mutual trade between colony and mother country in his defence of a budgetary increase for colonial administration. One-third of all imports entering the colony came from the Netherlands, he said. Delegates were impressed, probably without realising that this statistic mainly testified to the small scale of imports purchased by the colony. A more relevant statistic would have been the colony's share in total imports of the mother country but that was only 3%, a figure that Idenburg was careful not to cite (Baudet 1975: 438). Three decades after Idenburg's speech, even the misused statistic had become less impressive. By then only 15% of all imports entering the Indonesian archipelago originated in the Netherlands.

The declining share of exports from the Netherlands to its colony was matched by an even sharper decline in the reverse direction of exports from the colony to the Netherlands. The volume of exports to the Netherlands stayed roughly the same in absolute terms but, because the total volume of exports from the archipelago rose so dramatically, the Dutch *share* was ever lower (Figure 5.5; Korthals Altes 1991: 100–3). The Netherlands simply ceased to be the main market outlet for most exports from the archipelago, just as it ceased to be the major supplier of imports. This marked a commercial emancipation of the colony from the mother country. It presupposed a very liberal trading regime, which indeed prevailed in the colony up to the early 1930s.

Commercial emancipation from the Dutch implied that both exports and imports became increasingly oriented towards the USA, Singapore, other European trading partners such as Britain and Germany, and other markets in Asia, for instance India and China. There demand for sugar, oil and rubber was growing. This was a further step in an ongoing process of globalisation. The Indonesian archipelago claimed an impressive market share for several leading commodities such as rubber (37%), copra (27%), palm oil (24%), tea (19%), tin (17%) and sugar (11%). In addition, it

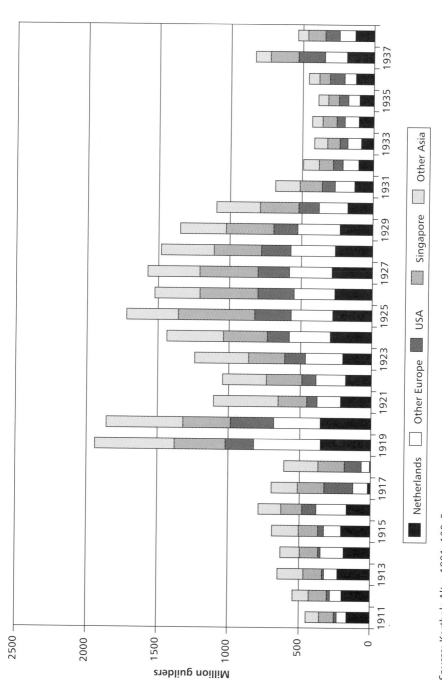

Million guilders

2500 — 2000 — 1500 — 1000 — 500 — 0

1911 1913 1915 1917 1919 1921 1923 1925 1927 1929 1931 1933 1935 1937

Netherlands   Other Europe   USA   Singapore   Other Asia

Source: Korthals Altes 1991: 100–3.

enjoyed a near-monopoly in world exports of minor commodities, such as cinchona (the main ingredient in quinine) and pepper, holding market shares at 91% and 86% respectively (Baudet & Fasseur 1977: 332). At the end of the colonial period Indonesia had thus become one of the world's foremost suppliers of tropical raw materials.

The globalisation especially favoured economic relations with the wider region of Southeast and East Asia. Singapore retained its position as the chief entrepôt distributing goods from the archipelago throughout the Asian market, especially for goods supplied by smallholder producers. Meanwhile Japan emerged as a major supplier of foreign imports, in particular cheap consumer goods such as textiles. By the early 1930s, Singapore alone absorbed one-fifth of all exports from the archipelago and Japan supplied one-third of all imports (Booth 1998a: 211; Chapter 6).

Another type of reorientation in geographical terms occurred inside the archipelago. Exports expanded especially fast in the Outer Islands, from about 300 million guilders ($120 million) in the 1910s to more than 750 million guilders ($300 million) in the second half of the 1920s (Figure 5.6; Korthals Altes 1991: 72–5). The share of the Outer Islands in total exports leaving the colony exceeded 50% from the early 1920s onwards. The Outer Islands then became the foremost earner of foreign exchange in the Indonesian archipelago, a tendency that was reinforced after Independence (see also Chapter 1).

As demand for imports in the Outer Islands lagged behind export revenues, a huge surplus was generated in the balance of trade of these regions with the outside world. On average more than 50% of the export revenues accruing to the Outer Islands was *not* spent on purchases of foreign imports. The corresponding percentage for Java was far lower, about 25% on average (Lindblad 1990). This divergence in trade performance, with a faster export growth but a slower import growth in the Outer Islands, had profound consequences for the interdependency between core and periphery in the Indonesian archipelago. The periphery, being the Outer Islands, therefore provided most of the surplus in the external balance, whereas the core of Java offered the political protection to facilitate the investment in export production that made the generation of the surplus possible in the first place.

Changing trading patterns inside the archipelago and in the world market formed the most tangible evidence that the export-driven expansion had profoundly altered the economy of the Indonesian archipelago. Meanwhile the vulnerability to possible adverse movements in terms of trade in the world market had been greatly increased, as was the case with neighbours specialising in exports of primary products (Manarungsan 1989). This path of economic development did not result in sustained economic growth, which can be understood by reviewing the economic structure in which the export expansion took place (see also Booth 1992a).

ECONOMIC INTEGRATION AND SEGMENTATION

In the early 20th century rapid advances were made in shaping an archipelago-wide economy that would eventually mature as the national economy of independent Indonesia. Economic integration followed in the wake of administrative integration, which included the extension of the Java-based system of colonial administration to large parts of the Outer Islands. A single customs area for the entire Indonesian archipelago was established in the 1900s after main free ports such as Makassar had lost their special status. The shipping lines of the KPM extended to even the most remote outports, ensuring regular communications throughout the archipelago (à Campo 1992). Monetary integration proceeded as foreign currencies were purged from the money circulation in main regions of the Outer Islands, including East Sumatra (1907/08) and West Kalimantan (1914). At long last, the Netherlands-Indies guilder became the sole legal tender in the colony (Potting 1987, 1997: 83–117). Nevertheless, such reforms laid only the foundations for economic and administrative integration. There remained deep structural cleavages between ethnic groups, individual regions and economic sectors.

Ethnic discrimination was marked. In the sphere of production, Western and Indonesian economies developed alongside one another, whereas distribution was dominated by Chinese traders. Specialisation along ethnic lines was most apparent in Java: Western firms focused on export production but the Javanese rural economy remained oriented towards food crop cultivation and local markets. In the Outer Islands the situation was more complex. Some sectors of export production, notably the oil industry and tin mining, were the exclusive domain of Western capital, but Indonesian smallholders often took the lead in export agriculture, such as the cultivation of copra and pepper. Parallelism was the most pronounced in the rubber industry, in which both Western estates and Indonesian smallholders were quick to expand production. Deli estates specialised in premium cigar-wrapper leaves, while smallholders in Bojonegoro and Madura supplied cheap *krosok* tobacco for Indonesian *kretek* cigarettes. Minangkabau coffee from West Sumatra differed markedly from higher-quality brands from hillside plantations in Java. Over the years there has been much discussion in the literature about the various types of dualism in production (Appendix 5.D).

The economy of the Indonesian archipelago has been widely conceived in stereotypes. Inward-looking stagnant Java contrasted with market-oriented smallholder economies in the Outer Islands, just as all rural economic activities of Indonesians appeared less dynamic than operations of the urban-based Western enterprises. Separate discussions have evolved in the literature about the structure of the local economy in Java as opposed to the Outer Islands. It is useful to apply that distinction also here.

According to the stereotype, rural Java was doomed to economic backwardness (Dick 2000: 198–201). The feudal organisation thwarted economic initiatives from below. Levels of income and consumption were almost pathetically low. Productivity lagged behind while population pressure on the land only increased. The economic structure was traditional, with a very high proportion of the total labour force engaged in agriculture. Land and labour were partly mobilised for work in Western export agriculture, especially in sugar production, but this was alleged to have had a retarding rather than a stimulating influence on the local Javanese economy. Such was the stereotype perpetuated by contemporary observers and colonial administrators. Against this background, in the 1900s the Ethical Policy aimed to raise the welfare of the Javanese population. Little appeared to have improved by the mid-1920s, and disillusionment abounded (see also the section on the Ethical Policy above).

The characteristics of rural Java in the late colonial period were, as said, a feudal social organisation, poverty, low productivity in agriculture, a traditional economic structure and impoverishment due to Western capital. They were encapsulated in two concepts that have stubbornly remained the pivot of much of the international literature over several decades. One is the 'diminishing welfare' (*mindere welvaart*), coined when the colonial government in 1903 ordered a large-scale investigation into the causes and extent of poverty in rural Java, only two years after the Ethical Policy had been launched. This term, which literally means 'declining *prosperity*', suggests that the liberalisation of economic life in Java since abandonment of the Cultivation System around 1870 had brought contraction rather than economic growth. It was even tacitly acknowledged that the simultaneous rise of Western export agriculture might at least in part be responsible for the impoverishment of surrounding villages (Hüsken 1994). The other concept is 'agricultural involution', proposed by the American anthropologist Clifford Geertz in 1963. This is literally the antithesis of evolution. Things changed in the rural economy of Java, but not for the better. The enforced sharing of land, labour and even water with adjacent Western estates deprived the Javanese peasants of an opportunity to increase productivity. They remained trapped in increasingly elaborate, even ornate arrangements for shared poverty in light of persistently low levels of productivity and rapid population growth (Geertz 1963a: 83–103). Although proven basically wrong, this idea has given rise to a generation of new research on the rural economy in Java (see Appendix 5.E; see also Chapter 6).

The liberalisation of economic life in Java after 1870 was underpinned by a far-reaching individualisation of property and labour relationships, which served to redress some of the distortions of the Cultivation System (see Chapter 3). This applied in particular to individual land rights, even if changes in legal terms often applied more in theory than in practice (Kano 1977). On occasion the colonial government took an active part in furthering defeudalisation. In Cirebon, West Java, agrarian reform was initiated in 1918 with the intention of creating a local middle class of peasants. Small, fragmented landholdings were abolished. But, as it turned out, the local elite was strengthened, and those without land became even more dependent than before on wage labour (Breman 1983: 39–71; Padmo 1993: 115–16). However, the social structure was loosening up and becoming less rigid in most of Java during the first two decades of the 20th century.

When the 'declining welfare investigation' concluded in 1914, after more than a decade of collecting data, it was apparent that poverty in rural Java was no longer as widespread as had originally been thought (Alexander & Alexander 1991). Of the 45 districts surveyed, 32 had experienced an improvement in living standards and only 13 had experienced decline. The evidence of rising prosperity was corroborated by later data on consumption, in particular non-food goods (Booth 1998a: 101).

The main problem of food crop agriculture in Java was to sustain growth in total output in line with the rapid growth of the population. Historically this had been accomplished mainly by extending cultivation into new areas, but around 1920 the land frontier was reached (Booth 1988: 38–9). Further expansion of the harvested area was confined to thinly populated parts of Priangan (West Java) and Besuki (East Java). Total land under cultivation increased from 5.6 million hectares in 1916 to eight million hectares in 1940, but three-quarters of the expansion occurred before 1926 (Boomgaard & Van Zanden 1990: 91–2). As the increase in *sawah* area was especially slow, most of this expansion was accounted for by an increase in dryland area. The proportion of *sawah* in total cultivated land dropped from 50% in 1916 to 43% in 1927.

About 1920, agricultural expansion in Java entered a second phase that was to last until the introduction of high-yielding varieties in the 1960s and 1970s. Intensification, primarily through double-cropping of land, now became the means to enlarge total output. A higher cropping ratio, meaning harvested area divided by total *sawah* area, accounted for at least 50% of the total increase in rice output during the 1920s and 1930s (Booth 1988: 37–43). This adjustment to the land constraint by definition raised the productivity of land employed in food crop agriculture. Labour productivity, however, remained constant at a low level (Van der Eng 1996). Intensification therefore represented a dynamic response to changing circumstances but did not enhance the capacity of agriculture to generate a food surplus. This was a prime disappointment to agricultural consultants committed to the Ethical Policy.

Intensification of rice cultivation in Java was accompanied by increasing diversification of food crop agriculture. Secondary crops (*palawija*) were planted on newly cultivated drylands. The main crops were maize and cassava, supplemented by sweet potatoes, peanuts and soybeans. All were produced in much smaller quantities than rice but all expanded faster than rice after 1920. Cassava in particular became a favoured secondary food crop. Total output grew by almost 40% between the early 1920s and the late 1930s, while rice grew with 25%, in part because sugar lands were in the 1930s released for rice cultivation. These figures need to be offset against the population increase, which can be estimated at approximately 30% for the 1920s and 1930s (Lindblad 1999: 240). The lag of rice output behind growth of population was therefore alleviated by the faster increase in the production of cassava and other dryland crops. The caloric equivalent of food consumption per person/day in Java fell from 2140 kilocalories (kcal) in the late 1910s to 1980 kcal in the early 1920s, but rose to 2040 kcal in the late 1920s (Boomgaard & Van Zanden 1990: 121, 126–7, 132).

Cassava is regarded as much inferior to rice as a staple food and also has had a bad reputation among agricultural economists. The protein content is lower than rice and rising consumption per capita is usually viewed as a sign of impoverishment. Yet this is not necessarily the case. Dried cassava chips (*gaplek*) may serve as a supplement to rice rather than as a substitute. Increased consumption could then be taken as a sign of improving rather than deteriorating standards of living. In addition, it appears that cassava was more profitable in terms of money value of the final product than other food crops (Van der Eng 1998a). The switch to cassava may therefore be further evidence of the dynamism of Java's food crop agriculture in the late colonial period.

The best test of structural change is the share of agriculture in the total labour force. Contemporary observers were pessimistic, but there is a growing appreciation that the stereotype of structural backwardness in the Javanese economy is misleading. A major difficulty in understanding the economic structure of rural Java stems from an all too stubborn application of categories derived from Western society. This applies in particular to the distinction between agricultural and non-agricultural pursuits. According to the 'declining welfare investigation', a large number of persons were registered without any specified occupation or position in the local economy. Their proportion was improbably high, for instance 25% in Kedu in South Central Java (Alexander & Alexander 1991: 75). It is likely that they found work outside agriculture but within the rural economy.

More careful investigation has unearthed evidence of a wide range of non-agricultural employment in the rural economy all over Java in the late 19th century and early 20th century (Fernando 1993). At first this represented a traditional kind of diversification in order to secure a local supply of consumer goods that would otherwise have been costly to obtain. This tendency towards diversification was reversed by the introduction of cheap foreign imports into the village economy in the early 20th century. But then a second wave of diversification ensued. Non-agricultural employment now formed a response to low returns to labour in agriculture (see also Dick 2000).

Structural diversification in the rural economy may be illustrated by the case of Cirebon, West Java. Here non-farm employment involved both families without landholdings of their own and families outside farming altogether. Rural industry and services accounted for an increasing proportion of total employment in Cirebon (Padmo 1993). In coastal areas the diversification often coincided with a modernisation of fishing activities. In the 1920s, for instance, the fisheries along the northern coast of Java matured into an industry with some modern features, such as formal institutions for financing and the organisation of marketing (Masyhuri 1995: 127–78).

Diversification of the rural economy boosted total labour productivity in Java by relieving the rural economy from excessive dependency on low and stagnating levels of productivity in farming (Van der Eng 1996). Off-farm employment supplemented farm incomes and forestalled a possible decline in standards of living. It may also have enhanced Javanese participation in local commerce. This in turn was stimulated in particular by the entry of Japanese traders into the rural economy of Java in the 1910s and 1920s. The Japanese traders proved far more successful than European trading firms in establishing direct connections with local retailers and customers. They thus became instrumental in fostering an embryonic Javanese business elite before the Pacific War (Post 1997).

That Western export agriculture impoverished rural Java is increasingly disputed. The image perpetuated in the literatures of economic dualism and agricultural involution presumes excessive claims on available land and labour from Western estates, particularly the sugar industry, as well as unlimited supplies of cheap Javanese labour. High productivity and prof-itability levels in Western estates were thus attained at the expense of the surrounding local economy. Critical examination shows that the situation was more complex and less unambiguous than the traditional stereotype may make us believe.

Western estates claimed 12% of the total arable land in Java. Sugar cane was harvested on about 200 000 hectares, corresponding to about 3% of the total arable land. Competition for land between Western estates and Javanese peasants therefore probably concerned the quality of the land rather than access to land as such. Since the abolition of the Cultivation System, Western estates increasingly made use of individualised contrac-tual agreements with Javanese farmers, both to rent land, the right to which was inalienable under the Agrarian Law of 1870, and to hire labourers. This reduced the influence of village heads as intermediaries. Still no more than 8%, at most, of the total rural labour force found employment in estate agri-culture, primarily in the sugar industry (Van der Eng 1993a: 188–91). This relatively modest claim on the total available labour by Western estates reflects the very high levels of productivity achieved in the sugar industry.

An unlimited supply of labour would allow wages to be fixed at very low levels. However, unlike densely populated Central Java, this generalisation may not necessarily hold true for West and East Java. In Pekalongan and Tegal (West Java) sugar estates competed both with employers outside farming and Javanese peasants looking for farm hands. Fierce competition gave rise to widespread use of cash advances and intermediaries. The estates often ended up importing seasonal workers from far afield (Knight 1993). In the Surabaya region the extension of sugar cultivation into new areas such as Mojokerto and Jombang stimulated immigration. At the same time population growth slowed down in Sidoarjo, where the land frontier had already been reached (Mackie 1993). Migration played a similar role in regulating supply in the local market for Javanese labour in the tobacco industry in Besuki, East Java, during its initial period of growth in the 1920s (Padmo 1994: 145–57). This all testifies to a rural economy driven by market forces rather than by coercion exercised by powerful Western estates.

The link between much use of local land and labour on the one hand and the high level of productivity in Western estate agriculture on the other was less clear-cut than has often been contended in the literature. The most spectacular gains in productivity were realised in the well-capitalised sugar industry. Here total output doubled between 1915 and 1930 but the harvested area remained virtually constant. Much of the productivity gain was due to technological innovation and improved organisation that bore little relationship to developments in the surrounding local economy (Van der Eng 1993a: 193–201). The late 1920s saw the introduction of new, high-yielding varieties, including the so-called 'wonder cane', labelled 'P.O.J. 2878' after the experimental laboratory in East Java (*Proefstation Oost-Java*) where it had been developed. This kind of technological improvement in agricultural production, based on scientific research, antici-pated the 'Green Revolution' in rice cultivation in Java by about half a century. Sugar cultivation in Java in the late colonial period has been aptly described as a 'first-world industry in a third-world field' (Knight 1996). It thrived by virtue of both its superior technology and its location in an en-vironment with often ready access to cheap land and labour. Yet, even if it had less detrimental effects on surrounding food crop agriculture than has often been presumed, it did little to further modernisation in the rural Javanese economy.

Business rationality and networks

The smallholder economies of the Outer Islands were quite different from those of Java. Food crop agriculture outside Java generally made use of drylands (*ladang*) and was often combined with production for export. The foremost examples were rubber from Sumatra and Kaliman-tan and copra from Sulawesi. Production expanded so fast that by 1930 output was three times as much as in 1920. This increase was far more rapid than in the production of oil and tin, the other two key export commodities supplied by the Outer Islands (Figure 5.6). The smallholder proportion of exports was virtually 100% in the case of copra, but grew fast for rubber, so that this export industry eventually became strongly dominated by smallholders. Oil and tin were both exclusively supplied by Western enterprises.

Both smallholders and Western enterprises were responsive to market signals. The initial phase of expansion with high and rising prices lasted until the mid-1920s. As world prices fell, producers sought to compensate

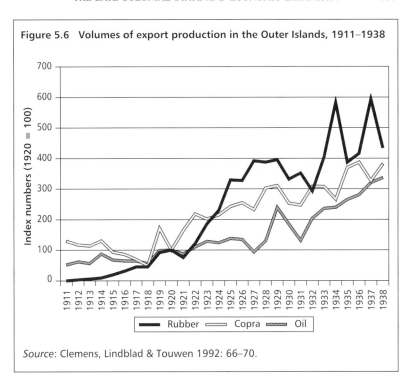

Figure 5.6   Volumes of export production in the Outer Islands, 1911–1938

Source: Clemens, Lindblad & Touwen 1992: 66–70.

by increasing the quantum of exports. Investment decisions were taken in the same context of profit expectations, even if the scale of investment was obviously much larger in capital-intensive industries such as oil and tin production than in rubber and copra cultivation. The swift reaction of smallholders to changing conditions in world markets testified to their entrepreneurial spirit (Ranken 1989; Touwen 1991; Zed 1996).

An important difference between smallholders and Western enterprises concerned the mobilisation of labour. Smallholders benefited from the seasonality of work in food crop agriculture, whereas Western estates relied on imported coolies. Rubber and copra cultivation expanded most rapidly in regions that were densely populated by the standards of the Outer Islands. In such regions there was a substantial demand for additional employment. Smallholders made extensive use of family labour and engaged additional labour on a short-run or part-time basis. Local coolies were recruited when the necessity arose. The popular base of smallholder production thus became very wide. It is estimated that half of all house-holds in the Hulu Sungai district of South Kalimantan was directly or indirectly engaged in rubber cultivation (Lindblad 1988a: 58–78). Thus smallholders enjoyed much flexibility in adjusting their labour force to the demands of production.

With only slight oversimplification, it can be said that Western enterprise adjusted the environment to production, whereas smallholder entrepreneurship adjusted production to the environment. Smallholders relied on existing local infrastructure, but Western estates often invested heavily in roads, harbours and other facilities, including recruitment of coolie labour. Local Chinese often served as intermediaries in contacts of smallholders with foreign markets. Financing of production was organised through profit-sharing arrangements or formalised contractual agreements. Examples are found in smallholder rubber cultivation in southern Sumatra and copra production in Manado (Purwanto 1996; Leirissa 1996).

Western planters and colonial administrators never ceased to complain about the 'untidy' appearance of the smallholders' rubber gardens and the deficient quality of the final product. This points at another difference in business operations between the two parallel lines of production. There was little incentive for smallholder producers to invest in future productivity growth or technological improvement. Their objective was to produce as much as possible while prices were still high, or at any rate before they had fallen further. The quality of smallholder rubber improved only in the 1930s, after the boom had passed.

The 1920s were the 'golden age' (*hujan emas* or 'golden rain') for smallholder rubber, long remembered among rural residents in Palembang, Jambi and West and South Kalimantan. Consumption of both local and imported goods quickly increased. The number of motor cars in Palembang rose from 300 in 1922 to 1300 in 1924, and more than 19 000 bicycles and 17 000 sewing-machines were imported into Palembang and Jambi in the 1920s (Purwanto 1996: 187–8). Another clear indication of suddenly rising incomes was the steep increase in the numbers of pilgrims leaving for Mecca. Conspicuous consumption was also observed in the Hulu Sungai in South Kalimantan, where several thousand bicycles and hundreds of cars were imported (Lindblad 1988a: 70). Houses were improved and wedding feasts competed in sumptuousness. In the mid-1920s Southeast Kalimantan counted the largest number of *haji* per thousand residents in the entire Islamic world. Much romantic nostalgia surrounded the *hujan emas* in the rubber regions of the Outer Islands.

The long-run effects were less impressive. Failure to generate sustained economic growth was a major weakness of the smallholder economies in the Outer Islands. The absence of a link between the external impetus to expansion through exports on the one hand and regional economic growth on the other is statistically confirmed (Lindblad 1993). Three reasons can be identified. First, little value-adding export processing took place in the Outer Islands. Second, as explained, most smallholder export proceeds were spent on immediate consumption, instead of being saved and invested. Third, a high proportion of consumption was of imported goods. In Palembang, smallholder exports led to some growth of light manufacturing such as textile production, but this was atypical of the rest of the Outer Islands and especially of the copra-producing eastern archipelago (Purwanto 1993). If anywhere in the region benefited from the smallholder rubber boom it was Singapore, which performed value-adding functions, supplied imported consumer goods and enjoyed some industrial linkages (Booth 1998a: 235). Significantly, these advantages accrued only minimally to Java. A similar pattern applied to Western export production such as the tobacco and rubber estates in Deli, the oil refineries in Palembang and East Kalimantan or the tin mines in Bangka and Belitung.

There was a regional dimension to the export-led expansion in the Outer Islands. We may distinguish between four clusters of regions: those where Western capital predominated, those where smallholder entrepreneurship was more important, those that saw a combination of the two and, finally, regions that appeared largely unaffected by the economic expansion (Touwen 1997: 63–87). East Sumatra remained the prototype of the first category, whereas Jambi, West Kalimantan, Manado and South Sulawesi all represented centres of 'Asian dynamics' — that is, the second category. Palembang and Southeast Kalimantan in the third category counted among the largest exporters of oil and rubber. In the fourth category, Bengkulu and Lampung in southern Sumatra as well as Bali, Lombok, Timor and the Moluccas all lagged hopelessly behind, trading little with the outside world and having pockets of endemic poverty.

The Western segment of the economy extended throughout the entire Indonesian archipelago but focused on export production, mining and services. It was based on a small part of the labour force but accounted for a very substantial proportion of total capital formation, even if the unrecorded investment in farm households and smallholder production units is underestimated (Booth 1998a: 249–50). Total accumulated foreign investment in export agriculture, oil refining, coal and tin mining and transport increased from 1.5 billion guilders in 1914 ($675 million) to four billion guilders ($1.6 billion) in 1930. The latter total was almost four times the annual value of exports. Investors in the Netherlands held about two-thirds of total accumulated foreign investment (Lindblad 1998: 13–15). These large commitments of Dutch private capital were a major stumbling block to Dutch acceptance of Indonesia's independence after the Pacific War.

Especially outside Java, Western estates and mines were often enclave economies that had few linkages with the surrounding local economy. Capital, technology, management and, in the case of the Outer Islands, even labour were all imported. The entire product was generally exported, coal being the main exception to the rule. Processing at the tobacco and rubber estates of Deli, let alone in the tin mines of Bangka and Belitung, only served to facilitate shipment abroad and thus failed to give rise to any further industrial production. The oil and sugar industries both formed special cases. An increasing proportion of crude oil was refined at the huge installations at Plaju (Palembang), Balikpapan (East Kalimantan) and Cepu (East Java). However, the refineries used such sophisticated technologies that few linkages could materialise with the surrounding local economy (Lindblad 1989b). The sugar refineries in Java made extensive use of advanced technology and facilitated the growth of a local engineering industry (Leidelmeijer 1997; Dick 1993c). The failure of Western export production to generate sustained regional economic growth in the Outer Islands can be verified by applying formal economic theory to the long-run development of leading export regions such as East Sumatra and Southeast Kalimantan (Thee 1977: 84–121; Lindblad 1988a: 171–215).

The most controversial part of Western enterprise outside Java was the use of imported coolie labour under legal arrangements that gave employers immense power over employees (see also Chapter 4). The number of coolies working for Western enterprises in the Outer Islands grew especially fast in the 1920s. In 1930, at the height of this system of labour mobilisation, the total labour force of coolies consisted of about 500 000 persons, of whom 60% were found in East Sumatra alone. Other regions accommodating large numbers of coolies were Southeast Kalimantan, Palembang, Bangka and Belitung. Conditions of coolie labour varied markedly across regions and between different industries. Some improvement occurred in material conditions, notably health and housing, whereas other aspects of treatment of coolies, as reflected in harsh punishments, still left much to be desired at the end of the 1920s (see further Stoler 1985; Houben, Lindblad et al. 1999).

The so-called 'coolie issue' occasioned much heated discussion, both among contemporaries and in the later literature (Appendix 5.F). Much of the public debate at the time concerned the repeal of the Coolie Ordinance and the penal clause associated with it (Taselaar 1998: 261–300). In the event, this did not occur until 1931 under pressure from the US Congress, which otherwise would have discriminated against tobacco produced by bonded labour and in favour of American plantations (Homan 1987). The dismantling of the system of coolie labour proceeded much faster than anticipated by the Dutch Parliament in 1931. The economic Depression was already making itself felt and the employers' need for flexibility in firing and hiring of labour was more urgent than their need to safeguard the long-run supply of cheap labour.

Distribution was dominated by Chinese businessmen (see further Vleming 1925; Cator 1936; Liem 1947). They were conspicuous in local commerce, often in trades that were not considered to be profitable by Europeans or where Indonesian merchants were slow to seize the opportunities. They could draw on two slightly different traditions dating from the 19th century. In the Outer Islands the Chinese formed nodes in a wider regional trading network, embracing all of Southeast Asia (see also Chapter 4). In Java, profits from revenue farms serving the colonial administration often became the base for further Chinese economic activity. The outstanding example of a successful Chinese businessman in the Indonesian archipelago in the late 19th and early 20th century was Oei Tiong Ham in

Semarang, who built up a widely diversified concern including sugar mills, light manufacturing and banking (Yoshihara 1989; Dick 1993e). Oei Tiong Ham counted as one of the colony's richest men when he died in 1924.

There were two types of Chinese residents — those who were themselves born in China or at any rate had retained the language and customs of their ancestors (*totok*), and those who were born in the Indonesian archipelago and had assimilated fully into colonial society (*peranakan*). The latter group continuously grew in importance, and by 1930 four-fifths of all Chinese were *peranakan*, possessing only a rudimentary knowledge of the Chinese language (Mackie & Coppel 1976: 6–7). Assimilation of the Chinese meant a stronger orientation towards Dutch society. Chinese-owned business in the archipelago thus acquired a character of its own. It was not foreign but it was also not fully domestic. In that sense Chinese firms formed an intermediate stage between European and Indonesian business.

Chinese capital investment towards the end of colonial rule has been estimated at 375 million guilders ($150 million) (Callis 1942: 36). In the 1920s the number of Chinese business firms registered as unlimited companies rose towards 700, mostly in commerce (Lindblad 1998: 74). Scrutiny of individual firms reveals that the paid-up capital of these enterprises increased little over time, suggesting that Chinese businessmen chose incorporation to gain access to European commercial law and business networks rather than to raise funds for investment (Lindblad 1998: 14, 78). In the early 1920s there were reportedly 1700 Chinese-owned firms in manufacturing employing at least five persons (Fernando & Bulbeck 1992: 254–9). Most of these firms were not part of the formal corporate network. Such data, piecemeal and incomplete as they may be, reaffirm that Chinese business played a very substantial role in the economy of the colony, even if the full extent of their operations remains to be explored.

Income by ethnic origin

The segmentation of economic structure along ethnic lines was marked by very different trends in income. In the 1920s per capita incomes rose much faster for Europeans and Chinese than for Indonesians (Figure 5.7). Between 1921 and 1929 nominal per capita incomes rose by 50% for Europeans and 80% for Chinese residents, but Indonesian incomes stayed more or less constant. The gap between European and Chinese incomes therefore narrowed, whereas that between these two groups and the Indonesian population further widened.

Around 1930 incomes per capita displayed extreme disparities between the population groups. Average incomes, expressed in guilders at current prices, were as follows:

- Indonesians   59.70
- Chinese   326.90
- Europeans   2700.00

The income of the average European therefore corresponded to that of 45 Indonesians, or eight Chinese. Only a small part of these differences was explained by the smaller size of European households.

The income distribution remained uneven throughout the 1920s and 1930s (Figure 5.7; Creutzberg 1979: 71). The share of Europeans, whether residents of the colony or not, oscillated around 20% of the total. This percentage should be compared with the minuscule 0.5% share of Europeans in the total population. The Chinese (together with a handful of Arab and Indian residents) received around 10% of national income, while constituting less than 2% of the total population. These discrepancies in the distribution of income impaired the capacity of the colonial economy to save for future investment.

Such calculations should also allow for income that originated in the Indonesian archipelago but flowed away in the form of overseas remittances. This is the so-called 'colonial drain', a controversial concept that was applied by contemporary critics of the colonial economic system. The argument has two dimensions. First, too much of the income generated through expanding exports was pocketed by overseas owners of factors of production, especially private Dutch corporations. Second, too little was done to make the Indonesian economy less dependent on exports of primary commodities for which prices in the world market

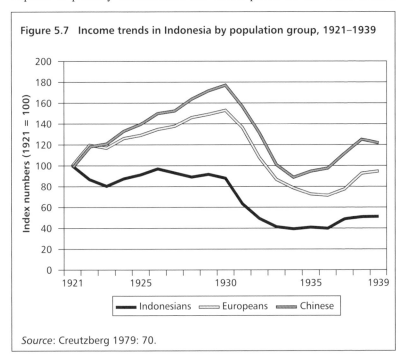

Figure 5.7   Income trends in Indonesia by population group, 1921–1939

Source: Creutzberg 1979: 70.

were likely to continue to decline also after 1945. Each warrants a separate comment.

At the end of the colonial period, the later Dutch Nobel Laureate Jan Tinbergen and an associate calculated that 14% of the national income of the Netherlands consisted of direct and indirect income from private investment in the Indonesian archipelago (Derksen & Tinbergen 1945; Sumitro 1946). This percentage is high by any international comparison and conveys not only how much the Netherlands gained but also how much the archipelago lost. It was used by politicians in the Netherlands to justify the continuation of colonial rule and by Indonesian nationalists to justify its overthrow.

As economic expansion during the late colonial period was export-led, the 'colonial drain' refers specifically to the surplus in the commodity balance of trade — that is, the proportion of export revenue not spent on foreign imports. This percentage averaged 38% throughout the late colonial period (see section on export-led expansion), which is also high by any international standard. The surplus of exports above imports translated into a substantial surplus on the current account of the balance of payments, which in turn financed the outflow of profits, interests and dividends. In the 1920s the surplus on current account corresponded to 5% of the estimated national income of the Indonesian archipelago. This surplus was very high by international standards and has been compared with the outflow of funds from major creditor nations at the peak of their overseas economic commitments, for instance Great Britain in the 1880s and Japan in the 1980s (Golay 1976; Booth 1998a: 213–14). Opinions vary as to whether this massive outflow of capital represented an 'adequate' remuneration to overseas factors of production or a 'drain' of resources that could otherwise have been used for investment in the Indonesian archipelago (Van der Eng 1993b; see also Appendix 5.G).

The second dimension of the 'colonial drain' argument touches on the economic structure as it was shaped by the expansion in the late colonial period. Contemporary estimates show that as much as 60% of the total domestic product originated in the primary sector. Manufacturing accounted for less than 15% and services for a little more than 25% of the total (Polak 1943/1979). Recent efforts to reconstruct the national accounts of Indonesia before and after Independence have underscored the lopsided sectoral composition of the economy at the end of the colonial period (Van der Eng 1992).

Some economic diversification did take place. The proportion of the labour force engaged in manufacturing rose from 7% in 1905 to 13% in 1930. Absolute numbers grew from less than one million to 1.7 million. Many of the new enterprises were small-scale and set up by European or Chinese businessmen. They catered to a local market and were not oriented towards foreign exports. The number of establishments registered under the so-called Factory Act increased by more than 50% between 1923 and 1929. Yet average employment per factory amounted to only 39 persons in the latter year

(Segers 1987: 24). The impact on long-run industrial development therefore remained limited. Some of the responsibility for this lay with the colonial government, which failed to formulate and implement an industrialisation policy at a time when export revenues were flowing in on a large scale. Such a policy emerged only during the Depression of the 1930s (see Chapter 6).

CONCLUSION

The three main themes of this chapter have been colonial state formation, globalisation through economic expansion, and integration in the direction of a national economy. It advances several propositions. One concerns the Dutch style of colonial rule. The Dutch colonial administration pursued two broad objectives simultaneously — providing a favourable environment for foreign trade and investment, and improving economic prospects for Indonesians. The Dutch colonial state succeeded in the former but failed in the latter. By perpetuating rather than alleviating ethnic disparities in income and economic opportunities, it carried the seeds of its own destruction. The 'colonial experiment' of the Dutch in Indonesia, with its apparent economic benefits for the Netherlands, could possibly have been more viable in the long run had a more enlightened effort been made to bridge the gap between Europeans and Indonesians. The contradiction between economic liberalism and increasing political repression in the late colonial state anticipated the situation during the New Order government of Soeharto several decades later.

A second proposition refers to the export-led type of economic expansion. This implied a commercial emancipation of the colony from the mother country and increased dependence on foreign markets. It resulted in a sharper dichotomy between core and periphery within the archipelago, and it failed to produce a solid basis for sustained economic growth because until the 1930s the multiplier effects continued to flow outwards. Thus the export boom was ultimately not sustainable. The expansion of exports was accompanied by enhanced vulnerability to adverse price movements in world markets. In the 1930s terms of trade worsened and losses with respect to export revenues became dramatic.

A third and final proposition links the continuing integration towards a national economy with the cleavages between ethnic groups, economic sectors and regions. In the early 20th century the colonial system of administration was extended from Java to the Outer Islands, backed up by a substantial investment in infrastructure and communication. Yet economic integration lagged behind administrative integration. In addition, economic integration reinforced the high degree of segmentation in ethnic, sectoral and regional terms. Funds were drained away from the colony and the scope for a structural transformation of the economy was reduced.

Why was Indonesia so poor in 1945 after having experienced sustained economic expansion during earlier decades of the 20th century? An answer requires asking what could have been different. A better alternative scenario

would have been a society more susceptible to modernisation through integration across economic sectors, ethnic groups and regions. In such a
scenario gains from the expansion of export production could have been
used to develop other sectors, most notably manufacturing, and to invest
more in physical infrastructure and, above all, far more in human capital —
the very point at which the Ethical Policy failed. Yet such a scenario presup-
poses a commitment to national economic development incompatible with
the very institution of colonial rule. Could more have been done during the
early decades of the 20th century given that the colony remained a colonial
possession? The answer is probably no.

APPENDICES

5.A   The colonial state

The concept of the colonial state is an evasive one. What exactly do we
mean by a *colonial* state? What is the difference from a state in general? A
preliminary answer is that a colonial state possesses a structure that
remains partly dependent on a nation-state elsewhere while at the same
time developing a character of its own. A colonial state is by definition
based on the domination of a tiny foreign elite above the majority of the
indigenous population.

As a theoretical concept the colonial state remains rather undeveloped.
To some it has appeared uninspiring, literally a 'historical dead-end'
(Cribb 1994: 2). Only in recent years has there been an increasing appreciation that the colonial state represented a system with a distinct character of
its own, separate from the mother country in Europe and the particular
department of government to which it was technically subordinated, even if
the construct of the colonial state as such represented a major type of technology transfer from Europe to Asia. The current perception was anticipated by à Campo and Van Doorn. The former describes the emergence of
overlapping political, economic and maritime networks in the Indonesian
archipelago around 1900 that represented a system in its own right
(à Campo 1992). The latter analyses the traumatic decolonisation of
Indonesia in the second half of the 1940s, insisting that there was an additional actor involved in this process, next to the one-time mother country
and the one-time colony. The third actor was the permanent Dutch settlement in Indonesia (*Indië*) prepared to cling to a continued Dutch presence
in the Indonesian archipelago also after independence and at virtually any
cost (Van Doorn 1985: 107).

Three features are commonly identified in the literature on the Dutch
colonial state in the Indonesian archipelago (Cribb 1994: 3–6):

1. Constitutional separation enhanced by a formal separation of financial
   responsibility between the Netherlands and the colony. As a result
   the deficit on the annual colonial budget was added to the debt of the

colony to the mother country. Even if this was a legal formality, it had repercussions when Indonesia negotiated its terms of independence with the Netherlands in the late 1940s (see further Chapter 6).

2. Administrative complexity through the elaboration of a colonial bureaucracy. Procedures took account of all intricacies of direct and indirect rule and left Javanese and Malay sultanates intact, though with much reduced real power. This was the most substantive achievement of the colonial state, but it fostered resentment on the part of its Indonesian subjects.

3. Political responsibility to Indonesian subjects, allegedly manifest in for instance the People's Council (*Volksraad*) installed in 1918. The Dutch colonial authorities paid lip-service to this principle, at any rate up to the collapse of the Ethical Policy in the mid-1920s. The Dutch, however, stayed short of substantive initiatives such as some measure of self-government, as introduced in the Philippines in 1935.

5.B   The Ethical Policy debate

The term 'Ethical Policy' was coined in 1901 by the Dutch journalist P. Brooshooft in Semarang. In a slim brochure he stressed measures to enhance the prosperity of Indonesians and decentralisation in colonial administration. He assumed a paternalistic attitude, referring to the Javanese as 'this childish people' (Furnivall 1939/1944: 232; Houben 1996b: 59–60). In the same year the ethic aspirations were elevated into official policy.

The ethical aspirations of Dutch colonial policy should be understood against the background of the so-called 'debt of honour' (*ereschuld*) of the Netherlands to its colony. In 1899, C.Th. van Deventer, member of the Dutch Parliament, calculated that the surplus in the colonial budget had enriched the Dutch treasury by at least 145 million guilders ($58 million) during the period 1867–1875 alone. There had already been sizeable gains during the preceding decades, especially returns from the Cultivation System in Java, but these gains were difficult to set off against expenditures as there was no separation of financial responsibility between the mother country and the colony prior to 1867. Shortly after 1875 the colonial enterprise started to run at a deficit, mainly because of the mounting costs of warfare in Aceh. Accumulated deficits caused an increasing indebtedness of the colony to the mother country. The idea of a 'debt of honour' meant that the Netherlands had an obligation to repay some of its previous gains in the form of expenditures on prosperity for Indonesians rather than amassing financial claims.

The discussion of the merits and achievements of the Ethical Policy began around that time. Contemporary observers shared the general disappointment with what the Ethical Policy had actually accomplished for the indigenous peoples of Indonesia (Furnivall 1948). The good intentions and genuine sincerity of the colonial administrators was usually not doubted. This standpoint is echoed in more recent studies on how the colonial administrators thought and acted (Prince 1989: 220; see also Locher-Scholten 1981;

Van Doorn 1982). The difference in sheer scale between the tiny mother country on the shores of the North Sea and the huge colony in Southeast Asia has often been mentioned as a reason why more could not be achieved. A less apologetic line of argument insists that the ethical aspirations of the colonial government only served the interests of private Dutch investors in the colony. Such opinions have been voiced but rarely substantiated in the literature.

There is a renewed interest in recent years to assess the performance of the Ethical Policy. The current approach is to look at targets and results in specific areas, notably education, irrigation and agricultural extension. Conclusions are often far from revolutionary but they do render a deeper understanding of the Ethical Policy and the functioning of the late colonial state. A major difficulty is to find the appropriate yardstick against which to measure achievements. One possibility is to examine the impact on productivity levels or standards of living. Another is to apply a comparative perspective and look at what was achieved elsewhere or at other times. The various case studies tend to complement each other rather than to dispute preceding assertions. Further debate may be expected as researchers move into more common ground.

Several examples of different approaches and foci of attention deserve to be mentioned. Booth considers the educational record. She contrasts the low level of literacy and small numbers of Indonesians in secondary, let alone tertiary education with the substantial enrolment in comparable institutions in British India (Booth 1989b: 117–18). Cribb reviews the entire package of 'welfare services'. He seeks explanation in an overly technocratic attitude, depriving the development strategy of a clear focus and direction (Cribb 1993).

Special attention is rightly given to improvements in agriculture. Van der Eng offers a thorough survey of all types of direct government interference in agricultural production. He concludes that irrigation had the largest impact in quantitative terms (Van der Eng 1993a). Both Van der Eng and Prince stress the great responsiveness of the Dutch agricultural consultants to local conditions and needs in the Javanese rural economy. This view is difficult to reconcile with the technocratic approach in the implementation of the Ethical Policy that Cribb describes (Van der Eng 1991; 1993a: 112; Prince 1995: 36–8).

So far the Ethical Policy has scarcely been studied in conjunction with economic liberalism. Was the Ethical Policy a correction of the outcome of the free play of market? Or was it rather an expression of the growing cleavage between advocates of the interests of private capital as opposed to those of the colonial state? A potential area for a clash between extreme economic liberalism and the Ethical Policy was the stimulation of industrialisation in the Indonesian archipelago. This was the part of the Ethical Policy where probably the least was achieved. A coherent industrialisation policy scarcely existed before the late 1930s (see also Fasseur 2000). Moreover, it was bound to fail unless accompanied by protective measures against imports. Yet such protection would have restricted the market for Dutch imports. Did the Ethical Policy serve as a surrogate for industrialisation?

5.C   Using trade statistics

The official records of foreign trade in the Indonesian archipelago during the late colonial period are exceptionally good. Annual details are provided by port, region, commodity and trading partner. This represents a wealth of information that may be used to shed light on the development of the colonial economy in both the short and long run. However, a word of caution is due for at least two reasons. Only trading that caught the eye of the colonial administrators was recorded, which implies that illicit or unofficial trade may have escaped registration. This may be of particular importance in the relationship between the eastern coast of Sumatra and the nearby Malay peninsula. In addition, final destinations are not always disclosed for exports going for instance to Singapore or the Netherlands. Re-exports were anticipated but it was apparently not yet known where the goods were to end up.

A special problem with using statistics of foreign trade concerns the evaluation of trade flows. This may be illustrated by looking at the situation in 1919 and 1920, during the immediate postwar boom in world trade. Extreme price rises for sugar pushed nominal export values upwards. The very high share of sugar in total exports at that time assured that the composite export price index to a very large extent reflected the price of sugar. This explains the extreme difference in total export values immediately after World War I when expressed in current as opposed to constant prices (Figure 5.3).

All trade values in the statistics are calculated from standardised prices supposedly reflecting current market prices at the time. This implies that a development in trade values over time will automatically contain an inflationary or deflationary component, depending on whether prices have risen or fallen in the meantime. For the purpose of comparisons over time, trade values need to be corrected for inflation or deflation with the use of a price index. The conversion of official export values from current into constant prices here applies an index with a different set of weighting factors for each decade. For imports entering colonial Indonesia, a separate and partly unweighted index is applied: 1913 is the base year for which the index number equals 100 (Korthals Altes 1994: 160–4; see also Van Ark 1988: 114–20).

5.D   On economic dualism

There is a strong tradition of dualism in the literature about Western and Asian modes of production. But what precisely do we mean by this term? Is it the dynamic Western sector against the stagnant indigenous one, as the

Dutch economist Boeke insisted already in the early 20th century? Or are we concerned with exclusive Western lines of production against exclusive Indonesian ones? Or does dualism refer to the coexistence of parallel lines of production, each in its own right?

The conventional concept of economic dualism was for decades at length reiterated by J.H. Boeke, professor of 'tropical-colonial economics' at the University of Leiden in the Netherlands. With its Kiplingesque undertones it offered a justification for investment by Western enterprises and a segregation along ethnic lines in the colonial economy (Boeke 1953). Originally the concept was applied only to Java, but later the emphasis shifted towards the Outer Islands. Here the gap between Western dynamic entrepreneurship and a stagnating Asian economy appeared even sharper than in Java.

The departure from the conventional conception was facilitated by a number of case studies on individual regions among the Outer Islands during the late colonial period. The case studies covered East Sumatra, Southeast Kalimantan, Aceh, southern Sumatra, Bangka and West Sumatra (Thee 1977; Lindblad 1988a; Ismail 1991; Purwanto 1992; Somers Heidhues 1992; Colombijn 1994). They have been accompanied by numerous articles on several topics concerning economic life outside Java (Clemens & Lindblad 1989). This rich harvest has led to a fuller appreciation of the dynamic smallholder economies in the Outer Islands.

A common denominator in recent case studies is the emphasis on successful smallholder entrepreneurship. This applied most notably to rubber cultivation in the 1910s and 20s. Smallholders reacted as swiftly as Western enterprises to signals from the world market. They were more flexible in adjusting production to changing circumstances but less inclined to invest in upgrading the technology of production (Lindblad 1988a: 58–78; Clemens 1989; Touwen 1991; Lindayanti 1994; Ismail 1996; Purwanto 1996; Zed 1996). Dynamic Indonesian entrepreneurship also explains the success of copra producers in Sulawesi (Heersink 1995; Leirissa 1996). These studies all point in the direction of a dualism of a different type from the one propagated by Boeke. The 'new' dualism is characterised by simultaneous and parallel paths of development, each with its own viability.

5.E   Agricultural involution

The large international literature on the economic development of Java in the late colonial period has until recently been heavily biased towards testing one provocative hypothesis — Clifford Geertz's idea of agricultural involution, or continuous agricultural change without progress. The hypothesis carried an instant appeal, partly because of its ecological undertones, when it was first presented in 1963. It gave rise to a generation of case studies. These studies have greatly enriched our knowledge of rural Java in the early 20th century and revealed the high degree of regional variation and heterogeneity across Java. They have also shown Geertz's hypothesis of agricultural involution to be basically wrong.

Geertz's idea appeared novel in 1963. In fact it was a recast and more elaborate version of the conventional notion of a fundamental dualism in the colonial economy (see also Appendix 5.D). Geertz describes the situation in Javanese agriculture around 1920. He attributes the lack of progress in Javanese production to traditional patterns of land use and labour mobilisation. These patterns were inherited from the Cultivation System (Geertz 1963a: 83–103). Numerous scholars looked for a causal link between the Cultivation System in the 19th century and agricultural involution in the early 20th century. They did not find it. There was even evidence to the contrary. The principalities of Yogyakarta and Surakarta (Solo), where the Cultivation System had never been implemented, displayed the dominant features of agricultural involution, such as high population densities, much *sawah* land and low productivity levels (White 1976; Hüsken 1982; Svensson 1988). Van Schaik undertook an in-depth study of two leading sugar-producing regions, Tegal in West Java and Pasuruan in East Java. He concludes that no agricultural involution was inherited from the Cultivation System (Van Schaik 1986).

5.F   The coolie issue

The expression 'coolie issue' (*koelievraagstuk*) has undergone several changes of meaning. At first it denoted the problem that employers in the Outer Islands faced in securing sufficient volumes of labour. This became the justification for the Coolie Ordinance for the Outer Islands (1880) and the associated penal clause. Then the term came to refer to problems with the treatment of coolie labourers by employers. The Labour Inspectorate, installed in 1908 by the colonial authorities in response to the evidence of widespread abuse on the estates of Deli in East Sumatra, was entrusted with solving this problem. In the more recent literature on the subject, the coolie issue refers to the impact of the Labour Inspectorate in actually improving conditions for coolie labour.

The modern discussion was sparked off by Stoler, an American anthropologist. She depicts coolie labour on Western estates in East Sumatra as a form of 'commodisation' of labour as a key factor of production. Coercion and abuse formed inalienable parts of this system of capitalist exploitation (Stoler 1985). This theme is pursued by Breman. He gave publicity to the so-called Rhemrev report, the document revealing abuse in Deli that was suppressed (but not destroyed) by the colonial authorities. Breman examines the public discussion at the time and argues that the institutionalisation of abuse and coercion by employers was not questioned (Breman 1987, 1989, 1997; for the original Rhemrev report, see Breman 1987: 315–408).

Two questions stand out in the debate on coolie labour. First, did maltreatment and abuse form an integral part of the Western mode of production as applied in the Outer Islands? Second, did conditions of coolie labour improve after 1908 when the colonial government installed the Labour Inspectorate? Stoler and Breman answer the first question affirmatively and the second question in the negative.

A distinction between material and non-material conditions of labour is convenient when arranging the available evidence. Material conditions of coolie labour concern health (mirrored for instance in mortality rates), wages and housing. Non-material conditions are indicated by the frequency of violence, coolie protests, punishment and desertion. The evidence itself is subject to discussion, as it was almost exclusively compiled by the Labour Inspectorate. The Breman-Stoler conception of sustained systematic abuse is challenged by an examination of the quantitative and qualitative evidence, interpreted with the necessary caution. This endeavour makes use of an analytical scheme containing four determinants of actual conditions of coolie labour: type of coolie, type of employer, region, and action taken by the Labour Inspectorate (Houben 1994a, 1995, 1996a; Houben, Lindblad et al. 1999; see also Kamphues 1988).

5.G   Colonial drain

The discussion about a possible drainage of resources away from the colony for the benefit of the mother country started already in the late 1940s. It was revitalised in the 1980s when an explicit link was established between the highly successful trade performance of the Indonesian archipelago and the increasing flow of remittances to the Netherlands. Booth contends that Indonesia could have embarked on the path towards sustained economic growth already before the Pacific War, had more of the gains from the expansion in foreign exports been employed in investment in the colonial economy. Following Maddison, she distinguishes between two types of drain. One consisted of profits accruing to Western, primarily Dutch enterprises operating in the colony. The other benefited Chinese intermediaries and recipients abroad. This gave rise to the idea of a 'double drain' thwarting opportunities for economic growth in the Indonesian archipelago in the early 20th century (Booth 1989a, 1990a; Maddison 1990).

A major difficulty in assessing the validity of the 'colonial drain' argument concerns the measurement of the drain. Booth and Maddison both use the surplus of exports above imports on the balance of trade as a crude measure of the size of the colonial drain. It was found to be very high by international comparison. Even more elusive is the Chinese part of the drain, although more primary evidence has become available on overseas Chinese remittances in the late colonial period (Hicks 1993). The most outspoken criticism has been articulated by Van der Eng. He argues that the export surplus overstates the drain. Opportunity costs of Dutch capital and labour employed in the colony should be deducted, as they reflect 'normal' payment for services and rates of return on invested capital. The resulting drain is much smaller and fails to offer a sufficient explanation for the absence of sustained economic growth. Dutch business did profit substantially from investment in the colony but rates of return were no higher than those from alternative uses of capital (Van der Eng 1993b, 1998b). The controversy about the colonial drain is not yet resolved.

6

Formation of the nation-state, 1930s–1966

Howard Dick

INTRODUCTION

Although the birth of modern Indonesia is conventionally dated from the Declaration of Independence on 17 August 1945, the turning-point in economic history was the world Depression of the 1930s, which became a crisis of the colonial economy and the colonial state. In 1929 the Nether-lands Indies was, as the name implied, a colonial appendage of the Netherlands, managed by a modest civil administration committed above all to *rust en orde* (peace and order) (Chapter 5). An open, *laissez-faire* trade regime was maintained on behalf of a pyramid of plantation big business, whose base rested on village society and whose apex was the management houses and banks in Jakarta, Surabaya and, ultimately, Amsterdam, The Hague and Rotterdam. When world commodity prices collapsed, this export–import economy with its elaborate infrastructure and finely tuned systems of production not only contracted but lost vitality. The export industries were crippled and Dutch imports all but eliminated by Japanese competition. Released from the constraint of the plantation interest, with its obsession about cheap labour, the colonial state responded creatively by charting an independent economic course. From 1933 it followed a protectionist policy that drew on Java's abundant labour to produce manufactures, while raising domestic self-sufficiency in rice and other food crops. The Netherlands Indies at last began to be managed as an autonomous economic unit by a government which, however narrowly, represented the interests of the Indies as well as the Netherlands.

When Germany occupied the Netherlands in May 1940, the Netherlands Indies became virtually a self-governing dominion. Subject to the Dutch government-in-exile in London, the Governor-General probably exercised more power than the founding president after 1935 of the self-governing Republic of the Philippines under American tutelage. After a decade of state-building, the Netherlands Indies government was well equipped to exercise its new powers. Its obvious weakness, shared with the rest of Southeast Asia, was defence. Despite limited American, British and Australian assistance, the Netherlands Indies lacked the equipment, manpower, command structure and will to resist the Japanese. The fundamental weakness, however, was one of legitimacy. In marked contrast with the Philippines, until the eve of invasion the Dutch colonial state steadfastly refused to enlist the support of the Indonesian people, whose leaders remained in prison. Towards Indonesian nationalism the Dutch maintained 'a studied, condescending indifference' (Benda 1966). Only *force majeure* of the Japanese invasion caused this repressive colonial state to collapse unexpectedly, leaving the apparatus of a modern state to be claimed by those it had ruled. The tragedy was not so much the Japanese invasion as the subsequent attempt by the Dutch to reclaim by force what had already been lost. The bloody strife which preceded the transfer of sovereignty compromised the terms of independence and distracted the energies of the nation well into the 1960s.

This chapter begins by looking at indicators of the severity of the 1930s Depression and its impact. It then examines the phenomenon of Japanese economic penetration before reviewing the policy shift towards protectionism and import substitution and assessing the impact on industrial development. It covers the strife-torn interregnum between the collapse of Dutch rule in March 1942 and the transfer of sovereignty to the United States of Indonesia in December 1949. It briefly reviews the Japanese occupation and considers the extent of the long-run disruption to the economy before the outbreak of the armed revolutionary struggle in August 1945. A longer section then examines Dutch attempts to restore the productive system and to find a political compromise that would safeguard Dutch interests in a guided transition towards self-government. Another section reveals the barren harvest that was reaped from the strife of 1945–1949. Efforts during the 1950s to restore the economy, pursue a modest program of import substitution and gradually Indonesianise the modern sector were thwarted by worsening political instability in the contest for control of the new nation-state. After 1959 in the period of Guided Democracy, economic development was sacrificed to political mobilisation, which eventually threatened the survival of the state itself. The periods are as follows:

Period	Politics	Economy
1930–42	Repression	Depression and recovery
1942–49	Occupation, revolution	Catastrophic decline
1950–59	Party politics	Rehabilitation
1959–66	Guided Democracy	Decline; macroeconomic chaos

THE 1930s DEPRESSION

Foreign trade

The Depression of the 1930s was the most severe global economic crisis of the 20th century. Its trigger was the collapse on New York's Wall Street stock exchange in October 1929, which within months flowed through to loss of confidence in the real economy, with declining orders and investment. This economic contraction accelerated the decline in commodity prices (Table 6.1; Indisch Verslag 1940: 360). Rapid growth in world production had caused prices to weaken after the mid-1920s, well before the actual Depression. Export values held up only because of growth in volume, which exacerbated the fall in prices. When world demand shrank after 1929, the impact on commodity prices was catastrophic. The countries hardest hit by the Depression were those heavily dependent on the export of primary products. That included colonies like the Netherlands Indies and Malaya alongside developed, rich countries like Australia and Canada. Even in the case of sugar and rubber, of which the Netherlands Indies was a leading supplier, there was little scope to force up prices by withholding supply. International restrictions on output were either too late or ineffectual.

Prices and real incomes

Relative to the great decline in export prices, the overall impact of the Depression on the Netherlands Indies seems to have been rather mild. In the USA and Canada, the epicentre of the crisis, real GDP fell almost one-third below the 1929 peak. The experience of the Netherlands Indies was close to that of Australia, where real GDP fell almost 10% (Gregory 1988). According to the estimates of Van der Eng, by 1934 real GDP had fallen almost 10% below 1929 and GDP per capita 16% below the 1928/30

Table 6.1   Impact of the Depression on commodity prices, 1923–1936

Commodity	Maximum Year	Price	1929 price	Minimum Year	Price	Minimum/ 1929 (%)
Rubber	1925	1.74	0.54	1932	0.08	15
Copra	1925	30.7	23.3	1934	4.75	20
Coffee	1925	105.2	89.6	1932	19.8	22
Sugar	1923	28.4	13.7	1934	3.7	27
Tin	1925	336.9	243.4	1932	115.7	47

Average wholesale prices at Jakarta, Semarang and Surabaya, guilders per 100 kg.

Table 6.2 GDP per capita, 1928/30–1941		
	GDP per capita	Index
1928/30 average	289	100
1931	264	91
1932	255	88
1933	248	86
1934	244	84
1935	250	86
1936	264	91
1937	285	98
1938	287	99
1939	284	98
1940	301	104
1941	309	107
Rp. 000, 1983 prices, oil at shadow price.		

average (Table 6.2; Van der Eng 2001). The sudden and bizarre crisis of the late 1990s was far worse: real GDP per capita fell by almost as much in 1998 alone, and was accompanied by 80% inflation that eroded living standards for a large part of the population (Chapter 7). What made the 1930s Depression so severe was not so much its magnitude as its duration and global impact.

Several reasons can be adduced why the Netherlands Indies suffered less than might have been expected for a small, open economy. First, the switch in imports from European to cheaper Japanese goods after the yen devaluation of December 1931 cushioned the decline in the terms of trade. Second, although the Dutch government resisted devaluation until 1936, the Netherlands Indies price level measured in Jakarta roughly halved over this period (CKS 1947: 122). The Java rice price index was by 1936 only 36% of its 1929 level (Creutzberg 1978: table 1). This deflation restored international competitiveness while cushioning the decline in real income. Third, on balance the colonial government stimulated the economy. The official aim of policy was to balance the budget, which had been more or less in balance in 1928 and was restored to surplus in 1936. However, the timing of expenditure reductions was important. Because expenditure cuts lagged behind the contraction in revenues (see Figure 5.2), the crude budget deficit actually rose to a peak of 26% in 1932 and was still 20% in 1933 (Creutzberg 1976). By the time the deficit reduction program began to bite, the government was stimulating the economy in another way by switching expenditure from imports to domestic production of manufactures and foodstuffs (Booth 1998a). Even if this timing was fortuitous, the benefits were nonetheless real. Unlike some Western countries, the Netherlands Indies was spared fiscal deflation during the worst phase of economic downturn. It was also relevant that in the 1930s the Netherlands Indies was a much less monetised economy than Western primary producing nations, and therefore less vulnerable to the monetary shocks and loss of confidence that hit so hard, for example, at the American economy.

Income distribution

The most important long-run consequence of the Depression was not the loss in GDP per capita, which was recovered by 1941 (Table 6.2), but the redistribution of income and accelerated structural change. The redistribution of income was a product of complex interactions. An immediate effect was loss of wage employment, especially in the plantation and urban manufacturing sectors. However, the large part of the workforce remained in wage employment and enjoyed rising real wages, because food prices fell much more than the modest decline in money wages (CKS 1947: 125; Booth 1998a: 110–11). A shift in demand towards cheaper goods and services boosted employment opportunities in a growing small-scale sector, in activities as diverse as urban public transport, street hawkers and *prahu* shipping. On Java subsistence incomes may have risen somewhat as the sugar plantations released irrigated riceland, though the land tax burden seems also to have risen (Booth 1980). In the Outer Islands the foreign exchange earnings of smallholders were taxed under the International Rubber Restriction Scheme (Touwen 1997: 260–301).

In terms of spatial redistribution, the salient feature of the 1930s was the sharp drop in Java's share of colonial exports. From 1913 until 1929 Java and the Outer Islands had each contributed about half of exports. By 1939 Java contributed only one-third, the Outer Islands two-thirds. This shift was due primarily to the contraction of the Java-based sugar industry, but the Outer Islands also improved their share of rubber, coffee, tea and copra exports while enjoying buoyant demand for oil products and tin (see Figures 5.4 and 5.6). Import shares, however, remained virtually unchanged, at two-thirds to Java and one-third to the Outer Islands. After Independence, Java's claims on the foreign exchange of the Outer Islands would become politically explosive.

The other important spatial feature was the emergence of Jakarta as the economic centre of Indonesia. From the Cultivation System of the 1830s until the 1920s, East and Central Java had been the heartland of Java's plantation economy, but by the 1920s the land frontier had closed. Further export development had to come from intensification. In West Java, however, jungle could still be cleared for rubber and tea plantations. In the 1930s West Java was least affected by the contraction of the sugar industry and most able to benefit from the recovery in rubber prices. It also benefited from proximity to the rubber and coffee districts of Lampung and South Sumatra. The impact can be seen from trade figures by main port. In 1929 Surabaya was Java's leading port for both imports and exports; 10 years later it had been eclipsed by Jakarta (CKS 1928–1940). Because of faster growth in purchasing power, Jakarta also led Surabaya in industrial development (see below).

The Japanese challenge

Well before Dutch rule collapsed like a house of cards in 1942, there had already occurred a decisive shift in the economic balance of power. The 'Japanese threat' was the *leitmotif* of foreign economic policy and diplomacy for the decade before the Pacific War. Fear of Japanese expansion among the European population, apprehension by the Chinese in light of events in their homeland, and a vague sense of shared pan-Asian destiny among Indonesian intellectuals also helped to shape identities in this tense final decade.

Japanese trade with the Netherlands Indies began to boom during World War I. Interruption of European exports and, after 1917, the Allied blockade of Dutch shipping, allowed Japan unchallenged access to the colonial market. Its share of imports rose to 12% by 1920 and almost maintained that share during the next decade. The yen's December 1931 devaluation of almost 60% against the US dollar and guilder made Japanese goods extremely competitive in the Netherlands Indies, as elsewhere in Asia. Japan's share of imports soared to a peak of 32% in 1934, exceeding that of the Netherlands, Britain and Germany combined. European textiles were all but driven from the market. Japanese goods also dominated pottery, bicycles and motorcycles, glassware and cement.

Official reaction was at first sanguine, on the grounds that cheap Japanese imports were a cushion against falling living standards. Dutch manufacturers, however, sought protection to regain lost markets and Dutch trading houses panicked that their vertically integrated distribution system was being undermined by an exclusive Japanese system of direct distribution from cities and towns to rural villages. The Dutch saw themselves as losing control of their colonial economy (Taselaar 1998). In a world increasingly organised in trading blocs, there was also concern at the soaring deficit in bilateral trade with Japan, which was not compensated by any increased demand for Netherlands Indies exports.

The policy response was the Crisis Import Ordinance (*Crisisinvoerordonnantie*), of September 1933, which gave the colonial government powers to impose quotas on categories of imports and to discriminate by country of origin (*Staatsblad* 1933: no. 349). 'General' quotas were set according to 'normal' (i.e. pre-Depression) levels, and these were supplemented for many items by 'specific' quotas according to country of origin (Saroso 1951). Publicly the government denied any discrimination but it was an open secret that the aim was to blunt the Japanese trade offensive and to restore the market share of local and Dutch manufacturers. For example, between 1932 and 1936 cement imports from Japan were reduced from 96.5% to 58% and cambric imports from 81% to 42.5%, while Japanese sarongs were almost shut out of the market. By 1937, assisted by the Chinese boycott in protest against the Japanese invasion of China, Japan's overall share of imports had been cut from 32% to 15%.

The quota system provoked fierce protests from Japan, leading in June 1934 to formal trade negotiations in Jakarta. At stake was not only Japan's share of Netherlands Indies imports but also the colonial distribution system, with the Dutch insisting that no more than 25% of Japanese imports be handled direct through Japanese resident in the colony. A third issue was the falling share of the Dutch-flag shipping on the Japan–Indonesia route. After tough and protracted negotiations, the Hart-Ichizawa agreement was signed in April 1937.

These trade disputes and negotiations marked a decisive and permanent shift in the economic balance of power between the Netherlands and Japan. Relieved of the burden of an overvalued exchange rate, Japanese firms could undersell European manufactures in Asia because they produced at lower unit cost and enjoyed lower margins on ocean transport and vertically integrated, direct distribution. The Dutch, like the British, French and Americans, could hold Japanese competition at bay by import tariffs and quotas, but only at the cost of reducing already modest purchasing power and raising the unit cost of primary exports. What made it harder for the Dutch than the British was that most Netherlands Indies exports were sold in unprotected markets and were therefore price-sensitive. Even without the Pacific War, the Dutch would have faced a difficult choice. The logic of the import–export economy was to maintain free trade and accept the growing economic dominance of Japan, so that ultimately the Dutch would have become landlords in a Japanese sphere of influence. The alternative was to abandon free trade and develop the cheap labour of the Netherlands Indies to produce manufactures in competition with Japan, thereby breaking the nexus of colonial dependence. Despite much discussion of closer economic cooperation between the Netherlands and its colony, the orientation of the two economies had become so different that no more than a marginal impact could be expected (Taselaar 1998: 462).

Structural change/industrialisation

In the large-scale industrial sector, the impact of the Depression was absorbed in reduced utilisation and employment. Industries that relied heavily on investment spending bore the brunt. On Java, and especially in Surabaya, the metals and machinery industry suffered acutely, because its main customer, the plantation sector, ceased investment and cut maintenance to the bare minimum, cannibalising idle plant. In 1932 the government brought forward some capital works programs, such as rail bridge replacement, and switched orders from the Netherlands to the Netherlands Indies, but this brought little relief (EWNI 25/1/47: 63). N.V. Braat, the largest engineering firm, saw turnover collapse from 6.3 million guilders in 1929 to less than 1 million in 1933, while the workforce was reduced to one-quarter of its normal size. The Surabaya Drydock Company reduced its workforce by two-thirds and work at the Naval Base was cut back to a minimum. No steady recovery was apparent in this sector until 1936.

After 1933, manufacturing output began to recover because of the new protection. Although the primary aim of quotas was to protect the market for the exports of Dutch industry against cheap Japanese goods, they also gave protection to local manufacturers. The Crisis Import Ordinance of 1933 was followed in 1934 by the Industry Regulations, which provided a legal basis for the introduction of capacity controls on industry to prevent 'destructive' competition (Van Oorschot 1956: 46). Capacity restrictions were also placed on machine-made white cigarettes to assist small-scale *kretek* (clove) manufacturers.

On welfare grounds, the government took measures to develop small-scale industry. The Textile Institute in Bandung (founded in 1919) had in 1926 produced an improved handloom with a capacity seven times greater than existing handlooms; in 1930 there followed a simple machine loom with a capacity four times greater again (Van Oorschot 1956: 43). Protection created a climate for the rapid diffusion of these 'appropriate technologies' throughout Java. In 1936 the government took a further step with the establishment of small industry centres (*centrales* — later known as *induk*) to upgrade technology and management. These initiatives were nevertheless too few and on too small a scale to have more than localised impact.

The most dramatic effect of the new protection was the emergence of a modern textile industry. There was strong demand for locally woven sarongs. In 1930 there were just 500 modern handlooms; by 1941 there were 49 000, mostly in West Java, plus 9800 machine looms (Sitsen 1943: 33). The large majority of mills had fewer than 15 looms, but a few were large enterprises (Rhyne 1954: 341). The Mualim mill near Surabaya was reported in February 1938 to have 2000 handlooms plus 350 second-hand machine looms from Japan and at full capacity employed 4000 workers, mainly women (Rothe 1938: 8–9).

Industrial development was most rapid in West Java. Contraction of the sugar industry depressed consumer purchasing power in East Java, whereas West Java benefited from the more buoyant rubber and tea plantations and from the proximity of Sumatra (Ziesel 1939: 54). Apart from textiles around Bandung, foreign investors established several new industries in the environs of Jakarta, including automobiles (General Motors), rubber tyres (Goodyear), margarine (Unilever), shoes (Bata), batteries and biscuits. Firms hitherto based in East Java such as paint and soap manufacturers also opened plants. The industrial centre of gravity therefore shifted west, especially for consumer goods industries. One rough indicator is the consumption by industry of electrical power: in 1938 and 1939 the level of consumption in West Java was double that in East Java (EWNI 16/5/41: 832–3). New projects in the late 1930s included light bulbs, bicycles, glycerine, vehicle assembly, confectionery, metal fittings, rubber sandals, coconut oil and soap. Most of these projects drew on Dutch capital but there were also American and Japanese ventures (NIF 10/38; NHM 1944: 75).

This burst of late colonial industrialisation resulted in striking gains from a very low base. Booth (1998a) argues that the best evidence is that the manufacturing share of GDP jumped, from 8% to 12% between 1931 and 1939. Much import substitution was achieved in a short time, albeit in a fairly narrow range of goods. By 1938 the Netherlands Indies was almost self-sufficient in cigarettes, frying pans, paint, toiletries, beer, shoes and confectionery; there was also significant local production of biscuits, margarine, batteries, and bicycles (NHM 1944: 40, 121). Under the quota system, much of these gains had been at the expense of Japanese imports. In the case of textiles, however, the level of self-sufficiency was still a mere 6%.

Protection, import substitution and controls were also extended to food crop agriculture. Until the world Depression, the colonial government had followed a cheap labour policy that sought to keep the price of rice low and to rely on imports to feed both the main cities and plantation and mining districts in the Outer Islands. Import prices then fell so low that in 1933 restrictive import licences and an import duty were imposed to support domestic agriculture (Creutzberg 1974). Rice self-sufficiency was achieved in 1936 (Van der Eng 1994b: 7). Measures were taken with some success to encourage domestic production of maize, cassava and soybeans. Formed successively to promote agricultural exports, the Coffee Fund (*Koffiefonds* 1937), Kapok Fund (*Kapokfonds* 1938) and Copra Fund (*Coprafonds* 1940) in the emergency conditions of 1940 took full control of buying and export (EWNI 18/10/41). In April 1939, as the international situation deteriorated, a Foodstuffs Fund (*Voedingsmiddelenfonds*) was also set up to protect food supplies; it quickly took on price stabilisation functions that foreshadowed the New Order's logistics agency, Bulog.

After the outbreak of World War II, domestic demand shifted back to local heavy industry for the first time since 1920. The Netherlands Indies was now again reliant on local production. In expectation of war with Japan, the Army and Navy placed urgent local contracts for items from basic field equipment such as helmets, gas masks, flasks and stainless steel kettles to armoured cars, tanks and minesweepers (EWNI 25/1/47: 63). Suddenly it was a sellers' market. However, because equipment and raw materials were unavailable or had to be shipped from the USA, installation was delayed into 1941 and many contracts were never completed. Nevertheless, for two years heavy industry, especially the metal and machinery and chemical industries, operated at full capacity. The boom was reflected in the overall level of economic activity. According to Van der Eng's revised figures, GDP per capita grew 6% in 1940 and 3% in 1941 (Table 6.2). Within such a short time, however, little investment was possible and, as during World War I, there was no long-term gain in industrial capability.

A similar fate befell the crash program announced by the Netherlands Indies government in 1940 for the development of heavy industry, including aluminium (Asahan), chemicals such as caustic soda, sulphuric acid, saltpetre and ammonia, cellulose, glass, spinning mills and a new cement plant (EWNI 9/5/41: 719–20). Planning to free the Netherlands Indies from dependence on foreign supplies of essential industrial inputs had begun in the mid-1930s, when the military threat from Japan became a serious concern, and was accelerated after the fall of the Netherlands (Taselaar 1998: 472–502). The estimated cost of the program was 50 million guilders, of which the government put forward 10 million under the 1941 budget (NHM 1944: 139). In the event none of these projects was completed — few were even commenced — before the outbreak of the Pacific War. The significance of the crash program is that the colonial government thereby moved beyond the protection of mainly light consumer goods industries to large-scale investment in industrial inputs, what are now known as 'upstream' industries. During World War I the colonial government had by default left it to the market to bring forth investment. In 1940 it took the initiative, and thereby foreshadowed a pattern of public intervention and emphasis on heavy industry that would be perpetuated after Independence.

Industrialisation consolidated the tightly knit structure of colonial capital. In the face of strong Japanese competition, Dutch firms clawed back control over the colonial economy and laid solid institutional foundations for rapid industrialisation. The entrepreneurial drive was provided by a small number of large colonial banks, trading houses and management agencies plus some direct foreign investors (see also Chapter 5). Especially prominent were the 'Big Five' trading houses, which provided capital and technical advice and looked after distribution of the product (NHM 1944). Behind the private sector was the economic general staff of the Department of Economic Affairs, formed in 1933 from the more loosely coordinated Department of Agriculture, Industry and Trade (Van Gelderen 1939; Hart 1942; EWNI 18/10/41, 6/12/41).[1] By 1941 it had moved beyond directing the economy to economic mobilisation with a panoply of controls, including capacity licensing, price controls (1939) and foreign exchange controls (1940). The Trade Section alone, which in 1933 had only 20 staff, now numbered 1000 (including the various funds) (EWNI 18/10/41: 1974). Had the Japanese invasion not eliminated Dutch political and economic power, it is plausible that in the 1940s the Netherlands Indies could have begun the kind of sustained industrial expansion that eventually occurred in the 1970s. In that event Indonesia — and Java in particular — would have led Southeast Asia's industrialisation. Instead, these institutional advantages were lost in the process of decolonisation. What did survive and grow into a monster was the emergency wartime model of an all-powerful, all-directing economic bureaucracy.

THE JAPANESE OCCUPATION, 1942–1945

The Japanese occupation of March 1942 to August 1945 is usually viewed as a tide of events in which Indonesia was swept along with the rest of Southeast Asia. The truth is more complex. Control of Indonesia's resources, in particular its oilfields, was Japan's rationale for the Pacific War. Although Japan had abundant coal deposits, neither its own islands nor its colonial empire produced oil. Once Japan launched its full-scale invasion of China in July 1937, the strategic constraint became apparent. The air force in particular was dependent on the continued import of high-octane fuel, the supply of which could no longer be regarded as secure against rising anti-Japanese feeling in the USA and Britain. After the German occupation of the Netherlands in May 1940, Japanese demanded much increased shipments of oil, rubber, bauxite and other strategic materials, leading in September 1940 to a new round of commercial negotiations. The Netherlands Indies government, which since 1940 had been party with local oil producers Shell and Stanvac to top-level negotiations in the USA and Britain, stonewalled until the Japanese broke off negotiations in June 1941 (Anderson 1975; Goto 1997: 59). A month later, after the fall of France, Japan moved troops into southern Indochina, the USA retaliated with a de facto oil embargo, and the Netherlands Indies followed suit (Van Mook 1944). Indonesia then became a prime military target.

Defence of the Netherlands Indies was precariously dependent on the USA and Great Britain, neither of whom retained a substantial navy or air force in the region (Gill 1957). All hopes rested on the perceived impregnability of Singapore and the strength of the US Pacific Fleet based at Pearl Harbor (Hawaii). The latter was eliminated by the surprise air strike on 7 December 1941, whereupon the Governor-General followed the USA in declaring war. No-one believed that the small Dutch forces with token Allied reinforcements could offer firm resistance. Belated attempts to enlist nationalist parties in defence of the colony came to nought. Desperate as they now were, the Dutch, unlike the British in India, were still not prepared to make political concessions, let alone to hand over weapons to the nationalists (Abeyasekere 1976). The blows soon fell. Japanese naval forces seized the oilfields of Tarakan on 12 January 1942, then Balikpapan (Gill 1957: 529–36). In mid-February, the fall of Singapore and the seizure of the Palembang oilfields and refinery in South Sumatra occurred almost simultaneously. With the Japanese occupying South Sumatra, South Kalimantan, South Sulawesi and Bali, Java was trapped in a Japanese vice. Air raids become increasingly frequent. Japan's naval triumph in the Battle of the Java Sea was followed on 1 March by landings in both West and East Java, whereupon the Dutch began systematically to destroy all surviving military and oil installations. Within barely a week the Dutch had ignominiously capitulated. The occupying Japanese forces were welcomed as liberators by many among the Indonesian population.

Over the next few months Dutch power was eradicated. Indonesia, as it now became known, was divided into three separate military administrations. The Sixteenth Army had arrived in Java with no specific guidelines as to how to govern its new territories, little detailed knowledge of them, and only 200 civilians to supplement the existing consular staff (Sato 1994: 10–12, 22). Of necessity the Japanese had therefore to rely on the existing administration. Before fleeing to Australia, senior colonial officials had urged Dutch civilians to remain at their posts, which could have led to a situation akin to Indochina, where the French colonial administration continued to govern on Japan's behalf (Sato 1994: 23). In fact, no working relationship was established and by late April all but a handful of Dutch officials had joined their military colleagues in internment camps (Van Dulm et al. 2000). They were replaced by Indonesians, who enjoyed sudden promotion by amalgamation of the Dutch bureaucracy (*Binnenlands Bestuur*) with the indigenous *pangreh praja* (Sato 1994: 26). Later, in 1944 this structure was extended down to the level of the neighbourhood association (now *rukun tetangga*, RT). The Dutch language was banned in favour of Japanese and Malay. Batavia became Djakarta, Buitenzorg became Bogor, streets were renamed. Chinese identified as Kuomintang supporters were arrested and in parts of the Outer Islands, especially Kalimantan, Chinese community leaders were killed; on Java the Chinese and Japanese managed to coexist (Goto 1997: 416–19).

Despite this taste of freedom, Indonesians discovered within months that they had exchanged one colonial power for another. The Japanese turned out to be more authoritarian than the Dutch. They delegated little real power and insisted on unquestioning obedience, to the point of bowing in the street to Japanese officers. Breaches of the Japanese code of behaviour were met by brutal physical punishment. However, the crushing burden that fell on the Indonesian population was a product of clumsy wartime mobilisation. What people remembered afterwards was first scarcity, especially of food, clothing, and medicines; and second the arbitrary requisition of forced labour and the appalling conditions under which people were made to work.

The causes of economic decline were structural and institutional. Physical damage was not the main problem, because Japanese bombing had been confined to military targets and last-minute Dutch sabotage was neither systematic nor effective. Rather, the colonial economy was like a sophisticated machine suddenly driven hard by an untrained crew. By 1942 Japan itself had become a controlled economy in which the power of the large business conglomerates (*zaibatsu*) was much circumscribed in the interest of wartime mobilisation. In view of the urgency, this was the obvious model to apply to the newly occupied colony. Thus industries were organised into guilds (*kumiai*) under government supervision. Responsibility for distribution was allocated to Japanese trading houses such as Mitsui with local networks. Production had to be drastically reorganised to meet the needs of the Japanese war effort. Most of the output of plantations and smallholders, the *raison d'être* of the colonial economy, was suddenly redundant. The main aim was no longer to extract commodities, for apart from a few strategic commodities such as oil, rubber and quinine, Japan's needs could be met from closer sources of supply. Instead policy sought to minimise the demands on imports and shipping by promoting regional self-sufficiency in food and manufactures.

Java and Malaya were seen as the only regions in the southern part of Southeast Asia able to meet the demand for more sophisticated manufactures (Miyamoto 1986: 237). Ambitious targets were set for a wide range of basic items, of which textiles were a key sector. Towards the end of 1942 a five-year plan was introduced to develop cotton cultivation in East and Central Java (Sutter 1959: 157, 160–1). However, local cotton cultivation was a failure and the worsening shipping shortage meant that almost no raw cotton could be imported. The military authorities drew on the huge stockpile of textiles confiscated from the Dutch, while denying them for civilian use (Miyamoto 1986: 248–9; Frederick 1989: 127–8, n. 147). The Indonesian population had to make do with gunny sacks. A widespread and angry recollection of the Japanese occupation was of having to dress in worn-out rags.

To overcome the shipping crisis, another high priority was shipbuilding, specifically small wooden-hulled motor vessels powered by locally manufactured diesel engines (Sutter 1959: 145). Because of its teak plantations, engineering capability and supply of skilled labour, Java was to be the main centre of production (Miyamoto 1986). Timber was cut ruthlessly, but production of hulls and engines fell far below targets (Sutter 1959: 197; Miyamoto 1986). By 1944 Allied submarines were relentlessly sinking the Japanese merchant fleet, not only preventing proper communication between Japan and Southeast Asia but also interrupting the flow of goods and raw materials, even between adjacent islands.

Food supply ought not to have been a problem for the Japanese administration. In 1941 the Netherlands Indies had been self-sufficient in rice and Java produced a considerable surplus, which the Japanese sought by various measures to increase (Kurasawa 1993; Van der Eng 1994b). In 1939 the colonial government had set up a Foodstuffs Fund to maintain floor prices and a buffer stock, for which in 1941 it bought up 22% of the crop (Mears 1961; Sato 1994: 116). The Japanese extended delivery quotas from surplus districts to every residency, while maintaining floor prices at the mill as an incentive to farmers to increase production. In fact production fell and delivery quotas were not met, despite increasing administrative pressure. Van der Eng (1994b) points to falling real purchase prices and the growing black market trade. Sato (1994) emphasises the virtual disappearance of trade goods, even textiles, and the great difficulties of local transport. With echoes of the Cultivation System, there was a reversion to handcarts and even human porterage. Labour mobilisation (see below) also affected food production. During 1943 officials banned private rice trade from surplus districts, depressing rice prices and further discouraging production (Sato 1994: 129–36). Without their usual imports, deficit areas were hard-pressed to meet rigid purchase quotas. In 1944 the situation became critical because of a prolonged dry season. Signs of famine appeared in some districts, especially in Madura and Indramayu (Sato 1994: 122). On average, in 1944 and 1945 calorie and protein intake seems to have been only two-thirds that of 1942 (Van der Eng 1994b: A3.1). Natural causes therefore played their part, but it was mainly administrative incompetence that within three years turned Java from a rice exporter into an island of hunger. The Outer Islands reverted to a subsistence mode of production. In the plantation districts of North Sumatra, workers planted out food crops, a right which they defended staunchly after Independence (Pelzer 1978, 1982).

In response to shortages, stringent rationing was introduced over most basic consumer items, especially food and textiles. As a means of control, registration was linked to the newly formed neighbourhood associations. The daily ration of rice was set nominally at only 200 grams per adult, with the balance of carbohydrate made up of corn and soybean (Soeparto Brata 1983). Only sugar, which no longer had an export market, was in plentiful supply. Urban dwellers therefore had just enough to eat, even if they could not enjoy their preferred diet. Small entrepreneurs seized opportunities to make articles such as softdrinks, soy sauce and toothpaste that were no longer available through normal channels (Frederick 1989: 102). Substitution also occurred in public transport. The commandeering of private motor vehicles created a niche for a new kind of vehicle, the *becak* (pedicab). What people could not obtain through rationing they tried to obtain on the black market.

No aspect of the Japanese occupation left more bitter memories than the forced labour (Kurasawa 1993). By November 1944 some 2.6 million Javanese were working as forced labourers (*romusha*) out of a total workforce of around 25 million. However, allowing for the turnover of temporary labourers and other work such as transportation services, Sato (Sato 1994: 157–9) suggests that well over half of the able-bodied male population of Java and Madura was at some stage affected by this 'total mobilisation'. Of these, no more than 200 000 seem to have been sent beyond Java. Most worked on labour-intensive construction projects on Java. Food rations were restricted to 250 grams of rice per day, health conditions were appalling and Japanese supervision brutal and inflexible. Some ran away. A large but unknown number died. And, like the notorious Thai–Burma railway, some of the biggest projects turned out to be a complete waste (Sato 1994).

Despite the Japanese declaration in 1944 of a New Economic Order, the reality was that Java was being impoverished by the unrealistic requirements of the Japanese war machine. Results were uneven but, because of so many bottlenecks in supply, industrial production must have fallen below prewar levels, at least as far as the factory sector was concerned. Propaganda drives to meet plan targets merely highlighted the problem. The reality was that if Japanese procurement targets could not be met from increased production, they were squeezed from reduced consumption. Those who suffered most were to be found in food-deficit districts; those in surplus districts survived somewhat better. Urban dwellers suffered least: their food supply was guaranteed, however minimally, by rationing, while there was also less risk of recruitment for forced labour and better job opportunities. The cities therefore became places of refuge, even for beggars. Between 1940 and 1945, Jakarta increased in population from about 600 000 to almost 850 000, Surabaya from around 400 000 to about 600 000 (Abeyasekere 1987: 140–1; Steele 1980: 58–9).

The brief but tumultuous period of Japanese rule proved once again that a command system could not manage the vast and complex economies that constituted Indonesia. That same lesson had been learned by the Dutch from the experience of the Cultivation System; but, knowing nothing of this history, the Japanese attempted to force the economic system into reverse. This futile experiment, which Kurasawa (1993) identifies as (economic) mobilisation and (political and social) control, had no evolutionary benefit. The suspension of international trade and the reversion to self-sufficiency involved a heavy loss in productive efficiency through sacrifice of the gains from specialisation. The human cost was compounded by administrative stupidity, arbitrary brutality and the burden of 'prestige projects'. Mass mobilisation of labour by the exercise of absolute power led to people being treated like cattle. In the end not even the food supply could be guaranteed. People starved, and in that condition succumbed to disease, including malaria, which again became rampant. The long dry season in 1944/45 became a calamity. Unfortunately the lessons were not learned. The Japanese occupation encouraged bureaucrats to believe that they had a responsibility to direct (*mengatur*) economic forces. At the same time, the proliferation of black markets, smuggling and corruption made the market economy much more chaotic.

Politically, however, the Japanese period was a watershed. For three and a half years the archipelago had been released from Dutch colonial rule, and during this time nationalist leaders and radical youth had begun to prepare for a future Indonesian nation. Some had gained experience in government or as officers in the auxiliary army PETA (*Pembela Tanah Air*). Many youth had joined mass organisations such as the Youth Corps (*Seinendan*) or Vigilante Corps (*Keibodan*) (Anderson 1972; Reid 1974). Neighbourhood associations (*tonarigumi* or *rukun tetangga*), introduced in 1944 as the lowest unit in the system of political control had strengthened local organisation (Kurasawa 1993; Cribb 1991: 40–1). In the final months, as defeat loomed, influential Japanese gave covert support to the nationalist movement. The prevailing mood was that there would be no return to Dutch rule.

NATIONAL REVOLUTION

Despite haphazard terror and general deprivation, Indonesia escaped comparatively lightly from the Pacific War. The rough calculations of Van der Eng (1992) based on agricultural output suggest that by 1945 income per capita may have fallen to about half the 1938 level (see Figure 1 in the Introduction), which would be comparable with the decline suffered by Japan itself (Uchino 1983). Damage to human and physical capital, however, was fairly light, in marked contrast with the Philippines, where the American reconquest and Japanese resistance exacted a horrific price. The only parts of the Indonesian archipelago that were the target of Allied military operations were the oilfields of Tarakan and Balikpapan and remote parts of Eastern Indonesia. On Java, Allied bombing caused only superficial damage to port facilities, military installations and factories. Perhaps the most severe dislocation was the sinking of most of the modern interisland shipping fleet. Otherwise, war damage to productive capacity was fairly light, worse problems being lack of maintenance and Japanese depredations, including removal of equipment. Total loss and damage was estimated at four billion guilders, requiring a period of rehabilitation to restore normal peacetime conditions (Fruin 1947).

Instead Indonesia, and especially Java, was convulsed for over four years by a bitter armed struggle. For Dutch leaders in exile, the restoration of colonial rule was not problematic. The Netherlands Indies was a colonial territory and its return was part of Allied planning. Allied forces would accept the Japanese surrender and release prisoners-of-war; as ships and men became available the Dutch would restore their efficient and benevolent colonial administration with vague promises of eventual self-government. None of these confident plans anticipated that Indonesian leaders, having tasted a degree of freedom and self-government under the Japanese, would declare Independence on 17 August 1945.

British officers landed at Jakarta on 29 September 1945, some six weeks after the Surrender in Tokyo, to find an Indonesian administration in control of the city. Indonesian leaders allowed the British to accept the surrender of Japanese forces and repatriate prisoners-of-war but the release of Dutch internees quickly led to violent skirmishes (Anderson 1972; Cribb 1991). In Surabaya, where the Japanese garrison had been disarmed by the local people, there was a pitched battle with British troops and assassination of the British commander (Frederick 1989). A British counterattack marked the first battle of the revolution, and paved the way for the return of the Netherlands Indies Civilian Administration (NICA), which on 30 November 1946 took over full authority (George 1980: 63). However, both Jakarta (now again known as Batavia) and Surabaya remained cities under siege, tiny Dutch enclaves in hostile Republican territory. Between January and March 1947 the Dutch gradually pushed out their perimeter, before in July launching a first military offensive (*Politionele Actie* or *Agresi*

Pertama) against Republican territory. It was so sudden and swift that most infrastructure and crops were captured without damage. The Republican government retreated to Yogyakarta in Central Java.

A division of Java between Dutch and Republican forces was confirmed in the Renville Agreement of January 1948, and the Dutch could soon congratulate themselves on the rapid rehabilitation of the vital export economy. Sugar mills and upland estates were reoccupied, a good harvest brought down rice prices, rice mills resumed operation, vegetables became more plentiful and fishponds were restocked. Rail services were gradually restored throughout much of the island. Bungalows were reoccupied in the hill resorts. Confident of their strength and believing that guerilla activity could be overcome by a final knock-out blow, on the night of 18 December 1948 the Dutch broke the ceasefire by launching a second 'Police Action' to seize all remaining Republican territory, including the capital of Yogyakarta. Militarily they achieved all objectives but found themselves occupying a much larger area than they could control. The southern hills became a kind of Ho Chi Minh trail, along which Indonesian guerillas could infiltrate the whole island (Nasution 1983a).

The strategic imperative in the two Dutch military actions was to regain control of the plantations and generate a flow of commodities and hard currency for rehabilitation of the Netherlands. In 1945 the Netherlands needed the lifebelt of colonial revenues as desperately as in 1830. The flaw in the Dutch military strategy was the vulnerability of these plantations to guerilla action. During the second offensive, Indonesian forces put much more effort into sabotage. Sugar mills and other plantations suffered more damage at this time than at the hands of the Japanese. Those recaptured intact had soon to be abandoned. Hill stations and road and rail traffic also became targets. Cooperating members of the 'native' civil service (*pamong praja*) were assassinated, paralysing the Dutch administration. The Dutch became bottled up in the towns, able to move only in daylight and even then not always in safety. This was very bad business. A negotiated settlement would have yielded a much better dividend.

Outer Islands   Despite fierce armed struggles in North Sumatra and South Sulawesi, the Dutch occupied most of the sparsely populated Outer Islands without much resistance. Sumatra was the richest prize because of its foreign exchange revenues. However, its coastline was so long, and access across the Straits of Malacca so easy, that enforcing a blockade was a huge task for the Dutch even after they had gained military control. And the British, who ultimately had assisted in restoring Dutch rule on Java, in Sumatra worked to frustrate it. Their prime concern was to restore the entrepôt trade of Singapore, especially the rubber trade of Sumatra and Kalimantan. Chinese traders in Singapore were sold cheap surplus military craft for conversion to commercial use. During 1946 and 1947 these vessels, sailing under the protection of the British flag, carried on a barter trade in a cat-and-mouse game with the Dutch navy (Twang 1998). Vessels were seized but the trade continued. After the second 'Police Action' of December 1948, however, only Aceh remained free of Dutch control.

Apart from securing foreign exchange, the Dutch strategy was to unite the Outer Islands in a federation of nominally self-governing states unbeholden to Republican Java (Schiller 1955). Sumatra was divided into several states, Kalimantan was another, and the largest and probably most successful was Eastern Indonesia (*Negara Indonesia Timur*), with its capital in Makassar. When it came to the choice, however, the states sided with the Republic.

FRUSTRATED EXPECTATIONS, 1950–1965

From the transfer of sovereignty in December 1949 to formation of the Ampera Cabinet in March 1966, Indonesia was preoccupied with politics. A period which began with high hopes ended in economic crisis, fear and bloodbath. That catastrophe, which gave rise to the contrived stability of the New Order, cast a dark shadow over the entire preceding period, which was rejected as the 'Old Order'. This crude periodisation is unworkable. History may be written after the event but the narrative need not be reversed. The phases of parliamentary democracy (1950–1958) and Guided Democracy (1959–1966) were as distinct as their different constitutions.

The terms of independence

Indonesia and Vietnam were the first colonies in Asia to declare independence, but the Philippines (1946), India (1947), Burma (1948) and Sri Lanka (1948) reached nationhood before international recognition was achieved in December 1949. Unlike any of these contemporaries, Indonesia's sovereignty was compromised by the stiff terms which the Dutch exacted at the preceding Round Table Conference. Reluctantly forced to concede independence by American threats to suspend NATO and Marshall Plan aid, the Dutch government directed its efforts to safeguarding its financial and economic interests. Indonesia contributed 8% to the national income of the Netherlands, and Dutch investments totalled around $1 billion (Meijer 1994: 648–9). This stubborn 'neocolonialism' caused great resentment and poisoned Indonesian–Dutch relations.

Four issues were particularly controversial, two political and two economic. First, the Dutch insisted on a Federation, the Republic of the United States of Indonesia (Republik Indonesia Serikat), in which the Republic, which had borne the brunt of the struggle for independence, was forced into partnership with a Dutch-inspired federation of 15 'puppet' states (Kahin 1952; Feith 1962). This complex arrangement began to unravel almost immediately as states seceded under popular pressure to the Republic. Despite a rebellion in Ambon, the unitary state of the Republic of Indonesia came into being under a revised constitution in August 1950. The second issue, Dutch refusal to transfer sovereignty over West New Guinea (Irian Jaya), proved insoluble and precipitated the complete breakdown of relations in 1958.

On the economic side, the Financial-Economic Agreement (Finec) guaranteed that Dutch firms could enjoy business as usual, including the remittance of profits. There was also an obligation on the Indonesian government to consult with the Netherlands on any monetary and financial measures likely to have an impact on Dutch interests, which was a definite limitation of Indonesian sovereignty (Meijer 1994: 157). Nationalisation of Dutch enterprises required mutual agreement, with compensation to be determined by a judge on the basis of actual worth (Meijer 1994: 46). The Minister of Foreign Affairs congratulated himself that he had secured the maximum protection for Dutch business (Baudet & Fennema 1983: 213).

Finally, the new nation was forced to take over $1.1 billion of public debt, comprising the entire internal debt of the colonial government of three billion guilders plus another 1.5 billion of the 3.5 billion external debt (Clerx 1992: 65). Although Indonesia refused Dutch claims for reimbursement of military outlays, this was still grossly unfair. While the Dutch enjoyed Marshall Plan aid in rebuilding their own country, they imposed what was tantamount to an indemnity on their former colony, at the same time demanding a guarantee to be allowed to continue to draw profits from it. Indonesia's leaders nevertheless saw no choice but to adhere to this obligation. When the Harahap cabinet abrogated the Finec agreements in February 1956, all but 18% of the debt had been paid off (Meijer 1994: 536). No other ex-colony in Asia had to shoulder such a burden, which was a drain on both the state budget and the balance of payments. It dwarfed the $100 million Export-Import Bank credit which was the independence gift from the USA. Had the debt of almost $1 billion been released for development, the economic situation in the mid-1950s would have been much brighter.

A further burden on the Indonesian budget was the obligation to maintain for two years at European pay scales the positions of some 17 000 Dutch officials (Meijer 1994: 169). This led to some uneasy relationships between senior Dutch bureaucrats and Indonesian ministers, whose authority was only grudgingly acknowledged (Higgins 1992: 48). The last senior officials were retired at the end of 1952 but the great shortage of qualified Indonesian officials meant that as late as 1955 there were still some 600 Dutch officials in specialist positions (Meijer 1994: 176). The Indonesian government had also to bear the costs of incorporating 26 000 out of the 65 000 soldiers of the Dutch colonial army (KNIL) into the Indonesian National Army, TNI (*Tentara Nasional Indonesia*), in addition to resettling around 100 000 Republican guerilla fighters who had not been part of the regular forces (Meijer 1994: 199–200). Administration would certainly have suffered if all Dutch personnel had been withdrawn in 1950, but the fact remains that the Netherlands was able to liquidate its colonial establishment largely at Indonesia's expense.

The continued rights and domination of Dutch enterprises in independent Indonesia was an affront to the self-respect of Indonesian nationalists. Most of Indonesia's top leaders were imbued by socialist ideals, as reflected in the Proclamation of Indonesia's Independence on 17 August 1945 and in the Preamble and Article 38 of Indonesia's 1945 Constitution 'to establish a just and prosperous society . . . based on social justice'. Vice-President Moh. Hatta, though regarded as moderate, had strongly espoused cooperatives rather than capitalist firms, especially in the villages, as the basis for a just society. Nevertheless, the main economic policy makers in the early 1950s were also pragmatic politicians, who realised that they could not quickly dismantle the colonial and capitalist economic structure without causing economic dislocation and hardship.

Once in government, leaders were therefore forced to make difficult compromises between restoring economic stability, to the benefit of foreign, private enterprise, and redistributing economic wealth and income to the Indonesian people. At root, it was the perennial dilemma of growth and equity. The Malaysian government faced similar problems in the late 1960s and confronted them with the New Economic Policy (NEP). Indonesian governments in the early 1950s were more circumspect. On the one hand they sought to peg back Dutch economic power by building up large-scale state enterprise (see below); on the other they tried to develop a smaller-scale, indigenous, private business sector. This dual approach also served to reassure the USA, then Indonesia's most powerful patron, that despite its socialist orientation Indonesia really would allow the development of free enterprise.[2]

State formation

The ideology and style of the new government were of the Republic. Above all it was nationalist, the crux of the new sovereignty of the people affirmed by the ongoing struggle with the Dutch. In spirit it was democratic, egalitarian, and secular, values enshrined in the Constitution and Pancasila (Five Principles). With the Ethical Policy the colonial state had accepted an obligation to protect the welfare of its subject people, but for the new nation-state this was its *raison d'être*. The means to that end was socialism. *Laissez-faire* economy had been discredited along with colonialism. Some of the senior ministers had been educated to tertiary level, including the Vice-President, Moh. Hatta, Prof. Sumitro Djojohadikusumo, the Sultan of Yogyakarta, Hamengkubuwono IX, and the Governor of Bank Indonesia, Sjafruddin Prawiranegara. Most senior Indonesian officials, however, were trained as lower- or middle-level bureaucrats. They had little experience of the practical difficulties of policy making, especially in the economic sphere, but a great deal of confidence in their ability to organise by decree.

The bureaucratic and legal system was a heritage of the colonial state, as in the urgency of transition there was no other viable or familiar model. The

rudimentary bureaucracy of the Republic merged into the larger unit, displacing Dutch officials. The legal codes, forms, titles and practices were taken
over almost *in toto* but brought under the Provisional Constitution, whereby
all citizens became equal under official law and customary law (*adat*) virtually lapsed. Bureaucratic and legal continuity should have ensured the consolidation of a strong state. Fatefully this did not happen. First, the new
democratic institutions did not graft easily onto the rigid bureaucratic system.
Second, the armed forces emerged as a rival locus of power.

Under the Provisional Constitution of 1949 (revised 1950), Indonesia
became a constitutional democracy along Dutch lines. The offices of Queen
and Governor-General were merged into a constitutional Presidency, whose
limited role was to convene Parliament and appoint a respected person
(*formateur*) to form a Cabinet. The Executive of Prime Minister and
Cabinet was chosen from and responsible to Parliament. Cabinets were
often brought down by motions of no-confidence in response to shifting
political alliances, giving rise to a good deal of instability, which was not
resolved by the 1955 election. From December 1949 to the formation of
the extra-parliamentary Djuanda Cabinet in April 1957 there were seven
cabinets, few lasting more than a year. Such instability would have been of
no great consequence had the powers of government still been wielded by
a strong bureaucracy. In fact its effectiveness greatly diminished. Contested
by rival political parties, the bureaucracy swelled in size but fragmented
into rival and increasingly corrupt patronage networks.

This growing power vacuum created opportunities for the military. The
Revolution had weakened the institutions of civilian rule but allowed a
National Army, TNI, to emerge as an autonomous political force with
popular legitimacy. After Independence the remnants of the colonial army
(KNIL) were absorbed into the structure and officer corps of the TNI.
During the 1950s this amalgam was gradually rationalised and profession-
alised, despite internal dissension and strong resistance from commands in
the Outer Islands (Nasution 1983b). Nationalist, centralist and authoritarian, its commanders looked with increasing disdain on civilian politicians
and bureaucrats, who were seen as squandering the fruits of the Revolution.
As guardians of the nation, these officers believed themselves under an
obligation to intervene politically in the event of national crisis.

Economic rehabilitation

In 1950 the immediate problems were political, but the crisis of the new
nation was also an economic one. For almost a decade the economy had
languished outside the mainstream of the world economy. These problems
were most apparent in Java, where prolonged neglect and guerilla sabotage
had done great damage to physical infrastructure, not only transport and
communications but also irrigation and power supplies. In the Outer Islands
roads had become impassable, forcing traffic back to waterways. Less

visible and more difficult to assess was the human dislocation. Especially in Java, many lives had been lost and large numbers of people become refugees, subsisting on makeshift employment. The high returns to smuggling and black market dealing, which during the Dutch blockade had been a patriotic duty, also led to breakdown of former social controls. Conscientious bureaucrats who tried to restore order were accused of being old-style colonialists. The background to all these problems was a highly unstable macroeconomic environment. Paauw (1960: 117) observed that 'Indonesia began its independence . . . with inflationary pressures on prices not offset to any significant extent by taxation or voluntary savings'. Rising budget deficits were funded by government borrowing from Bank Indonesia; the increase in money supply fuelled inflation and in turn weakened the balance of payments.

The new Indonesian government had the difficult task of rehabilitating a profoundly dualistic economy. A modern, large-scale sector constituting almost 25% of GDP was still dominated by Dutch firms and some British and American multinationals (Higgins 1992: 51). In 1952 eight Dutch trading firms handled about 60% of consumer goods imports; private banking was also dominated by foreign banks (Glassburner 1971: 78–9). Yet the rural economy was so little commercialised that in 1955 only 9.4% (in 1956 only 6.7%) of rice production in Java and Madura was commercially milled (Mears 1961: 75). Most paddies were still harvested stalk by stalk using the *ani-ani* knife. Villagers seldom travelled further than the nearest market town. In such an economy, the small, fully monetised, modern sector was highly sensitive to monetary and fiscal policy, while the rest of the economy was fairly sluggish. Credit and barter mechanisms via Chinese middlemen were the nexus between the two sectors. Economic theory offered little guidance as to how to manage such an economy, let alone to develop it (Higgins 1992).

At first the new government enjoyed good fortune. Outbreak of the Korean War in June 1950 caused a sudden boom in commodity prices, especially rubber and oil, which at these high prices constituted about two-thirds of export receipts (Paauw 1960: 452). Besides a good surplus on the balance of payments, in 1951 trade taxes also delivered a budget surplus. Unlike the oil boom of the 1970s, however, this windfall was shortlived. By 1952 the balance of payments was in worse deficit than 1950. Export producers had immediately converted their foreign exchange earnings into consumer goods, which in 1951/52 accounted for half of imports (Paauw 1960: 454). On the streets of Jakarta and provincial cities, motor cars became more numerous. This pent-up import demand could not be sustained by now depressed export receipts. As trade taxes fell, the budget also returned to deficit. There would be no more boom years until 1974.

The balance of payments thus became a perpetual constraint. Economic theory would have suggested devaluing to the market-clearing rate and stabilising it with tight monetary and fiscal policy, but the new Indonesian government set out down the apparently easier but still little-known path of multiple exchange rates (Appendix 6.A). Foreign exchange controls and an import licensing system had been inherited from the colonial administration. Export and import exchange rates were differentiated in March 1950 as a means of levying export taxes (Paauw 1960: 182). After collapse of the export boom, efforts turned in 1952 to restricting non-essential imports. Vast scope opened up for false classification and overinvoicing. Customs personnel could be bribed to turn a blind eye. Import licences became a lucrative form of political patronage.

This trade regime encouraged regional autonomy. To avoid export taxes, enterprising traders in the Outer Islands, some of whom had gained experience during the Japanese occupation and the Dutch blockade, sought military protection for routine smuggling with Singapore and Penang. They could afford to pay higher prices to export producers, brought back smuggled imports, and shared the profits with military commanders. As the gap widened between official exchange rates and the black market rates there was less and less incentive for traders to declare foreign exchange for virtual confiscation at arbitrarily low rates. Many shifted their business base and residence to Singapore, where they could deal in hard currency and operate beyond the uncertainties of Indonesian law. Businessmen who dealt in foreign currency had great incentive to earn undeclared margins and hold the funds in foreign bank accounts. Good profits were made, but they did not flow back to export producers, who had little incentive to expand production. The outcome was a kind of 'virtual reality', with high rewards for short-term opportunistic behaviour in markets grossly distorted by unstable bureaucratic intervention (Sumitro 1956). Statistics bore less and less relationship to what was actually being traded.

The budgetary problem was the inability of revenues to meet the inexorable demands for increased expenditure. Only in 1951, at the height of the Korean War boom, was the budget in surplus (Paauw 1960: 433). The root of the problem was contraction of the tax base: by 1956 and 1957 only one-fifth of revenues was raised as direct taxes, compared with almost twice this proportion in 1939 (Paauw 1960: 179–81, 434–5). Income taxes were constrained by the view that farmers, who constituted two-thirds of the workforce, were too poor to pay more than token taxes (Meiji Japan would have struggled to emerge as an industrial nation had its rulers been so generous in the 1870s). The Dutch had collected substantial revenues from the profits of state enterprises, including opium and pawnshop monopolies, railways, mines and plantations; by the mid-1950s many of these made losses and in total contributed only 2% to revenues.

The Indonesian government therefore came to rely excessively on trade taxes. These were regarded as 'equitable', as they were paid by business and their collection through a small number of customs points was fairly simple. In 1951, at the height of the Korean War boom, trade taxes — mainly export taxes — accounted for 70% of revenues (Paauw 1960: 181).

However, attempts to impose higher and higher rates of import duty and to raise quasi-taxes through the sale of foreign exchange certificates led to a burgeoning 'black economy' outside the tax system. In 1956 and 1957 trade taxes of all kinds still contributed just over half of revenues, but a plateau had been reached (Paauw 1960: 181). There was now a vicious circle between high trade taxes and a declining trade performance. The disincentives of high trade taxes discouraged investment in export sectors and encouraged smuggling, which by the mid-1960s was estimated to represent almost 30% of exports (Rosendale 1978: 151). This outcome may be contrasted with the virtuous circle of the New Order oil boom. In the early 1970s the government was still unable to mobilise domestic incomes through the tax system but enjoyed the windfall of high oil prices, which translated into a healthy balance of payments and high de facto trade taxes in the form of oil tax revenues. Such 'easy options' were not available after the Korean War.

Industrialisation

In industrial policy, the transfer of sovereignty in December 1949 marked no obvious discontinuity. The groundwork had been laid by the outgoing Dutch administration. The Industry Policy Guidelines of 1946 envisaged industrial rehabilitation and development being carried out on the basis of annual plans (Jonkers 1948: 121–2). In November 1949, on the eve of Independence, the Industry Section of the Department of Economic Affairs brought out a Special Industrial Welfare Plan (1950), which was intended as the basis for preparing a detailed industry plan (DEZ 1949). The first industry minister was economist Sumitro Djojohadikusumo, who became Minister for Trade and Industry in the Natsir Cabinet of September 1950 (Feith 1962: 46–7).

To recommend guidelines for industrial policy, in March 1951 Sumitro appointed an Industrialisation Committee (*Panitia Industrialisasi*). Taking its cue from the minister's own published views, the committee identified three aims of industrialisation: a more balanced economic structure, absorption of population growth, and the raising of national income (Van Oorschot 1956: 68–9). These apparently bland propositions betokened an important shift in emphasis. Whereas the Dutch had sought to strengthen an agrarian economy, the Indonesians foresaw its transformation into a modern industrial one. As in other newly independent countries, such as India and China, industry was regarded as the way of the future, the very essence of development. Industrial development was therefore now a matter of political prestige (Van Oorschot 1956: 67). Another new element was the view shared by all main political parties that 'key industries', still for the most part dominated by Dutch companies, should ultimately come under public ownership. Private capital, including foreign investment, would be allowed in 'non-essential' industries.

In April 1951, when the Industrialisation Committee had barely begun its work, Sumitro brought down the country's first development plan, the Economic Urgency Program. Fulfilling the promise of the Special Welfare Plan of 1949, the Urgency Program included an industrial development plan (Sutter 1959: 774–81). On the optimistic but then fashionable assumption that providing capital would call forth complementary factors of production,[3] this ambitious plan proposed to move forward simultaneously on the three fronts of large-, medium- and small-scale industry (Paauw 1963: 216–17). Significantly, assistance to small-scale industry was seen as more important than investment in large-scale industry, which was mostly foreign-owned (Van Oorschot 1956: 73–4). Measures to improve small-scale industry through simple mechanisation had begun during the 1930s and were renewed after the war through a Loan & Mechanisation Program, which involved simple pieces of equipment being lent to small and cottage industries on easy repayment terms (Mackie 1971: 47). Management centres (*induk*) were also set up to provide credit, technical assistance, and marketing outlets to cottage industries such as woodworking, ironworking, bronze, ceramics, textiles, leather and umbrellas (Higgins 1957: 68–9; Anspach 1969: 162–3). However, these centres were so few — only eight were in operation by the end of 1954 — so scattered, and in many cases so poorly managed as to be ineffectual in raising indigenous welfare (Sumitro 1954).

More obvious progress was made with the program for large-scale and mainly import-substituting industry, even though its role was specified to be only that of 'supporting and supplementary elements' (Van Oorschot 1956: 74–5). These projects, some of which had their genesis in the aborted 'crash program' of 1940, included rubber remilling, cotton spinning, cement, caustic soda and coconut flour. They were to be initiated and established primarily with government funds (for which the government allocated Rp. 160 million in 1952/53 alone, compared with only Rp. 30 million for the *induk* and Small-Scale Industrialisation Plan) (Anspach 1969: 163). These pilot projects proceeded slowly. The largest project, the cement plant at Gresik (East Java), financed out of the $100 million US Exim credit, was not completed until 1957 (Higgins 1957: 74). Programs were carried forward into the First Five Year Development Plan (1956–1960), but the rate of industrialisation actually slowed down.

Paauw (1960) argued that during the 1950s the Indonesian economy began to experience structural retrogression. According to official statistics, the manufacturing sector recovered to around 12% of NDP in 1957 and then stagnated (Suhadi 1967). Booth (1998a: 88) claims that the manufacturing share of GDP actually fell back, from 12% in 1939 to less than 10% in 1960. The primary sector remained stubbornly at just over half of national income. As seen in cities like Jakarta and Surabaya, the rapid influx of migrants from the countryside was absorbed not into manufacturing but into petty services, later to be known as the 'informal sector'.

The Indonesian economy still lacked an engine to drive economic development. Agriculture and trade just allowed it to survive.

Indigenous business: the *Benteng* program (1950–1957)

A third aspect of the Economic Urgency Program was the *Benteng* (fortress) program to build up an indigenous Indonesian business class. Introduced by the Hatta Cabinet in April 1950, it reserved certain categories of goods for indigenous Indonesian importers, who were provided with trade credits through the state-owned Bank Negara Indonesia (BNI) (Glassburner 1962). The rationale was to cut Dutch trading houses out of the lucrative import trade, using the leverage of import licences. While state enterprises would dominate the 'key sectors', importing was thought to suit indigenous business because only working capital was required. Over time, however, these businessmen could accumulate capital to invest in other sectors (Robison 1986: 44). The qualifications were to be a 'new Indonesian importer', legally incorporated and with at least 70% of the capital in indigenous hands (Sutter 1959: 1018–21). In June 1953 the program was extended to nationalisation of 70% of the import trade. Nominally this goal was achieved, but in early 1955 the head of the Central Office of Imports estimated that there were only 50 bona fide importers (Sutter 1959: 1025–6). Most others were 'briefcase importers' (*importir aktentas*), who just signed import licences on behalf of non-indigenous businessmen, most ethnic Chinese, in so-called Ali-Baba relationships. The program became a national scandal as the political parties exploited it as an easy form of patronage and graft. The new Minister of Economic Affairs, Roosseno, abolished discrimination on ethnic grounds (Anspach 1969: 171–5). The *Benteng* program was officially suspended in 1957, its main achievement having been to discredit the notion of indigenous free enterprise.

Assessment of the 1950s

The economic performance of the 1950s should not be judged only with the wisdom of hindsight. Until events began to run out of control in 1957 the economy showed signs of stress but was not obviously performing badly. Even allowing for rapid population growth, contemporary estimates suggested a respectable growth of income per capita of more than 2% per annum (Appendix 6.B). Governments were entitled to believe that the economic problems were being brought under control. Where they were unduly optimistic was in believing that the rapid recovery of the 1950s could be sustained without substantial increase in investment and productive capacity (ECAFE 1961: 109). This was not forthcoming. The domestic savings rate remained low, foreign investment was discouraged, and public expenditures were weighted heavily towards current consumption.

At the beginning of 1957 there were nevertheless grounds for guarded optimism. For the first time the macroeconomic situation had been held fairly stable for two years in succession. Money supply growth had been cut from 48% in 1954 to just 10% in 1955 and 1956, which enabled inflation to be brought back to around 10%, comparable with experience under the New Order (Mackie 1967b: 96; Paauw 1963: 205). The obvious unresolved problem was the balance of payments, with foreign exchange reserves at precarious levels (Paauw 1960: 119–20). Devaluation was resisted because it would raise the domestic prices of rice and textiles. Instead, great ingenuity was applied to an increasingly complicated system of multiple exchange rates, combining import surcharges of up to 400% with export incentives (see Paauw 1960: 185–90). The nation's propensity to import nevertheless remained stubbornly high. The solution was to boost exports, but this was vitiated by the breakdown of relations between the central government and the regions.

Java and the Outer Islands

'Unity in Diversity' was *the* challenge of Indonesia in the 1950s. Merging Java and the Outer Islands into a unitary state in 1950 was a revolutionary step to demolish a federal structure imposed by the Dutch after 1946 as a tactic to isolate the Republic. A workable system of centralised administration had yet to be devised. The task was all the more difficult because the economies of the Outer Islands were oriented to the outside world, in particular to Singapore and Penang, rather than to Java. The strong trend towards integration during the 1930s (see Chapter 1) had been reversed in the 1940s. After three years of enforced self-sufficiency, after 1945 trade revived across the Straits rather than with Java. Hence there were almost no economic foundations on which to integrate the new state. Efforts to extend the powers of the central government, and especially to tax the trade of the Outer Islands and to clamp down on smuggling, led to power struggles that could easily be polarised as the Outer Islands versus Java. Yet because the Outer Islands provided the dominant share of the nation's foreign exchange earnings, while Java absorbed the large share of its imports, some degree of redistribution was inevitable.

At the root of the regional crisis of the late-1950s was the taxation of export earnings and the restriction and taxation of imports by the multiple exchange rate and import licensing. In the colonial period smallholder producers had until the rubber restriction scheme enjoyed free disposal of their exports, which were exchanged directly for imports through local Chinese traders. That freedom had continued, albeit illegally, during the 1940s. Residual export taxes maintained after the collapse of the Korean War boom and the increasing cost of imports meant severe contraction in living standards, especially in areas where smallholders were heavily specialised in cash crops. After the high expectations of Independence, there ensued profound disillusionment and growing hostility to a central government perceived as dominated by Javanese.

One of the first flashpoints was East Indonesia, where the anti-trade regime was epitomised by the Copra Foundation (*Jajasan Kopra*). Set up by the Dutch in 1940 as the marketing board, formerly *Het Coprafonds*, like equivalent institutions in the British colonies, it was justified as a means of raising returns to farmers; in practice it was a mechanism to maximise and control foreign exchange and to collect tax revenues from the monopsony profit. The Foundation had little monopoly power, as Indonesia did not produce enough copra to influence the world price, but it held vast monopsony power over smallholder producers. Although the Foundation also operated in West Kalimantan and Riau, its role was most controversial in East Indonesia, especially Sulawesi and Maluku, which depended on copra for most foreign exchange. During the Korean War boom, smallholders in East Indonesia received from the Foundation little over half the free market price in Java and Sumatra (Harvey 1977: 34–5). Regional leaders claimed that these taxes were being siphoned off to fund expansion of the bureaucracy and luxury consumption in Jakarta. In January 1955 local leaders in the main copra-producing region of Minahasa (North Sulawesi) with army backing seized the assets of the Copra Foundation, then contracted with Hong Kong Chinese traders for direct barter shipments through the newly opened deepsea port of Bitung (Harvey 1977). Jakarta's response was ineffectual. By April 1956 the activities of the Foundation had been taken over throughout the rest of East Indonesia. Recognising the strength of regional feeling, the central government agreed to dissolve the bankrupt Foundation and pay off its debts to growers.

Unrest also broke out in Sumatra. In mid-1956 the army commander in North Sumatra openly shipped rubber and coffee, claiming the profits were for army projects (Feith 1962: 498–9). He was ordered to desist but no action was taken against him. Meanwhile smuggling proceeded as usual across the Straits of Malacca, with local army, navy and customs officers taking their cut of the spoils. The proximity of Singapore and Penang allowed for de facto free trade. Feith (1962) argues that the central government was willing to turn a blind eye as long as the smuggling was mainly of smallholder crops, and therefore conferred a welfare benefit. The exports of Sumatra's foreign-owned plantations, however, were still to be shipped officially through Indonesian ports.

These trade skirmishes became more serious after the resignation of Vice-President Moh. Hatta in December 1956. A Minangkabau from West Sumatra, Hatta was as popular in the Outer Islands as Sukarno, a Javanese, was unpopular. His presence in government alongside Sukarno had done much to maintain trust. After his resignation there was no check to the populist argument that the Outer Islands were being exploited for the benefit of Java and the Javanese. Demands for regional autonomy, even for a return to federation, proved irresistible. The split in civil society was matched by a split in the army. Commanders such as Ahmad Hussein (West Sumatra) and Warouw (East Indonesia) became leaders of the dissident movements (Leirissa 1991). Within the same month as Hatta's resignation, the provinces of North Sumatra and West Sumatra both declared autonomy. By February 1957 other 'officer-cum-veteran' councils had appeared in South Sumatra, Tapanuli (North Sumatra), Kalimantan, North and South Sulawesi, and Maluku (Feith 1962: 537). President Sukarno's attack on parliamentary government inflamed the situation. On 2 March the army commander of East Indonesia declared autonomy under martial law, the origins of the so-called Permesta rebellion (Feith 1962: 544–5). At this stage, however, it was not a secession but a political demand to renegotiate the balance of political and economic power within Indonesia.

Two new elements made the situation even more explosive. First, the American government, already disconcerted at Indonesia's hosting of the non-aligned conference at Bandung in 1955, the well-publicised visit of China's foreign minister Chou En-Lai and Sukarno's return visit to China in October 1956, took alarm at Communist Party (PKI) gains in the mid-1957 provincial and local elections (Kahin & Kahin 1995). In September 1957 the Eisenhower administration agreed to covert support for the regional movements as insurance against Java 'going Communist'. These supplies of funds and arms gave the potential rebels the means to challenge the central government militarily if negotiations yielded no satisfactory outcome.

Second, in December 1957 interisland shipping was crippled by trade union seizure of the Dutch-flag KPM fleet. In response to international pressure, the ships were returned three months later on condition of withdrawal from Indonesian waters, being replaced by chartered tonnage. However, there ceased to be any scheduled system of interisland shipping. East Indonesia, where the volume of cargo was very modest for the length of routes, was suddenly deprived of regular domestic connections. The sense of isolation combined with economic dislocation gave great impetus to arguments for secession.

Confident of American support, in February 1958 the dissident leaders in Sumatra announced a Revolutionary Government of the Republic of Indonesian or PRRI (*Pemerintah Revolusioner Republik Indonesia*), to serve until a return to constitutional government (Kahin & Kahin 1995: 140–1). Amid this worst crisis of the new Republic, the armed forces acted decisively to forestall American intervention. The Caltex oilfields of Pekanbaru (Central Sumatra) were recaptured, then the rebel forces driven from their strongholds of Padang and Bukitinggi (Kahin & Kahin 1995: 148–55). In Sulawesi the Permesta forces were better equipped but the rebellion collapsed at the end of June once central government forces had captured Menado. Despairing of their rebel allies, who had never been anxious to take up arms against the Republic, the Americans sought a rapprochement with Sukarno (Kahin & Kahin 1995: 217–20).

The PRRI-Permesta rebellion cast a long shadow. First, despite earlier local armed conflicts, this was the first and only time Outer Island provinces combined militarily to confront the central government. As in all previous cases the military strength and loyalty to the central government of Nasution's armed forces proved decisive. The unitary republic prevailed, militarily and ideologically. Second, although token concessions were made to interests in the Outer Islands, the military defeat of the rebellions also removed the pressure for a fairer redistribution of economic resources. Smuggling became even easier, which assisted Sumatra and West Kalimantan but was of less benefit to the more isolated region of East Indonesia. Third, and more ominously, PRRI-Permesta revealed Anglo-American collusion against the Republic and Sukarno in particular, who on 30 November in Jakarta narrowly survived an assassination attempt suspected to have had American backing (Kahin & Kahin 1995: 112–15; Leirissa 1991). These pigeons would come home to roost with Indonesian armed resistance to the formation of Malaysia in 1963. For all these reasons the Outer Islands would remain a turbulent frontier, Java the bulwark of the Republic.

Economic nationalism

Under the Finec agreements of December 1949, Indonesia reluctantly conceded full rights to Dutch enterprise in Indonesia. From an economic point of view, it might have been advantageous to encourage Dutch firms to reinvest in Indonesia. In the intellectual climate of that time, however, foreign investment, especially Dutch investment, was regarded as *prima facie* exploitative. That the concessions had been made under duress reinforced that view. Although Indonesia was obliged to allow free remittance of profits, in 1952 the government taxed those remittances by imposing a surcharge on the purchase of foreign exchange for that purpose. Price controls were applied to goods and services produced by Dutch firms, especially electricity (before nationalisation in 1954) and shipping (KPM). Permits for expatriate staff were subject to complicated bureaucratic approvals, while trade unions were applauded for strong pressure on Dutch companies to grant improved pay and working conditions. The general view was that Dutch firms had enjoyed very good profits in the past and should now be expected to make a contribution to the welfare of the Indonesian people.

Although the investment climate was deteriorating, Dutch business generally remained quite profitable into the mid-1950s. Once peace was restored, many firms were able to raise output fairly quickly to prewar levels. With the notable exception of sugar, most export industries were able to operate at near-full capacity and to pay good dividends. Meijer (1994: 529) cites profit remittances to the Netherlands of 0.8 billion guilders between 1954 and 1957. Such profits encouraged Dutch business to continue investing around 1.5 billion guilders between 1950 and 1958 (Meijer 1994: 497). Many smaller family-owned agricultural estates and manufacturing and non-oil mining firms nevertheless faced mounting

difficulties. Even some large firms like the KPM restricted further investment to the ploughback of profit, maintaining more or less a holding
operation.

Governments of the 1950s put high priority on achieving economic
sovereignty or 'Indonesianisation' (*Indonesianiasi*) of the economy.
Given the weakness of indigenous capital, in the early 1950s government
policy was to develop state enterprises to compete with Dutch firms at the
commanding heights of the economy. Business enterprises owned by
the former Netherlands Indies government, such as the Post Office, State
Railways, and various mining and plantation interests, were taken over
with political sovereignty. To these could be added state enterprises set
up by the Republic, such as the Bank Negara Indonesia (1946), which
competed with the Dutch commercial banks, and the Central Trading
Company (CTC) and Usindo, which competed with the 'Big Five' Dutch
trading houses. In 1953 the Java Bank was nationalised as Bank
Indonesia. The Rehabilitation Bank (*Herstelbank*), set up in May 1948,
became in 1951 the Industrial Bank (*Bank Industri Negara*, BIN; later
Indonesian Development Bank, Bapindo), which played the leading
role in financing industrial development under the Economic Urgency
Program (Siahaan 1996: 235–69). Dutch utilities such as the privately
owned railways and tramways on Java, as well as the gas and electricity
companies, were nationalised with full compensation. A number of
struggling Dutch estates and industrial enterprises were also taken
over and placed under control of the Government Estates Centre (*Pusat
Perkebunan Negara*, PPN).

In the case of domestic air transport, where the government required
continuing access to technology, the chosen form was the joint venture.
Garuda Indonesian Airways (GIA), Indonesia's new national airline, took
over the assets of the Royal Netherlands Indies Airlines, or KNILM (*Koninklijke Nederlandsch-Indische Luchtvaart-Maatschappij*) in a joint venture
with its former parent, the national airline KLM. The Indonesian government could take up the majority shareholding after 10 years. KLM was
required to train Indonesian personnel, who would gradually take over
(Anspach 1969: 146). More intractable was the status of the Dutch shipping
company KPM, which in 1950 held an almost complete monopoly of
interisland shipping and to nationalists epitomised colonial economic control.
The Round Table Conference negotiations deadlocked over the KPM's
insistence that it remain the 'central transport apparatus' and under the
Dutch flag (Dick 1987a: 14–16). After a Garuda-style joint venture had
been rejected, the Indonesian government set up its own state shipping
corporation, PELNI, which competed directly with the KPM and enjoyed
government patronage.

Indonesianisation could have achieved impressive results over a
10-year time horizon but the pace was too slow to assuage nationalist
aspirations. With government backing most of these enterprises soon

carved out a niche in the market, without challenging the supremacy of long-established Dutch firms, which usually provided better products and service. Accordingly, the first Sastroamidjojo government (1953–1955) sought to force the pace of nationalisation. In 1954 Garuda was summarily nationalised and KLM's management agreement terminated in favour of more limited technical assistance (Anspach 1969: 146). Certain fields were reserved for indigenous enterprise. This had already been attempted with the *Benteng* import licences. In 1954 it was extended to feeder shipping and stevedoring (with effect from 1956). Even these measures, however, merely underlined the frustration with the slow erosion of Dutch privileges, frustration fed by the Nationalist and Communist parties that could use the issue of foreign economic control to mobilise popular support.

Tensions over the status of Dutch investments in Indonesia were compounded by continued intransigence over West Irian. With widespread popular support, in February 1956 the Harahap government unilaterally abrogated the Round Table agreements. Bilateral negotiations having failed, Indonesia took the matter to the United Nations. Unlike in 1949, however, the USA did not back Indonesia's move to have the matter debated (Kahin & Kahin 1995: 109–11). In retaliation, on 1 December 1957 Dutch aircraft were prohibited from landing, Dutch-language newspapers and magazines were banned, and an official national strike was called for the following day, which became the pretext for militant trade unionists to seize the Jakarta headquarters and assets of the KPM, the prime symbol of Dutch economic control (Glassburner & Thomas 1965). In the following days more and more Dutch companies were taken over by the trade unions, including banks, the 'Big Five' trading companies, factories and plantations. A few enterprises such as Shell, Heineken Brewery and Unilever escaped seizure by transferring ownership to other European countries. After eight years of wrangling, 'the Gordian knot of Dutch capital' was finally cut (Feith 1962: 584). The claim on Indonesia for almost 1000 seized enterprises was 2.5 billion guilders (Clerx 1992). It was also the end of the Dutch presence in Indonesia. Of almost 50 000 Dutch nationals at the end of 1957, 34 000 had been repatriated by mid-1958, and a year later only 6000 remained (Meijer 1994: 592, 620).

Apparently taken by surprise at this swift turn of events, the government tried ineffectually to stop the seizures. To wrest control from Communist trade unions, on 13 December General Nasution ordered seized enterprises to be placed under supervision of local Army commanders (Feith 1962: 584). Day-to-day operations devolved on any Indonesian personnel with technical expertise. With formal nationalisation in February 1959, authority passed to various supervisory boards such as BPU (plantations) and BAPPIT (industry) (Siahaan 1996: 319–27). Under the State Enterprise Law 19/1960 the largest firms were reconstituted as state enterprises (*perusahaan negara*) and grouped under General Management Boards,

BPU (*Badan Pimpinan Umum*), while the rest were allocated to provincial governments as *perusahaan daerah* under supervision of Regional Enterprise Management Boards (BAPIPDA). The end of Dutch economic domination was therefore accompanied by a vast expansion of the state sector of the Indonesian economy. Performance rapidly worsened (Soehoed 1967: 72–3). The fundamental problems were lack of credit, lack of foreign exchange and bad management.

As Dutch business was eliminated, economic nationalism was redirected to the growing economic power of the ethnic Chinese, regardless of whether they were Indonesian or foreign nationals. Despite some criticism of their perceived pro-Dutch stance during the revolution, Indonesian–Chinese relations had been fairly good in the early 1950s. Most of Indonesia's leaders and notably President Sukarno and Vice-President Hatta stood firmly opposed to ethnic discrimination against 'non-indigenous' citizens (Anspach 1969: 129). However, Chinese businessmen were observed with envy to be prospering from measures to promote indigenous entrepreneurship, such as the *Benteng* program. In 1956 the businessman-cum-politician Assaat attacked the Chinese as privileged and opportunistic and called for discrimination in favour of indigenous business. The consequent Assaat Movement tapped a strong vein of resentment (Feith 1962: 481–7). Although these sentiments were submerged by the anti-Dutch actions of 1957/58, the economic vacuum caused by the elimination of Dutch economic interests and the inefficiency of state enterprise was to a large extent filled by Chinese business. In particular, Chinese merchants moved in to fill the vacancies left by the Dutch in the wholesale, import and export trade (Anspach 1969: 181–4). During 1959 there was a noticeable increase in popular anti-Chinese hostility, even in schools.

Restricting ethnic Chinese business was much more difficult than moving against Dutch economic interests. The ethnic Chinese population was not only much larger than that of the Dutch but many were also Indonesian citizens. Moreover, by virtue of long involvement in intermediate trade, the Chinese were much more intertwined with indigenous business. In the late 1950s measures were taken against 'foreign' pro-Taiwan Chinese in reprisal for Taiwan's alleged involvement in the PRRI-Permesta rebellion. Then in late 1959 Government Regulation 10/1959 banned 'foreign nationals' (in practice Chinese nationals) from engaging in retail trade in rural areas. After the decree had first been enforced in West Java, more than 100 000 Chinese accepted repatriation to the People's Republic (Mackie 1976). The huge gap in rural distribution could not readily be filled by cooperatives (Paauw 1963: 210) but in the long run probably did increase retail trading by indigenous Indonesians. More significantly, it increased the proportion of Chinese living in cities and towns and their role in urban economic life.

'Guided Democracy'

Between 1957 and 1959, against a background of turmoil, there was a decisive shift in the political balance of power and the constitutional basis of the nation-state. In February 1957 President Sukarno announced his *Konsepsi* of a new system of government: he would appoint and lead a consensus cabinet which, in place of the elected Parliament, would report to a National Council (Dewan Nasional) of 'functional groups', including the Communist Party (PKI) (Lev 1966). A month later, following outbreak of the PRRI-Permesta rebellions, Sukarno accepted army advice to declare martial law (literally a 'State of War and Siege'). The Ali Sastroamidjojo cabinet returned its mandate and Sukarno appointed an extra-parliamentary Working Cabinet (Kabinet Karya) under Prime Minister Djuanda. During this transitional phase, attention turned to the Constituent Assembly (*Konstituante*), which had the task of recommending the permanent constitution to replace the provisional one of 1950. Sukarno urged restoration of the 1945 Constitution, under which the president functioned as both head of state and head of executive government. When the Assembly failed to endorse this, he dubiously enacted it by Presidential Decree on 5 July 1959 and dissolved the Constituent Assembly (Nasution 1992). Almost without protest, the elected Parliament was dissolved in March 1960 and replaced by an appointed one representing the main political factions.

Indonesia thereby entered the period of 'Guided Democracy' and 'Guided Economy'. The rhetoric was what would now be called 'Asian values': Indonesia needed to develop its own form of democracy that fitted traditional values. The institutions, however, were modern, the 'functional groups' and corporatism a little reminiscent of 1930s populist European fascism. Its *realpolitik* was an alliance of convenience between Sukarno and the army, led by General Nasution (Bourchier & Legge 1994; Crouch 1978). However, the outcome was not strong government. Instability took a new form as Sukarno invoked the countervailing support of his own Nationalist Party (PNI) and Communist Party (PKI) to hold the army in check. In a theatre of revolution, he manipulated a national mood of crisis in both domestic and foreign policy in order to maintain the political initiative (Legge 1973). In succession came the West Irian campaign (1960–1962), confrontation against Malaysia (1963–1966), withdrawal from the United Nations (1965) and the self-reliance (*berdikari*) campaign (1965).

Foreign capital: the shutdown

'Guided Democracy' ushered in a period of increasing hostility towards both domestic private capital and what remained of foreign capital, mostly American and British. In his 1959 Independence Day speech calling for a 'Return to the Revolution', President Sukarno fulminated against 'national capitalism' as 'vulture capitalism' and warned against the dangers of 'liberalism', which he identified with exploitation. Instead he proclaimed a

'Political Manifesto' (*Manipol*) as the basis for Guided Economy, a socialist and cooperative path befitting Guided Democracy (Tan 1967). The
development of state-owned basic industry, especially fertiliser, cement,
paper, chemicals, spinning and shipbuilding, was accelerated under foreign
aid funding (Siahaan 1996). Private enterprise was to be supervised and
regulated through industry associations, or OPS (*Organisasi Perusahaan
Sejenis*) (Castles 1967).

The more hostile climate towards national private enterprise was
reflected in the promotion of state trading. Import of essential goods, about
70% of the total trade, was entrusted to nine state-owned trading houses
(*bhakti*, regrouped in 1964 into six *niaga*) as heirs of the nationalised Dutch
trading companies and the existing state trading companies, CTC and
Usindo (Panglaykim & Palmer 1969). These firms later acquired responsibility for domestic distribution and, in March 1961, for the bulk of exports.
Financing was provided through state banks. A rationing system was
introduced to ensure equity in consumption of basic commodities,
especially food and textiles (*sandang-pangan*). Domestic commerce nevertheless remained largely in private hands (Castles 1967).

Government control of production was also uneven. Around half
the output of the estate sector had passed into government hands
through the take-over of the Dutch-owned estates (Paauw 1963: 212–13;
Mackie 1967a), but food crop and cash crop agriculture, as well as small-
scale and cottage industries, remained in the private sector. Manufacturing
was also split between state enterprises, private firms and a large small-
scale sector. In principle the large-scale sector was organised under general
management boards (BPU), while the rationing of raw materials was biased
towards assisting the small-scale sector. The reality was very different, as
epitomised by the textile industry. By 1962 the country was nominally
self-sufficient in weaving, but capacity utilisation was estimated at only
36%: the small-scale sector, accounting for about two-thirds of capacity,
found it more profitable to trade its yarn allocation to the large-scale sector
than to produce (Palmer 1972). Similarly in other industries, traders set up
small manufacturing plant simply to qualify for foreign exchange licences
and raw material allocations. The outcome was a theatre economy in which
scarcity of foreign exchange and rapid inflation interacted with pervasive
but inconsistent regulation to give bizarre price signals and to reward
speculation more highly than production.

Nationalisation of Dutch enterprise by no means drew the teeth on
popular opposition to foreign enterprise. The Communist Party in particular
still needed foreign scapegoats. Passage in late 1958 of a new Foreign
Investment Law did not improve the investment climate. Sukarno promised
non-interference with the remaining foreign capital, but his increasingly
anti-Western tone was hardly reassuring. In 1959 he repealed the new law
and no further efforts were made to attract foreign private investment
(Hill 1988: 5). Western firms and consulates continued to be a target for

PKI/trade union mobilisation. On 18 January 1964, amid Confrontation against Malaysia and in a repeat of earlier action against Dutch firms, Communist-led unions began a wave of seizures of the assets of British firms (*SP* 24/1/64). A final wave of actions began on 3 December 1964, when a demonstration against American policy in the Congo became a pretext for a crowd of youths to sack the US Information Service library in Jakarta. Over the next few weeks assets of American firms were also seized. In May 1965 all remaining Western factories, German, Belgian, Swiss and Australian, were taken under government 'supervision', justified as protection against hostile labour unions (Sadli 1972: 202). Fifteen years after Independence, foreign investment was extinguished. No goose, no golden eggs.

There were two pragmatic exceptions to this trend towards anti-Western actions. First, economic relations with Japan had steadily been improving even before re-establishment of diplomatic relations in April 1958. The Reparations Agreement with Japan was signed on 8 December 1957, less than a week after the seizure of Dutch firms. This allowed for payment of $223 million in reparations over 12 years, $400 million of foreign aid and $176 million of trade credits (Nishihara 1976: 53). The largest project was Karangkates irrigation and hydropower system in East Java but there were also textile factories, paper mills and a student training program; loan funds were used to finance four luxury hotels, the Sarinah department store, the lifting bridge at Palembang, and interisland ships (Nishihara 1976). Other projects included the Monas independence monument in Jakarta. Despite much derision of prestige projects, they helped to define the face of modern Indonesia, especially Jakarta. There was also a personal element to this blooming relationship. Miss Nemoto Naoko (Ratna Sari Dewi), whom President Sukarno befriended in Tokyo in 1959 and took as his wife, served as an astute intermediary between the President and Japanese business. The Japanese did not make the mistake of investing but relied on loans, contracts and, in the 1960 deal with Permina (later Pertamina) for North Sumatran oil, 'production sharing'. Their extensive presence in Indonesia after all other foreign enterprise had been nationalised was a big advantage when foreign investment was liberalised in 1967.

The other exception was the role of American capital, notably in the oil industry. Through Stanvac, the USA had been vitally interested in Indonesia on the eve of the Pacific War. American attitudes were fundamental to the rhythm and outcome of the Revolution, and after Independence, in the context of the Cold War, the USA acted as godfather to the young nation. As Dutch influence declined, the USA used its aid, including educational and military aid, to try and stop the Communist Party from gaining power and to keep Indonesian oil under Western control. Apart from the miscalculation of 1958, when support was given to rebel movements in the Outer Islands, American policy in Indonesia was pragmatic, and most ambassadors managed to stay on good terms with President Sukarno. In 1962 the USA helped to broker the settlement between

Indonesia and the Netherlands over West Irian. However, disappointment arose from the US failure to commit the level of aid recommended by the Humphrey Mission (USESTI 1963; Mahajani 1970: 20).

Unlike the Dutch and the British, the USA had few 'hostages' in Indonesia in the form of direct investments, with the notable exception of the oil industry. Law 44/1960 on Petroleum and Natural Gas Mining specified that oil rights were vested in the state, for which foreign companies might act as 'contractors' (Hunter 1965: 16–17). During 1963, with intervention of a special emissary of President Kennedy (Hunter 1965: 17), production-sharing agreements were signed between the Indonesian government and the 'Big Three' oil companies, Caltex, Stanvac and Shell (which in 1965 sold out to Pertamina). Production was subcontracted for 20 years to the foreign oil companies, which were allowed managerial control over their operations, except for unprofitable domestic refining and distribution, which was transferred to state enterprise (Anspach 1969: 196). In this disguised way, American capital survived into the New Order.

As a non-aligned nation, Indonesia also accepted aid from the Communist bloc. A trade agreement was signed with the Soviet Union in August 1956. Generous civil and military aid flowed from Kruschev's visit to Indonesia in 1960, and military aid was stepped up after 1962 as Indonesian–US relations worsened (Mahajani 1970). Heavy industry projects included the Cilegon steel mill and Cilacap fertiliser plant (Siahaan 1996: 407). Many students were sent to Russian and East European universities. In 1966 the Communist bloc, including China and Eastern Europe, accounted for almost 60% of Indonesia's foreign debt (Panglaykim & Arndt 1966).

During 1965, Indonesian politics became manic as the economy stagnated and the modern sector collapsed. Withdrawal from the United Nations and closer alignment with the Asian Communist bloc was accompanied by a campaign for national self-reliance (*berdikari*). Large import-replacing industrial projects were launched (Siahaan 1996). Without foreign exchange reserves, however, Indonesia was living on credit, mainly from the Communist bloc. Capacity utilisation in the textile spinning industry, for example, fell from 82% in 1957 to just 26% in 1966 (Palmer 1972). Fuelled by expansion of the money supply to fund massive budget deficits, inflation reached a peak of 1500% in 1965/66 (Grenville 1981: 107). Speculation became rampant. As urban dwellers improvised their daily survival, the countryside was stirred into ferment by PKI-inspired land redistributions (*aksi sepihak*) to landless farmers. Government became paralysed. The Army and PKI, the only two disciplined mass organisations, faced off in shows of armed strength, amid rumours of death lists.

Following doubts over President Sukarno's health, on 30 September 1965 a small group of army officers kidnapped and murdered six senior generals and another officer in an attempt to remove the top army leadership. The coup leader, Colonel Untung, had links with the PKI but the putsch was bungled and may have been tactical rather than a full *coup d'état*. Next day, the commander of the Jakarta-based Strategic Army Command (*Kostrad*), General Soeharto, firmly quashed the revolt and in mid-March 1966 forced Sukarno to delegate executive power.[4] This marked the beginning of the New Order. Its first measure was to ban the Communist Party, followed by a bloody nationwide purge of PKI members and sympathisers. By 1967 income per capita had fallen back to the level of 1951.

CONCLUSION

The separate literatures of the colonial achievement, the triumph of the Revolution and the New Order 'miracle' do not connect into one narrative. At best they tell us something about the spirit of each age. Just as the 'Old Order' rejected the colonial experience, so the New Order in turn rejected political mobilisation and socialist ideology and discouraged intellectual inquiry. Nevertheless, the very force of that rejection is itself a phenomenon to be studied. Indonesia's modern (economic) history can be seen as morbidly extreme in all three periods, suggesting that a dialectic approach may be the best way of integrating them. If, as this volume proposes, political and economic development (or state and market) should be seen as related processes, their forced disjunction could be expected to lead to crisis. Thus, the intense political activity and experimentation of the 1940s–1960s was a reaction to colonial suppression, but its accompanying violence severely damaged the economy of the young Republic. Renewed suppression under the New Order created favourable conditions for economic development but sowed the seeds for another phase of instability.

The 'Old Order' became a lost era in Indonesian economic history and, until very recently, also in political history. Certainly it was a time of squandered opportunities. Yet it was not altogether a wasted time. The big political issues seemed to be settled. Establishment of the unitary state of Indonesia and acceptance of its territorial integrity were achieved after some bitter local campaigns won through the effectiveness of the Army's central command. Foreign economic control was virtually eliminated, though at tremendous economic cost. The power struggle for control of the state was also resolved by the bloody triumph of the Armed Forces. This was the last great issue to be determined and marked the dividing line between the Old and the New Order. With hindsight, both the demise of foreign capital and the eventual military hegemony can be seen to have flowed inexorably from the Dutch decision — or perhaps non-decision — to contest Indonesia's independence. The Revolution called the Indonesian National Army (TNI) into being as a legitimate and effective source of power and prevented a natural evolution of civil institutions, whether parliament, political parties, the bureaucracy or law. After 20 years the Army prevailed for the simple reasons that it was the only effective instrument of the state and had the most guns. In the struggle for control of Southeast Asia, the USA, Britain and

Australia were all relieved at the triumph of a strong anti-Communist government and turned a blind eye to the huge cost in human life. Thailand and Burma were already under military rule.

Over the period 1945–1966, macroeconomic instability, lack of investment and structural rigidity were not exogenous causes of political strife — though at times they exacerbated the situation — but symptoms of the intensifying power struggle. Mackie's perceptive analysis of the causes of the Old Order inflation identified three reasons why good policies were seldom carried through (Mackie 1967b: 19–21). First, there was the paradox that Sukarno's highly authoritarian and broadly based government was unable to apply policies which hurt its supporters, unless suddenly and indiscriminately. Second, budget deficits, however corrosive, acted as a 'safety valve' to avoid making difficult choices. Third, no influential group within government had a direct interest in stability per se. Redistribution therefore took precedence over growth and development. Any economic assets were cashed in that would give some political leverage. The power struggle could not be short-circuited, because the institutions of the new state were too weak to establish an equilibrium short of total victory by one or other party. Sukarno's romantic vision of the ongoing revolution, like that of Mao Tse-Tung, thus became a living nightmare that ended in catharsis with the massacres of 1966.

And yet we should not paint too bleak a picture. Despite the economic chaos of the mid-1960s, things were still much better than in 1944–45 at the end of the Japanese occupation, when there was mass starvation. Indonesia did not implode into civil war like Burma or Cambodia. Booth (1998a) argues that the period as a whole did yield some economic growth, which helps to explain why growth revived very quickly after 1966 once political stability was restored. Even if there had been a more stable macroeconomic climate in the 1950s and no attacks on foreign capital, economic growth would not necessarily have been rapid, although it would have been better sustained into the 1960s. After the shortlived Korean War boom there were no more big opportunities for primary producing nations until the dramatic oil price rise of 1973. Little foreign investment flowed into Southeast Asia, which was still the risky frontline of the 'War against Communism'. The 'Green Revolution' awaited the technological breakthroughs of the mid-1960s. Compared with its late colonial potential, the Indonesian economy performed poorly in the 1950s and especially in the 1960s, but it did not fall as far behind the rest of Southeast Asia as would Vietnam, Burma and Cambodia during the New Order.

APPENDICES

6.A   The multiple exchange rate debacle

Under postwar Bretton Woods rules, foreign exchange rates were fixed and devaluation was allowable only as a last resort, in the event of 'fundamental disequilibrium' in the balance of payments. Indonesian governments did devalue from time to time but were reluctant to devalue the rupiah to its market clearing level, partly because of pessimism as to the demand prospects for exports and partly to maintain cheap 'essential' imports. Partial devaluations could nevertheless be simulated by a set of differentiated import taxes and export subsidies. This system, whereby different exchange rates applied to different transactions, including capital flows and remittances, was known as a *multiple exchange rate* (Corden & Mackie 1962). Introduced in March 1950, when export prices were high, the original aim was to tax exports. In 1952, after the export boom had collapsed, devaluation removed exchange rate discrimination against exports but imposed differential surcharges (taxes) on imports, for luxury items reaching up to 200% on top of existing tariffs. Thereafter the exchange rate system became more and more byzantine.

The long-run impact of addressing symptoms rather than the causes of balance of payments disequilibrium was disastrous (Paauw 1963: 237). Official exchange rates and export and import prices ceased to act as signals of market scarcity. Now pegged to the American dollar rather than the Dutch guilder, the official rate became a reference point rather than an actual price. In 1952 the black market exchange rate was already double the official rate; by 1962 it was 19 times and two years later 29 times greater (Table 6.3; Booth 1998a; Van der Eng 1992; Mackie 1967b; Grenville 1981; Papanek & Dowsett 1975; Rosendale 1978; Panglaykim, Penny & Thalib 1968). By the mid-1960s foreign exchange reserves had shrunk to just two weeks imports: even nominally cheap 'essential' imports of food, cotton, and spareparts were virtually unobtainable. Rosendale (1978: 171–2) claimed that 'control over the allocation of official reserves ... passed from any central policy-making authority to individual officials,

Table 6.3   Economic indicators, 1951–1967

	1951	1957	1960	1962	1964	1965	1966	1967
Real GDP (1938 =100)	90	123	123	132	134	135	139	141
GDP per capita (Rp.)	2126	2320	2441	2441	2364	2324	2271	2141
Money growth (%)	16	41	39	99	156	280	763	132
Inflation (%)	65	5	26	167	93	284	898	192
Official exchange (Rp./$)	3.8	11.4	45	45	250	10000	10*	235*
Black market rate	16.5	45.8	150	850	7200	36000	122*	290*
Reserves ($ million)	511	224	337	135	35	26	23	53

* exchange rate new currency = 1/1000.

including the managers of government agricultural estates and the governor of the central bank, each of whom utilised the foreign exchange at his disposal as he saw fit'. After 1966 conventional macroeconomic policies of eliminating the budget deficit, restraining money supply growth, floating the rupiah and abolishing multiple exchange rates quickly restored internal and external equilibrium. By then Indonesia's share of world exports had shrunk from 1.7% in 1950 to just 0.4% (Rosendale 1978: 218).

6.B Pitfalls of estimating growth rates

Reconstructing growth estimates for the 1950s encounters formidable data problems. Booth (1998a: 55) cites a World Bank recalculation of 5.6% per annum for the period 1950/55; Van der Eng (1992) sets growth of output at 4.4% for the period 1949/57. Income per capita estimates require heroic assumptions as to population trends between the 1930 and 1961 censuses. Paauw (1963: 189–90) reckoned 1938 levels of income per capita to have been restored by 1959, but Van der Eng (1992) claims that income per capita in 1959 was still 9% below 1938 levels and 18% below peak 1941 levels.

Indonesia's recovery may be compared with that of Japan. Both countries may have suffered similar declines in output but Japan suffered far more damage to national wealth, estimated at about 25% (Uchino 1983). Japan's real GNP was estimated to have surpassed the peacetime level of the mid-1930s — though not the prewar peak of 1941 — by 1951. Indonesia, which was much worse affected by the Depression of the 1930s, also recovered its 1937/39 levels of output during the Korean War boom and surpassed its prewar peak (1941) in 1956 (Van der Eng 1992). Not much reliance can be placed on these figures but they suggest that Indonesia's postwar recovery in output was actually quite impressive. Attention thus shifts to the differential rates of population growth. In the late 1950s Japan's traditionally low population growth was just 1% per annum (Minami et al. 1994), while Indonesia's may have leapt to just over 2% (Hugo et al. 1987: 42–3). This crucial margin was at the expense of national savings and investment and hence future growth, but Sukarno, like Mao, regarded a large population as a source of national strength.

7

The Soeharto era and after: stability, development and crisis, 1966–2000

Thee Kian Wie

THE RISE AND FALL OF THE 'NEW ORDER'

Following widespread demonstrations by university and high school students against Sukarno for his alleged involvement in the coup of 30 September 1965 in Jakarta in early 1966, and the steady erosion of his power base, Sukarno on 11 March 1966 reluctantly signed a decree giving General Soeharto full authority to restore order, to facilitate the functioning of the government, to protect the President, and to safeguard the Indonesian Revolution. This decree (referred to as *Supersemar*, the acronym of *Surat Perintah Sebelas Maret*, the Presidential Decree of 11 March) provided Soeharto with some legitimacy to assume effective political power over the country. Following the dismissal of Sukarno and the appointment of Soeharto as Acting President in March 1967 by the Provisional People's Consultative Assembly, the country's highest state body, Soeharto was officially installed as Indonesia's second president in 1968. This event marked the emergence of the so-called 'New Order', in contrast to the 'Old Order' of the Sukarno government.

The difference implied by the name 'New Order' did not merely signify a change in political leadership but above all a significant philosophical shift of what constituted the fundamental mission of the government and what the appropriate methods were to achieve this mission. For the 'New Order' government, this fundamental mission was 'economic development'. In pursuit of this mission the discipline of economic science was given a prominence unimaginable during the 'Old Order' (Prawiro 1998: 79). Supported by his two most important civilian allies, Sultan Hamengkubuwono IX of Yogyakarta and Adam Malik, Soeharto quickly dismantled the architecture of 'Guided Democracy' established by Sukarno in the late 1950s. On the basis of this decree, Soeharto moved to eliminate the pro-Communist tilt of the previous government by banning the Indonesian

Communist Party and its affiliated organisations and arresting leftist ministers of Sukarno's cabinet, notably Subandrio, vice-premier and foreign
minister (Bresnan 1993: 35–6). Because of the alleged involvement of China
in the coup of 30 September 1965, the Jakarta–Beijing alliance forged
during the early 1960s was now dissolved.

On the foreign front Indonesia's new, anti-Communist political
leadership quickly abandoned the anti-Western policies of the Sukarno
government. Indonesia rejoined the United Nations, from which it had
withdrawn in January 1965 after Malaysia had been given a non-
permanent seat in the Security Council. As the Sukarno government
had left the economy in shambles, the new political leadership badly
needed economic assistance from Western countries and Japan. To qualify
for this aid, the armed confrontation with Malaysia was terminated in
May 1966. Indonesia also rejoined the International Monetary Fund
(IMF) and the World Bank, from which Indonesia had withdrawn in
August 1965 as part of Sukarno's efforts to cut links with the capitalist
world. Restoring links with these multilateral organisations was considered essential to assist Indonesia's economic recovery.

Facing the serious economic problems left by the Sukarno government,
notably a runaway inflation caused by unrestrained deficit spending,
Soeharto turned to a group of economists from the Faculty of Economics at
the University of Indonesia (FEUI) in Jakarta for economic advice.
Soeharto's confidence in the FEUI economists was strengthened by a series
of lectures on Indonesia's economic problems given by five of these economists (Widjojo Nitisastro, Ali Wardhana, Sadli, Emil Salim and Subroto) at
the Second Army Seminar in August 1966. This seminar was convened by
the late General Soewarto, then Commander of the Army Staff and
Command School, *Seskoad* (*Sekolah Staf dan Komando Angkatan Darat*),
where these five economists and other political and social scientists
had been teaching during the final years of the Sukarno government.
Among the senior army officers who followed the eight-month *Seskoad*
course was General Soeharto. Like the other participants, Soeharto
obtained his basic knowledge of economics from these economists at
Seskoad (Sadli 1993: 39).

At first the relationship between the military and the academics was
exploratory, but over time this bond became institutional because of the
regularity of the courses, which were later also given at the Airforce and
Navy Staff and Command Schools, *Seskoau* (from *Angkatan Udara*) and
Seskoal (from *Angkatan Laut*). However, the Army was the most committed to the non-military courses given at *Seskoad*, as it viewed these courses
as an essential input in preparing the military for the dual function
(*dwifungsi*) — the combined military and political/social roles — they
were preparing to perform during the post-Sukarno era (Sadli 1993: 39).
The institutional links between the military and the academics that developed as a result of these courses at *Seskoad*, *Seskoau* and *Seskoal* became

an important part of the military–civilian alliance which in 1966 overthrew Sukarno's 'Old Order' government and established the 'New Order' (Sadli 1993: 39).

In September 1966 Soeharto appointed a 'Team of Experts in the Field of Economics and Finance', consisting of the five FEUI economists and coordinated by the late Major-General Sudjono Humardani, an aide to General Soeharto (Subroto 1998: 75). This appointment marked the ascendancy of the so-called 'economic technocrats', sometimes referred to as the 'Berkeley Mafia', as several of these economists, including their leader Professor Widjojo, had pursued their postgraduate study in economics at the University of California in Berkeley. Over time this group was joined by other highly qualified economists.

Soeharto assigned this team of economists to draw up a Program for Stabilisation and Rehabilitation, which was incorporated in Decree no. 23 of the Provisional People's Consultative Assembly. Based on this Decree, on 3 October 1966 guidelines were set out for Indonesia's economic recovery, specifically policies on a balanced budget, the balance of payments, rehabilitation of the physical infrastructure, food production and agricultural development (Salim 1997: 57; Subroto 1998: 74–5).

By the late 1960s price stability had been achieved. With economic policy in the hands of a well-qualified group of economic technocrats, enjoying the full support and confidence of Soeharto and the strong support of the Inter-Governmental Group on Indonesia (IGGI), the international aid consortium chaired by the Netherlands, the Indonesian economy embarked in the late 1960s on a period of unprecedentedly rapid growth, which was sustained for the next three decades. The economic transformation that Indonesia experienced during this period transformed the country from the 'prime economic underperformer' among the Southeast Asian economies into a 'Newly Industrialising Economy' (NIE). Rapid industrial growth transformed Indonesia from an economy highly dependent on agriculture in the mid-1960s to one in which the manufacturing sector contributed more to GDP than agriculture in the mid-1990s.

In 1993 the World Bank, in its famous but controversial report on the 'East Asian Miracle', classified Indonesia, along with Japan, South Korea, Taiwan, Hong Kong, Singapore, Malaysia and Thailand, as one of the 'high performing Asian economies' (HPAEs) (World Bank 1993a: xvi). Other developing countries have grown equally rapidly, but not at such high and sustained rates for such a long period. As in other HPAEs Indonesia's economic growth was underpinned by high rates of investment in physical infrastructure, plant and equipment and human capital, and high rates of productivity growth (World Bank 1993a: 8). The HPAEs also experienced rapid demographic transition, strong agricultural growth and very rapid export growth (World Bank 1996b: 28–40). The rapid and sustained growth of the HPAEs was accompanied by a rapid decline in absolute poverty and a relatively equal income distribution.

Yet between 1997 and 1998 a serious financial and economic crisis which had started in Thailand engulfed all of Southeast and East Asia, including Indonesia, turning its 'miracle economy' into a 'melted-down economy' dependent for its very survival on international charity. By January 1998 the Indonesian rupiah had depreciated by 80%, inflation had risen to more than 50%, while the economy contracted sharply. Hundreds of thousands of workers were laid off, mainly in the modern, urban sector, while absolute poverty began to rise again. To make matters worse, Indonesia was also hit by a severe El Niño drought, which hurt agriculture and aggravated forest fires, and a falling oil price, which adversely affected export and government revenues.

The deep and protracted economic crisis led to serious political and social unrest, culminating in violent riots and demonstrations, which forced Soeharto to step down in May 1998 after a reign of 32 years, just as Sukarno had been forced to transfer his power in March 1966. Soeharto was succeeded as president by B.J. Habibie, his former vice-president. However, lacking political legitimacy, Habibie was widely regarded as a holdover of the New Order. At a Special Session of the People's Consultative Assembly in October 1999 to appoint a new president, Habibie was forced to withdraw his candidacy for president, opening the way for Abdurrachman Wahid to emerge as Indonesia's first democratically elected president. Thus the New Order government, which had emerged from the economic crisis left by Sukarno's Guided Democracy government, ended ignominiously in an even more serious economic and political crisis from which it was unable to extricate itself.

Indonesia's economic and political crisis released forces which could reverse the long-run trends towards a highly centralised nation state and an integrated national economy. With the collapse of the authoritarian, highly centralised New Order state, strong demands for greater regional autonomy and even outright independence were openly expressed, particularly in the resource-rich provinces. With greater authority to be delegated to around 300 sub-provincial regions (districts) by early 2001, including in the field of agriculture, industry and trade, and investment, the seeds for a fragmentation of the integrated national economy could be sown. This could happen if various districts, intent on maximising the economic benefits of their own regions, imposed barriers to interregional trade, investment and capital and labour movements. However, while the deep economic crisis was undeniably an unexpected consequence of the increasing globalisation or integration with the world economy, notably the huge flow of funds that had flooded into the country during the boom years of the early 1990s, it appears unlikely that this long-run trend will be reversed in the absence of a better alternative. In fact, despite the reversal in Indonesia's economic fortunes because of the crisis, there is widespread agreement that the benefits of international trade and foreign investment still outweigh the costs of engagement with the world economy.

FROM CRISIS TO 'MIRACLE' (1966–1996)

Rapid growth and transformation

During the period 1965–1996 the Indonesian economy experienced rapid and sustained growth, with Gross National Product (GNP) growing at an average annual rate of 6.7%. Meanwhile, a successful family planning program reduced population growth from an average of 2.4% in the period 1965–1980 to an average of 1.8% in 1980–1996 (World Bank 1992: 268; 1998a: 43). The resultant average population growth of 2.0% translated into a growth of GNP per capita at an average rate of 4.7%, one of the highest rates among the world's fast-growing economies (World Bank 1998a: 25). While per capita GNP was around $100 in the mid-1960s, it had reached $580 in 1982, enabling Indonesia to 'graduate' from the ranks of the 'low-income' into the ranks of the 'lower middle-income economies'. By the early 1990s per capita GNP had reached almost $1000.

Indonesia's sustained rapid economic growth during this period led to a considerable improvement in the economic and social welfare of Indonesia's population, as reflected in a sharp reduction in the incidence of absolute poverty as well as rising educational levels and higher life expectancies.

Rapid economic growth was underpinned by expansion of all three main sectors, namely agriculture, manufacturing and services (Table 7.1; World Bank 1992: 220, 222; 1998b: 177, 181).[1] The manufacturing sector grew faster than in the three other large ASEAN neighbours, Malaysia, the Philippines and Thailand, and only slightly slower than in South Korea. By 1995 Indonesia had, in terms of gross Manufacturing Value Added (MVA), the seventh-largest manufacturing sector among the developing countries after China, Brazil, South Korea, India, Argentina and Mexico (World Bank 1998b: 184–6).

Like Malaysia and Thailand a few years earlier, after the mid-1980s Indonesia also lessened its traditional dependence on primary exports by rapidly increasing its manufactured exports. For this reason the World Bank study on the 'East Asian Miracle' classified Indonesia as one of three

Table 7.1 Economic growth in Indonesia, 1965–1996			
	Average annual growth rate (%)		
	1965/1980	1980/1990	1990/1996
GDP	7.0	6.1	7.7
Agriculture	4.3	3.4	2.8
Industry	11.9	6.9	10.2
Manufacturing	12.0	12.6	11.1
Services	7.3	7.0	7.4

Figure 7.1   Composition of GDP in Indonesia, 1965–1996

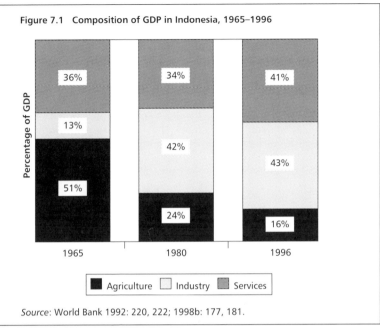

Source: World Bank 1992: 220, 222; 1998b: 177, 181.

Figure 7.2   Employment by sector in Indonesia, 1971–1996

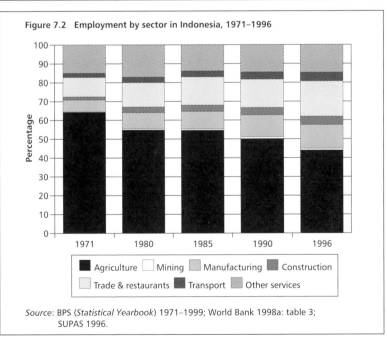

Source: BPS (*Statistical Yearbook*) 1971–1999; World Bank 1998a: table 3;
          SUPAS 1996.

'Newly Industrialising Economies' (World Bank 1993a: xvi). Over the three decades of the New Order the Indonesian economy also experienced rapid structural transformation (Figure 7.1). Even though agricultural outputrose steadily in absolute terms, by 1996 agriculture's relative share in Indonesia's GDP was less than one-third of that in 1965. Conversely, sustained double-digit growth enabled manufacturing to more than treble its relative share in GDP. In 1991 the share of manufacturing in GDP for the first time in Indonesia's economic history exceeded that of agriculture (Pangestu 1996: 104). This was a milestone in realising the long-held national aspiration for a 'more balanced' economy.

The transformation of the Indonesian economy was also accompanied by a transformation in the occupational distribution of the labour force (Figure 7.2). Agriculture's share of GDP declined much faster than its share of the workforce, which fell from 64% in 1971 to 44% in 1996. Yet the absolute number engaged in agriculture rose from a little over 25 million in 1971 to almost 40 million in 1990, when the number of agricultural workers began to decline, particularly in Java (Manning 1998: 88). The difference between the rapid decline in agriculture's relative share of GDP and the slower decline of the workforce share has been one important structural characteristic of Indonesia's development during the period 1971–1996. This difference is reflected in a more rapid increase in labour productivity in the non-agricultural sectors relative to that in agriculture compared with other developing economies (Manning 1998: 89). Conversely, employment growth in the industrial sector, including manufacturing, construction, mining and public utilities, has been high by developing-economy standards. This was largely the result of rapid employment growth in the small subsectors of industry, particularly construction, mining and public utilities, over the period 1971–1995 (Manning 1998: 93).

Indonesia's rapid economic growth was underpinned by high rates of domestic capital investment (Table 7.2; World Bank 1985b; 1997b). By the mid-1990s Indonesia had one of the highest rates of gross domestic capital investment among the developing countries. These high rates

Table 7.2	Gross domestic investment and gross domestic savings in Indonesia, 1965–1996		
	1965	*1980*	*1995*
Gross domestic investment as % of GDP	8.0	24.0	32.0
Gross domestic savings as % of GDP	8.0	30.0	33.0
	1965/80	*1980/90*	*1990/96*
Average annual growth rate of gross domestic investment (%)	16.1	6.7	9.9

of capital investment were in turn sustained by rising rates of gross domestic savings, corresponding to 33% of GDP in 1996. This savings rate was one of the highest among developing countries.

Gross domestic investment consisted of public, domestic private and foreign direct investment. The Foreign Investment Law of 1967 and the Domestic Investment Law of 1968 both improved the previously hostile climate for private, including foreign, investment by extending tax and other incentives to new investors. During the oil boom years of the 1970s huge resource rent taxes enabled the Indonesian government to undertake large investments, particularly in physical infrastructure and social development, primarily health and education. By the late 1970s large-scale, capital-intensive, resource-processing, basic industries, including the steel and aluminium industries, had become a main target of public investment. After the end of the oil boom in the early 1980s private investment (including foreign direct investment) began to play a more important role, and by 1996 private investment (including foreign direct investment) accounted for 61% of gross domestic fixed capital formation (World Bank 1998a: 255).

The efficiency with which capital was utilised, however, was disappointing. Compared with other developing countries at similar stages of development, Indonesia was often wasteful in its use of capital, reflected in frequent complaints about Indonesia's 'high-cost economy'.

Social development

Indonesia's achievements in social development were less impressive than its economic achievement and overall compared less than favourably with its neighbours (Table 7.3; World Bank 1998b: 68–9; World Bank *World Development Report* (various issues); see also Hill 1996/2000a: 7).[2] Much of the progress in social development has been eroded by the economic crisis of 1997/98 (see below).

In education the Indonesian government used some of the windfall oil tax revenues to expand education, particularly in rural primary schools (Jones 1994: 164). Universal primary education was achieved in the 1980s, assisted by slower growth of the primary school age population due to the successful family planning program. In turn this necessitated expansion of high school, vocational and tertiary education to meet the needs of the booming manufacturing and construction industries (Jones 1994: 165). Given that the New Order government began with such a low level of enrolments, its achievements in expanding primary education may be seen as better than those of Malaysia, the Philippines and Thailand, and comparable to those of South Korea. However, expansion of secondary and tertiary education has lagged behind most neighbouring countries. Standards of adult literacy among both men and women are lower than in other countries in the region (with the exception of Malaysia).

Table 7.3 Indonesia's social achievements during the New Order period in regional comparison

Indicators (%)	Beginning of New Order							End of New Order						
	Indonesia	Malaysia	Philippines	Thailand	Singapore	Hong Kong	South Korea	Indonesia	Malaysia	Philippines	Thailand	Singapore	Hong Kong	South Korea
School enrolments (1965 vs 1996)														
primary	72	90	113	78	105	103	101	115	102	116	87	101	94	94
secondary	12	29	41	14	45	29	35	48	61	77	56	67	73	102
tertiary	1	2	19	2	10	5	6	11	11	35	21	39	28	60
Adult literacy *(Beginning: Average 1960)*														
male }	47	23	72	68	—	71	71	90	89	95	96	96	96	99
female }								78	78	94	86	86	88	97
Infant mortality rate (per 1000) (1970 vs 1997)	118	45	67	73	20	27	46	47	11	35	33	4	4	9
Life expectancy at birth (1960 vs 1996) *(Beginning: Average 1960)*														
male }	40	52	49	49	63	63	53	63	70	64	67	74	76	69
female }								67	74	68	72	79	81	76
Per capita daily calorie supply (1974 vs 1989)	2126	2574	1971	2382	2819	2533	2630	2750	2774	2375	2316	3198	2853	2852
Crude birth rate (per 1000) (1965 vs 1996)	43	41	46	43	31	28	36	23	27	29	17	16	10	15
Crude death rate (per 1000) (1975 vs 1996)	20	12	12	12	6	6	12	8	5	7	7	5	5	6

Public health also improved markedly under the New Order. Rising incomes and the government's successful efforts to stimulate food production boosted per capita daily calorie supply. This level was comparable to Malaysia and the Asian 'Tigers' (South Korea, Hong Kong, Taiwan and Singapore) and higher than in the Philippines and Thailand. However, malnutrition among children under 5 years of age was more widespread than in the other countries.

Improved nutrition, environment and health care through local public health clinics led to a sharp fall in infant mortality rates. However, by 1996 these rates were still much higher than in other East Asian countries. Nevertheless, the substantial decline in infant mortality rates reinforced the family planning program by contributing to a reduction in the desired family size (Hull 1994: 139–40). The sharp fall in infant mortality rates also contributed to a substantial decline in the crude death rate.

In Indonesia as in most other developing countries social development followed in the wake of economic development. That Indonesia started economic development about a decade later than its ASEAN neighbours and the Asian Tigers helps to explain why in its social development Indonesia in general lagged behind those other countries.

Economic policies and outcomes during the Soeharto era

Whereas politics determines the periodisation between 1945 and 1966, a division of the Soeharto era into three major phases, each characterised by specific economic challenges, policies and performance, would be more appropriate. These phases are:

- *1966–1973*: stabilisation, rehabilitation, partial liberalisation and economic recovery;
- *1974–1982*: oil booms, rapid economic growth and increasing government intervention;
- *1983–1996*: post-oil boom, deregulation, renewed liberalisation and rapid export-led growth.

1966–1973: stabilisation, rehabilitation, partial liberalisation and economic recovery   Faced with the economic breakdown of the country left by the Sukarno government, the New Order government gave top priority to economic recovery. To achieve this objective, the new government adopted a pragmatic, non-ideological approach and entrusted economic policy making to the economic technocrats, led by Professor Widjojo Nitisastro. The pragmatic, non-ideological approach allowed the new government to implement various economic policies which in fundamental ways differed from the former government.

One basic feature that distinguished the economic policies of the new government from those of its predecessor was the reintegration of Indonesia into the global or world economy — that is, the creation of an open economy (Hollinger 1996: 25). While Indonesia had been an open economy since the late 19th century, economic policies during the last years of the Sukarno government could in a way be characterised as 'delinking policies', that is policies aimed at cutting or at least reducing links with the (Western) capitalist countries (Diaz-Alejandro 1978: 105; see also Chapter 6).

From the outset Soeharto recognised that these anti-Western or anti-capitalist attitudes were not only characteristic of the previous regime but were also part of the problem (Hollinger 1996: 25). Hence, the policy of reintegrating Indonesia into the world economy began almost immediately after the new government took office and was a cornerstone of the New Order government throughout its three decades in power. In consequence, the New Order government gradually reduced trade and investment barriers, particularly after the oil boom era had ended in the early 1980s, though more out of necessity than conviction.

In pursuing these policies the new government had to take political risks. Key elements of these policies ran counter to strongly held nationalist beliefs of large parts of the Indonesian people, including many political leaders and intellectuals. The potentially controversial elements of these policies included the role to be played by foreign aid, foreign direct investment and the private sector. Longstanding distrust of the private sector had arisen during the period of Dutch colonial rule (Hollinger 1996: 8; see also Chapter 5).

With the full support of Soeharto, these economic technocrats prepared a multi-year economic plan for economic recovery which was divided into three phases: stabilisation, rehabilitation, and development. A two-year stabilisation plan was drawn up containing four short-term objectives: halting hyperinflation; decontrol; rescheduling foreign debts and obtaining new credits; and a new, open-door policy towards foreign direct investment (Arndt 1984: 32).

Inheriting a crippling hyperinflation, the new government gave top priority to restoring macroeconomic stability, particularly price stability. To achieve this objective, the government introduced tight fiscal and monetary policies. As the hyperinflation had been caused by excessive money creation to finance the government's budget deficit, the New Order government enacted a 'balanced budget' law in 1967 to ensure fiscal discipline. This law prohibited domestic financing of the budget in the form of domestic debt or through money creation (Bhattacharya & Pangestu 1993: 6). Any shortfall in government revenues was to be supplemented by foreign aid inflows, thus treating Official Development Assistance (ODA) as government revenue. The stringent fiscal and monetary discipline imposed by the government quickly brought inflation down from 636% in 1966 to 112% in 1967, 85% in 1968, 10% in 1969 and 9% in 1970 (Grenville 1981: 108).

The decontrol objective involved dismantling the complex system of foreign trade and exchange controls which had proliferated during the final years of the Sukarno administration. These direct controls aggravated price distortions and interfered with market incentives (Arndt 1984: 32). Many import controls were replaced by fluctuating exchange rates, while the multiple exchange rates were gradually merged into a unified exchange rate which, if set at a competitive level, could induce rapid growth in exports (James & Stephenson 1993: 10). In 1972 capital account transactions were liberalised, which enabled capital to move freely into or out of the country (James & Stephenson 1993: 16). Domestic price controls were removed on various goods and services, except for basic goods and services including petroleum products, electricity, urban transport and drinking water (Hollinger 1996: 23). These decontrol measures restored the free market mechanism despite popular suspicion of the workings of the free market and much bureaucratic resistance.

The third stabilisation objective was to reschedule the foreign debt service payments and secure new inflows of foreign aid. As the economic technocrats realised that Indonesia's large foreign debt incurred by the Sukarno government put a large burden on the balance of payments, a rescheduling of the debt service payments and new inflows of foreign aid were urgently required (Prawiro 1998: 58–64). The technocrats realised that new foreign aid and foreign investment were crucial to the survival of the new government and that they could not afford to indulge in nationalist rhetoric (Mackie & MacIntyre 1994: 11).

Requests to reschedule debt service payments were met with sympathetic hearing by the Western countries and Japan, which wanted to give the new, strongly anti-Communist government all the support it needed. In September 1966 Indonesia attended a preliminary meeting with the so-called 'Paris Club countries', comprising the Western countries, and Japan, to which Indonesia was indebted. As Indonesia under the Sukarno government also had incurred a large debt with the Communist countries, including the Soviet Union and Eastern Europe, these countries were also invited to attend the Tokyo meeting. However, they chose not to attend, preferring to hold a separate meeting with Indonesia (Prawiro 1998: 63). In Paris in December 1966, representatives of Indonesia's new government, the Western countries and Japan reached agreement on a moratorium of debt service payments on long-term debts incurred before June 1966 (Bresnan 1993: 70). Negotiations with Communist countries, particularly the Soviet Union, were more protracted, but in 1971 a rescheduling agreement was reached on similar terms to those of the 'Paris Club countries' (Prawiro 1998: 69).

Once the obstacle of rescheduling had been overcome, new aid flowed into Indonesia in steadily rising amounts. Building on the goodwill towards the new Indonesian government, the Western countries, Japan and the multilateral aid organisations, including the World Bank, the IMF and the Asian Development Bank (ADB), in 1967 established the aid consortium IGGI. By 1970 Indonesia ranked as the second-largest aid-recipient country after India among the developing countries. This international goodwill persisted for the next two decades as Indonesia continued to receive large amounts of foreign aid. By 1990 Indonesia had become the largest aid-recipient country, followed by India and China (McCawley 1993: 3). These official aid flows turned out to be crucial, as the implementation of the balanced budget law was crucially dependent on continued annual inflows of foreign aid (Sadli 1984: 103–5).

The new government's economic advisers also realised that new foreign direct investment would be required to develop Indonesia's natural resources and to resume its long-delayed industrialisation efforts (Sadli 1972: 203). The hostile foreign investment policy of the Sukarno government was reversed by enacting a new Foreign Investment Law in 1967. This law contained attractive incentives and guarantees to foreign investors, including generous tax concessions, guarantees for the free transfer of profits and dividends and a guarantee against arbitrary national-isation (Sadli 1972: 204). This new law opened Indonesia's door wide to foreign direct investment, at least for a few years.

In 1968 the government also overturned policies hostile towards domestic private enterprise by enacting a Domestic Investment Law, which offered Indonesian entrepreneurs similar incentives and guarantees to those given to foreign investors.

The impending arrival of new foreign investors only a few years after the nationalisation of Dutch enterprises aroused renewed concern that Indonesia would again be dominated by foreign enterprise and the local non-indigenous entrepreneurs, mostly Sino-Indonesians. However, the economy was in such a shambles that there was no alternative for the new government but to restore the economy. The new government also had to reassure the Chinese businessmen that their investments would be safe and protected. This would also require a stable political climate in which pragmatism took precedence over economic nationalism and populism. The retreat from *étatisme* and the more favourable stance towards the private sector was reflected in some reduction in preferential treatment to state-owned enterprises (SOEs) (McCawley 1981: 64).

These pragmatic policies resulted in an impressive economic recovery. Over the period 1967–1973 economic growth averaged over 7%. Gross investment, financed for about two-thirds by private domestic savings and for one-third by foreign savings (i.e. foreign aid), rose steadily from 8% of GDP in 1967 to almost 18% in 1973 (Gillis 1984: 245–6). The relatively high share of private domestic savings during the period 1967–1972 may partly have been caused by the repatriation of capital by Indonesian residents, primarily Sino-Indonesians, who had fled the country during the turbulent years of the late 1950s and early 1960s but returned to Indonesia after political stability had been restored. Government savings, which had been negligible in the mid-1960s, also began to rise steadily as a result of tight control over government expenditures combined with a greater effort at collecting taxes (Gillis 1984: 246). Realised foreign direct investment jumped from a cumulative $83 million during the years 1967/69 to $271 million in 1972, which shows the benefits of an open capital account (James & Stephenson 1993: 16).

1974–1981: the oil boom years, rapid growth and increasing government intervention   Over the period 1974–1981 Indonesia experienced rapid and sustained economic growth, with real GDP growing at an unprecedented average annual rate of 7.7% (Hill 1996/2000a: 16). This was an impressive performance compared with the sluggish growth during the 1950s and early 1960s. It was also an impressive performance compared with most other developing countries (Booth 1992b: 1).

To a large extent this rapid growth was attributable to the substantial improvement in the country's international terms of trade (i.e. the ratio of the average price of a country's exports to the average price of its imports) as a result of the two oil booms in the 1970s. The first oil boom occurred in 1973/74 when the Organisation of Petroleum-Exporting Countries (OPEC), of which Indonesia was a member, was able to quadruple the export price of oil by cutting back its oil exports. The second oil boom of 1978/79 occurred when a revolution against the Shah's regime in Iran, the world's second-largest oil producer and exporter, led to a temporary closure of the country's oil industry. This created a short-term imbalance in the world oil supply and demand, which led to a further doubling of the price of oil to about $30 per barrel by early 1980 (Odell 1981: 255–6). In nominal terms the price of Indonesia's oil rose from $1.67 per barrel in 1970 to $35 in 1981 (Prawiro 1998: 101).

As a result of these oil booms, Indonesia's export earnings rose steeply, as did government revenues from the oil taxes paid by the foreign oil companies operating in Indonesia. The sudden oil windfall gain was an extraordinary bonanza for Indonesia which relieved both the balance of payments and the budget constraints that had greatly hampered economic policy throughout the 1950s and 1960s (Booth & McCawley 1981: 11–12). Oil export earnings rose steeply as the share of oil in total export earnings increased from about 17% before 1974 to between one-half and more for the rest of the decade. Government revenues from taxes paid by the foreign oil companies operating in Indonesia rose from about one-third of total government revenues before 1974 to more than than two-thirds by 1979 (Gillis 1984: 246). As a result, the public sector was able to play a greater role in the economy, as central government revenues as a share of GDP rose from 4.2% in 1966 to 22.1% in 1986, while government expenditures rose from 9.3% to 22.1% respectively (Booth 1989b: 120). However, in comparative perspective, the oil windfall was in one respect worth less to Indonesia than to the other oil-exporting, developing countries. In dollars per capita, because of its large population, Indonesia's windfall was quite modest compared to most other OPEC countries (Bresnan 1993: 190).

Due to the higher oil revenues, the Indonesian government was able to undertake substantial public investments and expand and improve the efficiency of the public administration sector (for instance by raising the salaries of public servants) which, in turn, contributed to economic growth. In addition, the increased foreign exchange earnings made it possible to import more raw materials, intermediate inputs and capital goods needed by the rapidly growing manufacturing sector. Economic growth was stimulated not only by increased investment, as reflected in increased imports of capital goods, but also by the more modern and sophisticated process and product technologies embodied in the imported capital goods (Sundrum 1986: 63–4).

By the mid-1970s a shift back towards more government intervention also affected policy on foreign and domestic investment. Two factors accounted for this shift. For one thing, since the early 1970s latent economic nationalism had re-emerged in response to the perceived 'sell-out' of the economy to foreign capital and the perceived preferential treatment accorded to a number of favoured non-indigenous (i.e. ethnic Chinese) entrepreneurs (pejoratively referred to as *cukong*), particularly by the provision of lavish credits by the state-owned banks. The public resentment against the perceived 'over-presence' of foreign, specifically Japanese, investment projects and dominance of non-indigenous capitalists culminated in anti-Japanese riots in January 1974 (the *Malari affair*) during a state visit by Japanese prime minister Tanaka (Bresnan 1993: 152–4).

The government responded to this serious incident by introducing more restrictive measures on foreign investment and preferential policies favouring indigenous businessmen. For instance, from 1974 new foreign direct investment could enter Indonesia only in the form of joint ventures with national businessmen or companies in which *pribumi* businessmen had majority ownership and/or majority control or were to obtain this in the near future. The second and more important factor leading to more government intervention was the vastly increased government revenue from oil company taxes, which largely removed the budget constraint on the government's development plans. Having largely overcome the economic difficulties left by the Sukarno government, the government felt able and confident to revise its erstwhile liberal, free-market policies in favour of more interventionist policies (Mackie & MacIntyre 1994: 35). These interventionist policies took the form of a more activist and direct role of the government in accelerating economic development.

The oil booms provided an opportunity for the central government to launch several ambitious development programs. These new programs included promoting development in the regions, social development, expanding physical infrastructure and establishing large-scale basic (heavy) industries. To promote regional development, the central government recycled part of its oil revenues through the so-called 'Presidential Instruction', or *Inpres* (*Instruksi Presiden*), programs to the various provinces.

Through both these *Inpres* grants and foreign aid programs, many of the more backward, resource-poor provinces in both Java and outside Java received a considerable boost in development assistance in the 1970s (Booth 1992b: 30). Most of these *Inpres* programs were allocated to the three tiers of local government — the province, district and subdistrict — to be spent on rural infrastructure development (Prawiro 1998: 175). A subsidiary aim of these *Inpres* programs was to improve the quality and effectiveness of local public administration. To qualify for grants, local governments had to prepare plans and budgets and, at the end of each fiscal year, submit reports. In view of the modest tax base of the regional governments, the rapidly expanding central government grants made possible by the oil revenues greatly enhanced the power of the central government vis-à-vis the provincial and sub-provincial governments, both in control of financial resources and decision-making authority (Mackie 1997: 29–30).

During the 1970s an increasing part of the government's oil revenues was also recycled into social development, particularly education, health care and family planning. Government spending on these three sectors rose steadily from 11% of the development budget during the First Five Year Development Plan, *Repelita* I (*Rencana Pembangunan Lima Tahun*) (1969/70–1973/74), to almost 15% during *Repelita* II (1974/75–1978/79), and further to 19% during *Repelita* III (1979/80–1983/84). The strong commitment to social development persisted even after the oil boom era was over in the 1980s (Prawiro 1998: 175). The outcome of this commitment to social development is shown in Table 7.3.

After the early 1970s first foreign aid and then oil revenues were spent on rehabilitating and expanding the long-neglected physical infrastructure (particularly in rural areas) and transport infrastructure (Dick & Forbes 1992: 265, 280). This rapid expansion and improvement of the physical and transport infrastructure involved roads, railways, bridges, harbours, airports and communications (Hill 1996/2000a: 179). During this period the telecommunications infrastructure was also vastly expanded and modernised, including the establishment of an International Direct Dialling (IDD) facility in 1974 and the launching of the Palapa telecommunications satellite in 1976. Through this telecommunications satellite an integrated telephone system covering the whole country, and linking this to the International Subscriber Dialling (ISD) system, was created (Dick & Forbes 1992: 274). As a result of these vast investments in physical infrastructure, the transport and communications industry grew at a rapid rate during the 1970s and early 1980s (Hill 1996: 179). The contribution of the transport sector to GDP rose from 4.4% in 1971 to 5.0% in 1985. Employment in the transport, storage, and communication sectors also rose, from 2.3% of the total workforce to 3.1% (Dick & Forbes 1992: 264).

The oil boom, which coincided in the mid-1970s with the completion of the first ('easy') phase of import-substituting industrialisation (i.e. substituting imported consumer goods by locally made ones behind protectionist barriers), led the government to embark on an ambitious state-led program of 'industrial deepening' or second-phase import substitution involving the establishment of state-owned, upstream, basic, resource-processing industries. In 1978 a new Minister of State for Research and Technology, B.J. Habibie, was appointed to develop a range of strategic, state-owned industries, notably a 'hi-tech' aircraft assembling industry.

The government's development plans experienced a setback in the mid-1970s because of the unexpected bankruptcy of Pertamina, the powerful state-owned oil company, when it defaulted on a short-term loan from a foreign bank. Under the strong leadership of General Ibnu Sutowo, Pertamina had grown into 'Indonesia's unofficial development agency', even 'a state within a state' (Prawiro 1998: 105). Because of Indonesia's open capital account, Pertamina had, without the knowledge of the government, been able to evade restrictions on long-term loans by state-owned enterprises by borrowing large amounts of short-term credit on the international capital market (McCawley 1978). These loans were used to finance a number of ambitious projects, including the huge Krakatau Steel plant, which cost at least $5.6 billion (Arndt 1984: 249; Hill 1996/2000a: 16). Because of Pertamina's bankruptcy, a considerable part of the government's oil revenues had to be wasted bailing out Pertamina.

1983–1996: post-oil boom, deregulation, renewed liberalisation and rapid export-led growth   As the price of oil began to fall in 1982, Indonesia's external terms of trade deteriorated. Other adverse factors affecting the Indonesian economy were the recession in the major industrial countries and the currency realignments of 1985, which aggravated Indonesia's foreign debt burden. Almost 40% of Indonesia's foreign debt was denominated in Japanese yen, while its export earnings were denominated in US dollars, which had depreciated steeply vis-à-vis the yen. As the large part of government revenues were obtained from oil company taxes, the government had fewer financial resources available for development projects. In effect, the virtuous cycle of prosperity that Indonesia had enjoyed during the 1970s was now reversing itself.

In response to the worsening external conditions, the government in early 1983 initiated a broad-based adjustment program aimed at restoring macroeconomic stability. To deal with the rising current account deficit, the government devalued the rupiah in March 1983. The problem of falling government revenues was dealt with by an austerity program, involving the deferral of several large-scale public sector projects. A new tax law was introduced in December 1984 aimed at increasing non-oil taxes, particularly personal and corporate income taxes and a new Value-Added Tax (VAT), to offset the decline in oil company taxes. To improve the efficiency of the banking system and the mobilisation of domestic funds, a banking deregulation measure was introduced in June 1983. To this end state-owned banks, which at that time still accounted for the bulk of bank assets, were now allowed freely to set their interest rates, while credit ceilings were lifted.

To encourage more non-oil exports and wean the economy away from its heavy dependence on oil, the economic efficiency of those sectors capable of generating non-oil exports had to be boosted. Because this required an internationally competitive private sector oriented towards export markets, the government introduced a series of deregulation measures to improve both the trade regime and the investment climate for private investors, particularly foreign investors. However, during the early post-oil boom years, the shift from an import-substituting pattern of industrialisation towards an export-oriented one was contested. Several vested interest groups waged an effective rearguard action against further reforms. Some industrial policy makers did not seem to realise that shifting to an export-oriented strategy required sacrificing the highly protected upstream industries, which penalised downstream, export-oriented assembly industries by forcing them to use more expensive, locally made inputs. Hence, the number of categories of products subject to quantitative import restrictions or outright import bans actually increased. This was justified by the rising current account deficit, which could not yet be closed by non-oil exports.

Despite half-hearted attempts to shift to export promotion during the period 1983–1985, the economy performed rather well. Indonesia also benefited from the economic recovery of the major industrial countries after 1983/84. The current account deficit fell from $7.0 billion in fiscal year 1982/83 (8.5% of GNP) to $1.8 billion in 1985/86, which was a manageable 2.4% of GNP. Over the same period non-oil exports also rose steadily, from $3.9 billion in 1982/83 to $6.2 billion in 1985/86. Meanwhile, the fiscal deficit was reduced from 6.3% of GNP in 1982/83 to 1.9% in 1983/84 (World Bank 1985a: 1–2). By 1985/86 macroeconomic stability had largely been restored, as inflation was brought down to below 5% per annum, and the economy appeared set to resume its rapid growth (World Bank 1987: 1; Pangestu 1996: 103).

Not until early 1986, when the price of oil fell even more steeply than in 1982, did the government at last find the resolve to push through the policy reforms that had been urged by Indonesian and foreign economists. The price of oil collapsed from $25 a barrel in 1985 to $13 a barrel in early 1986, while prices of other primary products also fell. Indonesia's commodity terms of trade suddenly worsened by 34%, resulting in a 5% decline in national income (World Bank 1987: 1–2). Export promotion was now imperative. The experience of the Asian Tigers had shown that the initial stages of export-oriented industrialisation depended on a supportive trade regime which approximated free trade conditions for export-oriented firms. This implied that export-oriented firms were able to purchase their inputs, whether imported or locally procured, at world market prices (Little 1979: 14, 34). To this end the government introduced a series of trade reforms aimed at reducing the policy impediments hampering export-oriented firms. A first major step was the introduction of a duty exemption and drawback scheme in May 1986. Firms exporting at least 85% (later 65%) of their output were exempted from all import duties and regulations on importing their inputs (Muir 1986: 22).

In addition to these trade reforms, the government pursued a supportive exchange rate policy, to improve the international competitiveness of non-oil exports. In September 1986 the government devalued the rupiah following the steep decline in the price of oil. Thereafter a managed floating exchange rate was allowed to depreciate by 4%–5% annually to offset the differential between Indonesia's higher inflation rate and those of its major trading partners. By keeping inflationary pressures under control and pursuing a active managed float, the government was able to prevent the real effective exchange rate from appreciating and to keep local cost levels in line with those of its main international competitors (Pangestu 1996: 19).

Further trade reforms were introduced in the following years. A major trade reform was the May 1995 package, which included significant and almost across-the-board reductions in average tariffs and a preannounced schedule for further tariff reductions to the year 2003. This package also replaced or abolished the remaining Non-Tariff Barriers (NTBs) by more transparent tariff surcharges (World Bank 1995: 38–9).

The quickening pace of Indonesia's trade deregulation reflected accelerating trade deregulation in the other ASEAN countries, most notably in Malaysia and Thailand, and the impending subregional, regional and multilateral trade liberalisation initiatives of the ASEAN Free Trade Area (AFTA) Common Effective Preferential Tariff (CEPT) Scheme, the APEC (Asia-Pacific Economic Cooperation) Leaders' Summit Meeting in Bogor, Indonesia, in November 1994, and the Uruguay Round of GATT (General Agreement on Tariffs and Trade) negotiations concluded in late 1994 (World Bank 1995: 39).

Besides trade reforms, the policy packages of the late 1980s and early 1990s also deregulated foreign direct investment, by removing the restrictions that had been introduced since 1974. These deregulation measures were aimed at improving the investment climate for foreign investors, particularly for those investing in export-oriented ventures (Pangestu 1996: 157–65). One important measure was the replacement in 1989 of the complicated Investment Priority List with a much simpler and clearer Negative Investment List, which listed merely the small number of fields closed to foreign investment. Over the years this number was steadily reduced.

The most significant liberalisation of foreign investment was contained in the June 1994 deregulation package. Foreign investment approvals had been declining in 1993 and early 1994, reflecting the increasing competition from China to attract foreign investment (Hobohm 1995: 10–11). The divestment rule, which had been a tenet of Indonesia's foreign investment regime since 1974, had been a major deterrent to foreign investors, who were clearly concerned at losing management control over their operations. Under the June 1994 package new foreign investors had the alternative of either forming a joint venture with 95% majority equity ownership without any further mandatory divestment or forming a fully owned subsidiary with the stipulation that within a period of 10 years some (not specified) divestment would take place in favour of an Indonesian partner or the public (Pangestu & Azis 1994: 21–2).

Deregulation also affected the financial sector. The financial deregulation of October 1988 opened up the financial sector to new entrants. New private banks could be established with relatively low entry requirements; existing banks were allowed to set up branch offices across the country; and foreign banks were allowed to operate outside Jakarta subject to certain restrictions. To stimulate the development of the capital market, bank deposits were charged a 15% witholding tax.

These financial reforms had a dramatic effect on the development of the financial sector but also contained the seeds of serious trouble, which would erupt in the financial crisis of 1997/98. Failure to enforce prudential regulations allowed rapid expansion of a weak banking system. Many banks, often controlled by leading businessmen, flouted Bank Indonesia's rules, such as the legal lending limit on intra-group lending (lending to companies of the same business group).

The extensive and far-reaching deregulation measures that were introduced during the post-oil boom years aimed at extracting the maximum benefits from the reintegration with the world economy which had started in the late 1960s. Their outcome can be seen in various indicators on the growing integration with the global economy during the decade 1987–1997 (Appendix 7.A).

Despite the resumption of rapid growth in the late 1980s, several commentators, including academic economists, began to voice concern about threats not only to long-term growth but also to the cherished national goal of establishing a 'just and prosperous society' (*masyarakat adil dan makmur*). These issues were interrelated and included the burgeoning corruption at all levels of the government bureacracy, collusive relationships between political powerholders and their business cronies, and the proliferation of policy-generated barriers to domestic competition. The 'KKN' (*korupsi, kolusi, nepotisme*) practices, as they later became known, distorted market incentives by rewarding 'rent-seeking' rather than productive entrepreneurial activities. These practices, as reflected by the blatant preferential treatment accorded to well-connected businessmen, also led to the explosive growth of large business groups (conglomerates) owned and controlled by the President's relatives and cronies. With rapidly expanding interests in various economic activities, including estate agriculture, forestry, manufacturing, banking and real estate, the stranglehold of these conglomerates in the economy was likened to that of an octopus. This development reinforced the view about the 'widening economic gap' between rich and poor, thereby undermining the social cohesion required for political stability and national development. The fact that many of President Soeharto's business cronies were ethnic Chinese tycoons also aggravated public resentment at the perceived economic domination by the Sino-Indonesian minority. More specific economic concern was raised about the growing disregard of economic analysis in policy formulation; the ascendancy of the so-called 'technologists' and the attendant promotion of costly high-technology ('hi-tech') projects; and the slower growth of non-oil exports, particularly manufactured exports.

These worrisome developments were attributed to the waning influence of the economic technocrats. Senior economic technocrats, most notably professors Widjojo Nitisastro and Ali Wardhana, had retired after long ministerial service and, although appointed as economic advisers to the President, no longer held executive power. Some senior economic posts then passed to non-economists, many of them engineers, the so-called 'technologists'. Economists worried that these technologists favoured hi-tech projects of questionable economic viability, without regard to the economy-wide scarcity of economic resources or seemingly the impact on the size distribution of income (Nasution 1995: 4–5; McLeod 1993: 4–5).

The rise of the technologists was greatly facilitated by the growing political influence of B.J. Habibie, the powerful Minister of State for Research and Technology. According to Habibie and his fellow technologists, the development of Indonesia's human resources was crucial to accelerate the mastery of science and technology and enable Indonesia to build hi-tech enterprises (McLeod 1993: 4–5). When concern arose in the early 1990s about the slower growth of non-oil manufactured exports, Habibie pushed strongly for the development of strategic, particularly hi-tech industries, including his pet aircraft industry, which in his view were imperative if Indonesia were to sustain the growth of its manufactured exports. Habibie argued that in the face of rising competition from China and India with armies of cheap workers, Indonesia could not continue to rely on its comparative advantage in resource- and labour-intensive manufacturing industries (Thee 1994: 14). Economists responded that the issue was one of means (Thee 1994: 19). Without prudent policy that took proper account of resource constraints, ambitious projects would become devouring 'tapeworms', as one critical economist termed it (Nasution 1995: 3–4).

Another source of great concern to Indonesian economists was the proliferation of regulations and restrictions on domestic competition and trade. Whereas the trade regime had undergone drastic deregulation since the mid-1980s, the domestic market was still highly regulated, especially agriculture. Restraints on domestic competition included cartels, price controls, entry and exit controls, exclusive licensing, dominance of SOEs in certain industries, and ad hoc government interventions in favour of specific firms or sectors (Iqbal 1995: 14). Such restrictions artificially raised the costs of doing business in Indonesia, giving rise to complaints about the 'high-cost economy'. Restraints on domestic competition also reduced economic efficiency and limited economic opportunities, in particular for small- and medium-scale enterprises, which lacked political and administrative connections (Thee 1998: 119). Many restrictions were initiated by politically well-connected rent-seekers. Aside from the policy-generated barriers to domestic competition, politically well-connected businessmen also received preferential access to credit provided by state-owned banks, protection against import competition, and tax and duty exemptions. Such factors obviously damaged the investment climate for bona fide entrepreneurs.

One blatant example of a rent-seeking barrier to competition was the establishment in late 1990 of a private consortium, the Clove Marketing Board, or BPPC (*Badan Penyangga dan Pemasaran Cengkeh*), led by Tommy Soeharto, the President's youngest son, which was given the monopoly right to purchase and distribute cloves, an essential raw material for the production of the *kretek* (clove) cigarettes very popular with Indonesians. Although the clove monopoly was ostensibly granted to protect the clove farmers from exploitation by the large clove cigarette manufacturers, as critics had predicted the farm-gate price of cloves fell substantially (Parker 1991: 34).

With continued emphasis on sound macroeconomic policies and effective exchange rate management, the wide-ranging deregulation measures of the late 1980s and early 1990s bore good fruit. Non-oil exports, especially manufactured exports, now began to drive the economy. In the late 1980s the economy once again grew rapidly, as it had during the 1970s. GDP grew by an astounding 9.0% per year in 1988–1991 and at a lower but still very impressive annual rate of 7.3% over the period 1991–1994. In the two last years before the crisis, growth was 8.2% and 7.8% in 1995 and 1996 respectively (World Bank 1997a: 2). This was even more impressive than the performance during the 1970s, because it was achieved without the windfall benefit of vast oil revenues (Hill 1996/2000a: 17).

Indonesia thus followed in the footsteps of the Asian Tigers and its ASEAN neighbours, Malaysia and Thailand, as a significant exporter of manufactures, particularly resource- and low-skill labour-intensive products. The main sources of these manufactured exports were domestic firms, many of them small- and medium-sized enterprises, and foreign investment projects mostly set up since the late 1980s by firms from the Asian Tigers, particularly South Korea and Taiwan (Thee 1991: 58–65). Unlike the Korean conglomerates (*chaebol*), Indonesia's conglomerates remained focused on the protected domestic market. In 1993, the contribution of the top 50 conglomerates to total manufactured exports was a mere 16% (World Bank 1994b: 59).

Agricultural development

Agricultural development, as reflected by greater agricultural productivity and output, can contribute to an economy's development by supplying foodstuffs and raw materials to other expanding sectors (e.g. manufacturing) in the economy; providing an 'investible surplus' of savings and taxes to support investment in other expanding sectors; selling for cash a 'marketable surplus' that will raise the demand of the rural population for products of other expanding sectors; and relaxing the foreign exchange constraint through agricultural exports or by saving foreign exchange through avoiding food imports (Meier 1984: 427). Underemployed labour in agriculture can also be more productively employed in other expanding sectors, notably manufacturing.

Because poor rice harvests had often led to widespread hunger, the economic technocrats with the full support of President Soeharto gave top priority to agricultural development in the First Five Year Development Plan, *Repelita* I, for the period 1969/70–1973/74, specifically setting the goal of achieving self-sufficiency in rice (Prawiro 1998: 127). Having grown up in a poor village in Central Java, Soeharto himself had a strong personal commitment to food self-sufficiency and rural welfare.

Overall growth of the agricultural sector was quite impressive during the period 1965–1980, but thereafter gradually slowed (Table 7.1). Rice output, which received top priority, rose much faster than that of non-rice food crops and cash crops. The progress of the other three subsectors, fisheries, animal husbandry and forestry, was less than satisfactory (Hill 1996/2000a: 124).

The foodcrop subsector   Rapid agricultural growth was generated by rapid growth in cereal production, particularly rice, the main food crop. Over the period 1972–1982 rice output grew at an average annual rate of 5.7%, accelerating from 3.7% in 1972–1977 to 7.2% in 1977–1982 (Glassburner 1988: 215). By 1985 Indonesia had reached self-sufficiency in rice. This was a remarkable achievement, as only six years earlier, in 1979, Indonesia had been the world's largest importer of rice, importing 2.9 million metric tons at a cost of $600 million (Tabor 1992: 172). The output of other food crops was also growing, although at a less rapid rate (Glassburner 1988: 215). This performance was in sharp contrast to that of the 1950s and early 1960s, when Indonesia's agricultural growth was the slowest among major Asian countries. According to the Food and Agricultural Organisation (FAO), Indonesia's growth in per capita cereal production between 1974/75 and 1984/85 was the second highest in Asia after Myanmar (Booth 1988: 1).

Indonesia's good agricultural performance during this period contrasted with other oil-exporting countries such as Nigeria, Algeria, Venezuela and Ecuador, where agricultural output had either stagnated or declined ('de-agriculturalisation') as a result of the adverse effects of the so-called 'Dutch disease' following resource booms (Booth 1988: 1–2). Indonesia was able to avoid the harmful effects of the 'Dutch disease', which normally afflicts countries during resource booms, including oil booms, because of the great importance which the New Order government had attached to agricultural development. Countries afflicted with the 'Dutch disease' in the wake of a resource boom, say an oil boom, experience a marked shift in the production structure of their economies away from the non-booming tradeable goods sectors, including agriculture, and towards the non-tradeable sectors, including construction or commerce (Booth 1988: 1–2; Gelb et al. 1988: 214–15).

Rice was important, not only because it was the key staple food of most Indonesians but also because it was a basic wage good. The rice crisis of 1967, when a severe drought resulted in a very poor dry season rice harvest, reminded the new government that the provision of adequate rice supplies was essential to the success of stabilisation policy. Rice's weight in the Jakarta cost of living index was then 31% (Mears & Moeljono 1981: 29–30). In 1967 the government established the Food Logistics Agency, Bulog (*Badan Urusan Logistik*). Successor to the *Voedingsmiddelenfonds* (Foodstuffs Fund), established in 1939 by the Dutch colonial government (Mears & Moeljono 1981: 24), Bulog was charged with building and maintaining a buffer stock of rice, managing rice distribution throughout the country and engaging in market intervention to preserve rice price stability (within a certain band) (Prawiro 1998: 44). By defending a floor price of unmilled rice (*gabah*), the government hoped to stimulate rice production and contribute to the farmer's welfare (Pearson & Monke 1991: 2–3; Mears & Moeljono 1981: 33–4). Conversely, Bulog was also charged with stabilising the ceiling price of rice for urban consumers by injecting stored or imported rice supplies into domestic markets when shortages caused the price to rise excessively (Pearson & Monke 1991: 3).

The Indonesian government was fortunate to be able to benefit from the 'Green Revolution', involving the development of high-yielding, fertiliser-responsive seed varieties developed by the International Rice Research Institute (IRRI) in Los Baños, the Philippines, in the late 1960s and early 1970s. In the 1970s and 1980s these new high-yielding varieties (HYVs) were rapidly disseminated in smallholder food crop agriculture throughout Indonesia, particularly in Java, Bali and the better irrigated parts of Sumatra and Sulawesi, such as West Sumatra and South Sulawesi. As a result, rice output rose rapidly (Figure 7.3) (Booth 1995: 23–4; Hill 1996/2000a: 124). The Green Revolution in Indonesia was an outstanding example of government-sponsored technology transfer to millions of small farmers, who proved responsive to new cultivation technologies despite the need for high-cost inputs.

The Indonesian government's success in expanding rice output can be attributed to the rice-intensification programs, most notably the Mass

Guidance, or Bimas (*Bimbingan Massal*), program introduced on a trial basis by the Sukarno government and the Mass Intensification, or Inmas (*Intensifikasi Massal*), program. These programs involved the subsidised provision of various inputs, including the new HYVs, fertiliser, pesticides and credit, a supporting infrastructure, particularly a widespread irrigation system, extension services and the guarantee of a stable floor price for rice (Booth 1995: 23–4).

The rehabilitation and expansion of existing irrigation systems was mainly carried out in Java. In Sumatra the government also attempted to increase rice cultivation on tidal lands (*pasang surut*) and to develop rice estates (Mears & Moeljono 1981: 34). In the late 1980s these efforts were extended to grow rice on peat soil (*tanah gambut*) areas in Kalimantan. The government turned to some of the largest conglomerates to help finance their development. After the fall of Soeharto, however, this program was discontinued because of the huge costs involved with this project and its adverse enviromental impact.

Large factor subsidies induced quick adoption of the new inputs. When the number of farmers using HYVs was small, the subsidy bill was manageable. However, the rapid growth of the number of farmers using HYVs caused the fiscal burden to grow faster than the government's ability to mobilise domestic resources. Furthermore, the adverse institutional effects of chronic price distortion reduced the economic effectiveness and

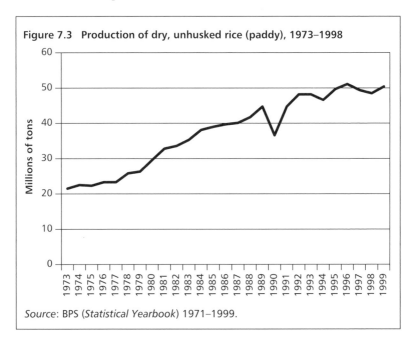

Figure 7.3   Production of dry, unhusked rice (paddy), 1973–1998

Source: BPS (*Statistical Yearbook*) 1971–1999.

efficiency of subsidies as a food policy tool (Tabor 1992: 177–8). This high-cost agricultural policy regime became a problem in the early 1990s, when agriculture was no longer the top-priority sector (Tabor 1992: 198), and the government was once again facing budget constraints.

At the height of the Green Revolution in the period 1978–1981 agricultural output, especially rice output, grew at the extraordinarily high rate of 6.1%. It then slowed down to a lower but still respectable 3.1% during the period 1982–1988 (Tabor 1992: 162). This slowdown was caused by the combined effects of depressed markets for agricultural commodities, slowdown in the expansion of the land frontier, ecological limits on further increases in cropping intensity, and technological limits to the Green Revolution for rice (Tabor 1992: 162). In the early 1990s agricultural growth slowed down because of the slowdown in irrigation investment and the technological limits of cropping intensities on irrigated land (Tabor 1992: 198).

The tree crop subsector   Similar government efforts to raise productivities and incomes of tree crop smallholders by transferring new technologies to the smallholder tree crop sector, most of it located in the islands outside Java, were less successful (Barlow & Tomich 1991: 50–1; Hill 1996/2000a: 142–3). Yields achieved by the smallholders in rubber, coffee and coconuts were little higher than the yields achieved during the Dutch colonial period (Booth 1998a: 284). Until the mid-1970s Indonesia lagged well behind Malaysia in replacing old rubber trees with new and more productive varieties.

From the mid-1950s to the mid-1970s government efforts to assist the tree crop smallholders were focused on the introduction of new yield- and quality-improving technologies to individual farmers. This was to be achieved by provision of tree crop extension services, improved planting materials from small scattered nurseries, and small loans for purchasing these materials and other modern inputs. The government also tried to regulate the trade in tree crops by introducing official marketing boards and limiting the activities of private dealers, most of whom were ethnic Chinese traders. In addition, it introduced subsidies to enable the smallholders to purchase fertilisers, pesticides and other material inputs (Barlow & Tomich 1991: 43).

The lack of success of these efforts led the government in the mid-1970s to introduce a radically different approach which, instead of assisting individual smallholders, involved the introduction of supervised plantings in large contiguous blocks. The Nucleus Estate Scheme, or PIR (*Perusahaan Inti Rakyat*), became the government's main vehicle to developing commercial farming by rubber, oil palm and sugar smallholders (Barlow & Johnston 1983: 9–10). The Nucleus Estates, often a large, state-owned estate enterprise, PTP (*Perseroan Terbatas Perkebunan*), assisted and supervised smallholders within a certain geographical area (referred to as a 'development block') of around 500 hectares in the planting or replanting of rubber seedlings, the processing of latex, and bulk sales (Barlow & Johnston 1983: 9).

Each smallholder, who could be a local farmer or a settler from Java, was provided with two hectares to grow tree crops. To cultivate a high-quality product, the smallholders were provided with key production inputs as well as with management advice, information and sometimes access to central processing facilities (Barlow & Tomich 1991: 44).

The shortcomings of the Nucleus Estate Scheme eventually became apparent. Being capital- and management-intensive, block development stifled the individual initiative of the rubber smallholders. Moreover, the tasks of developing the surrounding smallholdings put a heavy burden on the Nucleus Estate staff, which was not expanded in line with the additional duties (Barlow & Tomich 1991: 48).

By contrast, smallholdings and large private estates growing cocoa and particularly large, privately owned estates growing oil palm were quite successful. Here Indonesia had also lagged well behind Malaysia, which had diversified into oil palm in the 1930s. Until the mid-1980s most oil palm estates had been foreign- or state-owned. Subsequent investments were private estates, established by domestic private capital (particularly the large Salim and Sinar Mas business groups) and foreign capital, mostly from Malaysia (Sato 1997: 66–77).

The incentive for these private investors to establish oil palm estates was the rapid increase in world demand, including in Indonesia itself, for vegetable oils. Foreign and domestic demand for vegetable oils had been increasing rapidly because of the health benefits of vegetable oils over animal fats. Conglomerates that already operated oil palm processing plants set up oil palm estates on a large scale in order to secure a continuous supply of palm kernels. This development fostered the vertical integration of the oil palm processing industry with the plantation industry. It also forced the state-owned oil palm estates to raise their efficiency in order to survive (Sato 1997: 74–7). Indonesia emerged as the largest oil palm producer in the world, but at heavy environmental and social cost, as forest dwellers and small farmers had to be resettled — sometimes forcibly or without adequate compensation — to make way for these private estates.

Industrial development

Indonesia started its rapid industrialisation roughly two decades after the Philippines and one decade after three of the Asian 'Tigers' (South Korea, Taiwan and Singapore) and its two ASEAN neighbours, Malaysia and Thailand. Under the New Order government, however, rapid industrial development was initiated and sustained for three decades. In 1965 Indonesia had the third-smallest manufacturing sector in the region; by 1996 it had the second-largest manufacturing sector after South Korea (Table 7.4; World Bank 1991: tables 2, 3, 6, 16; 1998b: tables 4.1, 4.2, 4.4; 1999b: tables 4.1 to 4.3). This was achieved as Indonesian manufacturing

Table 7.4   Indonesia's industrial development in regional perspective, 1965–1996

	Manufacturing value added (MVA) (millions of current $)		Manufacturing average annual growth rate (%)			MVA as % of GDP		Manufactured exports as % of total exports	
	1970	1996	1965/80	1980/90	1990/96	1965	1996	1965	1996
ASEAN-4									
Indonesia	994	58 244	12.0	12.6	11.1	8	25	4	51
Malaysia	500	34 030	–	8.9	13.2	9	34	6	76
Philippines	1622	18 908	7.5	0.2	2.6	20	23	6	84
Thailand	1130	51 525	11.2	9.5	10.7	14	29	3	73
Three Asian Tigers									
South Korea	1880	125 314	18.7	13.0	7.9	18	29	59	92
Hong Kong	1013	10 352	–	–	–	24	9	94	92
Singapore	379	23 520	13.2	6.6	7.9	15	26	34	84

was growing at double-digit rates, one of the highest and most sustained among the developing countries.

In the late 1960s rapid industrial growth was stimulated by trade liberalisation and the restoration of macroeconomic stability. Attracted by the improvement in the investment climate, as reflected by the incentives and guarantees of the Foreign Investment Law of 1967 and the Domestic Investment Law of 1968, foreign and domestic investment rose rapidly, especially in manufacturing. Over the period 1967–1977 manufacturing received the second-largest amount of foreign investment after mining and petroleum (Hill 1988: 81). This new foreign direct investment brought not only capital but also valuable managerial, organisational and technical skills, as well as new industrial technologies.

During the 1970s Indonesia pursued one of the most inward-looking patterns of industrialisation among the Asian developing countries (Naya 1988: 87; Ariff & Hill 1985: 17). Under this industrial strategy, tariff and non-tariff protection enabled locally made light consumer goods and consumer durables to replace imported products. This phase is usually referred to as the first or 'easy' phase of import substitution. The policy tools included the highest nominal and effective rates of protection for consumer goods industries among the Southeast Asian countries, widespread use of non-tariff barriers, and even total import bans on some goods already being assembled or manufactured in Indonesia, including motor vehicles, electric appliances and consumer electronics products.

In the late 1970s Soehoed, the Minister of Industry, launched an ambitious, state-directed, second phase of import substitution. This involved 'deepening the industrial structure' by promoting the development of upstream industries, specifically basic, resource-processing industries. Fifty-two key basic industry projects were planned to be undertaken by SOEs. During the early years of the New Order, private enterprise was reluctant to enter the upsteam sector because of the smaller margins and higher risks involved, as well as the huge capital requirements (Soehoed 1988: 46).

Several economists expressed serious concern about the government's ambitious 'industrial deepening' plan, which was 'one massive exercise in import substitution' without any reference to efficiency or exportability considerations. Should this be the case, the potential damage to the economy would be far greater, as both the investment that would have to be protected and the number of downstream industries whose cost structures would be inflated by having to purchase higher-cost locally made inputs would be much greater than had been the case for protected light manufacturing during the 'easy' phase of import substitution (Gray 1982: 41–2). This concern was aggravated by the knowledge that this industrial strategy was strongly supported by the goverment/military bureaucracy, whose economic fortunes would be greatly advanced by the establishment and operation of new, large state-owned industries (Gray 1982: 49).

In addition to basic industries, Soehoed pushed the development of the engineering goods industry and its supporting industries making parts and components for the former assembly industries. To encourage the development of the supporting industries, in the late 1970s the Department of Industry introduced several mandatory 'deletion programs' (local content programs), under which the engineering goods industries were required to use progressively more locally made parts and components. These measures led to rapid but inefficient (and ultimately unsustainable) industrial growth. While the domestic market was still quite small, deletion programs seldom fostered economically viable supplier firms able to produce the high-quality parts and components required by export-oriented firms. By the early 1990s these deletion programs had been discontinued.

As mentioned above, it was only after the oil boom that the Indonesian government was forced to initiate a series of policy reforms, notably trade reforms and other deregulation measures, to stimulate the manufacturing sector to become export-oriented. This meant that the ambitious plan to set up a large number of large-scale, capital-intensive basic industries had to be deferred, if not scrapped altogether. The post-oil boom policy reforms were quite successful. After the late 1980s Indonesia followed Malaysia and Thailand in switching its traditional dependence on primary exports to reliance on manufactured exports (Figure 7.4). After 1987 the surge of manufactured exports was so remarkable that it can be considered a milestone in Indonesia's modern economic history (Hill 1987: 20). Industrial development was now being driven by manufactured exports and the private sector (Hill 1996/2000a: 154–5), in particular by low-skill labour-intensive exports, in which Indonesia has a strong comparative advantage.

In the case of the commercial vehicle industry, the deletion program was replaced in August 1993 by a so-called 'incentive program', under which the commercial vehicle assemblers were allowed to import fully built-up motor vehicles with progressively lower duties the higher the local content of their locally assembled motor vehicles. In early 1996 this incentive program was supplanted by the so-called 'national car policy', under which a company owned and controlled by Tommy Soeharto, the President's youngest son, was given exclusive rights to assemble a 'national car' with technical assistance from Korean automobile manufacturer Kia Motors. The joint venture company, *Timor Putra Nasional* (TPN), was given exclusive tax and duty exemptions to import the required parts and components from Korea (Manning & Jayasuriya 1996: 18–21). After the economic crisis of 1997 this economically unviable and highly unpopular project was terminated under the second agreement with the IMF in January 1998 (IMF II).[3]

The surge of manufactured exports after the late 1980s proved to be shortlived, as after 1993 the growth of Indonesia's manufactured exports began to slow down. Serious concern arose among policy makers that

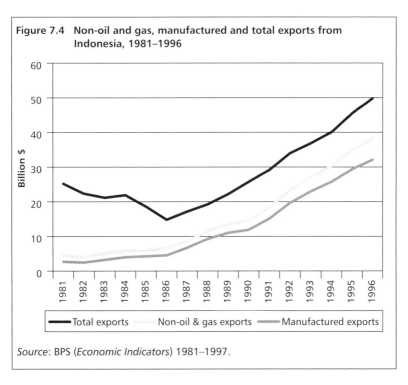

Figure 7.4   Non-oil and gas, manufactured and total exports from Indonesia, 1981–1996

Source: BPS (*Economic Indicators*) 1981–1997.

Indonesia could not continue to rely on resource- and labour-intensive manufactured exports in the face of strong competition from other low-wage rapidly industrialising countries, such as China, Vietnam, India and Bangladesh. This gave rise to demands on the part of the technologists and like-minded economists for an industrial policy to promote more technology- and skill-intensive industries in order to sustain the growth of manufactured exports. As mentioned above, some policy makers, notably the Minister for Research and Technology, Habibie, argued for a much faster entry to a range of high-technology industries, including the aircraft and shipbuilding industries, in order to sustain the growth of manufactured exports. Nevertheless, trade data showed that in the mid-1990s, even without explicit government intervention, the export base was already diversifying, most notably into technology- and skill-intensive products, including chemicals, electronics and other equipment (Table 7.5; James 1996; see also Manning & Jayasuriya 1996: 24). Economists critical of an explicit industrial policy therefore argued that the best economic incentives for sustaining manufactured export growth would be continued macroeconomic stability and a continuation of steady deregulation (James 1997: 13).

Table 7.5   Growth of Indonesia's manufactured exports by factor intensity, 1994–1995

No. of categories	Factor intensity	Manufactured exports (millions of $)		Growth rate (%) 1994/95
		1994	1995	
16	Natural resource–intensive products (NR)	12604.8	14617.4	16.0
11	Unskilled labour–intensive products (UL)	8028.0	8806.5	9.7
7	Human capital–intensive products (HC)	2688.2	3093.9	15.1
4	Technology–intensive products (TC)	1032.3	1304.4	26.3

Social welfare

Absolute poverty   One of the proudest achievements of the New Order government was its success in combining rapid growth with a sustained reduction in the incidence of absolute poverty. Estimates by Indonesia's Central Bureau of Statistics, BPS (*Biro/Badan Pusat Statistik*), indicate that the incidence of absolute poverty steadily declined from 40% of the population in 1976 to 11% in 1996. The decline took place in both urban and rural areas (Figure 7.5). The corresponding absolute number of people in poverty fell from around 54 million people in 1976 to 23 million people in 1996 (BPS 1999: 576). This steep reduction in absolute poverty was remarkable in comparison with other developing countries. A comparative study on poverty alleviation in a number of developing countries by the World Bank concluded that over the period 1970–1987 Indonesia was the most successful in reducing absolute poverty (World Bank 1990: 45).

Hence, in Indonesia no 'immiserising growth' took place: people did not become poorer as growth proceeded. This remarkable achievement can be attributed to the government's commitment to a broad-based rural development strategy, which targeted the rural areas in which the majority of Indonesia's poor were living and working. Much of the decline in absolute poverty between the mid-1970s and the mid-1990s was due to poverty alleviation in rural Java. The prime reason was the rapid growth in the availability of off-farm employment opportunities for rural households. This was made possible by the rapid growth of agricultural production, particularly rice, which had led to the generation of new jobs in agricultural processing, transport and commerce, and the rapid growth of the construction and manufacturing sectors in both rural and urban Java. Higher wage incomes contributed to higher household incomes and thus reduced poverty (Booth 1992c: 639).

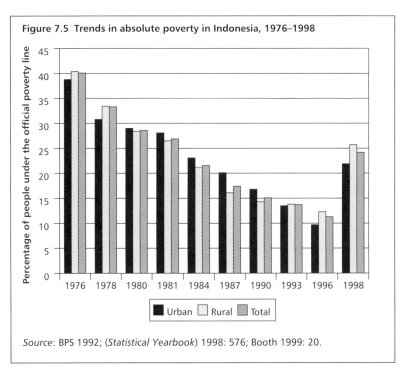

Figure 7.5 Trends in absolute poverty in Indonesia, 1976–1998

Source: BPS 1992; (*Statistical Yearbook*) 1998: 576; Booth 1999: 20.

Despite the undeniable fall in absolute poverty during the Soeharto era, estimates based on the official poverty line understate the incidence of absolute poverty. Indonesia's official poverty line is not only far lower than the ones used in neighbouring countries, such as the Philippines, which has approximately the same level of per capita income as Indonesia, but even lower than the ones used for the poorest countries in the world (Booth 1992c: 637). However, higher poverty lines would still show a clear downward trend in the incidence of absolute poverty, even though a higher poverty line, such as the one developed by the World Bank, would naturally show a higher incidence of absolute poverty than the official poverty line (Appendix 7.B).

Relative inequality

Another indicator of social welfare is relative inequality, which refers to the degree of inequality in the distribution of income in an economy. This is reflected in the percentage share of either income or consumption accruing to segments of the population ranked by income or consumption levels. The segments ranked lowest by personal income receive the smallest share of total income. Indonesia's performance in this regard was by and large comparable to that of neighbouring countries (World Bank 1999a: 70–3).

Table 7.6 Distribution of income in Indonesia, 1964/65–1996	
	Gini ratio
1964/65	0.35
1976	0.34
1987	0.32
1993	0.32
1995	0.34
1996	0.37

The extent to which the distribution of income (or consumption expenditures) deviates from a perfectly equal distribution can be expressed by a summary measure, the Gini ratio. This indicator reveals that income distribution in Indonesia remained fairly constant during the New Order era (Table 7.6; Hill 1996/2000a: 193; World Bank 1998b: 69–71; 1999b: 70–3).[4] In South Korea and Taiwan, by contrast, the Gini ratios were not only lower compared to most other developing countries, but also declined during the long period of rapid economic growth. Indonesia's higher Gini ratio may be due to the greater importance of large-scale capital- and resource-intensive industries during the early phases of industrialisation. As these industries require a higher proportion of highly skilled and professional employees, one might expect this to lead to a more unequal income distribution in Indonesia than in South Korea and Taiwan (Manning 1995: 76). The fact that Indonesia received more foreign direct investment (FDI) flows than these two countries may have contributed to a less equal income distribution through the effects of high remuneration paid to expatriate employees and flow-on effects on domestic managerial and professional manpower (Manning 1995: 77).

Despite such statistical evidence, the view was generally held that economic growth during the New Order era had widened economic disparities between the rich elite and the poor masses as well as between urban and rural areas and between western Indonesia and the much poorer eastern part of the archipelago. This perception was strengthened by the rise of the conglomerates, many of them owned and controlled by relatives or cronies of former President Soeharto.

Insofar as an unequal income distribution reflects an unequal distribution of wealth or productive assets (Ahluwalia & Chenery 1974: 43–4), rapid economic growth can be expected to lead to asset concentration in the privileged groups in society, in both physical assets (land, shares in companies, factories, banks and other economic entities) and non-physical assets (educational opportunities, particularly elite secondary school education and opportunities to pursue tertiary education overseas). However, in the absence of data on wealth or asset distribution, the evidence of widening economic disparities of wealth is circumstantial.

Urban–rural income disparities   Another disparity is that between urban and rural incomes. In his study on urban bias in world development, Lipton argues that the process of development in developing countries is characterised by a strong urban bias. In most developing countries the allocation of scarce resources between urban and rural areas and within the urban areas themselves often reflects urban priorities rather than equity or efficiency (Lipton 1978: 13). The disparity between urban and rural welfare is much greater in developing countries now than it was in the advanced countries during their early development (Lipton 1978: 16). Using expenditure data as a proxy for income data, Booth and Sundrum found that urban–rural income disparities grew between 1970 and 1976, especially in Java. While average urban incomes in 1970 were 42% higher than average rural incomes, this disparity had increased to 84% by 1976, clear evidence of a rising urban bias (Booth & Sundrum 1981: 202). Urban–rural income disparities stabilised in the 1980s and early 1990s, but the gap between average incomes in the Greater Jakarta Region and average rural incomes further widened. By 1993 urban incomes were 92% higher than rural incomes, but those in Jakarta were 205% higher (Booth 1998b: 10–11). Thus average incomes grew not only much faster in Jakarta than in the rural areas, but also faster than in other major cities (Booth 1998b: 11). Indonesia's development during the 1980s and early 1990s was therefore characterised not only by an urban bias but also by a pronounced 'capital city bias'. Investment in large and medium-scale manufacturing plants as well as in associated infrastructure was concentrated in the Greater Jakarta Region and towards Bandung, and to a lesser extent also around Surabaya.

Regional income disparities   Another aspect of relative inequality is the economic disparity between the various provinces in Indonesia. World Bank estimates indicate that per capita GDP and per capita consumption improved in all provinces of Indonesia during the years 1983–1993, a period for which consistent regional accounts are available. The incidence of absolute poverty also declined in all provinces, although it remained quite high in West and East Nusa Tenggara, the poorest provinces. Regional indicators on social development confirm these trends. Despite these improvements, some social indicators remained similar to low-income countries (World Bank 1996a: 92).

Despite rapid growth of Gross Provincial Product (GPP) in the poorer provinces, marked regional disparities in GPP per capita persisted into the mid-1990s, and were quite high by international standards (Booth 1992d: 41). This problem had several aspects. First, Java and Bali, which in the mid-1970s had counted as poor provinces, benefited from the rapid growth of the manufacturing and modern service sectors. This was one main factor behind the overall decline in regional income disparity (Booth 1998b: 9). The Greater Jakarta Region, however, advanced well ahead of the country, while West and East Nusa Tenggara lagged far behind (Hill 1998b: 32).

Second, in contrast to the deregulation of the manufacturing sector, agriculture continued to be subject to onerous regulations and restrictions. Although ostensibly imposed to benefit farmers, these measures usually depressed the incomes of poor farmers, particularly in Eastern Indonesia. A blatant example of such a regulation was the establishment of the Clove Marketing Board (BPPC) which, acting as a monopsonist, particularly hurt farmers in eastern Indonesia — particularly Sulawesi and Maluku, where most cloves (*cengkeh*) are grown — by depressed farm-gate prices (Hill 1998b: 31). Another example was the restriction on the trade in livestock, an important sector in eastern Indonesia, particularly in West Nusa Tenggara, where it accounted for more than 20% of GPP. By imposing a maximum quota for interisland export, this restriction prevented increased production of livestock in this and other provinces where livestock holding is an important economic activity. The worst-affected producers were smallholders, as the export permits were usually given to large traders (Azis 1995: 14).

Third, some of the country's most valuable natural resources, including oil, natural gas, minerals and timber, are concentrated in a few sparsely populated provinces outside Java (Booth 1992d: 41). Resource-rich provinces, specifically Aceh, Riau, East Kalimantan and Irian Jaya (Papua), were among the richest provinces in terms of GPP per capita, yet per capita consumption standards there were generally lower than per capita GPP levels would predict (Booth 1992d: 41). Moreover, in the oil-producing regions of Riau, South Sumatra and East Kalimantan, GPP per capita had actually been growing more slowly since the mid-1970s than national GDP per capita.

The explanation is that a substantial portion of these provinces' GPP was being transferred to other parts of the country, notably to the central government, as taxes, or to overseas (Booth 1992d: 41–2). Huge financial transfers of resources from these resource-rich provinces, as reflected by their large export surpluses, understandably led to serious discontent and the emergence of separatist forces, particularly in Aceh and Irian Jaya. These tensions would later explode after the fall of Soeharto, presenting the new central government with the challenge of reconciling national integrity with the granting of much greater autonomy to the regions.

In some provinces intra-regional income disparities were a problem, particularly in Java, where large concentrations of manufacturing industries had emerged within and around the big urban centres of Jakarta and Surabaya and to a lesser extent in Bandung. Other heavy industrial centres were also emerging, for instance the steel industry complex around the town of Cilegon at the western tip of the province of West Java and a chemical industry complex at the port of Cilacap on the south coast tip of Java. The emergence of these industrial centres was an inevitable consequence of the ongoing process of industrialisation, but most likely contributed to more rapid urbanisation as people living in relatively stagnant rural areas migrated to better-paying jobs in the manufacturing and the modern service sectors (Booth 1998b: 10).

The environmental impact of development

As in many other rapidly developing countries, Indonesia's rapid economic and population growth have done much damage to the environment. Resource degradation and resource depletion have been the two main problems. In the case of land and water resources, resource degradation involved ecological adjustment to a lower and often less stable level of productivity (Hardjono 1994: 179). Resource depletion has been a problem not only with non-renewable resources, like minerals, but also with renewable resources like timber. Because of the indiscriminate felling and burning of trees in these tropical hardwood forests, one of Indonesia's most valuable renewable resources has been gravely depleted.

During the first decade of the New Order, the government pushed rapid economic growth without much regard to environmental consequences. By the late 1970s, however, the environmental damage, especially air and water pollution, had become apparent even in Jakarta. In 1978 President Soeharto appointed economist Emil Salim as Indonesia's first Minister for the Environment. His task was to find a path of sustainable development in which economic development could be combined with protection of the environment (Salim 1997: 62). As a Minister of State, however, Salim was not an executive agent and had to work through the other ministers, who had their own sectoral concerns and were therefore indifferent, sometimes even hostile, to environmental concerns. Salim, however, was able to convince the President and the National Planning Board, *Bappenas* (*Badan Perencanaan Pembangunan Nasional*), that an agency was needed for implementing environmental protection (Salim 1997: 64). To this end an Environmental Impact Management Agency was established in 1990 to control air and water pollution. Over the years this agency enjoyed growing support from an urban middle class increasingly vocal about the right to live in a healthy environment. In the late 1980s the Minister for Environment also launched the Clean Rivers (*Prokasih*) project, which required industries to clean up the rivers they had polluted and install sewerage treatment facilities to prevent further pollution (Salim 1997: 63).

The three crucial issues faced by Indonesia in preventing further damage to the environment and achieving sustainable development are land use management, the growing threat of urban and industrial pollution, and the costs and consequences of environmental degradation (World Bank 1994a: xii–vi). The problem of land use has become pressing as a result of rapid population growth and changes in the nature and intensity of economic activity throughout Indonesia. In Java landless farmers have encroached on upland forests, causing erosion and floods during the rainy season and thus depleting the fertile topsoil; conversion of coastal wetlands to aquaculture has also led to soil erosion, flooding of coastal areas and loss of valuable marine resources (World Bank 1994a: xii–iii). In the Outer Islands forests and coastal wetlands have been converted to plantations (mostly oil palm) or agriculture, while reckless commercial exploitation of the tropical rain-forest has led to rapid depletion of this potentially renewable resource (World Bank 1994a: xiii).

Rapid industrialisation and urbanisation have led to serious industrial and urban pollution and consequent health problems. Lack of reticulated sewerage or treatment of industrial and household wastes has caused contamination of rivers, groundwater and coastal fishing grounds. In Jakarta uncontrolled groundwater use has also caused advanced saline intrusion. In large cities, and again especially in Jakarta, air pollution caused mainly by vehicle emissions has become an increasingly serious health problem (World Bank 1993b: 17).

With regard to resource depletion, however, public awareness is still limited (Hardjono 1994: 214–15). This is clearly evident in the common but illegal practice of burning forests to clear land in the islands outside Java, particularly Sumatra and Kalimantan. Of Indonesia's estimated 114 million hectares of land covered by forests, 97% are located in the Outer Islands. Government-sponsored programs (transmigration and tree crop develop-ment programs), spontaneous migration from densely populated Java to the other islands, and their lower land productivity, have led to great pressure on land. This has led to the progressive encroachment on forest lands and the conversion of unsuitable lands to agriculture (World Bank 1988: 92). In the 1980s the rate of deforestation caused by smallholder conversion, devel-opment projects, poor logging practices and natural and man-made disasters was estimated at nearly 900 000 hectares/year (World Bank 1988: 91–2).

In mid-1997 the reckless felling and burning of trees by operators of large estates, transmigration contractors, timber concessionnaires, and to a lesser extent shifting cultivators, led to devastating forest fires in Sumatra and Kalimantan, which were aggravated by the El Niño drought. These caused serious smog problems in the two islands and in peninsular Malaysia and Singapore. This led not only to a sharp fall in crop yields, lower incomes for farmers and a sharp drop in tourism but also to serious health problems (World Bank 1998a: 1.1).

THE CRISIS OF THE LATE 1990s

The course of the crisis

Since the early 1990s the Indonesian economy had been performing very well, growing at an average rate of 7.7%. In 1996 inflation was down to 6%, while approved domestic investment as well as foreign exchange reserves were growing rapidly (McLeod 1997a: 6–10). In May 1997 a cautiously upbeat World Bank Country Report had, on the assumption of continued rising domestic and foreign direct investment, projected a similar robust average growth rate of 7.8% for the remainder of the 1990s (World Bank 1997a: 28–9). The report, however, also identified a number of domestic and external risks facing the Indonesian economy. These risks included persistently high inflation, a weak banking sector, a slowdown in non-oil exports, a widening current account deficit and a rapidly rising private external debt (World Bank 1997a: xxvi). Looking ahead, the report warned, prophetically, that the current account was likely to worsen in the coming year, and that adverse developments in other Asian economies could spill over into Indonesia and lead to a reversal of capital inflows. These risks were magnified by Indonesia's large external debt and the increasing sensitivity of global capital flows (World Bank 1997a: xxvi). However, there was no inkling in the report that only two months later these problems would suddenly erupt and throw the Indonesian economy into a deep crisis.

Indonesia's financial crisis was precipitated by a crisis of confidence. Following the depreciation of the Thai baht in July 1997, which through the 'contagion effect' led to similar currency depreciations in the Philippines and Malaysia, foreign investors and creditors in Indonesia also became jittery and scrambled to reduce their exposure to Indonesia. Suddenly waking up to the large exposure of many Indonesian firms to large, unhedged, short-term offshore loans and the weakness of the banking system, these foreign investors and creditors started reassessing the risks of their Indonesian investments and loans. The newly perceived risk was that these firms would suffer big losses if the rupiah depreciated, like the baht, the peso and the ringgit. It was feared that this could lead to a proliferation of bad debts among the Indonesian banks, some of which were known to be very weak (McLeod 1997b: 42–3).

Concern turned to panic as domestic and foreign investors alike started selling shares in listed companies, especially those considered vulnerable to foreign exchange risk, and converted the rupiah proceeds from these sales into dollars or other strong foreign currencies (McLeod 1997b: 43). Indebted Indonesian firms also rushed to cover their unhedged and short-term external debts by purchasing foreign exchange in large quantities. This aggravated the downward pressure on the rupiah, as foreign exchange supplies had grown scarce because foreign creditors were increasingly reluctant to lend to Indonesian companies (World Bank 1998a: 1.4).

Despite concern about these developments, the initial response of Indonesia's economic policy makers was not to overreact. The country's economic and financial indicators still looked good, as reflected by single-digit inflation, a balanced budget, a manageable current account deficit, and buoyant savings and investment (Hill 2000: 120). Having witnessed the Bank of Thailand's costly failure to maintain the fixed exchange rate with the dollar by selling large amounts of its foreign exchange reserves, on 14 August 1997 Bank Indonesia floated the rupiah. The move to a floating exchange rate, however, did not succeed in stabilising the rupiah, and the free-floating rupiah further depreciated as people scrambled to get out of the currency as fast as possible (McLeod 1997b: 43–4). To stem ongoing depreciation, the government tightened monetary policy by steeply raising interest rates, but this weakened the fragile banking system and encouraged further capital flight, aggravating the downward slide of the rupiah (Montes & Abdulsalamov 1998: 180).

Unable any longer to deal with the crisis, the government on 13 October 1997 turned to the IMF for financial assistance. In return for a standby loan of \$43 billion, including a \$12.3 billion standby loan from the IMF itself and additional standby loans from the World Bank, the ADB and contingency loans from individual countries such as Japan and Singapore, the Indonesian government pledged to implement a comprehensive reform program, including sound macroeconomic policies, financial sector restructuring and structural reforms (Soesastro & Basri 1998: 16). It was hoped that with the availability of a large IMF standby loan, backed by a credible economic reform program sanctioned by the IMF, confidence in the rupiah would be restored (Sadli 1999: 17). Thus, as in 1966, the Indonesian government again came under the tutelage of the IMF. However, while in 1966 IMF assistance was primarily to lower inflation (Booth 1998a: 178), in 1997 it was sought to stem the erosion of market confidence in the rupiah.

The IMF package was to be implemented over a three-year period and to be tightly monitored by the Indonesian government, assisted by experts from the IMF, the World Bank and the ADB (Soesastro & Basri 1998: 18). The first step to implement the IMF reform program was in the field of financial restructuring. This step was considered necessary, as the weak banking system, saddled with large, non-performing loans, had been a major factor in causing the crisis. To this end the Indonesian government closed down 16 private insolvent banks, including some controlled by the President's relatives and cronies. However, in the absence of deposit insurance, these closures led to a run on all private banks, forcing Bank Indonesia to provide large liquidity credits to the remaining private banks to head off a banking crisis (World Bank 1998a: 1.6). By late January 1998 the rupiah had experienced a spectacular free-fall depreciation, from Rp. 2400 per dollar in early July 1997 to Rp. 17 000, an over 80% depreciation in just six months. Meanwhile, the stock exchange index had dropped by 50%.

Unlike Thailand and South Korea, the other two worst-affected Asian countries, which had from the outset vigorously implemented the agreed-on reform programs in return for IMF assistance, the Indonesian goverment did not seem fully committed to implementing the reform program. Hence, when the rupiah failed to strengthen and the economy continued its downward slide, the government in January 1998 reluctantly signed a second agreement with the IMF which contained a more detailed 50-point reform program, this time including provisions for a social safety net for those most severely affected by the economic crisis.[5] President Soeharto, however, still hesitated to implement the second agreement faith-fully, particularly the structural reforms aimed at eliminating various policy-generated barriers to domestic competition, including the notorious clove monopoly managed by his youngest son and the lucrative import monopolies of Bulog on rice, wheat, flour, soybeans and garlic. Many critics attributed the President's reluctance to implement the structural reforms to his unwillingness to harm the extensive business interests of his children. The President even seemed to backtrack on earlier commitments when he asserted that some of the IMF-mandated measures were 'unconstitutional'. It was at this time that the President lost confidence in his economic technocrats and started to see the IMF-mandated reforms as containing a 'hidden agenda' that was aimed at eroding the financial foundations of his children's businesses and his own political power.

Worsening economic conditions and greater flexibility on the part of the IMF led in early April 1998 to a third agreement. This allowed for large food subsidies for low-income groups and a budget deficit of 3.5% of GDP, instead of the 1% under the second agreement. The government's greater commitment to implementing the third agreement led to a gradual appreciation of the rupiah to Rp. 7500–8000 to the dollar.

In May 1998 massive student demonstrations against the government, sparked by a steep reduction in fuel subsidies, came to a head when four students were killed by unknown snipers, believed to belong to rogue elements of the army. This killing triggered large-scale riots, arson and mass looting all over Jakarta and some other towns, notably Solo in Central Java. Under threat of impeachment by the no longer compliant leaders of the Parliament, on 21 May 1998 President Soeharto resigned when 14 ministers in charge of economic affairs refused to join a reorganised cabinet. Ultimately, however, the fall of Soeharto was due to his inability to reverse the economic collapse of the country.

In June 1998 a fourth agreement with the IMF was signed by the new transitional government, now headed by President Habibie. By then the rupiah had fallen back to Rp. 16 000 per dollar and the dollar value of the stock market was only about 15% of mid-1997 levels (McLeod 1998: 42). Because of the government's reduced fiscal capacity, the approved budget deficit was raised to 8.5% of GDP (World Bank 1998a: 2.10). To finance this deficit, a huge aid package of $13.5 billion was provided by the Consultative Group on Indonesia (CGI), the new aid consortium which had been formed after the disbandment of the IGGI in 1992.

By late 1998 there were tentative signs of economic recovery in the strengthening of the rupiah, a rise in the Jakarta Stock Exchange Composite Index, a slight but positive growth since the last quarter of 1997, and a decline in the rate of inflation and interest rates (Pardede 1999: 3). However, one year later the Habibie government was still unable to solve the two most critical problems holding up economic recovery, namely the bank and corporate debt restructuring. Involvement of a number of Habibie's allies in the *Bank Bali* scandal also led the IMF to withhold payment of the next instalment of its standby loan.

Even the assumption of power in October 1999 of a new government under Abdurrachman Wahid, the first democratically elected president in Indonesia's history, failed to achieve significant progress in economic recovery. Being a coalition of ministers from different political parties, President Wahid's first cabinet was unable to provide strong and effective government (McLeod 2000: 3). Like Habibie's government, Wahid's government during its first year failed to achieve steady progress in bank and corporate restructuring as agreed on in the government's successive agreements with the IMF.

The origins of the financial crisis

What factors caused the sudden reversal of Indonesia's economic fortunes? Out of the financial and economic crisis that engulfed the East Asian countries in 1997/98 a general consensus emerged that the core technical factors causing the crisis were fixed or quasi-fixed exchange rates, rapidly rising short-term debt and weak financial systems (Hill 1999: 8).

Buoyed by the prospects of the booming Southeast Asian economies, including Indonesia, and encouraged by favourable assessments by the World Bank, the IMF and reputable credit-rating agencies, such as Moody's and Standard and Poor's, since the early 1990s foreign investors and creditors had recklessly provided huge loans to these economies for investment in the tradeable and non-tradeable sectors, particularly in property. In doing so, they had ignored systemic weaknesses in financial systems and distortions and inefficiencies in those economies. The Indonesian government too had ignored the early warning signals, partly because it had little, if any, information on the size of the capital flows, particularly short-term capital inflows, and partly because it was still euphoric about the booming economy.

Although Indonesia, unlike Thailand, had not pegged its rupiah exchange rate to the dollar, it did maintain, through its managed float, a quasi-fixed exchange rate pegged to the dollar and implicitly guaranteed by the government (Hill 1998a: 96). Because of this implicit guarantee, few overseas loans were hedged (Hill 1999: 8).

The borrowing spree of Indonesia's private sector since the early 1990s caused total external debt (public and private) to double, from around $70 billion in 1990 to around $140 billion in mid-1997, an amount equivalent to two years' worth of exports. About half was private debt, much of it both short-term (with an average maturity of only 1.5 years) and unhedged. The combination of an open capital account and high domestic nominal interest rates — about three times above international levels — encouraged such borrowing (Hill 1998a: 96). Much of the private sector's external debt was explicitly or implicitly guaranteed by the Indonesian government, as part of these foreign loans were used to finance large-scale infrastructure projects undertaken by SOEs and politically well-connected private investors (Vichyanond 1998: 19; Simanjuntak 1998: 3).

When the rupiah, following the fall of the Thai baht, began to depreciate sharply after July 1997, external debts in rupiah terms rose sharply. This led to enormous pressure on the banking system, and the proportion of its non-performing loans rose sharply. Once foreign exchange markets perceived that a serious problem was emerging, 'herd' behaviour led to a stampede out of the rupiah (Hill 1999: 9).

The currency crises that had hit the East Asian countries since mid-1997 were triggered by international speculators, who had been targeting the currencies of these countries for two main reasons. The first was that exchange rates with the dollar, including the quasi-fixed rupiah exchange rate with the dollar, which had been maintained since the mid-1980s, were perceived as no longer sustainable. In 1996 inflation differentials widened between the Southeast Asian countries, including Indonesia, and the USA, whereas the Japanese yen began to depreciate vis-à-vis the dollar. Real effective exchange rates, including the rupiah, began to appreciate, reducing export competitiveness and contributing to rising current account deficits (Komine 1998: 3).

The second reason was the burst of the 'bubble economy' which had been building up in Southeast Asia, particularly in Indonesia, Malaysia and Thailand, during the 1990s. The rise of this 'bubble economy' was caused by record capital inflows, particularly through the huge loans provided by foreign institutional investors and foreign banks. As in Japan in the late 1980s and early 1990s, it manifested itself in the form of a steep rise in the value of property and financial assets to levels that bore little relationship to income yields or rates of return in the real sector (Komine 1998: 3–4). After the 'bubble' had burst, the value of assets tumbled but not that of the debts, which were of course denominated in foreign currency. Balance sheets deteriorated and in many cases became negative (Komine 1998: 4).

While Indonesia's economic crisis was triggered by a sudden loss of investors and creditor confidence in the rupiah, its severity was attributable to political factors rather than economic factors alone (Sadli 1999: 16; MacIntyre 1999: 148–56). The massive centralisation of power that Soeharto had consolidated during his 32 years as President left the Indonesian government vulnerable to serious credibility problems due to unreliable policy commitments to economic reforms (MacIntyre 1999: 156). In the two other worst-afflicted Asian countries, South Korea and Thailand, a political and social crisis was averted by the speedy dismissal of a discredited government and the accession of a new, popularly elected government committed to wide-ranging economic reforms (Bhanoji Rao 1998: 1401–7). In Indonesia, however, a discredited government not seriously committed to implementing economic reforms tried to hang onto power. Economic crisis thereby escalated into a full-blown political and social crisis (Bhanoji Rao 1998: 1406–7).

The transition to a true democracy, as reflected by genuinely free general elections in June 1999 and the accession to power of a coalition government with a strong popular mandate, has been difficult and has not led to the restoration of political stability. As the new Wahid government was an inexperienced coalition cabinet without internal cohesion, no decisive action could be taken on the bank and corporate restructuring essential to economic recovery. Because of the lack of political and social stability, by late 2000 investment spending — the most basic indicator of confidence in Indonesia's near-term economic prospects — remained far below pre-crisis levels (McLeod 2000: 3), thereby hampering economic recovery.

The impact of the economic crisis

The economic impact   Although the financial crisis had hit Indonesia already in mid-1997, GDP in 1997 was still able to grow by 4.6%, as all the sectors were still able to achieve positive though slower growth. The full impact of the crisis on the economy was felt only in 1998, with construction, the financial sector and business services, trade, hotels and restaurants, manufacturing, and transport and communications recording the sharpest declines. Only agriculture and public utilities recorded slight growth. As a result, GDP contracted by an unprecedented 13.7% in 1998 (Figure 7.6). This economic contraction was much worse than in 1963, when the Indonesian economy contracted by nearly 3.0% (World Bank 1998a: 2.1; see also Booth 2000).

Besides the financial crisis, Indonesia in 1997 suffered the worst drought of this century because of the El Niño effect. The drought of 1997/98 was not only severe but occurred twice, in July/August 1997 and March 1998 (World Bank 1998a: 1.11). Because of this drought, total rice production in 1997 fell by 4%, causing the agricultural sector in 1997 to grow by only 0.6% (Johnson 1998: 16–17). To make matters worse, during this period the international oil price also declined sharply, hurting export and government revenues.

In 1999, however, macroeconomic stability was slowly being restored as the exchange rate, inflation and interest rates responded well to tight monetary policies (World Bank 1999a: 1.1–1.2). Construction, which had contracted the most in 1998, recovered slightly, as did manufacturing and services. As a result GDP began to recover slightly in 1999, as industrial output started expanding again (World Bank 2000a: 2). Positive growth was maintained during 2000, with GDP growing at 4.8%. Nevertheless, in mid-2000 real output was some 37% lower than it would have been if the pre-crisis growth rate of 7.5% had been maintained (McLeod 2000: 11–12).

The socioeconomic impact   The socioeconomic effects of the Asian financial crisis in Indonesia were transmitted via two channels. The effects through the first channel were caused by the impact of capital outflows, the steep rupiah depreciation, and the contractionary effects of tight fiscal and

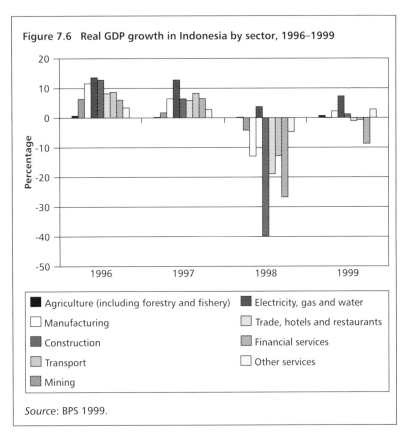

Figure 7.6   Real GDP growth in Indonesia by sector, 1996–1999

Legend:
- ■ Agriculture (including forestry and fishery)
- □ Manufacturing
- ■ Construction
- ■ Transport
- ■ Mining
- ■ Electricity, gas and water
- ■ Trade, hotels and restaurants
- ■ Financial services
- □ Other services

Source: BPS 1999.

monetary policies on GDP. The sharp contraction of sectors concentrated in urban areas (e.g. construction, financial services and manufacturing), led to many layoffs. The effects through the second channel were caused by the changes in relative prices, as prices of tradeable goods (including manu-factured goods) rose significantly vis-à-vis the non-tradeable goods and services as a result of the steep depreciation of the rupiah. Hence, inflation rates rose steeply in 1998 (Daimon & Thorbecke 1999: 2).

   The effects through these two channels suggest that urban households were affected more severely than rural households. First, the sectors hit hardest by the crisis were mostly located in the urban areas, which adversely affected urban employment. Second, inflation adversely affected net purchasers of foodstuffs (largely urban dwellers) because of the steep rise in food prices in 1998, while net producers of food (farmers) gained (Daimon & Thorbecke 1999: 2–3). Urban households in general may have suffered more than rural households, particularly farm households growing their own food.

As a result of the economic slowdown in 1997 and the severe economic contraction in 1998, large numbers of workers were laid off, particularly in the labour-intensive construction, manufacturing and modern services sectors, which are mostly located in the urban areas. Data from the National Socio-Economic Survey, *Susenas* (*Survei Sosial-Ekonomi Nasional*), held in February 1998 showed that employment in manufacturing had fallen by 13%, finance by 7% and electricity by 27%. However, as some sectors, such as finance, were employing only a small part of the labour force, even a relatively large reduction in employment in these sectors had only a slight impact on total unemployment (Poppele et al. 1999: 20). Employment in agriculture and the urban informal sector expanded because the labour market and the social structures in these sectors were sufficiently flexible to reabsorb the workers laid off in the formal sector activities (Poppele et al. 1999: 20). As a result, total open unemployment rose from 3.6% in August 1997 to just 4.1% in December 1999 (Booth 1999: 21). However, crowding of the informal sector with large numbers of displaced workers tended to depress work and earnings for everyone in this sizeable sector (Breman 1998: 2; ILO/UNDP 1998: 25–6).

The severe contraction of the economy and the hyperinflation and attendant drop in purchasing power since late 1997 led to a significant increase in the number of poor people in 1998. The surge in inflation in mid-1998 especially hurt the poor because food prices rose more rapidly than non-food prices (Booth 1999: 18). Hence, one of the proudest achievements of the Soeharto administration, namely the steady reduction in absolute poverty during its 32-year rule, was reversed as a result of the economic crisis.

Revised estimates by BPS suggested that the rise in poverty rates, though serious enough, was not as disastrous as indicated by earlier estimates. These later estimates were that the poverty rate in rural areas rose from 12.3% in 1996 to 17.6% in December 1998, while in the urban areas it rose from 9.7% to 15.4% over the same period. As a result, the total poverty rate rose from 11.3% to 16.7% (Booth 1999: 20). When the economy slowly began to recover in 1999, the poverty rate started to decline, reversing the trend of the previous two years (World Bank 2000a: 5). This reversal, however, was no reason for complacency. The slow economic recovery meant that it would take a long time for poverty rates to drop to pre-crisis levels.

While some regions outside Java initially benefited from the windfall rupiah proceeds of their primary exports, other regions outside Java, particularly East Nusa Tenggara, East Timor and Irian Jaya, were hit very hard by the adverse effects of the El Niño drought and the economic crisis. Even before the economic crisis, these three provinces had a much higher proportion of poor households (World Bank 1998a: 3.12).

Another casualty of the economic crisis was education. Various studies of the impact of the crisis on education showed that the fall in enrolment rates in secondary schools was much larger than in the primary schools. In fact, for the country as a whole, primary school enrolments had not changed much, although there were substantial declines in the poorer urban areas (Booth 1999: 23). As even before the crisis many children from the lower-income groups, having completed primary education, did not enrol in the secondary schools, it is not surprising that the crisis raised the dropout rate in lower and particularly in higher secondary schools rather than in primary schools (Poppele et al. 1999: 29). The government responded to this problem by abolishing entrance fees for public schools, providing scholarships for students from poor households, and through public campaigns to persuade parents to keep their children in schools. These measures proved successful, as net enrolment rates at lower secondary schools improved between August and December 1998 for all income groups (Booth 1999: 24).

Remedial steps   With substantial financial and technical assistance from the IMF, the World Bank, the ADB, the United Nations Development Program and the CGI, the Indonesian government in 1998 took measures to protect the poor from the worst effects of the crisis, notably by providing emergency Social Safety Net (SSN) programs to the most vulnerable groups in society, including the distribution of subsidised rice to poor households, creation of short-term job opportunities through labour-intensive public works, and preservation of critical social services (World Bank 1999a: 2.5–2.7). As the economy slowly recovered in 1999, these emergency programs were gradually phased out in favour of the pre-crisis poverty alleviation programs, including health and education programs.

CONCLUSION

Indonesia entered the third millennium without good prospects of a speedy economic recovery. Amid a serious economic and political crisis it became apparent that this crisis was more than a temporary economic misfortune. Long-run trends towards a strong, unified nation-state and an integrated national economy have, at least for the moment, been reversed, even as the foundations of a more democratic and decentralised state and a more open and tolerant society are being laid. The crisis has brought about an *Umwertung aller Werte* (reversal of all values), the self-serving ideology of the ossified New Order is being rejected, and the Indonesian people are slowly and with great difficulty trying to rebuild a 'New Indonesia' which should be quite different from the repressive, corrupt New Order.

During the period of rapid economic growth of 1966–1996 the now discredited New Order government laid strong foundations for a modern, unitary nation-state and an integrated national economy. Windfall profits from the oil booms of the 1970s and development of natural resources funded transport and communication networks linking regions together and funded *Inpres* programs and redistributive policies to poor regions. However, as the power of the centralised state accumulated at the expense of society and, if threatened, was sustained by violence, authoritarianism eventually led to self-serving policies, notably the exploitation of the natural resources of resource-rich regions for the benefit of the central government and the ruling elite. Eventually this led to discontent and even separatist movements, which undermined the foundations of the unitary state and an integrated national economy.

The consolidation of the highly centralised, unitary New Order state was made possible not only by its ability to raise the standard of living of the Indonesian people but also by its ruthlessness in suppressing any overt and covert political threat to its supremacy, both at the centre or in the regions. Accumulation of corrupt political power at the centre also gave rise to interventionist policies that eroded business competitiveness and rewarded unproductive rent-seeking policies. The outcome was the emergence of collusive partnerships between political powerholders and their business cronies, many of them Sino-Indonesians. Preoccupation with rapid economic growth and greed also led to severe environmental degradation and depletion of scarce, non-renewable resources, not only raising the social costs of economic growth but also endangering its sustainability.

The Asian crisis showed the importance of 'good governance', once dismissed by economists as irrelevant. Indonesia's underdeveloped institutions were its weak and outmoded legal system, an inefficient and venal bureaucracy, and the absence of democratic process. To this may be added a badly supervised and undercapitalised banking system, domestic policy distortions, and unproductive rent-seeking activities. Indonesia's lag in institutional development was reflected in the fact that the only strong institution seemed to be President Soeharto himself, who was not a sustainable institution (de Tray 1999: 1). This lag undermined not only the foundations and resilience of the national economy but also political life and public confidence. Neither society nor economy could weather an economic shock like the Asian crisis.

For many Indonesians the crisis also brought into question the strategy of integration with the world economy. Reintegration with the world economy had begun in the late 1960s and accelerated after the mid-1980s. By 1997 the Indonesian economy was better integrated with the global economy than in 1987 (Appendix 7.A). The resultant more open economy enabled the country to enjoy 'static' and 'dynamic' gains from trade as well as spillover benefits from foreign direct investment. Such integration was in line with the increasing pace of global economic integration (World Bank 1997b: 295). However, the dramatic events in Southeast Asia during 1997/98 showed 'globalisation' to be a two-edged sword for developing countries. Opening up their economies accelerated economic growth and reduced poverty, but volatile short-term capital and long-term portfolio capital movements proved destabilising (Arndt 1998: 76–8). Sound 'economic fundamentals' alone did not shield Indonesia from the Asian crisis. The Asian crisis also showed that globalisation may require institutions to change faster than they are able to (de Tray 1999: 2).

Indonesia's economic recovery and the resumption of rapid, equitable and environmentally sustainable economic growth depend not only on sound macro- and microeconomic policies but also on the evolution of strong, viable institutions which can establish and enforce basic rules on government, private corporations and the public at large. As Indonesia tries to establish a truly democratic and tolerant society, the challenge is to rebuild a unified, though not necessarily unitary, democratic state based not on force but on the democratically expressed will of the people in the various regions to work together for the common good as one country.

APPENDICES

7.A   Indonesia's integration with the global economy, 1987–1997

Table 7.A below shows that the Indonesian economy in 1997 was more integrated with the world or global economy than in 1987. This is reflected in the greater role of trade in goods in 1997 as a percentage of both purchasing-power parity (PPP) GDP and goods GDP compared to 1987; the growth in real trade of goods and services less the growth of real GDP over the period 1987/97; and the greater role of both gross private capital flows and gross foreign direct investment in 1997 as a percentage of both PPP GDP and goods GDP (World Bank 1999b: 324–7).

Table 7.A Indonesia's integration with the global economy, 1987–1997				
Indicators	% of GDP (PPP)		% of goods GDP	
	1987	1997	1987	1997
Trade in goods	11.1	13.7	66.4	75.9
Gross private capital flows	0.6	2.1		
Gross foreign direct investment	0.1	0.7		
	% 1987/1997			
Growth in real trade less growth in real GDP	1.9			

Notes:
1. Trade in goods as a share of PPP GDP is the sum of merchandise exports and imports measured in current dollars divided by the value of GDP converted to international dollars using PPP conversion factors.
2. Growth in goods as a share of goods GDP is the sum of merchandise exports and imports divided by the current value of GDP in dollars after subcontracting value added in services.

3. Growth in real trade less growth in real GDP is the difference between annual growth in trade of goods and services and growth in real GDP. Growth rates are calculated using constant price series taken from national accounts, expressed as percentages.
4. Gross private capital flows are the sum of absolute values of direct, portfolio and other investment inflows and outflows recorded in the balance of payments financial account, excluding changes in the assets and liabilities of monetary authorities and general government. The indicator is calculated as a ratio of GDP converted to international dollars using purchasing-power parities.
5. Gross foreign direct investment is the sum of the absolute values of inflows and outflows of foreign direct investment recorded in the balance of payments financial account. It includes equity capital, re-investment of earnings, other long-term capital and short-term capital. The indicator is calculated as a ratio of GDP converted to international dollars using purchasing-power parities.

7.B   Incidence of absolute poverty in Indonesia in regional perspective

As different countries use different poverty lines, international comparisons of the incidence of absolute poverty are difficult. To solve this problem, the World Bank has developed an international poverty line. This line was set at $1 a day or $2 a day at 1985 international prices when adjusted for purchasing-power parity (PPP).

The data in Table 7.B show the $2 a day international poverty line as a basis for regional comparisons. These data show that in 1996 the incidence of absolute poverty expressed as a percentage of the population living below the international poverty line in Indonesia was more than 50%, the second-highest among four selected ASEAN countries (after the Philippines) and almost five times as high as indicated by the official poverty line (World Bank 1999b: 67–9).

A supplementary approach applies the concept of poverty gap — that is, the mean shortfall below the poverty line, expressed as a percentage of this line. This measure reflects the depth of poverty as well as its incidence. These data also show that the depth of poverty in Indonesia ranks second after the Philippines.

Table 7.B Incidence of absolute poverty in Indonesia in regional perspective					
Country	Survey year	Population < $1 a day (%)	Poverty gap at $1 a day (%)	Population < $2 a day (%)	Poverty gap at $2 a day (%)
Indonesia	1996	7.7	0.9	50.4	15.3
Malaysia	1995	4.3	0.7	22.4	6.8
Philippines	1994	26.9	7.1	62.8	27.0
Thailand	1992	< 2.0	—	23.5	5.4

Epilogue

Looking back over 200 years of Indonesian economic history puts recent turmoil in perspective. These two centuries have been punctuated by crises, some involving great loss of life and human suffering. Yet there remain very clear trends. Out of a sprawling archipelago and a colonial empire there has emerged a modern nation-state, the fourth most populous in the world. Unlike some other Asian and European nations, it has rarely embraced isolation but has engaged vigorously with the world economy. The benefits of that engagement have fluctuated markedly, but since Independence have been harnessed to drive development, rising welfare, and falling poverty. The country's economy has evolved from being primarily an exporter of food and raw materials to that of an exporter of labour-intensive manufactures. The economy has also gradually become more integrated, so that Java and the Outer Islands are no longer just a collection of island or sub-island economies but a single economic unit.

What is still contested is the nature of the nation-state. All but a decade of the past 200 years have been under authoritarian rule, whether colonial (Dutch, British or Japanese), populist (Sukarno) or military-bureaucratic (Soeharto). The transition to democracy has therefore been even more protracted and painful than economic development. This has in turn retarded the emergence of institutions that would be appropriate to a modern-state and able to sustain a large, dispersed and technically sophisticated economy.

Nevertheless, here also a sense of perspective is needed. Some European nations were slow to make the transition to democracy: Greece, Spain and Portugal in the 1970s, Eastern European countries after 1989, Serbia/Yugoslavia only in 2000. South American countries, which seized independence from Spain and Portugal at the beginning of the 19th century, at the same time as Daendels introduced a modern form of government to Java, are still struggling to combine economic prosperity with a stable democracy. Indonesia may be lagging, but it is not exceptional.

The clear lesson of colonial rule, 'Guided Democracy' and the 'New Order', as indeed for all the countries referred to above, is that authoritarian rule, especially military-authoritarian rule, is reactionary. It offers the promise of peace, prosperity and security, but demands a very high price. However impressive the economic indicators, a society that is abused and plundered by a small elite with a monopoly of violence cannot realise its potential. The resources of the Indonesian archipelago have for centuries allowed small elites, foreign and domestic, to make themselves fabulously wealthy, a process which culminated under the New Order. Indonesia's democratic challenge is to realise the extraordinary energies and creativity of its two hundred million people according to the high ideals on which it was founded as a nation in 1945. In the 20th century the opportunities were squandered. At the beginning of the 21st there is new hope, mixed with fear and uncertainty. The fear that the *nation* itself may fragment is probably exaggerated. Indonesia is unlikely to become the Balkans of Southeast Asia. The problem is more the evolution of the *state* and civil society, and here world history is on the side of hope.

———

In August 2001, as this book went to press, Megawati Sukarnoputri, eldest daughter of Indonesia's founding president, Sukarno, was appointed as fifth president by acclamation of the People's Consultative Assembly (MPR), replacing Abdurrachman Wahid, the nation's first democratically elected president, whose erratic rule had impeded economic recovery and national reconciliation. Despite widespread misgivings about her capabilities and political acumen, President Megawati's early decisions were astute. She demonstrated her awareness that good relations with the international community were essential for Indonesia's economic recovery. Notwithstanding her strong commitment to a unitary state, as espoused by her father, she accepted that regional autonomy was the best way to keep the country together. And, despite her strong ties to the military, she affirmed the need to bring to prosecution military officers guilty of atrocities. All in all, after four years of political turmoil, bloody ethnic and religious conflicts, and economic deprivation, the Indonesian people could at last entertain some hope that the worst of the crisis was over and that the herculean task of building a strong, democratic, tolerant, socially just and economically prosperous nation could finally begin.

Notes

Chapter 1 — State, nation-state and national economy

1   Until 1795 the Dutch had controlled Ceylon, which became the greatest of the spice islands; in the 17th century they also controlled Taiwan, the pilot project for an export sugar industry in Asia. Java was actually the third choice for development as a plantation economy (Gaastra 1989: 122–3).

2   In the absence of exchange controls, the same outcome would have been produced had Sumatra continued to use the Straits dollar as currency instead of being integrated with Java in 1908 on the Netherlands Indies guilder.

3   The main concern was that locally produced textiles would be more expensive than imports and thereby force up the price of labour. Competing demands for labour were also unwelcome.

4   Output destination is final output. Input origin is intermediate inputs excluding capital goods.

Chapter 2 — The pre-modern economies of the archipelago

1   Elasticity is an economic term that refers to the proportionate change in quantity in response to a given change in price or income.

Chapter 4 — The Outer Islands in the 19th century

1   Information from Dr Lesley Potter of the University of Adelaide.

Chapter 5 — The late colonial state and economic expansion, 1900–1930s

1   The university's emphasis on understanding local culture and society for the benefit of those colonised was not popular among Dutch corporations with large interests in the colony. In 1925 a second, rival indological faculty was set up at the University of Utrecht, with generous sponsorship from the Royal Dutch/Shell and major sugar companies (Fasseur 1993: 423).

Chapter 6 — Formation of the nation-state, 1930s–1966

1   The term is borrowed from Johnson's (1982) study of Japan's MITI, which also had its origins in wartime mobilisation.

2   The USA, knowing very little about Indonesia, in 1952 sponsored two academic research teams. The Indonesia Project under Benjamin Higgins worked in Jakarta on high-level economic policy, a counterweight to the ubiquitous Dutch advisers; the 'Modjokerto' team of anthropologists and sociologists worked at the local level in East Java. Clifford Geertz's (1963b) *Peddlers and Princes* was the apotheosis of the search for the elusive Indonesian entrepreneur.

3   This assumption applied to postwar rehabilitation in Europe and Japan, but expectations that it would also be valid in Third World countries with largely illiterate and unskilled workforces were disappointed. Efforts to explain why opened up the new field of Development Studies.

4   Sukarno was stripped of his formal presidential title in March 1968 and remained under unofficial house arrest until his lonely death in June 1970 (Legge 1973).

Chapter 7 — The Soeharto era and after

1   Agriculture also includes forestry, livestock and fisheries. Industry comprises value added in mining, manufacturing, construction, electricity, water and gas.

2   Definitions (Table 7.3). School enrolments refer to gross enrolment ratio, that is the ratio of actual enrolment, regardless of age, to the population of the age group that officially corresponds to the level of education shown (i.e. this ratio can on occasion exceed 100%). Adult literacy rate is the percentage of adults aged 15 and above who can, with understanding, read and write a short statement about their everyday life. Infant mortality rate is the number of infants who die before 1 year of age per 1000 live births in a given year. Health and malnutrition are expressed as per capita daily calorie supply. Life expectancy is the number of years a newborn child would live if prevailing patterns of mortality at the time of his/her birth were to stay the same throughout his/her life. Crude birth rate and crude death rate are the numbers of live birth and number of deaths occurring during one year per 1000 of population. The difference between the crude birth rate and the crude death rate is the rate of natural increase. Total fertility rate is the number of children that would be born to a woman if she were to live to the end of her child-bearing years and bear children in accordance with current age-specific fertility rates.

3   After a visit to South Korea by President Abdurrachman Wahid in early 2000 the Indonesian government decided to revive the 'Timor' car project in cooperation with the Korean principal, Kia Motors — this time, however, without giving exclusive tax and duty exemptions.

4   The Gini ratio measures the extent to which the distribution of income (or consumption expenditures) among individuals or households within an economy deviates from a perfectly equal distribution. A Gini ratio of zero represents perfect equality, while an index of 1.0 implies perfect inequality.

5   Memorandum of Economic and Financial Policies, accompanying the Second Agreement between Indonesia and the IMF, 15 January 1998.

Bibliography

Abeyasekere, S. (1976). *One Hand Clapping: Indonesian Nationalists and the Dutch, 1939–1942*. Melbourne: Centre for Southeast Asian Studies, Monash University.

Abeyasekere, S. (1987). *Jakarta: A History*. Singapore: Oxford University Press.

Adam, A.B. (1995). *The Vernacular Press and the Emergence of Modern Indonesian Consciousness*. Ithaca, NY: Cornell University.

Ahluwalia, M.S. & Chenery, H. (1974). 'The Economic Framework', in: H. Chenery et al. (eds), *Redistribution with Growth*. London: Oxford University Press, 38–51.

Alexander, J. & Alexander, P. (1991). 'Trade and Petty Commodity Production in Early Twentieth-Century Kebumen', in: P. Alexander, P. Boomgaard & B. White (eds), *In the Shadow of Agriculture: Non-Farm Activities in the Javanese Economy, Past and Present*. Amsterdam: Royal Tropical Institute, 70–91.

Anderson, B. (1972). *Java in a Time of Revolution: Occupation and Resistance, 1944–1946*. Ithaca, NY: Cornell University Press.

Anderson, B. (1983). 'Old State, New Society: Indonesia's New Order in Comparative Historical Perspective', *Journal of Asian Studies* 42, 477–96.

Anderson, I.H. (1975). *The Standard-Vacuum Oil Company and United States East Asian Policy, 1933–1941*. Princeton: Princeton University Press.

Anspach, R. (1969). 'Indonesia', in: R. Anspach et al., *Underdevelopment and Economic Nationalism in Southeast Asia*. Ithaca, NY: Cornell University Press.

Ariff, M. & Hill, H. (1985). *Export-Oriented Industrialisation: The ASEAN Experience*. Sydney: Allen & Unwin.

van Ark, B. (1988). 'The Volume and Price of Indonesian Exports, 1823 to 1940: The Long-Term Trend and its Measurement', *Bulletin of Indonesian Economic Studies* 24 (3), 87–120.

Arndt, H.W. (1984). *The Indonesian Economy: Collected Papers*. Singapore: Chopmen.

Arndt, H.W. (1998). 'Globalisation', *Banca Nazionale del Lavoro Quarterly Review* 204, 73–89.

Azis, I.J. (1995). 'Growth and Regional Distribution in Indonesia: Recent Trends, Future Path and Policy Issues', Paper presented at the 'One Day Discussion Sessions Commemorating the 50th Anniversary of the Independence of the Republic of Indonesia', San Francisco.

van Baardewijk, F. (1993). *Changing Economy in Indonesia* XIV: *The Cultivation System, Java 1834–1880*. Amsterdam: Royal Tropical Institute.

Bakker, H. (1989). 'Het economisch belang van Noord-Sumatra tijdens de Atjeh-oorlog, 1873–1910', in: A.H.P. Clemens & J.Th. Lindblad (eds), *Het belang van de Buitengewesten: Economische expansie en koloniale staatsvorming in de Buitengewesten van Nederlands-Indië, 1870–1942*. Amsterdam: NEHA, 41–66.

Bappenas (Badan Perencanaan Pembangunan Nasional) (1991). *Regional Aspects of Industrialization in Indonesia*. Discussion Paper No. 23. Jakarta: Bappenas. October 1991.

Barlow, C. & Drabble, J. (1990). 'Government and the Emerging Rubber Industries in Indonesia and Malaya, 1900–1940', in: A. Booth, W.J. O'Malley & A. Weidemann (eds), *Indonesian Economic History in the Dutch Colonial Era*. New Haven, CT: Yale University Press, 187–209.

Barlow, C. & Johnston, B. (1983). *Focus and Dispersal Policies for Agricultural Development: Models Based on Indonesian Rubber*. Canberra: Research School of Pacific Studies, Australian National University.

Barlow, C. & Tomich, T. (1991). 'Indonesian Agricultural Development: The Awkward Case of Smallholder Treecrops', *Bulletin of Indonesian Economic Studies* 27 (3), 29–54.

Baudet, H. (1975). 'Nederland en de rang van Denemarken', *Bijdragen en Mededelingen betreffende de Geschiedenis der Nederlanden* 90, 430–43.

Baudet, H. & Fasseur, C. (1977). 'Koloniale bedrijvigheid', in: J.H. van Stuijvenberg (ed.), *De economische geschiedenis van Nederland*. Groningen: Wolters-Noordhoff, 309–50.

Baudet, H. & Fennema, M. (1983). *Het Nederlands belang bij Indië*. Utrecht: Spectrum.

Benda, H.J. (1966). 'The Pattern of Administrative Reforms in the Closing Years of Dutch Rule in Indonesia', *Journal of Asian Studies* 25, 589–605.

Bhanoji Rao, V.V. (1998). 'East Asian Economies: The Crisis of 1997–98', *Economic and Political Weekly* 33, 1397–416.

Bhattacharya, A. & Pangestu, M. (1993). *The Lessons of East Asia: Development Transformation and Public Policy*. Washington: World Bank.

Blussé, J.L. (1986). *Strange Company: Chinese Settlers, Mestizo Women and the Dutch in VOC Batavia*. Dordrecht: Foris.

Boeke, J.H. (1953). *Economics and Economic Policy of Dual Societies as Exemplified by Indonesia*. New York: Institute of Pacific Relations.

de Boer, M.G. & Westermann, J.C. (1941). *Een halve eeuw paketvaart, 1891–1941*. Amsterdam: De Bussy.

Bogaars, G. (1955). 'Singapore and the Opening of the Suez Canal', *Journal of the Malayan Branch of the Royal Asiatic Society* 28 (1), 99–143.

Boomgaard, P. (1986). 'The Welfare Services in Indonesia', *Itinerario* 10 (1), 57–82.

Boomgaard, P. (1989a). *Children of the Colonial State: Population Growth and Economic Development in Java, 1795–1880*. Amsterdam: Free University Press.

Boomgaard, P. (1989b). 'The Javanese Rice Economy 800–1800', in: A. Hayami & Y. Tsubouchi (eds), *Economic and Demographic Development in Rice Producing Societies: Some Aspects of East Asian Economic History 1500–1900*. Tokyo: Keio University, 317–44.

Boomgaard, P. (1993). 'Economic Growth in Indonesia, 500–1990', in: A. Szirmai, B. van Ark & D. Pilat (eds), *Explaining Economic Growth*. Amsterdam: Elsevier, 195–216.

Boomgaard, P. (1996). 'Fluctuations in Mortality in 17th Century Indonesia', Paper presented at the Conference on Asian Population History, Taipei.

Boomgaard, P. & Gooszen, A.J. (1991). *Changing Economy in Indonesia* XI: *Population Trends 1795–1942*. Amsterdam: Royal Tropical Institute.

Boomgaard, P. and van Zanden, J.L. (1990). *Changing Economy in Indonesia* X: *Food Crops and Arable Lands, Java 1815–1942*. Amsterdam: Royal Tropical Institute.

Booth, A. (1980). 'The Burden of Taxation in Colonial Indonesia in the Twentieth Century', *Journal of Southeast Asian Studies* 11 (1), 91–109.

Booth, A. (1988). *Agricultural Development in Indonesia*. Sydney: Allen & Unwin.

Booth, A. (1989a). 'Exports and Growth in the Colonial Economy, 1830–1940', in: A. Maddison & G.H.A. Prince (eds), *Economic Growth in Indonesia, 1820–1940*. Dordrecht/Providence: Foris, 67–96.

Booth, A. (1989b). 'The State and Economic Development in Indonesia: The Ethical and New Order Eras Compared', in: R.J. May & W.J. O'Malley (eds), *Observing Change in Asia: Essays in Honour of J.A.C. Mackie*. Bathurst: Crawford, 111–26.

Booth, A. (1990a). 'Foreign Trade and Domestic Development in the Colonial Economy', in: A. Booth, W.J. O'Malley & A. Weidemann (eds), *Indonesian Economic History in the Dutch Colonial Era*. New Haven, CT: Yale University Press, 267–95.

Booth, A. (1990b). 'The Evolution of Fiscal Policy and the Role of Government in the Colonial Economy', in: A. Booth, W.J. O'Malley &

A. Weidemann (eds), *Indonesian Economic History in the Dutch Colonial Era*. New Haven, CT: Yale University Press, 210–43.

Booth, A. (1991). 'The Economic Development of Southeast Asia: 1870–1985', *Australian Economic Review* 31, 20–52.

Booth, A. (1992a). 'International Trade and Domestic Economic Development: An Indonesian Case Study', in: M.A. Anwar, Thee Kian Wie & I.J. Azis (eds), *Pemikiran, Pelaksanaan dan Perintisan Pembangunan Ekonomi*. Jakarta: Gramedia, 99–152.

Booth, A. (1992b). 'Introduction', in: A. Booth (ed.), *The Oil Boom and After: Indonesian Economic Policy and Performance in the Soeharto Era*. Singapore: Oxford University Press, 1–38.

Booth, A. (1992c). 'Review Article: The World Bank and Rural Poverty', *Journal of International Development* 24, 633–42.

Booth, A. (1992d). 'Can Indonesia Survive as a Unitary State?', *Indonesia Circle* 58, 32–47.

Booth, A. (1995). 'Counting the Poor in Indonesia', *Bulletin of Indonesian Economic Studies* 29 (1), 53–84.

Booth, A. (1998a). *The Indonesian Economy in the Nineteenth and Twentieth Centuries: A History of Missed Opportunities*. London: Macmillan.

Booth, A. (1998b). 'Rural Development, Income Distribution and Poverty Decline in Southeast Asia' [Revised draft], Nairobi: African Economic Research Consortium.

Booth, A. (1999). 'Survey of Recent Developments', *Bulletin of Indonesian Economic Studies* 35 (3), 3–38.

Booth, A. (2000). 'The Indonesian Crisis of 1997–1999 and the Way Out: What Are the Lessons of History', *Lembaran Sejarah* 3 (1), 1–27.

Booth, A. & McCawley, P. (1981). 'The Indonesian Economy since the Mid-Sixties', in: A. Booth & P. McCawley (eds), *The Indonesian Economy during the Soeharto Era*. Kuala Lumpur: Oxford University Press, 1–22.

Booth, A. & Sundrum, R.M. (1981). 'Income Distribution', in: A. Booth & P. McCawley (eds), *The Indonesian Economy during the Soeharto Era*. Kuala Lumpur: Oxford University Press, 181–217.

Bossenbroek, M. (1992). *Volk voor Indië: De werving van Europese militairen voor de Indische koloniale dienst 1814–1909*. Amsterdam: Van Soeren.

Bossenbroek, M. (1996). *Holland op zijn breedst: Indië en Zuid-Afrika in de Nederlandse cultuur omstreeks 1900*. Amsterdam: Bert Bakker.

Bourchier, D. & Legge, J. (eds) (1994). *Democracy in Indonesia: 1950s and 1990s*. Melbourne: Centre of Southeast Asian Studies, Monash University.

BPS (1956). *Statistical Pocketbook of Indonesia 1955*. Jakarta: Biro Pusat Statistik.

BPS (1971–1999). *Statistical Yearbook of Indonesia*. Jakarta: Biro Pusat Statistik.

BPS (1981–1997). *Economic Indicators*. Jakarta: Biro Pusat Statistik.

BPS (1992). *Statistical Pocketbook of Indonesia 1991*. Jakarta: Biro Pusat Statistik.

BPS (1999). *Gross Regional Domestic Product of Provinces in Indonesia by Industrial Origin, 1995–1998*. Jakarta: Biro Pusat Statistik.

Breman, J. (1983). *Control of Land and Labour in Colonial Java: A Case Study of Agrarian Crisis and Reform in the Region of Cirebon in the First Decades of the Twentieth Century*. Dordrecht: Foris.

Breman, J. (1987, 1992, 1989, 1997). *Koelies, planters en koloniale politiek: Het arbeidsregime op de grootlandbouwondernemingen aan Sumatra's oostkust in het begin van de twintigste eeuw*. Dordrecht/Providence: Foris. Translated as: *Taming the Coolie Beast*. Delhi: Oxford University Press [1989] and as: *Menjinakkan Sang Kuli: Politik Kolonial pada Awal Abad Ke-20*. Jakarta: Grafiti/KITLV [1997].

Breman, J. (1998). 'Krismon in the Javanese Desa: The Dynamics of Inclusion and Exclusion in the Reconstruction of Indonesia's New Order Regime', Paper presented at the Workshop on the 'Impact of the Economic Crisis on Labour in Indonesia', Bandung.

Bresnan, J. (1993). *Managing Indonesia: The Modern Political Economy*. New York: Columbia University Press.

Brown, I. (1997). *Economic Change in South-East Asia, c. 1830–1980*. Kuala Lumpur: Oxford University Press.

Brugmans, I.J. (1950). *Tachtig jaren varen met de Nederland, 1870–1950*. Amsterdam: Stoomvaart-Maatschappij Nederland.

Bulbeck, D., Reid, A., Tan, Lay Cheng and Wu, Yiqi (eds) (1998). *Southeast Asian Exports since the 14th Century: Cloves, Pepper, Coffee, and Sugar*. Singapore: Institute of Southeast Asian Studies/Leiden: KITLV.

Burger, D.H. (1939). *De ontsluiting van Java's binnenland voor het wereldverkeer*. Wageningen: Veenman.

Burger, D.H. (1957/1975). *Sociologisch-economische geschiedenis van Indonesia*. Wageningen: Agricultural University/Amsterdam: Royal Tropical Institute/Leiden: KITLV. Translated as: *Sejarah ekonomis sosiologis Indonesia*. Jakarta [1957].

Butcher, J. & Dick, H.W. (eds) (1993). *The Rise and Fall of Revenue Farming: Business Elites and the Emergence of the Modern State in Southeast Asia*. London: Macmillan.

Callis, H.G. (1942). *Foreign Capital in Southeast Asia*. New York: Institute of Pacific Relations.

à Campo, J.N.F.M. (1992). *Koninklijke Paketvaart Maatschappij: Stoomvaart en staatsvorming in de Indonesische archipel 1888–1914*. Hilversum: Verloren.

à Campo, J.N.F.M. (1993). 'Perahu Shipping in Indonesia 1870–1914', *Review of Indonesian and Malaysian Affairs* 27, 33–60.

Carey, P.B.R. (1986). 'Waiting for the "Just King": The Agrarian World of South-Central Java from Giyanti (1755) to the Java War (1825–30)', *Modern Asian Studies* 20, 59–137.

Castles, L. (1967). 'The Fate of the Private Entrepreneur', in: T.K. Tan (ed.), *Sukarno's Guided Indonesia*. Brisbane: Jacaranda.

Cator, W.J. (1936). *The Economic Position of the Chinese in the Netherlands Indies*. Oxford: Blackwell.

CKS (1928–1940). *Jaaroverzicht van de in- en uitvoer van Nederlandsch-Indië*. Batavia: Centraal Kantoor voor de Statistiek.

CKS (1947). *Statistical Pocket Book of Indonesia 1941*. Batavia: Centraal Kantoor voor de Statistiek.

Clarence Smith, W.G. (ed.) (1997). *Hadhrami Traders, Scholars and Statesmen in the Indian Ocean, 1750s–1960s*. Leiden: Brill.

Clemens, A.H.P. (1989). 'De inheemse rubbercultuur in Jambi en Palembang tijdens het Interbellum', in: A.H.P. Clemens & J.Th. Lindblad (eds), *Het belang van de Buitengewesten: Economische expansie en koloniale staatsvorming in de Buitengewesten van Nederlands-Indië, 1870–1942*. Amsterdam: NEHA, 213–37.

Clemens, A.H.P. & Lindblad, J.Th. (eds) (1989). *Het belang van de Buitengewesten: Economische expansie en koloniale staatsvorming in de Buitengewesten van Nederlands-Indië, 1870–1942*. Amsterdam: NEHA.

Clemens, A.H.P., Lindblad, J.Th. & Touwen, L.J. (1992). *Changing Economy in Indonesia* XII B: *Regional Patterns in Foreign Trade 1911–1940*. Amsterdam: Royal Tropical Institute.

Clerx, J.M.M.J. (1992). 'De financiële verhouding tussen Nederland en Indonesië opnieuw bezien (1945–1967)', *Politieke Opstellen* 11/12, 59–71.

Colombijn, F. (1994). *Patches of Padang: The History of an Indonesian Town in the Twentieth Century and the Use of Urban Space*. Leiden: CNWS.

Colombijn, F. (1996). 'The Development of the Transport Network in West Sumatra from Pre-Colonial times to the Present', in: J.Th. Lindblad (ed.), *Historical Foundations of a National Economy in Indonesia, 1890s–1990s*. Amsterdam: North-Holland, 385–400.

Coolhaas, Ph. (1956). 'Ontstaan en groei', in J. Prins et al. (eds), *Gedenkboek van de Vereniging van Ambtenaren bij het Binnenlands Bestuur in Nederlands-Indië*. Utrecht: Oosthoek, 35–72.

Coppel, C. (1983). *The Indonesian Chinese in Crisis*. Kuala Lumpur: Oxford University Press.

Corden, W.M. & Mackie, J.A.C. (1962). 'The Development of the Indonesian Exchange Rate System', *Malayan Economic Review* 7 (1), 37–60.

Creutzberg, P. (1972–1974). *Het ekonomisch beleid in Nederlandsch-Indië*. Groningen: Tjeenk Willink.

Creutzberg, P. (1975). *Changing Economy in Indonesia*, I: *Indonesia's Export Crops 1816–1940*. The Hague: Nijhoff.

Creutzberg, P. (1976). *Changing Economy in Indonesia*, II: *Public Finance 1816–1939*. The Hague: Nijhoff.

Creutzberg, P. (1978). *Changing Economy in Indonesia*, IV: *Rice Prices*. The Hague: Nijhoff.

Creutzberg, P. (1979). *Changing Economy in Indonesia, V: National Income*. The Hague: Nijhoff.

Cribb, R. (1991). *Gangsters and Revolutionaries: The Jakarta People's Militia and the Indonesian Revolution, 1945–1949*. Sydney: Allen & Unwin.

Cribb, R. (1993). 'Development Policy in the Early Twentieth Century', in: J.-P. Dirkse, F. Hüsken & M. Rutten (eds), *Development and Social Welfare: Indonesia's Experiences under the New Order*. Leiden: KITLV Press, 225–46.

Cribb, R. (1994). 'Introduction: The Late Colonial State in Indonesia', in: R. Cribb (ed.), *The Late Colonial State in Indonesia: Political and Economic Foundations of the Netherlands Indies 1880–1942*. Leiden: KITLV Press, 1–9.

Cribb, R. (2000). *Historical Atlas of Indonesia*. Richmond: Curzon.

Crouch, H. (1978). *The Army and Politics in Indonesia*. Ithaca, NY: Cornell University Press.

Daimon, T. & Thorbecke, E. (1999). 'Mitigating the Social Impacts of the Indonesian Crisis: Lessons from the IDT Experience' [Unpublished paper].

Day, C. (1904). *The Policy and Administration of the Dutch in Java*. London: Macmillan.

Derksen, J.B.D. & Tinbergen, J. (1945). 'Berekeningen over de economische betekenis van Nederlandsch-Indië voor Nederland', *Maandschrift van het Centraal Bureau voor de Statistiek* 40, 210–16.

DEZ (1949). *Bijzonder industrieel welvaartsplan 1950*. Batavia: Departement van Economische Zaken.

Diaz-Alejandro, C.F. (1978). 'Delinking North and South: Unshackled or Unhinged?', in: A. Fishlow et al. (eds), *Rich and Poor Nations in the World Economy*. New York: McGraw-Hill, 87–162.

Dick, H.W. (1975). 'Prahu Shipping in Eastern Indonesia', *Bulletin of Indonesian Economic Studies* 11 (2), 69–107; (3), 81–103.

Dick, H.W. (1987a). *The Indonesian Interisland Shipping Industry: An Analysis of Competition and Regulation*. Singapore: Institute of Southeast Asian Studies.

Dick, H.W. (1987b). 'Prahu Shipping in Eastern Indonesia in the Interwar Period', *Bulletin of Indonesian Economic Studies* 23 (1), 104–21.

Dick, H.W. (1989). 'Japan's Economic Expansion in the Netherlands Indies between the First and Second World Wars', *Journal of Southeast Asian Studies* 20 (2) 244–72.

Dick, H.W. (1993a). 'A Fresh Approach to Southeast Asian History', in: J. Butcher & H.W. Dick (eds), *The Rise and Fall of Revenue Farming: Business Elites and the Emergence of the Modern State in Southeast Asia*. London: Macmillan, 3–18.

Dick, H.W. (1993b). 'East Java in Regional Perspective', in: H.W. Dick, J. Fox & J.A.C. Mackie (eds), *Balanced Development: East Java under the New Order*. Singapore: Oxford University Press, 1–22.

Dick, H.W. (1993c). 'Indonesian Economic History Inside Out', *Review of Indonesian and Malaysian Affairs* 27, 1–12.

Dick, H.W. (1993d). 'Nineteenth-Century Industrialization: A Missed Opportunity?', in: J.Th. Lindblad (ed.), *New Challenges in the Modern Economic History of Indonesia*. Leiden: Programme of Indonesian Studies, 123–48.

Dick, H.W. (1993e). 'Oei Tiong Ham', in J. Butcher & H.W. Dick (eds), *The Rise and Fall of Revenue Farming: Business Elites and the Emergence of the Modern State in Southeast Asia*. London: Macmillan, 272–80.

Dick, H.W. (1995). 'The Transformation of Comparative Advantage: East Java, 1920–90', *Bulletin of Indonesian Economic Studies* 31 (1), 41–72.

Dick, H.W. (1996). 'The Emergence of a National Economy, 1808–1990s', in: J.Th. Lindblad (ed.), *Historical Foundations of a National Economy in Indonesia, 1890s–1990s*. Amsterdam: North-Holland, 21–51.

Dick, H.W. (2000). 'Representations of Development in 19th and 20th-Century Indonesia: A Transport History Perspective', *Bulletin of Indonesian Economic Studies* 36 (1), 185–207.

Dick, H.W. & Forbes, D. (1992). 'Transport and Communications: A Quiet Revolution', in: A. Booth (ed.), *The Oil Boom and After: Indonesian Economic Policy and Performance in the Soeharto Era*. Kuala Lumpur: Oxford University Press, 258–79.

Diehl, F.W. (1993). 'Revenue Farming and Colonial Finances in the Netherlands East Indies, 1816–1925', in: J. Butcher & H.W. Dick (eds), *The Rise and Fall of Revenue Farming: Business Elites and the Emergence of the Modern State in Southeast Asia*. London: Macmillan, 196–232.

van Dijk, C. (1997). 'Sarongs, Jubbahs and Trousers: Appearance as a Means of Distinction and Discrimination', in: H. Schulte Nordholt (ed.), *Outward Appearances: Dressing, State and Society in Indonesia*. Leiden: KITLV Press, 39–83.

Dobbin, C. (1983). *Islamic Revivalism in a Changing Peasant Economy: Central Sumatra, 1784–1847*. London: Curzon.

van den Doel, H.W. (1994). *De stille macht: Het Europese binnenlands bestuur op Java en Madoera, 1808–1942*. Amsterdam: Bert Bakker.

van Doorn, J.A.A. (1982). *The Engineers and the Colonial System: Technocratic Tendencies in the Dutch East Indies*. Rotterdam: CASP.

van Doorn, J.A.A. (1985). *Het Nederlands/Indonesisch conflict: Ontsporing van geweld*. Amsterdam/Dieren: Bataafsche Leeuw.

van Dulm, J., Aalders-Vorstman, M. and van Diessen, J.R. (2000). *Geïllustreerde atlas van de Japanse kampen in Nederlands-Indië, 1942–1945*. Purmerend: Asia Maior.

Earl, G.W. (1937/1971). *The Eastern Seas*. Singapore: Oxford University Press.

ECAFE (1961). *Economic Survey of Asia and the Far East*. Bangkok: United Nations Economic Commission for Asia and the Far East.

Elson, R.E. (1984). *Javanese Peasants and the Colonial Sugar Industry: Impact and Change in an East Java Residency 1830–1940*. Singapore: Oxford University Press.

Elson, R.E. (1986). 'Sugar Factory Workers and the Emergence of "Free Labour" in Nineteenth-Century Java', *Modern Asian Studies* 20 (1), 139–74.

Elson, R.E. (1994). *Village Java under the Cultivation System, 1830–1870*. Sydney: Allen & Unwin.

Elson, R.E. (1996). 'From "States" to State: The Changing Regime of Peasant Export Production in Mid-Nineteenth Century Java', in: J.Th. Lindblad (ed.), *Historical Foundations of a National Economy in Indonesia, 1890s–1990s*. Amsterdam: North-Holland, 123–35.

Elson, R.E. (1997). *The End of the Peasantry in Southeast Asia: A Social and Economic History of Peasant Livelihood, 1800–1990s*. London: Macmillan.

Encyclopaedie van Nederlandsch-Indië (1917–1939). The Hague: Nijhoff.

van der Eng, P. (1991). 'An Observer of 65 Years of Socio-Economic Change in Indonesia: Egbert de Vries', *Bulletin of Indonesian Economic Studies* 27 (1), 39–56.

van der Eng, P. (1992). 'The Real Domestic Product of Indonesia, 1880–1989', *Explorations in Economic History* 29, 343–73.

van der Eng, P. (1993a/1996). *Agricultural Growth in Indonesia since 1880*. Ph.D. dissertation, University of Groningen. Published as *Agricultural Growth in Indonesia: Productivity Change and Policy Impact since 1880*. London: Macmillan [1996].

van der Eng, P. (1993b). *The 'Colonial Drain' from Indonesia, 1823–1900*. Canberra: Research School of Pacific Studies, Australian National University.

van der Eng, P. (1994a). 'Assessing Economic Growth and Standards of Living in Asia, 1870–1990', in: A.J.H. Latham & H. Kawakatsu (eds), *The Evolving Structure of the East Asian Economic System since 1700: A Comparative Analysis*. Milan: Universitá Bocconi, 95–108.

van der Eng, P. (1994b). *Food Supply in Java during the War and Decolonisation, 1940–1950*. Hull: Centre for Southeast Asian Studies.

van der Eng, P. (1996). 'A Revolution in Indonesian Agriculture? A Long-Term View on Agricultural Labour Productivity', in: J.Th. Lindblad (ed.), *Historical Foundations of a National Economy in Indonesia, 1890s–1990s*. Amsterdam: North-Holland, 351–68.

van der Eng, P. (1997). 'Gauging Growth: Development of National Accounting in Indonesia', *Newsletter of the Asian Historical Statistics Project* 4, 9–11.

van der Eng, P. (1998a). 'Cassava in Indonesia: A Historical Reappraisal of an Enigmatic Food Crop', *Tonan Ajin Kenkyu [Southeast Asian Studies]* 36, 3–31.

van der Eng, P. (1998b). 'Exploring Exploitation: The Netherlands and Colonial Indonesia 1870–1940', *Revista de Historia Económica* 16, 291–321.

van der Eng, P. (2001). 'Indonesia's Growth Performance in the 20th Century', in: A. Maddison et al. (eds), *The Asian Economies in the Twentieth Century*. London: Elgar.

EWNI (1941, 1947). *Economisch Weekblad voor Nederlandsch-Indië* [weekly]. Batavia.

Falkus, M. (1990). *The Blue Funnel Legend: A History of the Ocean Steam Ship Company, 1865–1973*. London: Macmillan.

Fasseur, C. (1975/1992). *Kultuurstelsel en koloniale baten: De Nederlandse exploitatie van Java 1840–1860*. Leiden: Universitaire Pers. Translated as: *The Politics of Colonial Exploitation: Java, the Dutch and the Cultivation System*. Ithaca, NY: Southeast Asia Program, Cornell University Press [1992].

Fasseur, C. (1993). *De Indologen: Ambtenaren voor de Oost 1825–1950*. Amsterdam: Bert Bakker.

Fasseur, C. (1994). 'Cornerstone and Stumbling Block: Racial Classification and the Late Colonial State in Indonesia', in: R. Cribb (ed.), *The Late Colonial State in Indonesia: Political and Economic Foundations of the Netherlands Indies 1880–1942*. Leiden: KITLV Press, 31–56.

Fasseur, C. (2000). 'Ethical Policy and Economic Development: Some Experiences of the Colonial Past', *Lembaran Sejarah* 3 (1), 210–21.

Feith, H. (1962). *The Decline of Constitutional Democracy in Indonesia*. Ithaca, NY: Cornell University Press.

Fernando, M.R. (1993). 'Growth of Non-Agricultural Indigenous Economic Activities in Java, 1820–1880', in: J.Th. Lindblad (ed.), *New Challenges in the Modern Economic History of Indonesia*. Leiden: Programme of Indonesian Studies, 89–109.

Fernando, M.R. (1996). 'Growth of Non-Agricultural Economic Activities in Java in the Middle Decades of the Nineteenth Century', *Modern Asian Studies* 30 (1), 77–119.

Fernando, M.R. & Bulbeck, D. (1992). *Chinese Economic Activity in Netherlands India: Selected Translations from the Dutch*. Singapore: Institute of Southeast Asian Studies.

Frederick, W.H. (1989). *Visions and Heat: The Making of the Indonesian Revolution*. Athens: Ohio University Press.

Fruin, Th.A. (1947). 'Het economische aspect van het Indonesische vraagstuk', *Vrij Nederland*.

Furnivall, J.S. (1939/1944). *Netherlands India: A Study of Plural Economy*. Cambridge: Cambridge University Press.

Furnivall, J.S. (1948). *Colonial Policy and Practice: A Comparative Study of Burma and Netherlands India*. Cambridge: Cambridge University Press.

Gaastra, F. (1989). *Bewind en beleid: De financiële en commerciële politiek van de bewindhebbers, 1672–1702*. Zutphen: Walburg.

Geertz, C. (1963a). *Agricultural Involution: The Processes of Ecological Change in Indonesia*. Berkeley: University of California Press.

Geertz, C. (1963b). *Peddlers and Princes: Social Development and Economic Change in Two Indonesian Towns*. Chicago: University of Chicago Press.

Gelb, A. and Associates (1988). *Oil Windfalls: Blessing or Curse?* New York: Oxford University Press.

van Gelderen, J. (1939). *The Recent Development of Economic Foreign Policy in the Netherlands East Indies*. London: Longmans.

George, M. (1980). *Australia and the Indonesian Revolution*. Melbourne: Melbourne University Press.

Gill, G.H. (1957). *Royal Australian Navy, 1939–1942*. Canberra: Australian War Memorial.

Gillis, M. (1984). 'Episodes in Indonesian Economic Growth', in: A.C. Harberger (ed.), *World Economic Growth*. San Francisco: Institute for Contemporary Studies, 231–64.

Glassburner, B. (1962). 'The Attempt to Foster Private Entrepreneurship in Indonesia', *Indian Economic Review* 6 (2), 71–92.

Glassburner, B. (ed.) (1971). *The Economy of Indonesia*. Ithaca, NY: Cornell University Press.

Glassburner, B. (1988). 'Indonesia: Windfalls in a Poor Rural Economy', in: A. Gelb et al. (eds), *Oil Windfalls: Blessing or Curse?* New York: Oxford University Press, 197–226.

Glassburner, B. & Thomas, K.D. (1965). 'Abrogation, Take-Over and Nationalization: The Elimination of Dutch Economic Dominance from the Republic of Indonesia', *Australian Outlook* 19 (2), 158–79.

Golay, F. (1976). 'Southeast Asia: The "Colonial Drain" Revisited', in: C.D. Cowan & O.W. Wolters (eds), *Southeast Asian History and Historiography*. Ithaca, NY: Cornell University Press, 368–87.

van Goor, J. (1994). *De Nederlandse koloniën: Geschiedenis van de Nederlandse expansie 1600–1975*. The Hague: SDU.

Goto, K. (1997). *Returning to Asia: Japan-Indonesia Relations, 1930s–1942*. Tokyo: Ryukei Shyosha.

Gray, C.S. (1982). 'Survey of Recent Developments', *Bulletin of Indonesian Economic Studies* 18 (3), 1–51.

Gregory, R. (1988). 'An Overview', in: R. Gregory & N. Butlin (eds), *Recovery from the Depression: Australia and the World Economy in the 1930s*. Cambridge: Cambridge University Press, 1–32.

Grenville, S. (1981). 'Monetary Policy and the Formal Financial Sector', in: A. Booth & P. McCawley (eds), *The Indonesian Economy during the Soeharto Era*. Kuala Lumpur: Oxford University Press, 102–25.

Hall, K.R. (1985). *Maritime Trade and State Development in Early Southeast Asia*. Honolulu: University of Hawaii Press.

Hardjono, J. (1977). *Transmigration in Indonesia*. Kuala Lumpur: Oxford University Press.

Hardjono, J. (1994). 'Resource Utilisation and the Environment', in: H. Hill (ed.), *Indonesia's New Order: The Dynamics of Socio-Economic Transformation*. Sydney: Allen & Unwin, 179–215.

Hart, G.H.C. (1942). *Towards Economic Democracy in the Netherlands Indies*. New York: Institute of Pacific Relations.

Harvey, B.S. (1977). *Permesta: Half a Rebellion*. Ithaca, NY: Cornell University Press.

van den Haspel, C.Ch. (1985). *Overwicht in overleg: Hervormingen van justitie, grondgebruik en bestuur in de Vorstenlanden op Java 1880–1930*. Dordrecht/Providence: Foris.

Heersink, C.G. (1995/1999). *The Green Gold of Selayar: A Socio-Economic History of an Indonesian Coconut Island c. 1600–1950: Perspectives from a Periphery*. Ph.D. dissertation, Free University of Amsterdam. Leiden: KITLV Press [1999].

Hicks, G.L. (ed.) (1993). *Overseas Chinese Remittances from Southeast Asia 1910–1940*. Singapore: Select Books.

Higgins, B. (1957). *Indonesia's Stabilization and Development*. New York: Institute of Pacific Relations.

Higgins, B. (1992). *All the Difference: A Development Economist's Quest*. Montreal: McGill-Queen's.

Hill, H. (1987). 'Survey of Recent Developments', *Bulletin of Indonesian Economic Studies* 23 (3), 1–33.

Hill, H. (1988). *Foreign Investment and Industrialization in Indonesia*. Singapore: Oxford University Press.

Hill, H. (1994). 'The Economy', in: H. Hill (ed.), *Indonesia's New Order: The Dynamics of Socio-Economic Transformation*. Sydney: Allen & Unwin, 54–122.

Hill, H. (1995). *Indonesia's Industrial Policy and Performance: 'Orthodoxy' Vindicated*. Canberra: Research School of Pacific and Asian Studies, Australian National University.

Hill, H. (1996/2000a). *The Indonesian Economy since 1966: Southeast Asia's Emerging Giant*. Cambridge: Cambridge University Press.

Hill, H. (1998a). 'The Indonesian Economy: The Strange and Sudden Death of a Tiger', in: G. Forrester & R.J. May (eds), *The Fall of Soeharto*. Bathurst: Crawford, 93–103.

Hill, H. (1998b). 'The Challenge of Regional Development in Indonesia', *Australian Journal of International Affairs* 25 (1), 19–34.

Hill, H. (1999). 'An Overview of the Issues', in: H.W. Arndt & H. Hill (eds), *Southeast Asia's Economic Crisis: Origins, Lessons, and the Way Forward*. Singapore: Institute of Southeast Asian Studies, 1–15.

Hill, H. (2000). 'Indonesia: The Strange and Sudden Death of a Tiger Economy', *Oxford Development Studies* 28 (2), 117–39.

Hobohm, S. (1995). 'Survey of Recent Developments', *Bulletin of Indonesian Economic Studies* 31 (1), 3–41.

Hollinger, W.C. (1996). *Economic Policy under President Soeharto: Indonesia's Twenty-Five Years Record*. Washington: United States Indonesia Society.

Homan, G.D. (1987). 'That "Beautiful Tobacco"': The Sumatra Cigar Wrapper and the American Tariff, c. 1880–1941', *Economisch- en Sociaal-Historisch Jaarboek* 50, 145–56.

Houben, V.J.H. (1994a). 'Profit versus Ethics: Government Enterprises in the Late Colonial State', in: R. Cribb (ed.), *The Late Colonial State in Indonesia: Political and Economic Foundations of the Netherlands Indies 1880–1942*. Leiden: KITLV Press, 191–211.

Houben, V.J.H. (1994b). 'Trade and State Formation in Central Java 17th–19th Centuries', in: G.J. Schutte (ed.), *Trade and State in the Indonesian Archipelago*. Leiden: KITLV Press, 61–76.

Houben, V.J.H. (1994c). *Kraton and Kumpeni: Surakarta and Yogyakarta, 1830–1870*. Leiden: KITLV Press.

Houben, V.J.H. (1995). 'Labour Conditions on Western Firms in Colonial Indonesia: Outline of an Approach', *Jahrbuch für Wirtschaftsgeschichte* 1, 93–108.

Houben, V.J.H. (1996a). 'The Labour Inspectorate and Labour Conditions in the Outer Islands and Java, 1900–1940', in: J.Th. Lindblad (ed.), *Historical Foundations of a National Economy in Indonesia, 1890s–1990s*. Amsterdam: North-Holland, 193–206.

Houben, V.J.H. (1996b). *Van kolonie tot eenheidsstaat: Indonesië in de negentiende en twintigste eeuw*. Leiden: Vakgroep Talen en Culturen van Zuidoost-Azië en Oceanië, Leiden University.

Houben, V.J.H., Lindblad, J.Th. et al. (1999). *Coolie Labour in Late Colonial Indonesia: A Study of Labour Relations in the Outer Islands, c. 1900–1940*. Wiesbaden: Harrassowitz.

Houben, V.J.H., Maier, H.M.J. & van der Molen, W. (eds) (1992). *Looking in Odd Mirrors: The Java Sea*. Leiden: Vakgroep Talen en Culturen van Zuidoost-Azië en Oceanië, Leiden University.

Hugo, G.J., Hull, T.H., Hull, V.J. and Jones, G.W. (1987). *The Demographic Dimension in Indonesian Development*. Singapore: Oxford University Press.

Hull, T. (1994). 'Fertility Decline in the New Order Period: The Evolution of Population Policy, 1965–1990', in: H. Hill (ed.), *Indonesia's New Order: The Dynamics of Socio-Economic Transformation*. Sydney: Allen & Unwin, 123–45.

Hunter, A. (1965). 'Oil Exploration in Indonesia', *Bulletin of Indonesian Economic Studies* 4, 68–71.

Hüsken, F.A.M. (1982). 'Regional Diversity in Javanese Agrarian Development: Variations in the Pattern of Evolution', in: D. van den Muijzenberg (ed.), *Focus on the Region in Asia*. Rotterdam: Erasmus University Press, 167–91.

Hüsken, F.A.M. (1994). 'Declining Welfare in Java: Government and Private Inquiries, 1903–1914', in: R. Cribb (ed.), *The Late Colonial State in Indonesia: Political and Economic Foundations of the Netherlands Indies 1880–1942*. Leiden: KITLV Press, 213–28.

Hyde, F.E. (1957). *Blue Funnel: A History of Alfred Holt and Company of Liverpool from 1865 to 1914*. Liverpool: Liverpool University Press.

ILO/UNDP (1998). *Employment Challenges of the Indonesian Economic Crisis*. Jakarta: International Labour Organisation/United Nations Development Programme.

Indisch Verslag (1931–1940). Batavia: Centraal Kantoor voor de Statistiek.

Ingleson, G.W. (1979). *Road to Exile: The Indonesian Nationalist Movement 1927–1934*. Singapore: Heinemann.

Iqbal, F. (1995). 'Deregulation and Development in Indonesia', Paper presented at the Conference 'Building on Success: Maximising the Gains from Deregulation', Jakarta.

Ismail, M.G. (1991). *Seuneubok Lada, Uleëbalang, dan Kumpeni: Perkembangan Sosial Ekonomi di Daerah Batas: Aceh Timur, 1840–1942*. Ph.D. dissertation, Leiden University.

Ismail, M.G. (1996). 'Aceh's Dual Economy during the Late Colonial Period', in: J.Th. Lindblad (ed.), *Historical Foundations of a National Economy in Indonesia, 1890s–1990s*. Amsterdam: North-Holland, 229–48.

James, W.E. (1996). 'Indonesia: Non-Oil and Non-Gas Export Performance in 1995 and Prospects for 1996', Paper prepared for the Seminar on 'Non-Oil Export Performance', Department of Industry and Trade, Jakarta.

James, W.E. (1997). 'Indonesia's Non-Oil exports: Market-Led Growth and Diversification', Paper prepared for the 'North American Economics and Finance Association Meeting', New Orleans.

James, W.E. & Stephenson, S.M. (1993). 'Indonesia's Experience with Economic Policy Reform: Reversing the Conventional Wisdom about Sequencing' [Discussion paper], Jakarta.

Johnson, C. (1982). *MITI and the Japanese Miracle: The Growth of Industrial Policy, 1925–1975*. Stanford, CA: Stanford University Press.

Johnson, C. (1998). 'Survey of Recent Developments', *Bulletin of Indonesian Economic Studies* 34 (2), 3–57.

Jones, G.W. (1994). 'Labour Force and Education', in: H. Hill (ed.), *Indonesia's New Order: The Dynamics of Socio-Economic Transformation*. Sydney: Allen & Unwin, 145–78.

Jonkers, A. (1948). *Welvaartzorg in Indonesië*. The Hague: Van Hoeve.

Kahin, A.R. & Kahin, G.M. (1995). *Subversion as Foreign Policy: The Secret Eisenhower and Dulles Debacle in Indonesia*. New York: New Press.

Kahin, G.M. (1952). *Nationalism and Revolution in Indonesia*. Ithaca, NY: Cornell University Press.

Kamerling, R.N.J. (1982). *De N.V. Oliefabrieken Insulinde in Nederlands-Indië: Bedrijfsvoering in het onbekende*. Franeker: Wever.

Kamphues, A. (1988). 'Na Rhemrev: Arbeidsomstandigheden op de westerse ondernemingen in de Buitengewesten van Nederlands-Indië', *Economisch- en Sociaal-Historisch Jaarboek* 51, 299–337.

Kano, H. (1977). *Land Tenure System and the Desa Community in Nineteenth-Century Java*. Tokyo: Institute of Developing Economies.

Kathirithamby-Wells, J. (1986). 'The Islamic City: Melaka to Jogjakarta, c. 1500–1800', *Modern Asian Studies* 20, 333–51.

Kathirithamby-Wells, J. (1993). 'Restraints on the Development of Merchant Capitalism in Southeast Asia before c. 1800', in: A. Reid (ed.), *Southeast Asia in the Early Modern Era: Trade, Power and Belief*. Ithaca, NY: Cornell University Press, 123–48.

Kindleberger, C.P. (1962). *Foreign Trade and the National Economy*. New Haven, CT: Yale University Press.

Knaap, G.J. (1986). 'Coffee for Cash: The Dutch East India Company and the Expansion of Coffee Cultivation in Java, Ambon and Ceylon 1700–1730', in: J. van Goor (ed.), *Trading Companies in Asia 1600–1830*. Utrecht: Hes, 33–49.

Knaap, G.J. (1989). *Changing Economy in Indonesia IX: Transport 1819–1940*. Amsterdam: Royal Tropical Institute.

Knaap, G.J. (1995). 'The Demography of Ambon in the Seventeenth Century: Evidence from Colonial Proto-Censuses', *Journal of Southeast Asian Studies* 26, 227–41.

Knaap, G.J. (1996). *Shallow Waters, Rising Tide: Shipping and Trade in Java around 1775*. Leiden: KITLV Press.

Knaap, G.J. & Nagtegaal, L. (1991). 'A Forgotten Trade: Salt in Southeast Asia 1670–1813', in: R. Ptak & D. Rothermund (eds), *Emporia, Commodities and Entrepreneurs in Asian Maritime Trade, c. 1400–1750*. Stuttgart: Steiner, 127–57.

Knight, G.R. (1993). 'Gully Coolies, Weed-Women and "Snijvolk": The Sugar Industry Workers of North Java in the Early Twentieth Century', in: J.Th. Lindblad (ed.), *New Challenges in the Modern Economic History of Indonesia*. Leiden: Programme of Indonesian Studies, 67–88.

Knight, G.R. (1996). 'Did "Dependency" Really Get it Wrong? The Indonesian Sugar Industry, 1880–1942', in: J.Th. Lindblad (ed.), *Historical Foundations of a National Economy in Indonesia, 1890s–1990s*. Amsterdam: North-Holland, 155–73.

Komine, T. (1998). 'Currency Crisis and Financial Turmoil in Asia and the Potential for Future Growth', Paper presented at the 'International Symposium on Foreign Direct Investment in East Asia', Tokyo.

Korthals Altes, W.L. (1991). *Changing Economy in Indonesia, XII A: General Trade Statistics 1822–1940*. Amsterdam: Royal Tropical Institute.

Korthals Altes, W.L. (1994). *Changing Economy in Indonesia, XV: Prices (Non-Rice) 1814–1940*. Amsterdam: Royal Tropical Institute.

van der Kraan, A. (1980). *Lombok: Conquest, Colonization and Under-development, 1870–1940*. Singapore: Heinemann.

van der Kraan, A. (1993). 'Bali and Lombok in the World Economy, 1830–1850', *Review of Indonesian and Malaysian Affairs* 27, 91–105.

Kuitenbrouwer, M. (1985). *Nederland en de opkomst van het moderne imperialisme: Koloniën en buitenlandse politiek 1870–1902*. Amsterdam: Bataafsche Leeuw.

Kuntowijoyo (2000). 'The Making of a Modern Urban Ecology: Social and Economic History of Solo, 1900–1915', *Lembaran Sejarah* 3 (1), 163–85.

Kurasawa, A. (1993). *Mobilisasi dan Kontrol: Studi tentang Perubahan Sosial di Pedesaan Jawa, 1942–45*. Jakarta: Gramedia.

van Laanen, J.T.M. (1980). *Changing Economy in Indonesia* VI: *Money and Banking 1816–1940*. Amsterdam: Royal Tropical Institute.

Laarhoven, R. (1994). *The Power of Cloth: The Textile Trade of the Dutch East India Company (VOC) 1600–1780*. Ph.D. dissertation, Australian National University, Canberra.

Lee, J. (1999). 'Trade and Economy in Preindustrial East Asia, c. 1500–c. 1800: East Asia in the Age of Global Integration', *Journal of Asian Studies* 58, 2–26.

Legge, J.D. (1973). *Sukarno: A Political Biography*. Harmondsworth: Penguin Books.

Legge, J.D. (1980). *Indonesia*. Sydney: Prentice-Hall.

Leidelmeijer, M. (1997). *Van suikermolen tot grootbedrijf: Technische vernieuwing in de Java-suikerindustrie in de negentiende eeuw*. Amsterdam: NEHA.

Leirissa, R.Z. (1991). *PRRI Permesta: Strategi Membangun Indonesia tanpa Komunis*. Jakarta: Grafiti.

Leirissa, R.Z. (1993). 'The Structure of Makassar-Bugis Trade in the Pre-Modern Moluccas', *Review of Indonesian and Malaysian Affairs* 27, 77–90.

Leirissa, R.Z. (1996). ' "Copracontracten": An Indication of Economic Development in Minahasa during the Late Colonial Period', in: J.Th. Lindblad (ed.), *Historical Foundations of a National Economy in Indonesia, 1890s–1990s*. Amsterdam: North-Holland, 265–77.

van Leur, J.C. (1934/1983). *Indonesian Trade and Society: Essays in Asian Social and Economic History*. Dordrecht: Foris.

Lev, D.S. (1966). *The Transition to Guided Democracy: Indonesian Politics, 1957–1959*. Ithaca, NY: Cornell University Press.

Liaw, Yock Fang (1976). *Undang-Undang Melaka. The Laws of Melaka*. The Hague: Nijhoff.

Lieberman, V. (1995). 'An Age of Commerce in Southeast Asia? Problems of Regional Coherence: A Review Article', *Journal of Asian Studies* 54, 796–807.

Liem Twan Djie (1947). *De distribueerende tusschenhandel der Chineezen op Java*. The Hague: Nijhoff.

Lindayanti (1994). 'Perkebunan Karet Rakyat di Jambi, 1920–1928: Aspek Sosial-Ekonomi', *Sejarah* 5, 34–44.

Lindblad, J.Th. (1988a). *Between Dayak and Dutch: The Economic History of Southeast Kalimantan 1880–1942*. Dordrecht: Foris.

Lindblad, J.Th. (1988b). 'De handel tussen Nederland en Nederlands-Indië, 1874–1939', *Economisch- en Sociaal-Historisch Jaarboek* 51, 240–98.

Lindblad, J.Th. (1989a). 'Economic Aspects of the Dutch Expansion in Indonesia, 1870–1914', *Modern Asian Studies* 23 (1), 1–23.

Lindblad, J.Th. (1989b). 'The Petroleum Industry in Indonesia before the Second World War', *Bulletin of Indonesian Economic Studies* 25 (2), 53–78.

Lindblad, J.Th. (1990). 'The Process of Economic Development in the Outer Provinces of the Dutch East Indies', *Journal of the Japan-Netherlands Institute* 2, 208–34.

Lindblad, J.Th. (1991). 'Foreign Investment in Late-Colonial and Post-Colonial Indonesia', *Economic and Social History in the Netherlands* 3, 183–208.

Lindblad, J.Th. (1993). 'Economic Growth in the Outer Islands, 1910–1940', in: J.Th. Lindblad (ed.), *New Challenges in the Modern Economic History of Indonesia*. Leiden: Programme of Indonesian Studies, 233–63.

Lindblad, J.Th. (1994). 'The Contribution of Foreign Trade to Colonial State Formation', in: R. Cribb (ed.), *The Late Colonial State in Indonesia: Political and Economic Foundations of the Netherlands Indies 1880–1942*. Leiden: KITLV Press, 93–115.

Lindblad, J.Th. (1996). 'Between Singapore and Batavia: The Outer Islands in the Southeast Asian Economy during the Nineteenth Century', in: C.A. Davids, W. Fritschy & L.A. van der Valk (eds), *Kapitaal, ondernemerschap en beleid: Studies over economie en politiek in Nederland, Europa en Azië van 1500 tot heden*. Amsterdam: NEHA, 529–48.

Lindblad, J.Th. (1998). *Foreign Investment in Southeast Asia in the Twentieth Century*. London: Macmillan.

Lindblad, J.Th. (1999). 'Macro-economische beschouwingen over de voedselproductie op Java, circa 1914–1940', *Economisch- en Sociaal-Historisch Jaarboek* 62, 231–48.

Lipton, M. (1978). *Why Poor People Stay Poor: Urban Bias in Development*. London: Temple Smith.

Little, I.M.D. (1979). *The Experience and Cause of Rapid Labour-Intensive Development in Korea, Taiwan, Hong Kong, and Singapore and the Possibilities of Emulation*. Bangkok: International Labour Organisation.

Locher-Scholten, E.B. (1981). *Ethiek in fragmenten: Vijf studies over koloniaal denken en doen van Nederlanders in de Indonesische archipel 1877–1942*. Utrecht: Hes.

Locher-Scholten, E.B. (1991). '"Een gebiedende noodzakelijkheid": Besluitvorming rond de Boni-expeditie 1903–1905', in: H.A. Poeze & P. Schoorl (eds), *Excursies in Celebes: Een bundel bijdragen bij het afscheid van J. Noorduyn als directeur-secretaris van het Koninklijk Instituut voor Taal-, Land- en Volkenkunde.* Leiden: KITLV Press, 143–64.

Locher-Scholten, E.B. (1994a). 'Dutch Expansion in the Indonesian Archipelago around 1900 and the Imperialism Debate', *Journal of Southeast Asian Studies* 25, 91–111.

Locher-Scholten, E.B. (1994b). *Sumatraans sultanaat en koloniale staat: De relatie Djambi-Batavia (1830–1907) en het Nederlandse imperialisme.* Leiden: KITLV Press.

Locher-Scholten, E.B. (1996). 'The Establishment of Colonial Rule in Jambi: The Dual Strand of Politics and Economics', in: J.Th. Lindblad (ed.), *Historical Foundations of a National Economy in Indonesia, 1890s–1990s.* Amsterdam: North-Holland, 137–51.

Lombard, D. (1990). *Le Carrefour Javanais: Essai d'Histoire Globale.* Paris: Editions de l'École des Hautes Études en Sciences Sociales.

MacIntyre, A. (1999). 'Political Institutions and the Economic Crisis in Thailand and Indonesia', in: H.W. Arndt & H. Hill (eds), *Southeast Asia's Economic Crisis: Origins, Lessons, and the Way Forward.* Singapore: Institute of Southeast Asian Studies, 142–57.

Mackie, J.A.C. (1967a). 'The Government Estates', in: T.K. Tan (ed.), *Sukarno's Guided Indonesia.* Brisbane: Jacaranda, 58–72.

Mackie, J.A.C. (1967b). *Problems of the Indonesian Inflation.* Ithaca, NY: Cornell University Press.

Mackie, J.A.C. (1971). 'The Indonesian Economy, 1950–1960', in: B. Glassburner (ed.), *The Economy of Indonesia: Selected Readings.* Ithaca, NY: Cornell University Press, 16–69.

Mackie, J.A.C. (1976). 'Anti-Chinese Outbreaks in Indonesia, 1959–68', in: J.A.C. Mackie (ed.), *The Chinese in Indonesia: Five Essays.* Melbourne: Thomas Nelson, 77–138.

Mackie, J.A.C. (1993). 'Regional Demographic History as a Clue to Socio-Economic Changes: The Residency of Surabaya 1890–1990 as a Case Study', in: J.Th. Lindblad (ed.), *New Challenges in the Modern Economic History of Indonesia.* Leiden: Programme of Indonesian Studies, 216–32.

Mackie, J.A.C. (1997). 'Indonesia: Economic Growth and Depoliticization' [Unpublished paper], Canberra.

Mackie, J.A.C. & Coppel, C.A. (1976). 'A Preliminary Survey', in: J.A.C. Mackie (ed.), *The Chinese in Indonesia: Five Essays.* Melbourne: Thomas Nelson, 1–18.

Mackie, J.A.C. & MacIntyre, A. (1994). 'Politics', in: H. Hill (ed.), *Indonesia's New Order: The Dynamics of Socio-Economic Transformation.* Sydney: Allen & Unwin, 1–53.

Maddison, A. (1990). 'Dutch Colonialism in Indonesia: A Comparative Perspective', in: A. Booth, W.J. O'Malley & A. Weidemann (eds), *Indonesian Economic History in the Dutch Colonial Era.* New Haven, CT: Yale University Press, 322–35.

Mahajani, U. (1970). *Soviet and American Aid to Indonesia, 1949–68*. Athens: Southeast Asia Program, Ohio University.

Manarungsan, S. (1989). *Economic Development of Thailand, 1850–1950: Response to the Challenge of the World Economy*. Bangkok: Institute of Asian Studies.

Manguin, P.-Y. (1993). 'The Vanishing *Jong*: Insular Southeast Asian Fleets in Trade and War (Fifteenth to Seventeenth Centuries)', in: A. Reid (ed.), *Southeast Asia in the Early Modern Era: Trade, Power, and Belief*. Ithaca, NY: Cornell University Press, 197–213.

Manning, C. (1995). 'Approaching the Turning Point? Labor Market Change under Indonesia's New Order', *Developing Economies* 33 (1), 52–81.

Manning, C. (1998). *Indonesian Labour in Transition: An East Asian Success Story?* Cambridge: Cambridge University Press.

Manning, C. & Jayasuriya, S. (1996). 'Survey of Recent Developments', *Bulletin of Indonesian Economic Studies* 32 (2), 3–43.

Mansvelt, W.M.F. (1924). *Geschiedenis van de Nederlandsche Handel-Maatschappij*. Haarlem: Enschedé.

Margono Djojohadikusumo (1970). *Herinneringen uit drie tijdperken*. Amsterdam: Nabrink.

Masyhuri (1995). *Pasang Surut Usaha Perikanan Laut: Tinjauan Sosial-Ekonomi Kenelayanan di Jawa dan Madura, 1850–1940*. Ph.D. dissertation, Free University of Amsterdam.

McCawley, P. (1978). 'Some Consequences of the Crash of Pertamina', *Journal of Southeast Asian Studies* 9 (1), 1–27.

McCawley, P. (1981). 'The Growth of the Industrial Sector', in: A. Booth & P. McCawley (eds), *The Indonesian Economy during the Soeharto Era*. Kuala Lumpur: Oxford University Press, 62–101.

McCawley, P. (1993). 'Development Assistance in Asia', *Asian-Pacific Economic Literature* 7 (2), 1–13.

McLeod, R.H. (1993). 'Survey of Recent Developments', *Bulletin of Indonesian Economic Studies* 29 (2), 3–42.

McLeod, R.H. (1997a). 'Survey of Recent Developments', *Bulletin of Indonesian Economic Studies* 33 (1), 3–43.

McLeod, R.H. (1997b). 'Postscript to the Survey of Recent Developments: On Causes and Cures for the Rupiah Crisis', *Bulletin of Indonesian Economic Studies* 33 (3), 35–52.

McLeod, R.H. (1998). 'Indonesia', in: R.H. McLeod & R. Garnaut (eds) (1998). *East Asia in Crisis: From Being a Miracle to Needing One?* London: Routledge, 31–48.

McLeod, R.H. (2000). 'Survey of Recent Developments', *Bulletin of Indonesian Economic Studies* 36 (2), 3–38.

Mears, L.A. (1961). *Rice Marketing in the Republic of Indonesia*. Jakarta: Pembangunan.

Mears, L.A. & Moeljono, S. (1981). 'Food Policy', in: A. Booth & P. McCawley (eds), *The Indonesian Economy during the Soeharto Era*. Kuala Lumpur: Oxford University Press, 23–61.

Meier, G.M. (1984). *Leading Issues in Economic Development*. New York: Oxford University Press.

Meijer, H. (1994). *Den Haag-Djakarta: De Nederlands-Indonesische betrekkingen, 1950–1962*. Utrecht: Aula.

Meilink-Roelofsz, M.A.P. (1962). *Asian Trade and European Influence in the Indonesian Archipelago between 1500 and about 1630*. The Hague: Nijhoff.

van Miert, H. (1995). *Een koel hoofd en een warm hart: Nationalisme, javanisme en jeugdbeweging in Nederlands-Indië, 1918–1930*. Amsterdam: Bataafsche Leeuw.

Milner, A. (1982). *Kerajaan: Malay Political Culture on the Eve of Colonial Rule*. Tucson: University of Arizona Press.

Milner, A. (1995). *The Invention of Politics in Colonial Malaya: Contesting Nationalism and the Expansion of the Public Sphere*. Cambridge: Cambridge University Press.

Minami, R. et al. (1994). *The Economic Development of Japan: A Quantitative Study*. London: Macmillan.

Miyamoto, S. (1986). 'Jawa Shusen Shoriki (An Account of the Cessation of Hostilities in Java)', in: A.J.S. Reid & A. Oki (eds), *The Japanese Experience in Indonesia: Selected Memoirs of 1942–1945*. Athens: Centre for Southeast Asian Studies, Ohio University.

Moedjanto, G. (1988). *Indonesia abad ke-20*, I: *Dari Kebangkitan Nasional sampai Linggajati*. Yogyakarta: Kanisius.

Montes, M. & Abdulsalamov, M.A. (1998). 'Indonesian: Reaping the Market', in: K.S. Jomo (ed.) (1998), *Tigers in Trouble: Financial Governance, Liberalisation, and Crises in East Asia*. London: Zed Books, 162–80.

van Mook, H.J. (1944). *The Netherlands Indies and Japan*. London: Allen & Unwin.

Muir, R. (1986). 'Survey of Recent Developments', *Bulletin of Indonesian Economic Studies* 22 (2), 1–27.

Nagazumi, A. (1972). *The Dawn of Indonesian Nationalism: The Early Years of the Budi Utomo, 1908–1918*. Tokyo: Institute of Developing Economies. Translated into Indonesian as: *Bangkitnya Nasionalisme Indonesia: Budi Utomo 1908–1918*. Jakarta: Grafiti.

Nagtegaal, L. (1993). 'The Pre-Modern City in Indonesia and its Fall from Grace with the Gods', *Economic and Social History in the Netherlands* 5, 39–59.

Nagtegaal, L. (1996). *Riding the Dutch Tiger: The Dutch East Indies Company and the Northeast Coast of Java, 1680–1743*. Leiden: KITLV Press.

Napitupulu, B. (1968). 'Hunger in Indonesia', *Bulletin of Indonesian Economic Studies* 9, 60–70.

Nasution, A. (1995). 'Survey of Recent Developments', *Bulletin of Indonesian Economic Studies* 31 (2), 3–40.

Nasution, A.B. (1992). *The Aspiration for Constitutional Government in Indonesia: A Socio-Legal Study of the Indonesian Konstituante, 1956–1959*. Jakarta: Sinar Harapan.

Nasution, A.H. (1983a). *Memenuhi Panggilan Tugas: Kenangan Masa Gerilya*. Jakarta: Gunung Agung.

Nasution, A.H. (1983b). *Memenuhi Panggilan Tugas: Masa Pancaroba Pertama*. Jakarta: Gunung Agung.

Naya, S. (1988). 'The Role of Trade Policies in the Industrialization of Rapidly Growing Asian Developing Countries', in: H. Hughes (ed.), *Achieving Industrialization in East Asia*. Cambridge: Cambridge University Press, 64–94.

NHM (1944). *De industrialisatie in Nederlandsch-Indië na 1918* [Internal report]. Amsterdam: Nederlandsche Handel-Maatschappij.

NIF (1934–1940). *Officieël Orgaan der Vereeniging Nederlandsch-Indisch Fabrikaat* [monthly]. Batavia.

Nishihara, M. (1976). *The Japanese and Sukarno's Indonesia: Tokyo–Jakarta Relations, 1951–1966*. Honolulu: University Press of Hawaii.

Odell, P.R. (1981). *Oil and World Power*. Harmondsworth: Penguin.

van Oorschot, H.J. (1956). *De ontwikkeling van de nijverheid in Indonesië*. The Hague: Van Hoeve.

Paauw, D.S. (1960). *Financing Economic Development: The Indonesian Case*. Glencoe: Free Press.

Paauw, D.S. (1963). 'From Colonial to Guided Economy', in: R. McVey (ed.), *Indonesia*. New Haven, CT: Southeast Asian Studies Program, Yale University, 155–247.

Padmo, S. (1993). 'The Development of Non-Farm Employment Opportunities in the Residency of Cirebon, 1830–1930', in: J.Th. Lindblad (ed.), *New Challenges in the Modern Economic History of Indonesia*. Leiden: Programme of Indonesian Studies, 110–22.

Padmo, S. (1994). *The Cultivation of Vorstenlands Tobacco in Surakarta Residency and Besuki Tobacco in Besuki Residency and its Impact on the Peasant Economy and Society, 1860–1960*. Yogyakarta: Aditya Media.

Palmer, I. (1972). *Textiles in Indonesia: Problems of Import Substitution*. New York: Praeger.

Pangestu, M. (1996). *Economic Reform, Deregulation and Privatization: The Indonesian Experience*. Jakarta: Centre for Strategic and International Studies.

Pangestu, M. & Azis, I.J. (1994). 'Survey of Recent Developments', *Bulletin of Indonesian Economic Studies* 30 (2), 3–48.

Pangestu, M. & Sato, Y. (eds) (1997). *Waves of Change in Indonesia's Manufacturing Industry*. Tokyo: Institute of Developing Economies.

Panglaykim, J. & Arndt, H.W. (1966). 'Survey of Recent Developments', *Bulletin of Indonesian Economic Studies* 4, 1–35.

Panglaykim, J. & Palmer, I. (1969). *State Trading Corporations in Developing Countries*. Rotterdam: Rotterdam University Press.

Panglaykim, J., Penny, D.H. & Thalib, D. (1968). 'Survey of Recent Developments', *Bulletin of Indonesian Economic Studies* 9, 1–33.

Papanek, G. & Dowsett, D. (1975). 'The Cost of Living, 1938–1973', *Ekonomi dan Keuangan Indonesia* 23 (2), 181–216.

Pardede, R. (1999). 'Survey of Recent Developments', *Bulletin of Indonesian Economic Studies* 35 (2), 3–39.

Parker, S. (1991). 'Survey of Recent Developments', *Bulletin of Indonesian Economic Studies* 27 (1), 3–38.

Pearson, S. & Monke, E. (1991). 'Introduction', in: S. Pearson et al. (eds), *Rice Policy in Indonesia*. Ithaca, NY: Cornell University Press, 1–7.

Pelzer, K. (1978). *Planter and Peasant: Colonial Policy and the Agrarian Struggle in East Sumatra, 1863–1947*. The Hague: Nijhoff.

Pelzer, K. (1982). *Planters against Peasants: The Agrarian Struggle in East Sumatra, 1947–1958*. The Hague: Nijhoff.

Perlin, F. (1983). 'Proto-Industrialization and Pre-Colonial South Asia', *Past and Present* 98 (1), 30–95.

Poelinggomang, E.L. (1991). *Proteksi dan Perdagangan Bebas: Kajian tentang Perdagangan Makassar pada Abad ke-19*. Ph.D. dissertation, Free University of Amsterdam.

Poelinggomang, E.L. (1993). 'The Dutch Trade Policy and its Impact on Makassar's Trade', *Review of Indonesian and Malaysian Affairs* 27, 61–76.

Poeze, H.A. (1994). 'Political Intelligence in the Netherlands Indies', in: R. Cribb (ed.), *The Late Colonial State in Indonesia: Political and Economic Foundations of the Netherlands Indies 1880–1942*. Leiden: KITLV Press, 229–45.

Polak, L.L. (1943/1979). 'Het nationaal inkomen van Nederlands-Indië, 1921–1939', *Statistische en Economische Onderzoekingen* 2. Translated as: 'The National Income of the Netherlands Indies, 1921–1939', in: P. Creutzberg, *Changing Economy in Indonesia* V: *National Income*. The Hague: Nijhoff [1979].

Poppele, J., Sumarno, S. & Pritchett, L. (1999). 'Social Impacts of the Indonesian Crisis: New Data and Policy Implications: A SMERU Report' [Draft].

Post, P. (1996). 'Characteristics of Japanese Entrepreneurship in the Pre-War Indonesian Economy', in: J.Th. Lindblad (ed.), *Historical Foundations of a National Economy in Indonesia, 1890s–1990s*. Amsterdam: North-Holland, 297–314.

Post, P. (1997). 'The Formation of the Pribumi Business Elite in Indonesia, 1930s–1940s', in: P. Post & E. Touwen-Bouwsma (eds), *Japan, Indonesia and the War: Myths and Realities*. Leiden: KITLV Press, 87–110.

270   THE EMERGENCE OF A NATIONAL ECONOMY

Potter, L. (1993). 'Banjarese in and beyond Hulu Sungai, South Kalimantan:
A Study of Cultural Dependence, Economic Opportunity and Mobility',
in: J.Th. Lindblad (ed.), *New Challenges in the Modern Economic
History of Indonesia*. Leiden: Programme of Indonesian Studies,
264–98.

Potting, C.J.M. (1987). 'De muntvoorziening in Nederlands-Indië,
1877–1913', *Economisch- en Sociaal-Historisch Jaarboek* 50, 111–44.

Potting, C.J.M. (1997). *De ontwikkeling van het geldverkeer in een
koloniale samenleving: Oostkust van Sumatra, 1875–1938*. Ph.D.
dissertation, Leiden University.

Pramoedya Ananta Toer (1982). *Anak Semua Bangsa: Dengan Penjelasan
Istilah Bahasa Indonesia*. Melaka: Wira Karya.

Prapanca, M. (1995). *Desawarnana (Nagarakrtagama)*. S.O. Robson
(trans.). Leiden: KITLV Press.

Prawiro, R. (1998). *Indonesia's Struggle for Economic Development:
Pragmatism in Action*. Kuala Lumpur: Oxford University Press.

Prince, G.H.A. (1989). 'Dutch Economic Policy in Indonesia, 1870–1942',
in: A. Maddison & G. Prince (eds), *Economic Growth in Indonesia,
1820–1940*. Dordrecht: Foris, 203–26.

Prince, G.H.A. (1993). 'Economic Policy in Indonesia, 1900–1942', in:
J.Th. Lindblad (ed.), *New Challenges in the Modern Economic History
of Indonesia*. Leiden: Programme of Indonesian Studies, 161–81.

Prince, G.H.A. (1995). 'Dutch Economic Policy in Colonial Indonesia
1900–1942', *Jahrbuch für Wirtschaftsgeschichte* 1, 23–44.

Purwanto, B. (1992). *From Dusun to the Market: Native Rubber Cultivation
in Southern Sumatra, 1890–1940*. Ph.D. dissertation, University of London.

Purwanto, B. (1993). 'The Economy of the Native Population of Southern
Sumatra between 1850 and 1910', *Review of Indonesian and Malaysian
Affairs* 27, 106–33.

Purwanto, B. (1996). 'The Economy of Indonesian Smallholder Rubber,
1890s–1940', in: J.Th. Lindblad (ed.), *Historical Foundations of a National
Economy in Indonesia, 1890s–1990s*. Amsterdam: North-Holland, 175–92.

Ranken, E.A. (1989). 'De niet-Europese bijdrage tot de economische
ontwikkeling van West-Borneo, 1900–1940', in: A.H.P. Clemens &
J.Th. Lindblad (eds), *Het belang van de Buitengewesten: Economische
expansie en koloniale staatsvorming in de Buitengewesten van Nederlands-Indië, 1870–1942*. Amsterdam: NEHA, 177–209.

Reid, A.J.S. (1969). *The Contest for North Sumatra: Atjeh, the Netherlands
and Britain, 1858–1898*. Kuala Lumpur: Oxford University Press.

Reid, A.J.S. (1974). *The Indonesian National Revolution, 1945–1950*.
Victoria: Longman.

Reid, A.J.S. (1984). 'The Pre-Colonial Economy of Indonesia', *Bulletin of
Indonesian Economic Studies* 20, 151–67.

Reid, A.J.S. (1988). *Southeast Asia in the Age of Commerce 1450–1680*,
I: *The Lands below the Winds*. New Haven, CT: Yale University
Press.

Reid, A.J.S. (1993a). *Southeast Asia in the Age of Commerce 1450–1680, II: Expansion and Crisis*. New Haven, CT: Yale University Press.

Reid, A.J.S. (1993b). 'The Unthreatening Alternative: Chinese Shipping in Southeast Asia, 1567–1842', *Review of Indonesian and Malaysian Affairs* 27, 13–32.

Reid, A.J.S. (1996). 'Chains of Silver, Chains of Steel: Forcing Politics on Geography, 1865–1965', in: J.Th. Lindblad (ed.), *Historical Foundations of a National Economy in Indonesia, 1890s–1990s*. Amsterdam: North-Holland, 281–96.

Reitsma, S.A. (ed.) (1925). *Gedenkboek der Staatsspoor- en Tramwegen in Nederlandsch-Indië, 1875–1925*. Weltevreden: Topografische Inrichting.

Reitsma, S.A. (1928). *Korte geschiedenis der Nederlandsch-Indische Spoor- en Tramwegen*. Batavia: Kolff.

Rhyne, R.F. (1954). *Social and Political Changes Associated with the Dutch Program of Technological Development Carried out in Java, 1918–1942*. Ph.D. dissertation, University of California.

Ricklefs, M.C. (1981). *A History of Modern Indonesia, c. 1300 to the Present*. London: Macmillan.

Ricklefs, M.C. (1993). *War, Culture and Economy in Java, 1677–1726: Asian and European Imperialism in the Early Kartasura Period*. Sydney: Allen & Unwin.

Rigg, J. (1991). *Southeast Asia: A Region in Transition*. London: Unwin Hyman.

Robison, R. (1986). *Indonesia: The Rise of Capital*. Sydney: Allen & Unwin.

Robson, S.O. (1992). 'Java in Malay Literature', in: V.J.H. Houben, H.M.J. Maier & W. van der Molen (eds), *Looking in Odd Mirrors: The Java Sea*. Leiden: Vakgroep Talen en Culturen van Zuidoost-Azië en Oceanië, Leiden University: 27–42.

Rosendale, P. (1978). *The Indonesian Balance of Payments, 1950–1966: Some New Estimates*. Ph.D. dissertation, Australian National University, Canberra.

Rostow, W.W. (1960). *The Stages of Economic Growth: A Non-Communist Manifesto*. Cambridge: Cambridge University Press.

Rothe, C. (1938). *Industrieën in Nederlandsch-Indië: Textielindustrie*. Amsterdam: Koloniaal Instituut.

Rush, J.R. (1990). *Opium to Java: Revenue Farming and Chinese Enterprise in Colonial Indonesia, 1860–1910*. Ithaca, NY: Cornell University Press.

Sadli, M. (1972). 'Foreign Investment in Developing Countries: Indonesia', in: P. Drysdale (ed.), *Direct Foreign Investment in Asia and the Pacific*. Canberra: Australian National University Press, 201–25.

Sadli, M. (1984). 'Masalah-Masalah Ekonomi-Moneter Sita yang Struktural', in: *Jalur Baru Sesudah Runtuhnya Ekonomi Terpimpin*. Jakarta: Sinar Harapan, 98–109.

Sadli, M. (1993). 'Recollections of My Career', *Bulletin of Indonesian Economic Studies* 29 (1), 35–51.

Sadli, M. (1999). 'The Indonesian Crisis', in: H.W. Arndt & H. Hill (eds), *Southeast Asia's Economic Crisis: Origins, Lessons, and the Way Forward*. Singapore: Institute of Southeast Asian Studies, 16–27.

Salim, E. (1997). 'Recollections of My Career', *Bulletin of Indonesian Economic Studies* 33 (1), 45–74.

Saroso Wirodihardjo, R. (1951). *De contingenteeringspolitiek en hare invloed op de Indonesische bevolking*. Jakarta: Nijhoff.

Sartono Kartodirdjo (1986). 'The Historical Novel "Pak Troeno". A Mirror of Social Realities in the Colonial Past', in: Taufik Abdullah & Sartono Kartodirdjo (eds), *Papers of the Fourth Indonesian–Dutch History Conference*. Yogyakarta: Gadjah Mada University Press, 165–83.

Sato, S. (1994). *War, Nationalism and Peasants: Java under the Japanese Occupation, 1942–1945*. Sydney: Allen & Unwin.

Sato, Y. (1997). 'The Palm Oil Industry in Indonesia', in: M. Pangestu & Y. Sato (eds), *Waves of Change in Indonesia's Manufacturing Industry*. Tokyo: Institute of Developing Economies, 63–94.

van Schaik, A. (1986). *Colonial Control and Peasant Resources in Java: Agricultural Involution Reconsidered*. Ph.D. dissertation, University of Amsterdam.

Schiller, A. (1955). *The Formation of Federal Indonesia, 1945–1949*. The Hague: Van Hoeve.

Schouten, M. (1995). 'Eras and Areas: Export Crops and Subsistence in Minahasa, 1817–1985', Paper presented at the First Conference of the European Association of Southeast Asian Studies, Leiden.

Schrieke, B.J.O. (1955–1957). *Indonesian Sociological Studies: Selected Writings of B. Schrieke*. The Hague: Van Hoeve.

Schulte Nordholt, H. (1981). 'The Mads Lange Connection: A Danish Trader on Bali in the Middle of the Nineteenth Century: Broker and Buffer', *Indonesia* 32, 17–47.

Segers, W.A.I.M. (1987). *Changing Economy in Indonesia, VIII: Manufacturing Industry 1870–1942*. Amsterdam: Royal Tropical Institute.

Shiraishi Takashi (1990). *An Age in Motion: Popular Radicalism in Java, 1912–1926*. Ithaca, NY: Cornell University Press.

Siahaan, B. (1996). *Industrialisasi di Indonesia: Sejak Hutang Kehormatan sampai Banting Stir*. Jakarta: Pustaka Data.

Simanjuntak, D.S. (1998). 'The Indonesian Financial Crisis: Causes, Effects, and Challenges of Reconstruction' [Unpublished paper], Jakarta.

Sitsen, P.H.W. (1943). *Industrial Development of the Netherlands Indies*. New York: Institute of Pacific Relations.

Soehoed, A.R. (1967). 'Manufacturing in Indonesia', *Bulletin of Indonesian Economic Studies* 8, 65–84.

Soehoed, A.R. (1988). 'Reflections on Industrialisation and Industrial Policy in Indonesia', *Bulletin of Indonesian Economic Studies* 24 (2), 43–57.

Soeparto Brata (1983). 'Surabaya; 40 tahun yang lalu', *Jawa Pos*, May-June.

Soesastro, H. & Basri, M. Chatib (1998). 'Survey of Recent Developments', *Bulletin of Indonesian Economic Studies* 34 (1), 3–54.

Somers Heidhues, M. (1992). *Bangka Tin and Mentok Pepper: Chinese Settlement on an Indonesian Island*. Singapore: Institute of Southeast Asian Studies.

SP (1964). *Surabaya Post* [daily]. Surabaya.

Staatsblad (1933). *Staatsblad van Nederlandsch-Indië*. Batavia.

Steele, R.M. (1980). *Origins and Occupational Mobility of Lifetime Migrants to Surabaya, East Java*. Ph.D. dissertation, Australian National University, Canberra.

Steensgaard, N. (1973). *The Asian Trade Revolution of the Seventeenth Century: The East India Companies and the Decline of Caravan Trade*. Chicago: University of Chicago Press.

Stoler, A.L. (1985, 1995). *Capitalism and Confrontation in Sumatra's Plantation Belt 1870–1979*. New Haven, CT: Yale University Press.

Subroto (1998). 'Recollections of My Career', *Bulletin of Indonesian Economic Studies* 34 (2), 67–92.

Sugihara, K. (1986). 'Patterns of Asia's Integration into the World Economy, 1880–1913', in: W. Fischer, R.M. McInnis & J. Schneider (eds), *The Emergence of a World Economy 1500–1914*. Wiesbaden: Steiner, II: 709–28.

Suhadi, M. (1967). *Industrialization Efforts in Indonesia: The Role of Agriculture and Foreign Trade in the Development of the Industrial Sector*. Ph.D. dissertation, University of California, Berkeley.

Sumitro Djojohadikusumo (1943). *Het volkscreditwezen in de Depressie*. Haarlem: Bohn.

Sumitro Djojohadikusumo (1946). 'Apa arti Indonesia bagi Nederland, diukur dengan uang?', *Patriot* 28 September.

Sumitro Djojohadikusumo (1954). 'The Government's Program on Industries', *Ekonomi dan Keuangan Indonesia* 7 (11), 702–36.

Sumitro Djojohadikusumo (1956). 'Stabilization Policies in 1955', *Ekonomi dan Keuangan Indonesia* 9 (1), 40–75.

Sundrum, R.M. (1986). 'Indonesia's Rapid Economic Growth: 1968–81', *Bulletin of Indonesian Economic Studies* 23 (3), 40–69.

SUPAS [Survei Penduduk Antar Sensus] (1996). *Labour Force Situation in Indonesia*. Jakarta: BPS.

Sutherland, H.A. (1976). *Between Conflict and Accommodation: History, Colonialism, Politics and Southeast Asia*. Amsterdam: Free University.

Sutherland, H.A. (1979). *The Making of a Bureaucratic Elite: The Colonial Transformation of the Javanese Priyayi*. Singapore: Heinemann.

Sutter, J.O. (1959). *Indonesianisasi: Politics in a Changing Economy, 1940–1955*. Ithaca, NY: Cornell University Press.

Svensson, T. (1988). 'Contradictions and Expansions: Agrarian Change in Java since 1830', in: M. Mörner & T. Svensson (eds), *Classes, Strata and Elites: Essays on Social Stratification in Nordic and Third World History*. Gothenburg: Gothenburg University, 191–231.

Tabor, S. (1992). 'Agriculture in Transition', in: A. Booth (ed.), *The Oil Boom and After: Indonesian Economic Policy and Performance in the Soeharto Era*. Singapore: Oxford University Press, 161–203.

Tan, T.K. (1967). 'Sukarnian Economics', in: T.K. Tan (ed.), *Sukarno's Guided Indonesia*. Brisbane: Jacaranda, 29–45.

Taselaar, A. (1998). *De Nederlandse koloniale lobby: Ondernemers en de Indische politiek, 1914–1940*. Leiden: CNWS.

Thee Kian Wie (1977). *Plantation Agriculture and Export Growth: An Economic History of East Sumatra, 1863–1942*. Jakarta: LIPI.

Thee Kian Wie (1991). 'The Surge of Asian NIC Investment into Indonesia', *Bulletin of Indonesian Economic Studies* 27 (3), 55–88.

Thee Kian Wie (1993). *Industrial Structure and Small and Medium Enterprise Development in Indonesia*. Washington: World Bank.

Thee Kian Wie (1994). 'Reflections on Indonesia's Emerging Industrial Nationalism' [Working paper 41], Asia Research Centre, Murdoch University, Perth.

Thee Kian Wie, 1998. 'Determinants of Indonesia's Industrial Technology Development', in: H. Hill & Thee Kian Wie (eds), *Indonesia's Technological Challenge*. Canberra: Research School of Pacific and Asian Studies, Australian National University. Singapore: Institute of Southeast Asian Studies, 117–35.

van Tijn, Th. (1971). 'Een nabeschouwing', *Bijdragen en Mededelingen betreffende de Geschiedenis der Nederlanden* 90, 79–89.

Touwen, L.J. (1991). 'Voordeel van veelzijdigheid: De economische ontwikkeling van Palembang en Djambi tussen 1900 en 1940', *Economisch- en Sociaal-Historisch Jaarboek* 54, 143–82.

Touwen, L.J. (1997/2001). *Extremes in the Archipelago: Trade and Economic Development in the Outer Islands of Indonesia 1900–1942*. Ph.D. dissertation, Leiden University. Leiden: KITLV Press [2001].

de Tray, D. (1999). 'The World Bank's Lessons from the Indonesian Economic Crisis', Speech given at a farewell luncheon hosted by the Indonesian Forum Foundation, Jakarta.

Twang Peck-Yang (1998). *The Chinese Business Elite in Indonesia and the Transition to Independence, 1940–1950*. Kuala Lumpur: Oxford University Press.

Uchino, T. (1983). *Japan's Postwar Economy*. Tokyo: Kodansha.

Uemura, Y. (2000). 'The Food Shortage and Javanese Society from the End of 1910s to 1920', *Lembaran Sejarah* 3 (1), 124–62.

USESTI [United States Economic Survey Team for Indonesia] (1963). *Indonesia: Perspectives and Proposals for United States Economic Aid* [Humphrey Report]. New Haven, CT: Yale University Press.

van der Veur, P. (1969). *Education and Social Change in Colonial Indonesia*. Athens: Centre for International Studies, Ohio University.

Vichyanond, P. (1998). 'Management of Financial Flows in Southeast Asia', Paper presented at the UNU-AERC Conference on 'Asia and Africa in the Global Economy', Tokyo.

Vlekke, B.H.M. (1945). *Nusantara: A History of the East Indian Archipelago*. Cambridge, MA: Harvard University Press.

Vleming, J.L. (1925). *Het Chineesche zakenleven in Nederlandsch-Indië*. Weltevreden: Landsdrukkerij.

Vos, R. (1993). *Gentle Janus, Merchant Prince: The VOC and the Tightrope of Diplomacy in the Malay World, 1740–1800*. Leiden: KITLV Press.

Warren, J.F. (1981). *The Sulu Zone, 1768–1898*. Singapore: Singapore University Press.

Watson Andaya, B. (1993). *To Live as Brothers: Southeast Sumatra in the Seventeenth and Eighteenth Centuries*. Honolulu: University of Hawaii Press.

Watson Andaya, B. & Andaya, L.Y. (1982). *A History of Malaysia*. London: Macmillan.

Wertheim, W.F. (1956). *Indonesian Society in Transition: A Study of Social Change*. The Hague: Van Hoeve.

Wesseling, H.L. (1988). 'The Giant that was a Dwarf or the Strange History of Dutch Imperialism', *Journal of Imperial and Commonwealth History* 16 (3), 58–70.

White, B. (1976). 'Population, Involution and Development in Rural Java', *Economic Development and Cultural Change* 24, 267–90.

Willner, A.R. (1981). 'Repetition in Change: Cyclical Movement and Indonesian "Development"', *Economic Development and Cultural Change* 29, 409–17.

Wisseman Christie, J. (1995). 'State Formation in Early Maritime Southeast Asia: A Consideration of the Theories and the Data', *Bijdragen tot de Taal-, Land- en Volkenkunde* 151, 235–88.

Wolters, O.W. (1982). *History, Culture and Region in Southeast Asian Perspectives*. Singapore: Institute of Southeast Asian Studies.

Wong Lin Ken (1960). 'The Trade of Singapore 1819–1869', *Journal of the Malayan Branch of the Royal Asiatic Society* 33 (4), 5–315.

World Bank (1985a). *Indonesia: Policies for Growth and Employment*. Washington.

World Bank (1985b). *World Development Report 1985: International Capital and Economic Development*. New York: Oxford University Press.

World Bank (1987). *Indonesia: Strategy for Economic Recovery*. Washington.

World Bank (1988). *Indonesia: Adjustment, Growth and Sustainable Development*. Washington.

World Bank (1990). *World Development Report 1990: Poverty*. New York: Oxford University Press.

World Bank (1991). *World Development Report 1991.* New York: Oxford University Press.

World Bank (1992). *World Development Report 1992.* New York: Oxford University Press.

World Bank (1993a). *The East Asian Miracle: Economic Growth and Public Policy.* New York: Oxford University Press.

World Bank (1993b). *Indonesia: Sustaining Development.* Washington.

World Bank (1994a). *Indonesia: Environment and Development.* Washington.

World Bank (1994b). *Indonesia: Industrial Policy. Shifting into High Gear.* Washington.

World Bank (1995). *Indonesia: Improving Efficiency and Equity Changes in the Public Sector's Role.* Washington.

World Bank (1996a). *Indonesia: Dimensions of Growth.* Washington.

World Bank (1996b). *Industrial Development for a Competitive Edge.* Washington.

World Bank (1997a). *Indonesia: Sustaining High Growth with Equity.* Washington.

World Bank (1997b). *World Development Indicators 1997.* Washington.

World Bank (1998a). *Indonesia in Crisis: A Macroeconomic Update.* Washington.

World Bank (1998b). *World Development Indicators 1998.* Washington.

World Bank (1998c). *World Development Report 1997.* Washington.

World Bank (1999a). *Indonesia: From Crisis to Opportunity.* Washington.

World Bank (1999b). *World Development Indicators 1999.* Washington.

World Bank (2000a). *Indonesia: Seizing the Opportunity.* Washington.

World Bank (2000b). *Entering the 21st Century: World Development Report 1999/2000.* New York: Oxford University Press.

Yong Mun Cheong (1982). *H.J. van Mook and Indonesian Independence: A Study of his Role in Dutch–Indonesian Relations, 1945–48.* The Hague: Nijhoff.

Yoshihara Kunio (ed.) (1989). *Oei Tiong Ham Concern: The First Business Empire of Southeast Asia.* Kyoto: Centre for Southeast Asian Studies, Kyoto University.

Young, K.R. (1990). 'The Cultivation System in West Sumatra: Economic Stagnation and Political Stalemate', in: A. Booth, W.J. O'Malley & A. Weidemann (eds), *Indonesian Economic History in the Dutch Colonial Era.* New Haven, CT: Yale University Press, 90–110.

Zed, M. (1996). 'The Dualistic Economy in the Late Colonial Period', in: J.Th. Lindblad (ed.), *Historical Foundations of a National Economy in Indonesia, 1890s–1990s.* Amsterdam: North-Holland, 249–64.

Ziesel, J.H. (1939). 'Soerabaia als industriestad', *Locale Techniek* 8 (2), 52–4.

Index

Menggala, 91
Menggarai, 90
metals and machinery, 159, 161
Mexico, 198
migration, 136, 177
Minahasa, 19, 25, 95
Minangkabau, 91, 94, 131, 180
Mindanao, 36
mining, 47, 88, 95–7, 100, 104, 118, 131,
139, 200
Mojokerto, 135
Moluccas, 17, 21, 44–7, 49, 84, 99, 139
monetisation, 35, 45, 50, 53–4, 68, 76–7; *see
also* currency
money supply, 179, 192; *see also* inflation
motor car, 138, 223
Muara Dua, 91
Muara Muntai, 90
Muhammadiyah, 121
Multatuli, 65
multiple exchange rate, 175, 179, 191–2, 205;
see also balance of payments, foreign
exchange controls
multiplier, 144
Muntok, 19, 84
Myanmar, 216; *see also* Burma

Nagara, 47
Nagtegaal, L., 55
Napoleon, 3
Nasution, A.H., 182, 184, 186
national car policy, 223
national income, 5–7, 10–13, 143, 170; *see
also* GDP
nationalisation, 171, 177, 182, 206
nationalist movement, Indonesian, 111–14,
119–22, 154, 163, 167
Natsir, Moh., 176
Negara Indonesia Timur, 170
neighbourhood associations, 164, 167
Nemota Naoko, *see* Ratna Sari Dewi
neocolonialism, 170
Netherlands, The, 3, 10, 14, 16–18, 20–1, 25,
28, 59, 63, 66, 80, 87, 97, 103–4, 113, 116,
118, 121, 128–9, 139, 143–6, 148–9, 151,
153, 158–9, 162–3, 169, 171, 182, 189,
196
New Guinea, 21, 37, 99, 122, 171; *see also*
Irian Jaya
New South Wales, 88
New York, 155
New Zealand, 18
NHM, 15, 65–6, 69, 91, 103
NICA, 168
Nienhuys, J., 95, 103
NIEs, 196, 198–200
Nigeria, 216
NISN, 20, 22, 99

non-oil exports, 31, 211, 215, 232
non-oil taxes, 210
non-performing loans, 233, 236
non-tariff barriers, 212, 223
North America, 5, 25, 31
North Sea, 147
nucleus estate scheme, 219–20
Nusa Tenggara, 12–13, 18, 29–30, 46, 228–9,
239; *see also* Lesser Sunda islands
nutmeg, 40, 45–6

Oei Tiong Ham, 140–1
off-farm labour, 75–6, 78–9, 134, 225
official development assistance, 204
offshore loans, 232
oil, 13, 97, 99, 104–5, 126–8, 131, 136–7,
139, 163, 165, 168, 174, 181, 188–9; *see
also* Caltex, Pertamina, Shell Transport and
Trading, Stanvac
oil taxes, 176
Ombilin, 96
onthoudingspolitiek, 93
OPEC, 207
opium, 74, 77, 87, 118, 175

Paauw, D., 4, 174, 177, 193
Pacific War, *see* World War II
'pacification', *see* imperialism
Padang, 19, 91, 93, 113, 181
Padri War (1821–37), 83, 91, 94–5, 100
Pagatan, 90
Pakubuwana I, 52
palawija, 120, 133
Palembang, 41, 45, 19, 84, 88, 91, 93, 127,
138–40, 163, 188
palm oil, 126, 128, 219–20
pamong praja (pangreh praja), 164, 169
Panarukan, 72
Pancasila, 170
Pangkalan Brandan, 105
Papua, 13, 229
Papua New Guinea, 12
Paris, 205
Paris Club, 205
Parliament, Dutch, 93, 104, 128, 140, 146
Pasai, 50
Pasisir, 40, 48, 58–9, 62–3, 73
Pasundan, 62–3
Pasuruan, 59, 150
Pearl Harbor, 163
peasant, 57–8, 64–6, 71, 73, 77–9, 132, 135
Pekalongan, 135
Pekanbaru, 181
penal clause (*poenale sanctie*), 103, 140, 150;
see also Coolie Ordinance
Penang, 13, 18–20, 22–3, 84, 87–8, 92, 95,
101, 107–8, 175, 179, 180
People's Council (*Volksraad*), 114, 121, 146